Backroads of TEXAS

THIRD EDITION

Map Index

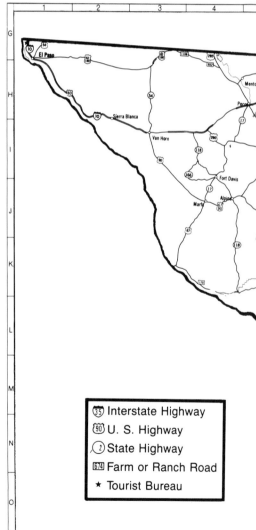

35 Interstate Highway
90 U. S. Highway
2 State Highway
674 Farm or Ranch Road
★ Tourist Bureau

Mileage Chart

Courtesy of Texas Department of Transportation

Example: El Paso to Orange 834 miles

266	Amarillo																																					
213	478	Austin
412	637	238	Beaumont
392	484	474	474	Big Bend
107	222	289	519	281	Big Spring
516	765	325	437	636	567	Brownsville
77	342	137	350	398	174	471	Brownwood
253	503	100	158	559	360	382	191	Bryan
154	116	367	521	483	204	671	231	388	Childress
387	636	192	288	524	438	159	329	237	542	Corpus Christi
343	82	536	719	525	294	842	420	503	197	713	Dalhart
180	361	192	276	559	287	517	157	165	245	377	443	Dallas
246	450	232	434	253	231	378	231	318	382	268	520	297	Del Rio
235	348	287	321	606	341	592	237	232	452	429	75	452		Eagle Pass
298	505	220	421	309	286	324	260	306	437	237	575	412	55	481	El Paso
439	418	573	810	329	332	801	493	660	482	691	417	617	424	666	478	Fort Stockton
250	338	335	572	136	143	563	260	422	347	453	398	416	185	479	240	238	Fort Worth
150	337	187	301	529	257	512	127	167	222	317	419	30	358	94	387	385		Gainesville
195	309	252	345	584	301	577	185	232	193	437	391	69	416	40	446	625	436	65	Galveston
398	646	206	78	651	493	374	336	145	531	219	728	288	393	361	380	774	536	309	307	Houston
348	596	162	86	603	449	352	286	95	480	207	678	238	349	310	336	730	492	259	50	Huntsville
144	380	139	376	332	182	386	107	237	299	257	457	264	124	328	154	435	197	233	292	340	296	Junction
397	646	206	317	602	448	119	340	263	552	39	723	398	260	473	205	445	393	358	442	357	291	Kingsville
373	609	232	396	434	406	199	330	318	528	141	686	424	179	499	124	602	364	416	480	341	311	365	230	Laredo
305	482	256	194	649	412	557	278	177	366	411	564	125	488	150	178	742	535	155	178	253	203	Longview
162	119	368	574	360	104	655	232	415	139	526	102	316	322	332	328	387	344	290	292	530	466	269	536	Lubbock
336	529	219	108	675	443	470	274	121	414	325	611	168	439	213	427	761	523	199	238	166	170	72	346	350	429	Lufkin
480	728	300	430	578	531	56	423	364	634	130	805	481	342	555	287	384	349	113	143	541	618	463	McAllen
167	255	334	567	222	60	609	219	408	263	480	315	347	247	401	301	274	83	317	360	538	494	458	224	490	472	490	Odessa
434	649	262	24	715	541	459	372	181	533	310	731	288	455	335	418	596	318	358	98	108	136	404	244	178	407	296	542	Orange
170	336	229	466	236	117	476	178	325	300	347	406	334	114	397	169	344	106	303	357	289	456	218	431	432	133	490	Ozona
281	403	294	292	665	388	615	257	234	287	475	446	103	485	103	515	717	516	101	77	297	434	Paris
240	320	388	625	190	133	616	293	475	337	506	374	420	261	493	265	57	43	390	434	545	526	250	498	41	546	203	565	560	Pecos
89	293	203	436	300	87	481	96	277	225	272	187	458	82	352	205	212	402	161	427	383	363	209	San Angelo
244	493	79	281	406	295	272	187	165	398	143	570	271	154	346	142	548	310	262	326	241	197	71	114	153	154	334	382	285	236	303	204	373	363	209	San Antonio
501	779	349	451	644	251	27	473	396	684	172	855	531	392	605	337	334	399	163	216	570	668	484	73	622	472	490	629	630	495	286	South Padre Is.
181	444	67	230	430	288	392	119	72	329	255	526	126	299	198	217	646	361	146	185	267	595	357	121	386	195	146	406	Temple
359	495	340	256	744	446	634	335	261	379	489	576	178	566	157	559	796	209	188	308	283	235	442	515	72	92	599	430	418	548	273	Texarkana
277	457	219	382	196	187	344	167	384	526	242	145	342	381	53	449	714	500	127	159	247	197	130	338	406	456	36	419	430	408	246	31	Tyler
328	401	454	690	199	221	682	378	540	425	571	447	508	304	562	359	119	119	478	522	654	610	315	563	483	83	291	642	626	161	714	225	608	88	282	428	696	476	686	605	Van Horn
328	600	122	209	502	402	230	259	152	489	65	671	292	264	367	344	487	334	116	244	178	244	178	407	296	542	Victoria
183	423	102	242	518	290	427	123	85	307	287	504	101	334	166	322	610	320	86	151	230	180	211	308	334	183	157	401	340	253	194	413	209	181	441	36	244	128	490	202	Waco
141	225	283	412	513	234	608	169	270	109	474	307	136	386	123	429	552	376	112	84	421	371	303	276	488	490	257	208	304	572	292	454	424	311	178	366	230	636	621	230	270	232	454	399	198	Wichita Falls

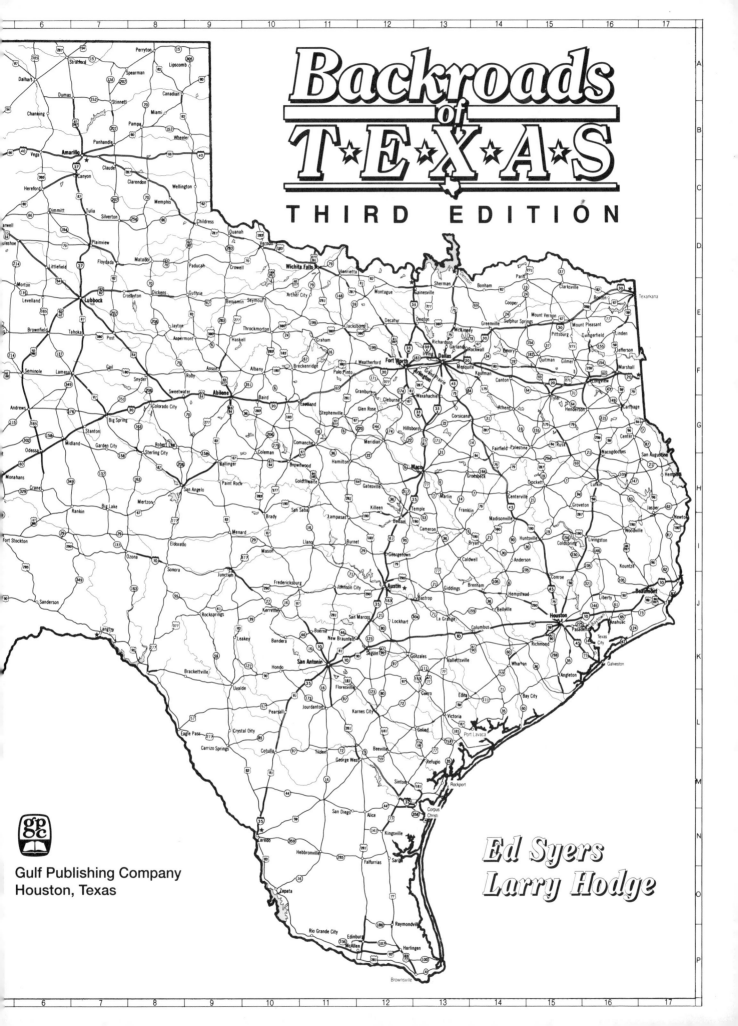

THIRD EDITION

Library of Congress Cataloging-in-Publication Data

Syers, William Edward, 1914–1987
    Backroads of Texas / Ed Syers. — 3rd ed. / revised by Larry D. Hodge.
      p. cm.
    Includes index.
    ISBN 0-88415-095-X
    1. Texas—Tours. 2. Automobile travel—Texas—Guidebooks. I. Hodge, Larry D. II. Title.
F384.3.S9 1993
917.6404′63—dc20   93-15530
                                  CIP

Gulf Publishing Company
Book Division
P.O. Box 2608 □ Houston, Texas 77252-2608

10 9 8 7 6 5 4 3 2

Special thanks go to the Texas Department of Transportation Travel & Information Division, for assistance with photographs, and to the hundreds of chambers of commerce throughout Texas for their cooperation.

Tour Maps by David T. Price

Contents

Region IV

REGION IV (map), page 106

For Betty, who encouraged *Off The Beaten Trail,* and all you
Texans who traveled it with me.

E. S.

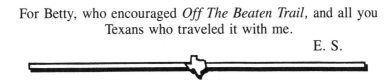

Introduction

How to Use This Book

The purpose of this book is to provide you the most comprehensive and interesting tourguide of Texas available. The amount of information contained herein is such that four divisions of the state are required for proper presentation.

Backroads divides Texas into four regions: Region I—Northeast; Region II—Southeast; Region III—South; and Region IV—Central and West. The divisions are arbitrary, following the highways that most closely cut the state along these regional lines. Beginning at the top (north) of each region, highways are traversed first from east to west, then from north to south. Because of the density of roads in the northeast and southeast sections of the state, Regions I and II have separate maps for east-west and north-south tours. By reference to the regional map at the beginning of each region (pages I-9, 26, 44, 64, 82, 106), it will be easy for you to shift from one highway to another and thus pursue your tour in whatever direction you choose.

Mileage on each tour (varying with odometers) is cumulative, but the distance between any two towns can be computed easily. For each town of importance, the altitude and population are listed, as well as the intersection with other tour routes, where such intersections occur. Each tour is accompanied by its own strip map.

Embedded throughout the text are brief and some not-so-brief indented sections that are set off with horizontal rules. These are "mini-tours" that splinter off the main tours and take you down farm, ranch, and county roads that are truly the backroads of Texas.

For an extensive trip, you may find it easiest to start with a Texas Highway map. Note the highways—Interstate, U.S., or Texas—that you will employ, then locate them by referring to the regional map at the head of each division of the book. Specific highways may be located quickly by use of the highway index that follows.

Maps can be obtained from most service stations at a small cost or free by writing the Texas Department of Transportation, P.O. Box 5064, Austin, Texas 78763-5064. Maps and complete tourist information are available free at any of the 12 Texas Travel Information Centers listed later. Or, you may call 1-800-452-9292 daily from 8 to 5. A counselor at one of the information centers will speak with you. County maps may be obtained at low cost from any Department of Transportation district office.

For quick reference to any town, you may find it most convenient to use the complete *Backroads* index.

A final word about *Backroads'* approach in this guide. Most guidebooks merely list the towns encountered, the distance between, and a few points of interest or special events. Here we also tell you why the town is where and what it is, why it is interesting, and we note the legends, rarities, landmarks, and scenic wonders along the way. Happy traveling!

The Highways

The Texas Highway system is second to none in America. With more than 250,000 miles of roads and streets, it is also America's largest system.

One rule of thumb applies as you travel the state: don't hesitate to select any Texas road in pursuit of your tour. The secondary road system, including farm and ranch roads, is paved, well marked, and provides easy and interesting travel.

A unique feature of the Texas Highway system has been the creation, mapping, and marking of ten Texas "Trails," each of which provides a relatively brief tour of scenic-historic interest. Brochures and maps of these trails are no longer available, but you will encounter the blue-and-white signs marking the trails still in place on Texas highways.

The tours each designed around a geographic-historic region, are as follows (east to west, north to south): Forest Trail, Lakes Trail, Brazos Trail, Independence Trail, Hill Country Trail, Tropical Trail, Forts Trail, Plains Trail, Mountain Trail.

On each of these, you can start at any point along the trail, spend a day, a weekend or as long as you like, enjoying every minute of your time.

The highways used in *Backroads,* and listed conveniently on each regional map, are as follows:

US Highways

US 59:	Tours 9, 10, 25, 35
US 60:	Tour 44
US 66:	Tour 45
US 67:	Tours 2, 2A, 52
US 69:	Tours 12, 24
US 70:	Tour 47
US 75:	Tours 13, 26
US 77:	Tours 15, 29, 37
US 79:	Tours 6, 18B
US 80:	Tours 3, 51
US 82:	Tours 1, 48
US 83:	Tours 42, 42A, 59
US 84:	Tours 7, 53
US 87:	Tours 33, 61
US 90:	Tours 19, 20, 34, 57
US 90A:	Tour 21
US 96:	Tours 9, 23
US 175:	Tour 5

US 180:	Tours 3, 50, 50A
US 181:	Tour 38
US 183:	Tour 31
US 190:	Tours 18, 54
US 259:	Tour 10
US 271:	Tour 11
US 277:	Tours 43, 58
US 281:	Tours 17, 32, 39, 39A
US 287:	Tours 16, 24, 46
US 290:	Tours 19, 55
US 377:	Tour 3B
US 380:	Tours 2, 49
US 385:	Tours 60, 62

Texas Highways		Interstates	
TX 6:	Tours 14, 28	I-10:	Tours 20, 56
TX 14:	Tour 14	I-20:	Tours 3A, 51
TX 16:	Tour 40	I-30:	Tour 2A
TX 21:	Tours 8, 18A	I-35:	Tours 15, 15A,
TX 31:	Tour 4		30, 41
TX 35:	Tours 27, 36	I-37:	Tour 39A
TX 36:	Tour 28	I-40:	Tour 45
TX 87:	Tour 22	I-45:	Tours 13, 26
TX 159:	Tour 28		

The Texas Travel Information Centers

Primarily at major points of entry in the state, the Texas Department of Transportation maintains 12 fully and competently staffed Texas Travel Information Centers. These centers provide a complete range of free maps, literature, and tourist information covering all parts of Texas. You may also call 1-800-452-9292 for information. The bureaus are located as follows (telephone numbers in parentheses):

Amarillo, I-40 east (806/335/1441)
Anthony (beyond El Paso), I-10 (915/886/3468)
Austin, State Capitol (512/463/8586)
Denison, US 75/69 north (214/465/5577)
Gainesville, I-35 north (817/665/2301)
Langtry (west of Del Rio), US 90/Loop 25 (915/291/3340)
Laredo, I-35 north (512/722/8119)
Orange, I-10 east (409/883/9416)
Texarkana, I-30 west (214/794/2114)
Valley (Harlingen), US 77/83 (512/428/4477)
Waskom (east of Marshall), I-20 east (214/687/2547)
Wichita Falls, US 277/287 north (817/723/7931)

Available on request from these centers or by writing the Texas Department of Transportation, P.O. Box 5064, Austin, Texas 78763-5064 is a 264-page full color guide, *Texas.*

Department District Offices, also providing information, are as follows: Abilene, Amarillo, Atlanta, Austin, Beaumont, Brownwood, Bryan, Childress, Corpus Christi, Dallas, Del Rio, El Paso, Fort Worth, Houston, Lubbock, Lufkin, Odessa, Paris, Pharr, San Angelo, San Antonio, Tyler, Waco, Wichita Falls, Yoakum.

State Parks and Recreation Areas

At this printing, over 100 state parks, historic sites, and recreation areas are in operation. They are located throughout Texas. *Texas Public Campgrounds,* available from the address above or from any Texas Travel Information Center, lists all state parks with camping facilities as well as parks operated by federal, city, county, or other government authorities. Or write Texas Parks and Wildlife, 4200 Smith School Road, Austin, Texas 78744.

The Texas park system is among America's very finest. The parks are clean, patrolled, and well-equipped, providing all facilities for camping, from hot showers to—in many cases—playground facilities. You will find them beside big lakes, at clear-running streamsides, along the Gulf Coast, in the picturesque Texas hills and in the western mountains. Several are located on sites of historic importance and maintain museums that are both informational and educational. Entry fees are charged; rates for overnight camping vary according to facilities required. Camp-sites range from primitive to complete hookups.

In addition to the state park system, the U.S. Army Corps of Engineers maintains parks at many of the scores of Texas lakes and offers camping and recreational facilities. The National Park Service administers five parks: Big Bend National Park, Guadalupe Mountains National Park, Padre Island National Seashore, Lake Meredith National Recreation Area, and Amistad National Recreation Area. A number of attractive county and city parks are available, and private campgrounds abound through the state. Texas' four national forests (all in East Texas) provide 25 excellent recreation areas. For complete information, see Mildred Little's *Camper's Guide to Texas Parks, Lakes, and Forests* (Gulf Publishing Co.).

The roadside park, for picnicking or a quick travel break, is a Texas innovation; and there are more than 1,100 such scenic rest stops along the highways. Each is clean and well-maintained with shelters, garbage disposal, grills and, often, firewood. The first such installation (which introduced America to the concept) is on a scenic hilltop southeast of Smithville (see Region II). Camping is not permitted in roadside parks.

The Face of Texas

Most newcomers think of Texas as big; they are right. If you fold the state map northward, Brownsville reaches almost to Canada. Fold it east and El Paso lies in the Atlantic; west, and Orange is beyond our Pacific shoreline. With a population approximating 17 million, Texas is the nation's third most populous state.

Newcomers often picture Texas as a vast, flat expanse; in this, they are wrong. You can find scenery for every taste, from deep woodland to soaring mountains, from spectacular desert to rich croplands that seem endless green seas. The 624-mile Texas seacoast is the third longest in America.

The easiest way to comprehend the face of Texas is to imagine that you can take hold of the state as you would a tabletop. Hold it at sea level along the Gulf Coast from Port Arthur on the east, around to Brownsville on the south.

Lift the north edge slightly. Texarkana rises some 300 feet above your coastline and the slope from south to north is gradual.

Now lift the west side more sharply, an upslope that climbs from sea level to more than 8,000 feet in the westward mountains around El Paso (in the Trans Pecos region are 91 mountains of a mile or more in altitude, the highest being Guadalupe

Peak at 8,751 feet). As you lift the west edge of your table you will note that the Panhandle (or High Plains) has elevated accordingly. That level upland approximates some 4,000 feet altitude.

The land itself is also varied. Inshore approximately 100 miles, the coastal prairies are flat, rising imperceptibly. Beyond them lie the blackland prairies and their rich farms. Northwest of San Antonio is the Edwards Plateau, the rugged, scenic Hill Country of Texas. West of the Pecos River, you enter mountain country: the relative height of peaks in the Big Bend, for example, is such that they rise above their surrounding terrain as formidably as any in America. Along the northern reaches of Texas, your ascent is more gradual but steady, crossing from rolling pineland to central prairies and, as you near the Panhandle and top the bluff-like Cap Rock escarpment, achieving the great, green reach of the High Plains.

The face of this terrain is equally varied. Eastward, both to the south and north, you wind through deep forest—pine and hardwoods. Gradually this timber thins: some 200 miles westward you travel blackland prairie, here and there timber-mottled. An equal distance beyond, you are within rougher, rolling land of post oak and blackjack. Halfway across the state, you traverse mesquite savannah. Beyond that, to the north lie the High Plains; to the south, the great mountain ranges and desert country. In the very southern tip of the state lies the bountiful, sub-tropic Lower Rio Grande Valley.

The Texas climate is the best balanced of all the Sun Belt. Summers are warm, winters, generally mild. January and February comprise "winter" for most of Texas; July and August are the hot months. Rain is heaviest in the east and south, ranging from 56 inches a year at Port Arthur to 7 inches at El Paso, from 43 inches at Texarkana to 20 inches at Amarillo. The growing season is long: in the Rio Grande Valley, a three-crop year is usual.

Ethnic diversity in Texas is as composite as any area of America and much more than most—32 nationalities claim a part in settling the state. From fledgling America itself, colonization was principally from the lower and middle south. More recently, the Texas newcomer hails from the Northeast, Midwest, Mexico, or the Orient.

Racially, anglos (whites minus Hispanics) comprise about 61 percent of the population; Hispanics about 26 percent; blacks about 12 percent, and all others about 1 percent.

English, Irish, German, Czech, Polish, and to a degree, Norwegian, Swedish, Alsatian and the Slavic Wendish are identifiable in whole communities. French, Belgian, Italian, Greeks, Russian, Japanese, Chinese and recently Vietnamese have introduced themselves more as individual citizens than in block settlements.

Communities bearing the most identifiable stamp are the German towns, such as Fredericksburg and New Braunfels and many small villages. Czech flavor is found around El Campo, Granger, and West. Most clearly bearing the Polish stamp is tiny Panna Maria. Bosque County around Clifton is Norwegian settled, just as the area near Hamlin is Swedish flavored. In all of South Texas (below San Antonio) as well as along the Rio Grande, the Spanish influence is predominant. Blacks are found principally in major cities and in East Texas.

An Outline of Texas History

Prehistoric man has been traced back 40,000 years in Texas, the oldest find being near Lewisville, close to Dallas. Traces of major settlements (Alibates National Monument) dating back 12,000 years have been found along the Canadian River on the High Plains. Other ancient people have been identified as cave dwellers along the Pecos and Rio Grande gorges and in similar shelters within the Big Bend.

At the time of Spanish penetration in the 1500s, Texas Indians became identifiable to us. In the northeast forests lived the Caddoan Confederacy (*Tejas* to the Spaniards), a friendly and relatively advanced people. West of them, along the Red River, were the Wichita. In east Central Texas lived the less advanced Tonkawa, and along the coast from east to west were the backward Attakapas and other small, somewhat kindred tribes. From the Galveston beaches westward coastally were the fierce Karankawa, later known to be cannibals.

Between the coast and San Antonio, a near-Stone-Age man known as the Coahuiltecan was encountered, and pressing upon him from the north were the warlike Lipan Apache, who later gave way to the Comanche. More than any other, this last Indian nation would dominate Texas Indian history and comprise the major barrier to settlement. In early far West Texas were the peaceful Jumano, displaced later by the predatory Apache.

Spanish exploration began in 1519 with the coastal survey of Alonzo Alvarez de Pineda, whose landing at the mouth of the Rio Grande resulted in a temporary settlement (Garay) there. Notably, Garay's brief existence coincided with Cortez' occupation of Mexico City, and the Texas settlement was Spain's first in today's United States. The opener of Texas was the redoubtable Cabeza de Vaca, who wandered across the state (and half the continent) in the 1520–30s, returning tales of treasure which induced Spanish exploration (Coronado in 1541–42; DeSoto-Moscoso in 1542).

Spain's first permanent settlement was at Ysleta (within today's El Paso), actually a 1680 way station to early Spanish villages up the Rio Grande in New Mexico.

In 1685, Rene Robert Cavelier Sieur de la Salle lodged Fort St. Louis (which failed in four years) below today's Victoria and claimed Texas for France; Spain immediately countered with settlement of missions in the East Texas area around Nacogdoches. Continued French pressure into the 1700s from Louisiana forced Spanish attempts to strengthen their isolated East Texas front—as in the settlement of San Antonio as a way station—but by 1750, distance and relentless Indian attacks (primarily the Comanche) had very nearly stabilized the Spanish northward boundary along the Rio Grande (San Antonio, Goliad and distant Nacogdoches being weakly held enclaves).

With the rise of America eastward, pressure on Texas increased. Philip Nolan scouted the region for a decade from the 1790s and Zebulon Pike reconnoitered the empty land in 1805–06. The 1803 Louisiana Purchase had raised the question of Texas' inclusion in that parcel, and by 1812–13 a series of unsuccessful filibustering expeditions (Gutierrez-Magee and James Long) sought to win independence from Spain. By 1821, a now-independent Mexico, seeking a buffer against west-pushing America, introduced non-Mexican colonization. Stephen F. Austin was the first and by far the most successful colonizer, and within 10 years a Texas which for three centuries had remained virtually uninhabited could count upwards of 20,000 colonists.

Distance, differences in language, law, and custom, and a tendency of early Mexican government toward dictatorship resulted in the Texas Revolution, 1835–36. Early clashes had occurred in 1832 at Velasco on the coast and at Nacogdoches. In 1835, the Battle of Gonzales became Texas' Lexington. Winning there, Texans pushed on to San Antonio, stormed and captured that city. A massive invasion by the Dictator Antonio Lopez de Santa Anna resulted in early 1836 Texas disasters at The Alamo and the Goliad Massacre. However, on April 21, 1836, Sam Houston, Texan commander-in-chief, ended a long retreat, turned on Santa Anna at San Jacinto, and inflicted a crushing defeat resulting eventually in Texas independence.

The ten years of Texas' life as a republic were consumed with a struggle for democratic institutions, fiscal stability, and efforts to clear its land of the Indian (primarily the Comanche) and to ward off further Mexican invasion while bringing law and order within its own borders. Some ill-fated attempts were made to extend Texas boundaries far westward; still, by 1845, successful colonization had increased the population to 150,000. On December 29 that year, the United States, concluding a long and difficult endeavor by Sam Houston, annexed Texas into the Union.

The Mexican War resulted from this annexation, and that war brought the acquisition of much of America's West. By 1860, however, the fires of American Civil War reached this state and despite the fact that only a small percentage of its people were slaveholders, proximity and custom kinship with the South resulted in Texas secession. A Texas brigade under General H. H. Sibley invaded the far West but fell back for lack of support. Most Texans fought eastward, and the state successfully resisted all attempts at invasion, although a few coastal beachheads were established by Union forces.

Reconstruction was less painful here than in other southern states, and by the 1873 gubernatorial election, the so-called "Carpetbag Rule" (the Republican hold on government) was thrown off with the election of Democrat Richard Coke as governor.

Until the late 1880s, Texas' recovery was bound up in the great cattle drives which pushed Longhorn cattle (worth $3 a head in Texas, $30–40 in the East) to Midwest railheads.

The twentieth century was ushered in, prophetically for Texas' future, with the great Spindletop Oilfield discovery in 1901 (see Beaumont, Port Arthur). In a few short years Texas was America's petroleum capital, and the resulting industrialization spinoff has brought about today's vast and varied economy as well as an enormous leap in population. In 1960 Texas was America's sixth most populous state, and in 10 years jumped to fourth, passing Illionis and Ohio. In 1974 Texans outnumbered Pennsylvanians, and today only California and New York rank ahead of this state. In 1992, population was estimated at 17,469,248.

More than 200,000 Texans served in World War I, and the state's topography and climate resulted in a concentration of many military installations. Texas continued as America's major military center into World War II, when 750,000 Texans were under arms, among them General Dwight D. Eisenhower (born in Denison) and Fleet Admiral Chester W. Nimitz of Fredericksburg.

The half-century since World War II has been marked by urban development. The Space Age fueled Houston's growth in the 1960s and '70s. In the '80s Austin boomed with the growth of the personal computer market. Maquiladoras made El Paso a center of international activity. In the mid-80s the Oil Patch went bust, and Texans found they were not immune to economic ills.

Six Flags . . . and More

Spain, 1519–1821
France, 1685–1762
Mexico, 1821–1836
Republic of Texas, 1836–1845
Confederate States of America, 1861–1865
United States of America, 1846–present

Spain's claim began with the 1519 landing of Pineda at the mouth of the Rio Grande. The French claim occurred with the lodgement of La Salle's Fort St. Louis on Matagorda Bay in 1685. Despite the recurring question of Texas' inclusion in the 1803 Louisiana Purchase, Mexico's dominance occurred with her independence from Spain and continued until the Texas Revolution, effectally ending with the Battle of San Jacinto. In 1846 the Republic of Texas passed into the United States as the nation's 28th state, the only admission to U.S. statehood by treaty between two sovereign republics. With this annexation, Texas retained the right—and still does—to divide itself into as many as five states. In 1861, Texas seceded and joined the Confederacy, being readmitted to the Union in 1865.

There have been other flags. In 1812–13, the green banner of the Gutierrez-Magee Expedition proclaimed a short-lived first Texas Republic, an alliance between Americans and Mexicans which fell before Spanish arms. In 1819–21, the James Long Expedition briefly proclaimed another Texas Republic, but the effort failed quickly. In 1826, the red and white banner of the Fredonian Republic flew over little Nacogdoches, a revolt against Mexico which allied Anglo settlers with Cherokee Indians. The Fredonians were quickly put down.

In 1841–42, a flag (still displayed at Laredo) announced another independent nation—the Republic of the Rio Grande, a proposed alliance between Northern Mexico and the Southwestern United States; it, too, was short-lived. Several other flags appeared during the Texas Revolution—the Come and Take It flag at the Battle of Gonzales, the Goliad Flag, and the 1824 Banner which flew above the Alamo. The Lone Star Flag was adopted by the Third Congress of the Republic in 1839 at Houston.

Some Facts About Texas

Aside from its great size and colorful history, Texas possesses many natural riches to interest the traveler. Here, briefly, are some facts that will help you see the state more clearly as you explore it with us. For convenience, the topics are listed alphabetically.

Agriculture

Despite its heavy recent industrialization and urbanization, Texas is America's third largest agricultural producer (California and Iowa preceding). Agribusiness—food, fiber, and forest, from processing to transporting and marketing—is almost a $40 billion business here.

Texas leads in dairy and beef cattle, sheep and wool, goats and mohair, cotton, grain sorghum, watermelons, cabbage and spinach, and ties with Louisiana in rice production. Chief exports include wheat and flour, cottonseed oil, fruits, poultry, soybean oil, and vegetables.

Much of the agricultural production lies in the South and High Plains region around Lubbock and north to Amarillo's area. Interestingly, before the discovery of great water reserves at shallow depths, this entire plains country was regarded as virtually uninhabitable. Early American explorers, traversing the then treeless and apparently barren land called it the "Great American Desert" and predicted that it could never be settled.

Cattle and Cowboys

The Longhorn is perhaps the symbol most associated with Texas, and with a reason. From the earliest Spanish explorers to today, particularly in South and West Texas, this has been "cow country." Today, cattle is a $3 billion industry, providing 50 percent of Texas farm and ranch income.

The great Spanish captain, Coronado, brought a sizable herd in his 1540s explorations, and from that and later conquistadores, the Spanish "black," forerunner of the six-foot, horned, tough, hardy and half-wild Texas steer, emerged. The industry began with modest trail drives across from South Texas to New Orleans, but it really grew along the dusty trails of the late 1860s to 1880s, and the Texas trail-driver saved this state from financial ruin resulting from the Civil War.

Wild in the Texas brush, cattle outnumbered men. Here, a cow brought $3 to $4, but in beef-hungry Northern markets, ten times that amount; the Missouri and Kansas railheads to those markets had to be reached. So began the period of the great drives—over the Shawnee Trail through Dallas, the Chisholm Trail through Fort Worth, the Dodge and Western Trail farther to the west.

Literally by the millions, up the trail they came: sinuous, mile-long, bawling, dust-churning, 50-foot wide, rope-like herds, trailing along behind point riders and lead steers, pinched compact by swing and flank riders, drag men tailing in the stragglers. With them rattled the chuck and hoodlum wagons for bedrolls and ditty bags, clanging coffee and bean pots with iron ovens for sourdough biscuits, and rawhide cooneys slung underneath for cookfire's wood or chips.

And the riders? They were first-trail, slatty kids, or grizzled, dusty-eyed, bent-legged old ones who'd sworn to their last trail two . . . five years ago. They gentled night herds, singing songs like *Bury Me Not* and *Cowboy's Dream.* They were fast guns and easy-riders, ones that Dodge or Abilene liquor would mean-up or maybe just get to dancing—the whole slouch-hatted, loose-vested, jingle-booted, Durham-rolling, dust-eating bunch, Texas drovers.

The great ranches emerged, from million-acre spreads like Richard King's and Shanghai Pierce's southward, or Goodnight's J. A., the XIT, and the Matador, far north.

Weather and rustlers were the ranchers' principal foes. Blizzards could freeze a herd, and drought, killing slower, was just as bad. No one has ever been able to tame the capricious Texas weather, but a combination of the six-gun, the hanging rope, the cattle brand, and the law-enforcing Cattleman's Association checked rustling.

The brand, known for more than 4,000 years, came to Texas from Spain's use of a coat-of-arms. By the latter 1800s, this had been reduced to a kind of monogram. Today the Texas Cattle Raiser's Association keeps track of more than 2,000 different brands.

The open range came to an end in the 1880s with the introduction of barbed wire. The big ranches were the first to fence their pastures, and smaller operators soon followed.

The quarter horse, today as yesterday, has remained the cowman's prize possession. Given to quick-footed, maneuverable speed for brief distances—a quarter-mile was and is sufficient range to manage his bovine charges—he is best known for his ability to "think right along with his rider." Today, fine quarter horses often command $50,000 or more.

The rodeo is the cowboy's circus. It derives from the great Spanish riders and their love for saddled gamesmanship. The towns of Pecos and Canadian both claim to have brought the sport to Texas.

The original Texas cowboy was legendary Pecos Bill, famed in song and story. Raised by coyotes, Bill was tough: he ate prickly pear and rode wild buffalo. Fearing his bite, the mountain lion and rattlesnakes alike hid from him. As Bill grew, so did his skills. On one bet he rode a Texas cyclone and traveled across three states. He leveled mountains, leaving the flat Texas Panhandle, but the twister finally bested him by raining out from under him. Bill is also credited with digging the Rio Grande with a stick (to water his spread), and with building a cattle pipeline from his ranch to the Chicago stockyards—too big, as it turned out: cattle hung their horns in the threads and starved.

Today's cowboy is less flamboyant, his work dress usually denim. When on the town he is more often than not quietly dressed, his boots topped by khaki pants, his usually-checkered shirt, by a jacket of the same khaki color. In town you will find him wearing a Bandera-creased silverbelly Stetson. His mount, quite often, will be a pickup, and the gun cradled behind him is for "varmints," not rustlers or Indians. He is definitely not the sequin-bespangled character so often portrayed in film. The King Ranch, near Kingsville, offers tours, even though its cowhands no longer work cattle on horseback. The Encinitos Ranch of Alice offers week-long working trail rides.

The Coast and its Recreation

The Texas coastline, America's third longest (behind Florida and California), stretches 624 miles from Sabine Pass on the east below Port Arthur to the mouth of the Rio Grande below Brownsville at the southern tip of the state.

Every saltwater activity may be found. Principal resorts are Galveston eastward, Corpus Christi at the middling coastal bend, and the satellite beaches out from Brownsville. Magnificent Padre Island, with resorts at either tip, reaches from Corpus Christi to Brownsville.

Beaches are broad and the swimming is excellent, with little undertow. Surfing is less than formidable; scuba diving is good. Birding and beachcombing are exceptional.

Fishing facilities literally cluster along the entire coast, with the areas around Port Arthur, Galveston, Freeport, Port O'Connor, Port Aransas, Corpus Christi, Port Mansfield, and all along Padre Island to Brownsville, most outstanding. Drum, redfish, flounder, king, sea trout, and red snapper are principal catches. Galveston, Port Aransas, Corpus Christi, and South Padre Island offer excellent facilities for deepsea fishing, from tarpon to swordfish. In commercial fishing, a substantial Texas industry, shrimp and oysters lead the way.

For the nature lover, 10 national wildlife refuges (coastal or inland and comprising 175,000 acres) offer tranquil rewards. These are located near Anahuac, Austwell, Eagle Lake, Angleton (2), Buffalo Lake at Umbarger, Sherman, Rio Hondo, Muleshoe, and Alamo. The Rockport area is one of America's major flyway crossroads for migratory birds. For the hunter, duck and geese abound in the rice fields around Eagle Lake and El Campo.

Fees for hunting and fishing licenses have become more complicated and expensive in recent years with the addition of stamps for specific kinds of game. A resident hunting or fishing license costs $13 (combination $25). A non-resident fishing license is $20; a general hunting license is $200. A special non-resident spring turkey hunting license is $75, as is a non-resident special hunting license required to hunt exotic animals and a variety of game birds other than turkeys.

Flora and Fauna

Texas displays more than 5,000 varieties of wildflowers, more than any other state. These bloom in spring, summer and fall, appearing in profusion as early as March in southern regions. They range the spectrum: blues, lavenders, reds and orange-reds, pinks, yellows, whites, and scores of delicately intermediate shades. Particularly in spring, they blanket the landscape. A rough rule of thumb is to look for the delicate blues and pinks early in the seasons, these deepening to warmer colors—oranges and yellows—as summer wears on.

Most familiar and famous is the Texas state flower, the bluebonnet (buffalo clover, *el conejo,* or *Lupinus texensis*). A close second is the orange-pink Indian paintbrush so often seen in massed company with the bluebonnet. Central and south coastal locales are your best sites for these displays.

Other flowers commonly seen are the red-edged Indian blanket or firewheel, the hardy purple verbena, the showy blue horsemint, yellow buttercup and lavender winecup, the white and yellow daisies, the jaunty Mexican hat and the multi-colored blooms of various cacti. Virtually every bloom known to

forest regions may be found in East Texas, including several varieties of rare orchids (see Big Thicket).

For detailed information consult any library's many wildflower books. A free copy of the *Wildflowers of Texas* folder may be obtained from the Texas Department of Transportation, P.O. Box 5064, Austin, Texas 78763, or from any Travel Information Center.

Texas is far more forested than most Americans realize. East Texas, from the Red River to the coast, is woodland. The pine is the state's most important tree, with the pecan (the state tree) a close second, and the many varieties of oak (particularly the majestic liveoak), a strong contender. More than 60 varieties of trees (not counting the various oaks and pines) from the anaqua to the yaupon are native, and among them are several national champions. Texas' four national forests embrace more than 650,000 acres; several smaller state forests are maintained, and there are more than 1,700 commercial tree farms to ensure timber permanence. The estimated market value of standing timber is some $4 billion.

The mesquite (*Prosopis juniflora D.C.*), that lacy thorn-wielder found almost everywhere south amd west, deserves special mention among Texas trees. Today considered a pest by farmer or rancher, and its iron-hard wood little used though it polishes beautifully, the mesquite was a friend to Indian and early settler alike. Its wood or extensive root system fueled camp and cookfire (it still barbecues deliciously). The boiled roots eased stomach ailments and served as a laxative as well as a dressing for wounds. Leaves made poultices, kept the head cool under your hat, and when boiled with clothing, whitened them. The beans, mortar-ground, made a palatable flour and a tolerable drink.

Finally, no handier weather forecaster can be found. A heavy crop of beans means a cold winter ahead, and once the mesquite buds in early spring, you need fear no further frosts.

An excellent guide to Texas trees, both those of championship size and historic story may be found in *Famous Trees of Texas* (Texas Forestry Service).

Some 600 species of birds (three-fourths of those known in America) are found in Texas. Some 142 different animals may be seen, including some rare species. Approximately 100 varieties of reptiles can be encountered.

The Texas mockingbird may be seen anywhere. Beyond such other common varieties as the cardinal, dove, quail, sparrow, and countless shore-nesting birds, the list is so extensive that you should consult *Peterson's Field Guide to the Birds of Texas.* Best locales for wildlife study are the numerous refuges: national, state and a few privately-endowed. For locations, see *Birder's Guide to Texas* by Ed Kutac (Gulf Publishing).

Many species in the world of mammals are commonly encountered. The armadillo is found almost anywhere, as is the common skunk. Various species of deer, from the smaller whitetailed (East, Central and South Texas) to the larger mule deer (West Texas, Panhandle) abound. The rabbit, particularly the big, rangy jack, may be seen anywhere, and the opossum, raccoon, and various squirrels are also common.

The bison (buffalo), once found in vast herds, now are limited to a few preserves (see index, individual tours). Other somewhat rare species include the pronghorn antelope (West Texas), the black bear (rare, even in the Trans Pecos mountains), the mountain lion (occasional, in the Hill Country or

Trans Pecos), and the Texas lynx or bobcat. The coyote is seen principally in South Texas brush country, as is the javelina (collared peccary). The gray wolf, once numerous, is very nearly extinct. Consult your library for details on Texas mammals. The *Texas Almanac* provides a good list.

Bass, perch, crappie and catfish are the common Texas catches. All varieties of saltwater fish may be found.

Among reptiles most often encountered are the four poisonous snakes known to America—the rattlesnake (several varieties, the western diamondback measuring up to 9 feet), the copperhead, cottonmouth moccasin, and the coral snake. Except for the coral, the bite is less deadly than commonly supposed. Directions from an up-to-date first-aid book and prompt medical attention will protect you.

The alligator can be found in East Texas lakes and streams. The horned toad, a harmless lizard, is a Texas resident.

Among the troublesome "varmints" are the ordinary spiders, tarantulas, and scorpions—all arachnids (again, less poisonous than supposed—particularly in the case of the tarantula), and the wormlike centipede. All are best avoided.

Lakes

With more than 6,000 square miles of lakes and streams, Texas is second only to Alaska in the volume of its inland water. At present some 350 lakes and reservoirs exist or are under construction. Concentration is heavier in the eastern half of the state; however, you can find a good lake close by almost anywhere in Texas.

These lakes range from such giants as East Texas' Toledo Bend (181,000 acres), Sam Rayburn (114,000 acres), and Livingston (82,000 acres) to big Texoma (89,000 acres) on the Red River, and Amistad (85,000 acres) and Falcon (87,000 acres), international projects on the Rio Grande.

Significantly, Texas can boast few natural lakes, only big Caddo Lake being naturally formed (though a dam exists today). In 1913 only eight major reservoirs dotted the state, a situation reflecting the immense expansion of water conservation and recreation in the last half century.

Nearly all this inland water provides recreation. Many lakes offer excellent camping and recreational facilities, these being maintained either by the Texas Parks and Wildlife Department, the U.S. Army Corps of Engineers, by county or community facility, and by many private camps.

Some of America's best fishing, particularly for bass and catfish, awaits you. See individual tours for details, or see complete listing of lakes in the Appendix.

Mexico

Interior Mexico is the destination of many out-of-state tourists, and the trip can be delightful. Mexicans are courteous, friendly and helpful to any who show appreciation for their intriguing country.

Principal points of entry (east to west) are Brownsville-Matamoros, Laredo-Nuevo Laredo, and El Paso-Juarez. Others, no less interesting, are McAllen-Reynosa, Eagle Pass-Piedras Negras, Del Rio-Ciudad Acuna, and Presidio-Ojinaga. Visits limited to Mexican border cities (not the interior) can be made

with no stop at customs. For the interior trips, count on one to three hours with Mexican customs. The most scenic route is Highway 85 (Mex.) from Laredo through Monterrey, Ciudad Victoria (where Highway 101 south from Brownsville joins), and the mighty sierra beyond. The fastest route, Highway 57 along the valleys west of Sierra Madre, is south from Eagle Pass via Saltillo and San Luis Potosi. Most Mexican highways lead to Mexico City; the major routes are well-paved if somewhat narrower than our roads.

For information, most major oil companies' tourist bureaus or the American Automobile Association will provide route maps on request. Perhaps the best source is Sanborns, at each major border city; you can obtain maps and very detailed road logs with complete information on lodging and meals (both generally excellent) and points of interest (countless) along the way. Also available is Mexican insurance, which you must carry when traveling into the interior.

To travel more than 12 miles into the interior of Mexico, you must plan ahead, as regulations adopted in 1992 for taking cars into Mexico are very stringent. (1) The driver or owner of the vehicle must pay a $10 fee using a major internationally accepted credit card. Cash, checks, or money orders are NOT accepted. (2) You must have a driver's license and title or registration papers for the vehicle. (3) The registered owner of the vehicle must be in the vehicle itself. (4) If you are driving a rental car, company car, or a vehicle that has a lienholder, you must have a letter giving you permission to take the car into Mexico. Upon completion of the requirements, you will be issued a permit good for six months which must be returned upon leaving Mexico.

Most major credit cards (not gasoline cards) are widely accepted, and American currency is accepted along the border.

Minerals

With its still vast petroleum and natural gas reserves, Texas is the nation's leading producer of crude minerals, its recent annual production valued at some $17.5 billion.

Petroleum-Gas: America's leader. The fields occupy much of the state from the High Plains to the Rio Grande and from East to West Texas.

Sulfur: Texas' second great mineral resource is found in honeycomb limestone along the Gulf Coast plain. Texas produces most of the world's sulfur.

Lignite Coal: Significant deposits are found in north central, east central, South and West Texas.

Stone: Primarily in the centrally-located Edwards Plateau or Central Mineral Region are substantial deposits of marble, granite, limestone, graphite, gypsum.

Clays: East and north central Texas deposits make the state a national leader in clay products.

Helium, magnesium and salt are also substantial Texas resources.

Silver and quicksilver (mercury), mined to a considerable degree in the past (primarily in West Texas mountains), are produced to a limited degree, if at all. Extraction costs are too high.

Rivers

By comparison with many other states, Texas rivers are not impressive, except in the hilly areas of the state where their clarity and scenic beauty compensates for their unimposing flow.

Texas counts 14 major rivers—the Rio Grande, Nueces, San Antonio, Guadalupe, Lavaca, Colorado, Brazos, San Jacinto, Trinity, Neches, Sabine, and Red (south to north). West is the Pecos, and far north, the Canadian. The Rio Grande, at 1,248 miles, is Texas' longest, with the Red River second, extending 726 miles.

The Rio Grande, like its tributary Pecos, has been described as "too thick to drink; too thin to plow"; however, its historic and scenic attributes have few equals. In all, Texas counts some 3,700 streams, with a combined length of some 80,000 miles, draining some 263,000 square miles of terrain. For more about Texas waterways see *A Guide to Texas Rivers and Streams* by Gene Kirkley (Gulf Publishing Co.).

Tex-Mex Foods

Mexican food, as we know it on this side of the Rio Grande, is more properly "Tex-Mex" food. Though its origin is unquestionably Mexican-inspired, you will find it—and it is delicious—more easily north of the border and, with a few notable exceptions, limited to Texas.

The food came about from early Texans who learned from their Mexican neighbors the art of spicing otherwise bland menus with seasoning, primarily the chili pepper. In fact, when the Mexican speaks of "chili," he refers to his red pepper. In Texas, chili is the state dish—ground or diced meat in a thick, hot gravy seasoned with that red pepper. Most of the Tex-Mex dishes build up around chili in some form.

Without attempting recipes, staples in a typical Tex-Mex meal consist of tortillas, tamales, enchiladas, beans, rice, and guacamole (avocado) salad. Side dishes, ranging from tacos and burritos to chili con queso and nachos, are delicious.

San Antonio ranks first in Tex-Mex food, with Austin in close competition. Most Texas cities and towns have good restaurants, and rare indeed is the cafe which does not offer a good bowl of chili.

Across the Rio Grande, you can order this kind of "Mexican food," but the menu of interior Mexico is more cosmopolitan in selection, and Tex-Mex food is really a concession to visiting Americans.

Top Historic Sites in Texas

Any list of "must-see" historic sites in Texas must begin with the Alamo and the other old Spanish missions in San Antonio. The greatest such concentration north of the Rio Grande, the sites are linked by the Mission Trail. Four missions and several acequia (irrigation canal) sites comprise the San Antonio Missions National Historical Park (2202 Roosevelt Ave., San Antonio 78210, 210/299-5701).

In the far western corner of the state is El Paso's Missions Trail (San Elizario, Socorro, Ysleta; El Paso Convention and Visitor's Bureau, One Civic Center Plaza, El Paso 79901, 1-800-351-6024; in Texas 1-800-592-6001). The Upper Rio Grande Valley holds the evidence of the earliest European influence in Texas. The mission churches and the Tigua Indian Reservation (119 S. Old Pueblo Rd., 915/859-3916) offer superb photographic possibilities; the two Tigua Indian restaurants serve some of the best Mexican food in Texas.

Fort Davis National Historic Site (Box 1456, Fort Davis 79734, 915/426-3224) offers not only history but also scenery—mountains, fantastic rock formations, trees, flowing streams, daytime skies a blue you'll never see anywhere else, and nighttime skies that may be the darkest in the United States. There's also much to see and do—McDonald Observatory, the Prude Guest Ranch (Box 1431, Fort Davis 79734, 1-800-458-6232), and Davis Mountains State Park (Box 786, Fort Davis 79734, 915/426-3337) are right at hand.

In Big Bend National Park (Big Bend National Park 79834-9999, 915/477-2291), history blends with fantastic scenery to create a tourist's paradise in the Big Bend. The Rio Grande played an important part in Texas history, and it is delightful to have it displayed in such a sublime setting, hemmed in on one side by the Chihuahuan Desert and on the other by the Chisos Mountains. Nearby is the ghost town of Terlingua; a little farther down the road is Lajitas, a ghost town come back to life.

At Seminole Canyon State Historical Park (Box 820, Comstock 78837, 915/292-4464), ruggedly beautiful scenery vies with ancient Indian rock art for superlatives. Both are fantastic.

Fort Leaton State Historic Site (four miles southeast of Presidio on Farm Road 170; Box 1220, Presidio 79845; 915/229-3613) is unique in Texas. It is one of the largest adobe structures in terms of the area it covers. The fact that it was built as a private fort makes it all the more remarkable. Its interpretive center, with all displays in both Spanish and English, provides an indepth look at the early history of the area. North of Presidio on US 67 is the ghost town of Shafter, the only place where significant amounts of the gold and silver the conquistadores sought in Texas were ever found.

The Petroleum Museum (1500 I-20 West, Midland 79701; 915/683-4403) portrays a part of the Texas heritage as important as any. In fact, it might be argued that but for oil, money might not have been available to preserve evidence of other aspects of Texas history.

Texas Symbols

State Nickname—Lone Star State

State Motto—Friendship, from *Tejas,* the Spanish version of a Caddo Indian word meaning "friends."

State Flower—The bluebonnet, *Lupensis texensis,* which blankets most of the state beginning with the Big Bend area in January through central areas of the state in March through May.

State Tree—The majestic Hicoria Pecan was named state tree in 1919. Its selection was urged by Texas' first native-born governor, James Stephen Hogg, who requested that a pecan be planted at his grave and that the children of Texas gather its nuts and plant them statewide.

State Bird—The Texas mockingbird, *Mimus polygottos,* became state bird in 1927. This bird is a skilled mimic of sounds from the songs of other birds to the meows of housecats.

State Gem—The topaz, found only in Mason County.

State Grass—Sideoats gramma

State Song—Contrary to popular belief, *The Eyes of Texas, the* song of The University of Texas at Austin, is not the state song. That honor belongs to *Texas, Our Texas,* rarely heard and usually not seen outside Texas history textbooks, where it is printed by law.

Region I
East-West: Tours 1 through 8

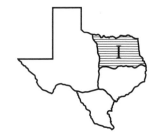

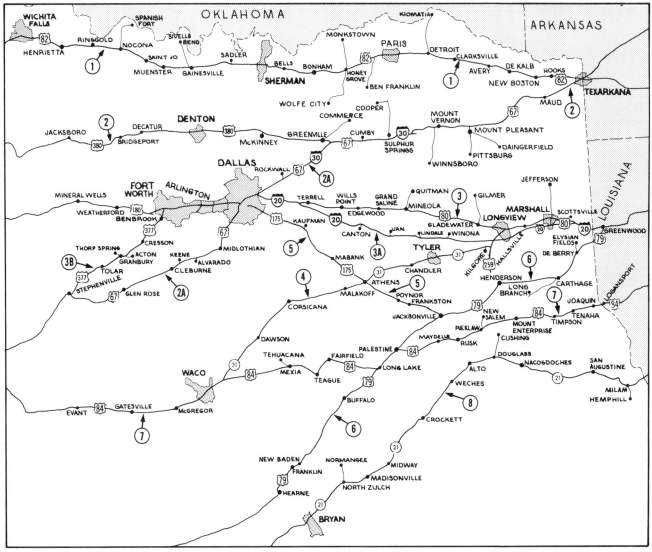

(Also see page 26)

Tour 1: Texarkana to Wichita Falls, **1**
Tour 2: Texarkana to Jacksboro, **4**
Tour 2A: Greenville to Stephenville, **6**
Tour 3: Waskom to Mineral Wells, **9**
Tour 3A: Marshall to Terrell, **13**
Tour 3B: Fort Worth to Stephenville, **14**

Tour 4: Longview to Waco, **15**
Tour 5: Jacksonville to Dallas, **17**
Tour 6: Carthage to Hearne, **18**
Tour 7: Logansport, La. to Evant, **19**
Tour 8: San Augustine to Bryan, **21**

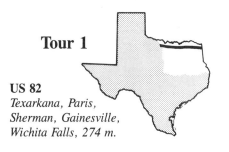

Tour 1

US 82
*Texarkana, Paris,
Sherman, Gainesville,
Wichita Falls, 274 m.*

On US 82 westward, you begin in the deep pine forests of the ancient Caddo mound-builders and parallel the storied old Red River Valley below the area first penetrated by French traders in the mid-1700s and—between Clarksville and Paris—where Americans first entered Texas in the early 1800s.

Beyond, as timber thins, you cross the Republic of Texas' blockhouse frontier at Bonham and Sherman, beginning to cut the northbound cattle trails, from the Shawnee and Chisholm to the Dodge and Western. By Gainesville, the land opens and vegetation thins and at Wichita Falls, where you enter Region IV, you have reached the lean, lonely land of Big Ranch Country.

Texarkana, 0 m. (alt. 295; pop. 31,656 Texas city). The approach to any gateway city excites, and this beautifully forested Siamese twin, straddling the Arkansas and Texas line and close to both Louisiana and Oklahoma, is no exception. The four-state trade, industrial and transportation center is unique in that the state line runs down the middle of its main street, and its post office, as well as its nationally-unique Bi-State Justice Center, literally—and impartially—straddles that line. The city operates under two closely-cooperating sets of government.

Displaying broad residential avenues lined with sycamores, oaks and box elders, Texarkana centers an area early inhabited by the relatively advanced Caddo mound-builders, and was among the first regions of America explored by Spain. Later explorations accompanied the 1690 founding of Spanish missions around Nacogdoches.

American colonists came up the Red River in the early 1800s, but the city was founded late—in 1873 with the arrival of railroads. Growth was rapid thereafter, and today Texarkana is a rail and highway hub—four US routes (one interstate) intersecting here.

A branch of East Texas State University is located here, as is Texarkana College. The Texarkana Historical Museum concentrates on the Caddoan period and the late 1800s. The big Four States Fair is held early each October.

Several interesting turn-of-the-century homes, churches and buildings lie within a few blocks of downtown. The Chamber of Commerce (C of C) has a map guide. South of the city, big Lake Wright Patman offers camping and all recreational facilities.

Immediately south of the highway and just within Texas is pretty Spring Lake Park. Here you may see the spring which, according to tradition, quenched the thirst of the survivors of De Soto's expedition more than four centuries ago (see Weches).

Texarkana is home to the outstanding Perot Theater, its restoration a gift of native son, H. Ross Perot. Also native was "King of the Ragtime Composers," Scott Joplin, a downtown mural depicting his life and accomplishments.

Across the line in Arkansas via US 71 south, 13 m., you can explore the eerie banks of Boggy Creek, home of the legendary Boggy Creek monster.

Westward, your route enters an area once rich in earlier homes—the antebellum plantations. The beautifully remodeled Pryor House (1847/private) on the New Boston Road is an example, and several old homes are near **Hooks,** 17 m. west.

Also at Hooks, the Red River Army Depot stores and repairs many types of arms and equipment. Call the depot information agency for tours.

New Boston, 23 m. (alt. 352; pop. 5,057). Due to a shifting county seat, there are three Bostons: to the south are Boston, then Old Boston, which deserves its name, founded in 1821. Tiny Boston holds the neat white courthouse now. Approximately 70 burnt-rock middens—Caddo trash dumps—have been found in this area. North, toward the Red River, excavation of one mound 150 feet long has indicated occupation by an ancient people. Each June, the Bostonians celebrate Pioneer Days.

At New Boston, veer from I-30/Tour 2.

De Kalb, 36 m. (alt. 350; pop. 1,976), is a little hilltop town, a pioneer settlement which took its name from the German general who aided American Revolutionary troops. Intersect US 259/Tour 10.

Avery, 46 m., pop. 430. Typical of early colonists' homes is the Williams House here. Just north is tiny English, once a leading community (1840). The old Oliver English home, dating from the 1850s, still stands.

Clarksville, 62 m. (alt. 442; pop. 4,311). Spreading out from a circular central park, its statued Confederate rifleman and its close-by, castle-like Victorian courthouse, this staunch little city, with several interesting old homes, is an outgrowth of the oldest American settlement in Texas—the 1814–16 Red River colony of Pecan Point, northeast. One block north of the "square" is the 1833 DeMorse home, just behind the site of the *Northern Standard*, a prominent 1841 Texas paper founded by Charles DeMorse, considered "the father of Texas journalism."

On the square, a marker honors Rev. William Stevenson, Methodist circuit rider, who, despite Spanish law,

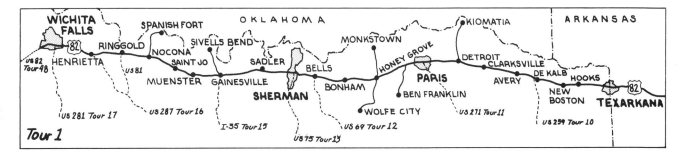

preached near here in 1815. Stephen Austin warned him he would be jailed if he carried Protestantism deeper into Texas.

A statue of Texas Republic's provisional president, David G. Burnet, presides over the high school grounds. Convenient to the old city cemetery is a huge, 200-year-old post oak, Clarksville's onetime "hanging tree."

South 4 m. on TX 37 is the tall, white-columned McKenzie home, site of old McKenzie College, which grew from an 1841 log cabin to one of Texas' largest colleges. By 1861, the entire student body had left for Confederate service and the school closed in 1886. North on TX 37, 6 m., is the site of Shiloh Cumberland Presbyterian Church, founded in 1833, one of the first protestant churches in Texas. Three of its members signed the Texas Declaration of Independence.

Farther north where FM 410 reaches the Red near tiny Kiomatia, a roadside park marks the site of old **Jonesborough,** centering the Pecan Point settlement. Here, sometime before 1820, Ben Milam landed a riverboat where some of the old tree stumps stand well clear of the water now. Leading settler Claiborne Wright, whose family flatboated here, was typical of other settlers. Uncertain as to whether they were in Arkansas' Miller County or Texas' Red River municipality, more than one family sent a member to Little Rock to write the Arkansas state constitution, while another journeyed south to Washington-on-the-Brazos to draft the Texas Declaration of Independence.

Dispute as to legal location continued for some time. It was nothing to find a Jonesborough court in session on some matter while, down the road, Clarksville was considering the same case. At one time, a US marshal from Arkansas pursued a man here, found himself arrested by a Texas sheriff and clapped into Clarksville jail. The United States finally held for Texas, and Jonesborough lost her dual citizenship.

At 67 m., you descend a gentle slope to Becknell's Prairie. Just south of the highway in a grove of trees, a large marker designates the grave of Capt. William Becknell who in 1821 blazed the Sante Fe Trail from St. Louis. Later, as a veteran of the Texas Revolution, he received considerable land nearabout. Old story adds that he later traded 1,000 acres of this land for 1,000 malaria pills.

Detroit, 74 m. (alt. 482; pop. 706), shows its age in the number of weathered brick buildings, half-hidden in trees. As a young man, former U.S. Vice-President John Nance Garner lived in the two-story frame home just south of the highway.

Paris, 92 m. (alt. 592; pop. 24,699), cultural, industrial and agricultural center for the Red River Valley, has a modern, clean look, particularly in its business area—the result of two great fires which brought about rebuilding. It is a city of wide streets and numerous parks. The beautiful Italian white marble Culberson Fountain graces Paris' downtown plaza.

Settled in 1824, Paris was another offshoot of the Pecan Point settlements, and it knew rough-and-tumble times. From Paris, John Chisum (buried here) drove cattle west to a New Mexico empire. The lady outlaw Belle Starr was jailed here; and Paris is the place where the Women's Christian Temperance Union was established in Texas in 1882. With no church admitting them, the ladies convened in the opera house.

Just west of the courthouse is the route of the Republic of Texas Central National Road, once the main route to the United States from San Antonio, running north to the Dallas area, and then across to the site of Texarkana today. Here FM 195 follows the old route, early specifications for which detailed the exact height that stumps might be left in the roadway for proper wagon clearance.

Walking/driving tour maps available from the visitors and convention council at 1651 Clarksville St. will guide you to 34 points of interest. Evergreen Cemetery, at S. Church St. and Jefferson Rd., contains graves of early Texas pioneers. The Sam Bell Maxey State Historic Structure, 812 S. Church, is fine example of Victorian architecture and landscaping.

At Paris, intersect US 271/Tour 11.

Northwest is Gambill Wildlife Refuge, where thousands of wild birds are fed twice daily. Northward, Lake Crook provides water sports and Pat Mayse Lake offers camping and all facilities.

Southwest via FM 38, sitting on the county line, is **Ben Franklin,** an 1890 railroad boomer whose population moved on with the tracks. West of there is **Wolfe City,** a secluded little town that boasts one of America's oldest working

blacksmith shops its forge worked by an old-time leather bellows. Between the two towns is dense scrub cedar, Jernigan's Thicket, an early-day hideout for badmen—still an area that can lose you.

Honey Grove, 113 m. (alt. 668; pop. 1,681), named for its long-ago bee trees, clusters some interesting old buildings around its square. North on FM 100, near **Monkstown,** are three resort lakes. South, frontier heritage is reflected in earthy names of tiny villages such as **Bugtussle, Seed Tick** and **Greasy Neck.**

Bonham, 129 m. (alt. 568; pop. 6,686), is an old-fashioned-looking town, deep-shaded around its high-curbed square, all of it having maintained a changeless dignity through the years. On the courthouse lawn is a statue of the Alamo's heroic messenger, James Butler Bonham. Also located here is the home of the longtime speaker of the house and dean of the U.S. Congress, Sam Rayburn, as well as the white Georgian marble Rayburn Memorial Library, with its replica of the speaker's office and a large display of congressional memorabilia.

Sam Rayburn Memorial Library, Bonham.

The settlement grew up around an 1837 blockhouse, Fort Inglish. During the Civil War Bonham was raided by Jayhawkers and visited by the unpredictable guerrilla leader, Quantrill, of bloody Kansas repute.

An excellent replica of the old fort has been erected and a number of historic buildings are being assembled on the grounds. Bonham honors Sam Rayburn each January and June. The Kueckelhan Ranch Rodeo is held in July, and the home-touring Bois d'Arc Festival in May. Each October, Bonham stages the Fannin County Fair, and in the summer of 1987 it opened its county museum in a refurbished railroad depot.

Just south (TX 78/FM 271) is Bonham State Park, camping and all facilities. Northeast are the Caddo National Grasslands; north on TX 78 are water sports at Lake Bonham. The ghost of **Old Warren,** another blockhouse settlement and first Fannin County seat, is 13 m. northwest, near Anthony. **Orangeville,** still another pioneer town that prospered into the 1900s, is now fading away, 15 m. southwest.

At **Bells,** 144 m., intersect US 69/Tour 12.

Sherman, 157 m. (alt. 728; pop. 31,601), an industrial, marketing and educational center, is also a handsome, shaded city of fine old homes, with a comfortable, lived-in air. Despite the apparently leisurely pace of its life, the city grows aggressively, a growth predicted in 1857, when John Butterfield agreed to route his mail stages this way: Sherman had a transcontinental road.

Here is the home of old Austin College, whose 60-acre campus will fill older visitors with nostalgia: the quiet feel of colleges of their youth. The school was founded at Huntsville in 1846, with Sam Houston an early trustee. It moved here in 1876 and continues to maintain highest academic standards, as well as offering major cultural attractions to the area throughout the year.

A historical driving tour brochure is available from the C of C at 1815 S. Sam Rayburn, and the Red River Historical Museum at 301 S. Walnut displays Grayson County history in a restored Carnegie Library with 1930s murals. Kelly Square, a restored three-story turn-of-the-century building at 115 S. Travis, houses art, antique, food, and other shops. Other antique shops can be found in the vicinity of Lamar and Travis streets.

In the area also see McKinney, Denison and Lake Texoma.

At Sherman intersect US 75/Tour 13.

Sadler, 172 m. Just north is Hagerman National Wildlife Refuge, tipping Lake Texoma, a winter home for numerous geese and ducks.

Whitesboro, 175 m. (alt. 783; pop. 3,209), provides a route to Lake Texoma via US 377, north 15 m. Just east of here, Henry B. Sanborn's ranch was the first large spread enclosed by barbed wire. Sanborn was the Texas salesman for Joseph Glidden, one of the inventors of "the devil's rope." The success of barbed wire meant the end of the open range and the great trail drives.

Gainesville, 190 m. (alt. 738; pop. 14,256). In the broad valley of the Trinity's Elm Fork, this city of wooded homes (many red brick Victorian) and bright gardens grew up with forty-niners who stopped on what became California Street. During the Civil War, Gainesville was repeatedly hit by Jayhawkers; citizens hunted them down, hanged 19 in one drumhead verdict. In all, 42 men died in Gainesville's mass hangings. The hanging elm, itself long dead, stood near the entrance to Leonard Park.

The city gained national fame as home of the Gainesville Community Circus, 1930–58, all of its expert performers being amateurs—everyday citizens. A fire, destroying nearly all equipment, ended the project. Adjacent to Leonard Park is the Frank Buck Zoo, dedicated to a native son. Here also is the Cooke County College and the Gainesville State School for Girls, a correctional institution.

Most intriguing is the Morton Museum of Cooke County, a restoration of the first city hall, with the addition of a magnificent stained glass skylight. Through the museum and C of C, excellent maps will tour you to Gainesville's fine old homes and buildings: even its downtown displays handsome structures adorned with intricate masonry and ornamental iron columns. A historic tour is conducted each April.

North via FM 1201 is **Sivil's Bend,** original Chisholm Trail crossing of the Red River.

At Gainesville, intersect US 77/I-35/Tour 15.

Lake Kiowa (southeast on FM 902) and Moss Lake (northwest on FM 1201) offer water sports.

Muenster, 203 m. (alt. 970; pop. 1,387), a pin-neat German Catholic community established in 1889, is dominated by lofty-steepled, beautiful Sacred Heart Church, whose carillon bells may be heard for miles. The church is called

one of the purest examples of Gothic architecture in Texas. Muenster's Germanfest, each April, is pure fun and good food.

St. Jo, 212 m. (alt. 1,146; pop. 1,048), in wooded hills, is an old trail town turned farm trade center. The Stonewall Saloon Museum is an interesting stop.

Nocona, 226 m. (alt. 988; pop. 2,870), leathergoods center for the Southwest, is named for a Comanche chief, husband of Cynthia Ann Parker of tragic memory (see Groesbeck). Away from its main street, the highway, it is a pretty town with neat homes set on well cared-for lawns. It has been the legitimate home of cowboy boots since 1881, when H. J. Justin began manufacturing them here. At that time Nocona was the last settlement of consequence before the Chisholm Trail crossed into Indian Territory. A Chisholm Trail Rodeo is held each mid-July. Lake Nocona, north via FM 103, offers all recreational facilities.

North on FM 103 is **Spanish Fort,** 17 m., a tiny village today, once the site of a large, important Taovaya Indian city that in 1759 reversed the course of Spanish colonization in Texas. A large Spanish force marched north from San Antonio to pacify this area and here encountered a walled city with some 2,000 Wichita and Comanche warriors entrenched under a French flag. The Spaniards were badly beaten, abandoning their cannon in a 400-mile flight— an event that began the downturn of mission colonization. Today the site is a farm field close by the Red River. Many artifacts from the site are displayed in Nocona.

Red River Station, 3 m. west, is the major crossing of the Chisholm Trail. From 1860–85, some 600,000 Longhorns crossed to a Kansas railhead at Abilene. The settlement and crossing waned with the opening of Dodge Trail, westward. The bank is worn where cattle herds plunged into the river.

Belcherville, 233 m., pop. 34, is a fading village now, but in 1900 it was a major cattle and cotton shipping point for northwest Texas and Indian Territory. The railroad that brought its promise led on to larger towns.

At **Ringgold,** 239 m. (alt. 890; pop. 100), boxy red brick on a bare hill, intersect US 81/Tour 16 with US 287.

Henrietta, 254 m. (alt. 886; pop. 2,896). Gathered about its red brick courthouse, this resolute little town tried three times before sinking its roots. In 1857 settlers were driven out by Indians, as were Illinois families in 1865. By 1873, Col. Ranald Mackenzie's troops had pushed the Indians onto the High Plains west, and Henrietta held on.

At Henrietta, merge with US 287/Tour 16.

Wichita Falls, 274 m. (alt. 946; pop. 96,259 city). The "Buckle on the Sun Belt," as this brisk petroleum hub calls itself, began as a remote trading post, grew as a ranch town, boomed with oil, and has now settled into substantial cosmopolitanism. On the route of 1768 Spanish exploration seeking a San Antonio-Santa Fe road, the new city became Wichita County seat in 1883.

Caught up in the boomingest of oil booms (Burkburnett, north), the city drew—for its number of saloons in the 1920s—the nickname "Whiskeytaw Falls." Now it is home of Midwestern State University, Sheppard Air Force Base, the Wichita Falls Museum and Art Center, and Lake Arrowhead State Park, just south, with camping and all facilities. Other recreational lakes nearby include Diversion, Kemp, Kickapoo, and Wichita.

A friendly, handsome city, proud of its rough-and-ready heritage as well as its maturity, Wichita Falls offers many metropolitan and university cultural events;

Museum and Art Center, Wichita Falls.

check with the C of C. The Red River Rodeo is staged for four days early each June.

Each December, Fantasy of Lights fills the lawns of Midwestern State University.

Today a substantial industrial center, the city still wears the easy grace of Big Ranch Country, which sprawls westward from here. Close by, however, are ghosts from its oil-boom past, almost traceless today, such as **Bridgetown,** north, a mile-long tent town of 10,000 with a church at one end of its single street, a call house at the other. The old bridge remains near Burkburnett.

Bradley's Corner, another boomtown ghost, called itself the wickedest town on earth. Others were Burk Station and Morgan Center.

At Wichita Falls intersect US 287/Tour 16; US 281/Tour 17. In the area, see Windthorst, Burkburnett.

Beyond Wichita Falls, enter Region IV, West Texas. US 82 continues at Tour 48.

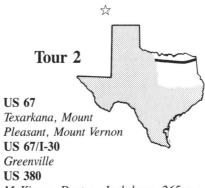

Tour 2

US 67
Texarkana, Mount Pleasant, Mount Vernon
US 67/I-30
Greenville
US 380
McKinney, Denton, Jacksboro, 265 m.

From Texarkana's deep pine woodlands, you travel southwest into the rich blackland prairies around Greenville, then due west across an area still known as the Bible Belt, a region settled under the Republic of Texas' major land grant—the Peters Colony—its towns yet inhabited by descendants of a people

deeply concerned with both religion and education. East Texas' Deep South accents begin fading beyond Denton. As your road pushes west, the land roughens and, beyond Decatur, vegetation—long since changed from forest to cross timbers, then grassland—thins to the mesquite-studded breaks of old ranch country. At Jacksboro you leave Region I on the original line of U.S. western frontier outposts.

Texarkana, 0 m. See Tour 1.

Near **Maud,** (alt. 284; pop. 1,049), 20 m., an old settlement, is Lake Wright Patman and Atlanta State Recreation Area, camping and all facilities; also Union Hill, just west, site of one of Texas' earliest schools, several old homes.

At 50 m., intersect US 259/Tour 10.

Mount Pleasant, 65 m. (alt. 416; pop. 12,291), took its name properly from these beautifully wooded hills: its location is best viewed from a southern approach. Before 1846 settlement, it was a Caddo Indian health resort and council ground, its red mineral springs believed of medicinal value, and the entire area marked by numerous Indian mounds. In the horse and buggy era, Dellwood Park on the south side of town was a major spa, complete with hotel, bath houses and muledrawn streetcar transportation. The city boasts a number of handsome old homes, one of which, the Florey-Meriwether Home at 702 S. Lide St., is open with advance notice (903/572-8567).

The downtown area still reflects something of that earlier age in its time-mellowed buildings; however, on the square, a handsome shopping mall has gone up, and just south of the interstate is a big new civic center; the city is fast becoming a trade and manufacturing hub for its area.

Close by, Lakes Welch and Monticello provide camping facilities and excellent bass fishing. Highly-developed Lake Bob Sandlin offers all fishing facilities

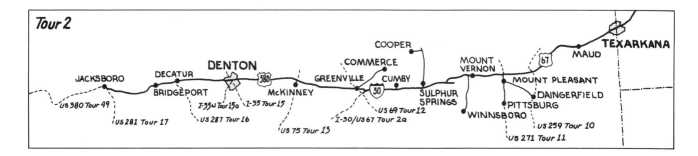

Crapemyrtles grace the roadside on US 67 near Mount Pleasant.

plus the 130-foot riverboat, Queen Maria, featuring weekend dinner cruises (reservations).

In the area, also see Daingerfield, Pittsburg.

At Mount Pleasant intersect US 271/ Tour 11.

Mount Vernon, 80 m. (alt. 476; pop. 2,219). On the eastern edge of piney woods, this pretty little town clusters serenely about a classically simple courthouse, its colonial style in keeping with the town's name. Although television has brought change, traces of old customs still prevail in outlying countryside— community sings, fiddler contests, and marvelous superstitions—charms against evil spirits and sensitivity to the haunting of houses and cemeteries.

Via TX 37 south 5 m. is Lake Cypress Springs, all facilities centering an area beautiful for fall woodland drives. Beyond, 13 m., is **Winnsboro** (alt. 533; pop. 2,904), gateway to a region beautiful with Autumn Trails each October. Nearby are Lakes Winnsboro, Quitman, and Fork, the latter the hottest bass-fishing lake in Texas, yielding 17-pounders.

At Weaver, 100 m., merge west with I-30.

Sulphur Springs, 101 m. (alt. 530; pop. 14,062). On rolling blackland prairie, around its handsome old brownstone courthouse, this town is a mixture of old and new—sedate, shaded homes and brisk new enterprise for this leading dairy county (a weeklong Dairy Festival is observed early each May). Heritage Park houses the Hopkins County Museum and a number of historic houses, shops, and mills. In the city library at 201 N. Davis St. is the Music Box Gallery, a collection of over 150 music boxes started by a gift from the Belgian royal family to Leo St. Clair.

North 5 m. via TX 19 is the rowdy ghost of **Tarrant.** First Hopkins County seat (1842–71), the town led a boisterous life. Its 1862 jail was built from funds raised by sale of cattle brought in the county illegally. During the Civil War, Tarrant saw its share of hangings, many of the outlaws flushed from hideouts in dense Jernigan Thicket, northwest near **Cooper.** A church and cemetery remain.

Cumby, 118 m., is the site of an old Republic of Texas ranger camp, later a principal stop for teamsters on the eastbound road for the riverport of **Jefferson.**

Campbell, 125 m., pop. 683, in 1904 envisioned a great educational future, enlarging an older school to become Henry College, with an enrollment equal to the village's population today. Two years of drought and no endowment closed the ambitious project in 1906.

Greenville, 133 m. (alt. 554; pop. 23,071) exhibits an air of ease in its handsome, shaded residential areas, of clamor in its big railroad yards, and of bustle in its downtown streets. Recently several manufacturing plants—from electronic parts to drill bits and aircraft modification—have changed the region's economy from its early blackland cotton farming to one of business and industry. Audie Murphy, America's most-decorated soldier of World War II, is honored with a room at the Harrison Public Library, 3716 Lee St. The Hunt County Museum, 2418 Lee St., includes exhibits on cotton industry as well as Jeana Yeager, copilot of first plane to circle the globe without refueling. Lake Tawakoni, south of town, offers all facilities.

Northeast 14 m. via TX 24 is **Commerce** (alt. 548; pop. 6,825). In 1853, as its name declares, this was projected as a major business center. Today, however, its dominant feature is East Texas State University, overlooking the little city from a commanding hill. The school, with all activities, was founded privately in 1888 and taken over by the state in 1917. A downtown marker honors native son, Gen. Claire Chennault, leader of WW II's famed Flying Tigers.

At Greenville, intersect US 69/Tour 12. I-30/US 67 continues southwest as Tour 2A. Follow US 380 west.

McKinney, 168 m. (alt. 612; pop. 21,283), reflects a warm, lived-in look, church spires rising above the treetops of quiet streets. Here you have reached early Republic of Texas frontier, the town having been settled in the mid 1840s by Collin McKinney, a signer of the Texas Declaration of Independence. Before his death at 95, this redoubtable patriot liked to boast that he had lived under eight flags—British, Colonial, Spanish, Mexican, Texas Provisional, Texas Republic, United States, and Confederate. He died Confederate in 1861. A number of historic buildings—from the old county prison to the Two-Bit House, a stagecoach stop for 25 cents a night—are displayed on McKinney's drive-through historic tour (C of C guidemap).

Nearby, the handsome Heard Natural Science Museum and 256-acre Wildlife Sanctuary—privately endowed—provide many exhibits and an interesting nature trail.

On the square is a statue of James W. Throckmorton, eleventh Texas governor and native son.

Lavon Lake, near Wylie southeast, offers camping and all facilities, good fishing.

At McKinney, intersect US 75/Tour 13. In the area also see Sherman, Dallas.

Denton, 200 m. (alt. 620; pop. 66,270). The towering buildings of the University of North Texas guide you into this fast-growing city of gracious homes with green lawns and bedded roses. From its 1857 beginnings, Denton has centered an area whose people have remained concerned with religion and education. In 1890, Texas Normal College—now the University of North Texas— was founded. In 1903, Texas College of Industrial Arts was established, later to become Texas State College for Women,

Denton County Courthouse, Denton.

and now Texas Woman's University, the largest women's college in America.

On its campus is the beautiful Little Chapel in the Woods, built and financed through students and ex-students in 1939. From the stained glass windows to the pews, much of the work was done by students. The chapel is open to all for individual meditation or group worship. Also on this campus is the glistening white statue of a pioneer woman; from her heavy shoes to the lines of resolve in her face, this is a moving, realistic tribute to the first ladies of Texas.

The Denton County Historical Museum (in the courthouse) depicts area history with displays of a kitchen, parlor, music room, farm tools, and folk art. The courthouse itself, an 1895 structure restored in 1987, has been called "the most picturesque pile of rocks in North Texas." Evers Hardware, 109 W. Hickory, is an old-time hardware store with goods and displays dating back 100 years. On the TWU campus at 117 Bell Ave. is display Gowns of the First Ladies of Texas, with inaugural gowns of wives of presidents of the Republic of Texas and state governors.

Four miles south on US 377 is Pilot Knob, once shelter to outlaw Sam Bass.

Denton's early homes are interestingly grouped along Silk Stocking Row: the Denton C of C provides a guide to "A Walk on Main Street."

As might be expected, the city enjoys a wide range of activities from its two universities, and each August, Denton plays host to the big North Texas State Fair and Rodeo.

Lake Lewisville and its state park as well as Grapevine Reservoir, just south, offer camping and all facilities for water sports.

At Denton, intersect I-35/Tour 15.

Beyond Denton, you cross an invisible boundary where the land grows rougher, the trees thinner, the cowboys' drawl more pronounced: you are beyond the line where the west begins—a real treaty line drawn just south at Arlington, between Sam Houston and the retreating Indians.

Decatur, 227 m. (alt. 1,097; pop. 4,252), spreads age-mellowed over its rolling hills. The town grew up with the Chisholm Trail drives, and some of its old rock homes show that age. The pink Texas granite Wise County Courthouse is an 1895 showpiece. East of the business district is the Waggoner Mansion, a great

stone home resembling a castle. Built in the 1870s by Dan Waggoner, pioneer rancher, it is one of the state's most interesting Victorian structures. Decatur Baptist College, established in 1892, one of the world's first junior colleges, now houses the Wise County Heritage Museum, which recalls trail drive days.

Each June, Decatur goes western, celebrating Chisholm Trail Days.

At Decatur intersect US 287/Tour 16.

Bridgeport, 238 m. (alt. 754; pop. 3,581), is an old town with a new face—a coal miner turned tourist center. In 1860 W. H. Hunt built a bridge over the Trinity River's West Fork for Butterfield's Overland stages. However, Bridgeport had achieved but one store and a saloon, the Buckhorn, when the Civil War intervened, and shortly thereafter the bridge collapsed.

A new bridge was built and, with arrival of the railroad, coal mining began. Now the town is gateway to Lake Bridgeport, a recreation center with a handsome resort at Runaway Bay. Each July Bridgeport celebrates Butterfield Stage Days with a three-day rodeo, barbecue, and street dancing.

At little Vineyard, 253 m., FM 1156 bends north to **Wizard Wells,** pop. 69, a rustic village, an ancient and picturesque health spa built around several mineral wells frequented by the Kiowa Indians.

Jacksboro, 265 m. (alt. 1,074; pop. 3,350). Lacy mesquite shades Jacksboro's many age-yellowed buildings, some dating back to the 1867 establishment of big Fort Richardson (see Fort Richardson State Park, camping, excellent facilities). The fine old Opera House, entertainment center for Fort Richardson's officers on Saturdays, still graces Jacksboro's square.

The courthouse and square wear a frontier look, and rightly so: for a bloody time this was the western front. Indian atrocities nearly depopulated this area during the Civil War—its men gone. The fort, a major anchor on the postwar line, experienced a grim and dramatic moment with the Salt Creek Massacre, west toward Fort Belknap (Region IV, Tour 49).

Jacksboro then witnessed the trial of two Kiowa chieftains, Satanta and Big Tree. A third, Satank, had been killed at-

Indian face carved in an oak tree at Fort Richardson, Jacksboro.

tempting escape. The Kiowa had ambushed and mutilated 8 army teamsters and were convicted of murder—the first time that America brought Indians to trial. Sentenced to hang, they were paroled instead, and Satanta, sent to Huntsville for breaking parole, committed suicide. Big Tree lived out his latter years seeking Christianity for his people.

The trial was held in Jacksboro's old courthouse. Of the posts' 40 original buildings, seven remain in restored condition, with a good museum reflecting those Indian frontier days.

At Jacksboro, intersect US 281/Tour 17. Beyond, enter Region IV, West Texas, where this route becomes Tour 49.

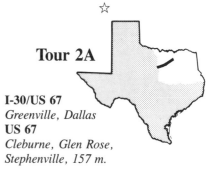

Tour 2A

I-30/US 67
Greenville, Dallas
US 67
Cleburne, Glen Rose, Stephenville, 157 m.

Sloping southwestward, your highway traverses rolling, rich blackland prairies, once almost entirely devoted to cotton. Shortly beyond Greenville you sense the urban outreach of the vast Dallas-Fort Worth metroplex; you dip southwest of it en route to Cleburne, the road at this point traveling a land where family farms reappear. Beyond Cleburne, the terrain billows up to a sudden line of

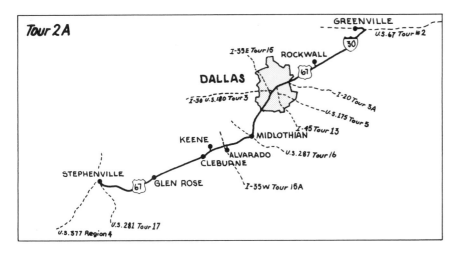

Tour 2A

hills that cup little Glen Rose in its Brazos valley. Shortly before reaching Stephenville, you will have left the blacklands behind, entering rougher, cross-timbered country—the beginning of ranchland which extends beyond into Region IV, West Texas.

Greenville, 0 m. See Tour 2.

Near tiny **Fate,** 21 m., pop. 475, is the site of famed Hobo Ranch, once 1,600 acres of rich farmland which until recently was dedicated for almost a century to the conviction that man is indeed his brother's keeper. The Henry Zollner family made a home for any man willing to work, within his ability, for board and keep.

The buildings—chapel, bunkhouse, dining room—were kept spotless, the food was always excellent; the men were part of the Zollner "family." Though many lived here for 50 years, some remained only long enough to regain the confidence to rejoin society. The "family" ranged from former executives who experienced failure to men just down on their luck. Without subsidy of any kind, the ranch paid its own way and counted as many as 200 residents at a time.

Zollner's death forced abandonment of the remarkable project, but the old buildings remain as a memorial to Hobo Ranch's brotherhood of man.

Rockwall, 27 m. (alt. 596; pop. 10,486). This seat of Texas' smallest county (147 square miles) rambles across a low, hackberry-covered hill, only the breadth of Lake Ray Hubbard (water sports), just west, separating it from the outmarching suburbs of Dallas. The town derived its name from the 1852 discovery of an extraordinary subterranean rock wall, vertical in position and varying from an inch to 18 inches in thickness. Extending over 4 miles, apparently fitted with beveled stones of regular size, it is seen by one school of thought as the work of a prehistoric race of men. Against the sides of the wall have been found numerous fossilized remains, apparently the neck and spinal bones of giant prehistoric reptiles.

Here, to many an honest investigator, was a walled city of dimmest antiquity. To geologists, however, the wall is simply a dike resulting from natural causes.

Dallas, 51 m. (alt. 512, pop. 1,006,877 city). Your highway will penetrate the heart of the city, crossing all intersecting routes. An alternate outer loop, I-635, will accomplish the same transfers, skirting the city.

Ever since 1907 when this city erected its baroque 15-story Praetorian Building, the first impact of Dallas has been its concentrated, soaring skyline.

This is the brisk, cosmopolitan, high-fashion Manhattan of Texas, with the notable distinction of operating in the black. Seventh largest in America, it is a city of banking and finance, of parks and beautiful residential areas, of intense community pride tied together with common belief that whatever is done here must be better than that done elsewhere—Dallas even claims its women America's loveliest—and with a perspective balanced between respect for its pioneer heritage, deep religious conviction, and a certainty as to its destiny as a leader in this nation.

Dallas is a center for national and world commerce, ranking second in the nation as an insurance center, third in the number of firms with a net worth exceeding $1 million dollars. Its manufacturing plants total some 2,500, ranging from electronics to fashion design. It is one of America's top five in convention attraction—its convention center a huge showcase—and its October State Fair compares with most international expositions.

Sixteen institutions of higher education stamp Dallas' emphasis on learning. Most notable among them are Southern Methodist University, the University of Dallas, the University of Texas at Dallas, the University of Texas Health Science Center, and Baylor University College of Dentistry.

Entertainment, recreation facilities and special events are almost limitless (begin with C of C Visitors Center). The magnificent Reunion Tower dominates an area recalling early French settlers, who originally stamped this as a city of culture. It is also one demanding bigness. Four church denominations—Baptist, Christian, Methodist, and Presbyterian—claim their congregations to be the world's largest.

Mini-Tour Guide

Biblical Arts Center: Paintings, sculptures, replicas. 7500 Park Lane.

Bryan Cabin: Main and Record.

Dallas Arboretum: Gardens, DeGolyer Estate. 8525 Garland Rd.

Dallas Firefighters Museum: 3801 Parry Ave.

Dallas Museum of Art: 1717 N. Harwood.

Dallas Theatre Center: Designed by Frank Lloyd Wright. 3636 Turtle Creek Blvd.

Dallas Zoo: 25-acre Wilds of Africa exhibit. 621 E. Clarendon Dr.

Frontiers of Flight Museum: Love Field.

McKinney Avenue Trolley: Tour shops and restaurants from St. Paul St. to McKinney Ave.

Meadows School of the Arts: Best collection of Spanish art in U.S. SMU campus.

Meyerson Symphony Center: I. M. Pei designed. 2301 Flora St.

Museum of African-American Life and Culture: Science Place II Bldg., Fair Park

Old City Park: 1717 Gano St.

Sixth Floor: John F. Kennedy exhibit. Houston and Elm Sts.

State Fair Park: Numerous exhibits and museums. Fair Park Exit off I-30.

Visitor Centers: 1201 Elm St., 400 S. Houston St., West End Marketplace.

West End Historic District: Market St. from Pacific to McKinney.

Fair Park is the site of the Texas State Fair each October, but many buildings are open year-round. Visit the Age of Steam Museum, the Aquarium, the 7-acre Southwestern Garden in the Civic Garden Center, Texas history displays in the Hall of State, the Museum of Natural History, Science Place I and II. Also at Fair Park is the Cotton Bowl, scene of annual football battle on New Year's Day.

Professional sports teams in the area include the Dallas Cowboys (football), Texas Rangers (baseball), Mavericks (basketball), and Sidekicks (soccer).

The satellite city of **Irving**, (pop. 155,037) houses the famous Dallas Cowboys Stadium with its hole in the roof as well as the National Museum of Communications (6305 N. O'Connor Rd.) and the North Texas Ice Arena, Olympic-sized (10101 Cowboys Parkway, Valley Ranch). The 12,000-acre Las Colinas development is noted for striking Mustangs of Las Colinas sculpture, larger-than-life-size horses running through fountains of Williams Square. The Mandalay Canal Walk features Venetian-built water taxis; a monorail also moves visitors through the complex.

Nearby **Grand Prairie** (pop. 99,616) features the drive-through International Wildlife Park (601 Wildlife Pkwy.), as well as the Palace of Wax and Ripley's Believe It or Not! (601 E. Safari Pkwy.). Traders Village, a huge flea market, opens every day at 2602 Mayfield Rd.

In 1841, John Neely Bryan built his log cabin beside the Trinity, apparently naming his town Dallas from the beginning. He was quick to publicize its future, and he did it well—three years later, a Missouri family noted, "We soon reached the place we had heard of so often, but the town, where was it?" Neeley's cabin (reconstructed) stands in the Dallas County Historical Plaza.

Nearby, at Main and Market Sts., is the white cenotaph memorial to President John F. Kennedy, slain in Dallas in 1963. The Sixth Floor Exhibit in the former Texas School Book Depository (Houston and Elm Sts.), from whence the fatal bullet came, details his life and legacy with photos, artifacts, and films.

Today the Dallas Market Center is a national focus of wholesale fashion and home furnishings markets, hosting some 32 shows each year. For the personal shopper, a visit to the West End Historic District and the West End Marketplace (Market St. at Munger Ave.) will delight.

For a time, Dallas contested with a rival community, Hord's Ridge, narrowly winning the county seat and gradually absorbing its neighbor, known today as Oak Cliff. To Oak Cliff, in 1854, came an unusual colony—La Reunion, its site near a cliffside cement plant today. This was a Utopian Socialist French undertaking which brought highly cultivated minds in virtually every field of endeavor . . . except that of withstanding harsh frontier life. Again, Dallas absorbed its neighbors and with them the cultural base that so distinguishes the city today.

In early days the city was part of the Republic of Texas' Peters Colony grant—an enormous undertaking in the settlement of 16,000 square miles, of which Dallas would become hub. The Civil War brought a cotton boom, and Dallas shortly reached for a career as inland port—navigation of the Trinity. Ruins of old locks exist today in the southeast part of the city. Some small sternwheelers did arrive—one completing the journey from Galveston in one year, four days.

By 1872, the *Texas Almanac* reported that Dallas, population 1,200 "was beginning to put on the airs of a city." An enormous city plan for that time was undertaken as railroads arrived; in one year 725 buildings went up. Despite occasional slowdowns such as the Panic of '73, this city has not stopped growing. Nor—as any Dallasite will tell you—does it intend to.

At Dallas, intersect (clockwise) I-20/Tour 3A; US 175/Tour 5; US 75, I-45/Tour 13; I-35E/Tour 15; US 67/Tour 2A; I-30 (Turnpike), US 180/Tour 3.

Continue Tour 2A southwest on US 67.

At **Midlothian**, 76 m. (alt. 749; pop. 5,141), a small manufacturing town in rich, rolling blackland, intersect US 287/Tour 16.

Little **Venus**, 82 m., pop. 977, was known as "the cotton capital of the world" in the early 1900s.

At **Alvarado**, 91 m. (alt. 693; pop. 2,918), surrounded by longtime family-owned farms, intersect I-35W/Tour 15A. Alvarado holds a Pioneer Settlers Reunion each August.

Keene, 97 m. (alt. 752; pop. 3,944). It will be hard for you to buy coffee, tobacco or alcohol in much of this pin-neat little city; it is almost entirely Seventh Day Adventist and entirely unique in Texas in that the town is closed on Saturday—a day of worship—and open busily on Sunday, an ordinary workday. Settled in 1852, it grew up around Southwestern Junior College in 1894 and has long been notable not only for thrift and enterprise but, until very recently, for the absence of police, judge or jail: there has been virtually no crime in Keene.

Cleburne, 102 m. (alt. 764; pop. 22,205) is beautified by park-banked West Buffalo Creek and nearby Lake Pat Cleburne, where hunting and fishing are good. A railroad and industrial center situated on rolling prairie land, the city is surrounded by a dozen ghost townsites dating from Civil War days. Two of them, Wardville, now under Lake Cleburne, and Buchanan, 5 m. northwest, preceded Cleburne as county seat.

In 1867, Camp Henderson—chosen for the new Johnson County seat—was renamed by returning veterans for Confederate General Pat Cleburne. By 1881 the city had begun its role as railroad center, and growth has been steady thereafter.

Cleburne boasts a number of fine old homes and churches dating to and before the turn of the century. The C of C furnishes a drive-by map, and home tours are scheduled in early May on even-numbered years. On odd-numbered years, the city celebrates "Promenade to Spring" with a county fair on the courthouse square. The Christmas Candlewalk, a home tour, is scheduled each December.

Interestingly, this city manufactured the Chaparral automobile in 1911–12—a total of nine cars. The company closed, but the old auto is on display today at Six Flags Over Texas (see Arlington).

Layland Museum, downtown, displays an outstanding collection of Indian artifacts.

Six miles west is Cleburne State Park, camping and all facilities; and to the south, the head of scenic Lake Whitney and Ham Creek Park in that recreation area. Around Cleburne see Blum, Cresson.

Replica of the ferocious carnivore, Tyrannosaurus rex, at Dinosaur Valley State Park near Glen Rose.

Westward the rolling land ridges up to a line of hills that barrier the Brazos valley and, without it, at 126 m., the intriguing old health spa of **Glen Rose** (alt. 680; pop. 1,949). This little resort tucks into lazy hills, its valley meandered by the Brazos and clear-running Paluxy rivers—difficult to visualize as strange swampland 135 million years ago. But paleontologists say that the great spoor of dinosaur tracks found here dates to that period. At Dinosaur State Park, just northwest, the slab bottom of the Paluxy is clustered with fossilized tracks of both the 30-ton brontosaur and the smaller, talon-toed, meat-eating cousin to the tyrannosaur, its deadly neighbor.

The American Museum of Natural History in New York calls Paluxy the most dramatic dinosaur trail ever found, and quarried 50 feet of that stream's bottom for its major exhibit in the Hall of the Dinosaur. The park has erected frighteningly lifelike models of both monsters as they might have appeared here.

Glen Rose became a health resort in the early 1900s, counting over 300 mineral springs. The old resort has used petrified wood, plentiful nearby, in many of its buildings and offers an interesting museum in town. The old stone mill, built during the Civil War, still stands. An intriguing item in Glen Rose history is the story of an 1870 citizen, John St. Helen, who thought himself dying and confessed his real identity as John Wilkes Booth, assassin of President Lincoln (see Bandera). St. Helen recovered and disappeared, only to commit suicide in Oklahoma.

West 2 m. is Shaky Springs, where the ground trembles as you walk it, a phenomenon due to subterranean spring flow. Nearby is the Comanche Peak Nuclear Plant, with an excellent and informative visitors center and a van tour that puts nuclear power into perspective. Just west of town is Fossil Rim Wildlife Ranch, an interesting game preserve for exotic animals.

West 10 m. the roadside-park overlook at Chalk Mountain offers a panoramic view.

Stephenville, 157 m. (alt. 1,283; pop. 13,502), rambling over a slight elevation, is an educational, industrial, agricultural and livestock center, established as Erath County seat in 1856. The town was flattened in its early days by one red-eyed trail herd stampede. Development of its area was slow due to repeated raids by Comanche and Kiowa Indians, not completely expelled until the 1870s. Here is the red brick campus of Stephenville-Tarleton State University.

A large mural in the city hall reflects Stephenville's growth from early days. At an interesting historical complex, 10 nineteenth century structures have been restored and furnished. The Chapel on the Bosque (late 1800s) preserves Stephenville's heritage of faith. The Center Grove School's two rooms reflect early education. There's an 1854 log cabin, a native stone cottage, a carriage house barn, an 1861 vintage corncrib, a well house, a dogtrot cabin, and a homestead cabin. 525 E. Washington St.

Southward on FM 914, 12 m. is reputedly one of Texas' most haunted sites—the McDow Hole on Green's Creek. The spectre of a young pioneer wife, murdered here, roams the gloomy nights, according to old story.

At Stephenville intersect US 281/Tour 17. Enter Region IV, West Texas, where your route continues as Tour 52.

☆

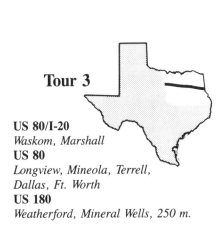

Tour 3

US 80/I-20
Waskom, Marshall
US 80
Longview, Mineola, Terrell, Dallas, Ft. Worth
US 180
Weatherford, Mineral Wells, 250 m.

Tour 3 is a main east-west thoroughfare spanning the upper width of the state. You begin in Texas' Old South— deep redland pines and hardwood forests, soft accents, once-plantations that now are small farms. Before leaving, you will have crossed one of the world's historic oilfields—the 1930s-famed East Texas fields. Beyond Gladewater both timber and derricks thin, and the farms are larger and richer as, near Terrell, you reach the blackland belt.

All at once you are absorbed in the fast-paced, glistening metroplex of Dallas and, without pause, Fort Worth. At that point—as the roughening land reflects but an Indian Treaty stipulated— the West has begun. By Mineral Wells, where you enter Region IV, you have penetrated the brief barrier hills beyond which lie the great old ranches.

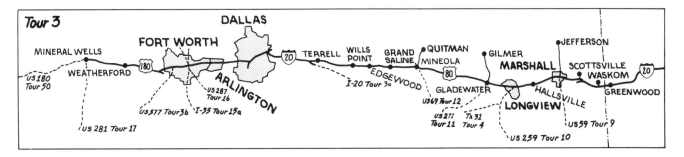

Across Region I, much of this tour can be sampled more rapidly if you wish from I-20, just south. But watch for exit ramps: the interesting towns lie along US 80.

Louisiana line (16 m. west of Shreveport), 0 m.

Waskom, 2 m. (alt. 299; pop. 1,812), greets you with a string of service stations, once "gas warriors." Deep forest surrounds. A Travel Information Center serves visitors daily with an excellent staff of travel counselors, free travel literature, information and maps. A little west of town is T. C. Lindsey and Company, an old general store and museum that has been used in several Disney films.

Scottsville, 12 m. Before the Civil War, the Scott plantation was headquarters for one of Texas' largest slaveholders. The 1840 elevated frame house is well preserved. Close by is the Youree Memorial Church, one of the oldest camp-meeting sites in the state. Here Sam Houston began attempts to settle the bloody Regulator-Moderator War, a power struggle between rival vigilante groups (see Shelbyville).

Pine and hardwood forests border US 80 near Scottsville.

Marshall, 19 m. (alt. 375; pop. 23,682), rests serenely in forested red hills, the Old South city, a place of tradition, manners, and fine old homes; of brick-cobbled streets named for Confederate heroes, and of a grassy square guarded by a Southern rifleman. In 1842, not far from where the soldier's

statue stands today, Peter Whetstone produced a jug of whiskey from a spring, thereby convincing Texas Republic commissioners that this woodland was not too dry for a queen city northeast.

While still frontier, Marshall was recognized as the Athens of Texas—churches, schools, and a cultured way of life. By 1861 it was one of the largest and wealthiest towns in the state. During the Civil War it became the seat of the Confederate government west of the Mississippi, housing the departments of post office, ordnance, quartermaster and commissary. Just off the square, at the old Capitol Hotel (now a store), the Marshall Conferences were held to determine whether the Trans-Mississippi states would go it alone after Appomattox. Three blocks south is the site of what was once the absentee-capitol of Missouri—its elected officials refugees of the war. Marshall suffered through Reconstruction, held on with the railroads and, with the discovery of oil close by, prospers today.

The old Harrison County courthouse, now one of Texas' best historical museums, has exhibits covering a time-range from the Caddo Indian to the Civil War. North—just above your highway—is Marshall's nationally-registered historic district, with several fine old homes, the beautifully restored Ginocchio Hotel, and the ornate old depot. The classic plantation-style Magnolia Hall and outlying Mont Hall are examples of the more than 50 homes exceeding a century in age. Downtown is the Houston Campaign Oak, where old Sam pleaded in 1857 against the secession he foresaw.

Late each May, Marshall celebrates Stagecoach Days—the coaches tour the streets. Late April-early May sees the city's Azalea Trail, and July, its thoroughbred horse show. In October, tongue firmly in cheek, Marshall observes a zany "Fire Ant Festival," where almost anything—including "calling" the pugnacious creatures—goes.

At Marshall Pottery and Red River Pottery Village, you can watch expert potters at work. The Michelson-Reves Art Museum and the Franks Doll Museum (some 1,200 dolls on display) are interesting attractions.

Each year from Thanksgiving to New Year's, the Wonderland of Lights blazes forth with over 3 million lights, one of the largest such displays in the nation.

North are beautiful Caddo Lake and Lake O' The Pines, both with camping and all facilities.

In this area also see Jefferson, Caddo Lake, Carthage and Tatum.

At Marshall, intersect US 59/Tour 9. Follow US 80 west.

Hallsville, 32 m., pop. 2,288, is the 1839 site of Fort Crawford, pioneer Indian-guarding outpost. North 5 m. via FM 450 is Noonday Campmeeting Grounds, a restful spot where early pioneers worshipped under a brush arbor. Each August, the meetings are still observed.

Heavy industry amid piney woods, Longview.

Longview, 42 m. (alt. 339; pop. 70,311), a smart and beautiful city, is a product of the prodigal East Texas oil boom. In antebellum days, Longview was the center of a rich plantation area straddling the military road eastward (approximately your route); and in 1930 it was a cloistered little city of 6,000, where a traveler always seemed to change trains at night. Then Lathrop No. 1 blew in, January 16, 1931. Wildcatters surmised that the well drew from the same pool as Kilgore's (just south) month-earlier gusher, which would make it a big field. Perhaps it drew from the same pool as the even more distant Joinerville well, near Henderson. That would make the field enormous. Within two years—by 1933—East Texas would be the world's biggest oil producer.

Today, Longview is a city of churches, fine schools and industry—from recreation vehicles to heavy equipment, mobile homes to a major brewery (tours conducted). Here also is industrial-minded LeTourneau College, as well as the loading end of World War II's Big Inch pipeline. The Gregg County Historical Museum and the R.G. LeTourneau Museum house many artifacts of local note. The Longview Museum and Arts Center features regional artists. On the north side of town just off FM 1844 is the Old Country School of East Mountain, showcasing handmade items of over a hundred craftspeople.

In this area also see Henderson, Kilgore, Tyler and Gilmer.

At Longview, intersect US 259/Tour 10; TX 31/Tour 4.

Gladewater, 55 m. (alt. 333; pop. 6,027), like Longview, occupies the heart of the East Texas oilfield. Overnight, during that frantic boom, this crossroads village exploded with 500 producing wells. The city's oil-inspired growth is evidenced even today by a somewhat meandering sprawl across its hilly terrain. Arrange oilfield tours at the C of C. Lake Gladewater, with all facilities, lies just north.

At Gladewater, intersect US 271/Tour 11.

Big Sandy, 65 m. (alt. 336; pop. 1,185), is home of Annie's, a complex of beautifully-restored Victorian homes providing a gift shop, antiques, a tearoom, needlecraft displays, and an attractive country guest house.

At 70 m., Lake Hawkins and water sports are close by, just northwest.

Mineola, 89 m. (alt. 414; pop. 4,321), like most of its neighbors, grew with the railroad's arrival in the 1870s and has remained brisk and clean with wide, tree-lined streets. It occupies a burgeoning tourist area, both spring and fall: a region already possessed of several lakes. Big Lake Fork boasts excellent fishing and all facilities, while the woodlands all about—dogwood flowered each Spring and ablaze with color each Fall—provide scenic drives. The downtown Civic Center is site of many festivals, and a museum at the old depot displays railroading memorabilia.

Near the Civic Center, downtown, is the old home of Gov. James Stephen Hogg, birthplace of his daughter, Miss Ima Hogg. South, on your highway, a marker designates the site of the governor's first law office.

At Mineola, intersect US 69/Tour 12.

Via TX 37 north, **Quitman,** 10 m. (alt. 414; pop. 1,684), is a quiet and pretty town edged about by forest and farm clearings. Here is Governor Hogg State Park, 26 acres with a restoration of the home of Texas' first native-born head of state. Several other family buildings also occupy the grounds. Hogg edited a two-fisted newspaper here briefly, then moved in stairstep elections from Justice of the Peace to Governor. Quitman's Old Settlers Reunion has been held at this site each August since 1898. The town hosts a national singing convention in early February and greets spring each March-April with a month-long Dogwood Fiesta. Autumn Trails wind up around Winnsboro and boast spectacular views of red and gold foliage against the evergreens. The nearby Collins-Haines House is an antebellum showpiece.

Grand Saline, 102 m. (alt. 407; pop. 2,630), first yielded salt to the 1820 Cherokee, and then—as Jordan's Saline, with big evaporating kettles—to the pioneer. Now it displays one of the largest salt mines in the United States—Morton's Kleer mine. Salt deposits cover a 30-mile area; the mine penetrates what amounts to a three-mile-high mountain, the peak of which is some 200 feet below the ground!

A shaft descends 700 feet with all-direction lateral tunnels reaching like a vertical checkerboard of room and column—more than 13 miles of tunnel. Within this gigantic block of salt, the impression is that of an ice cavern, but the temperature is moderate, the air slightly pungent. The galleries, mined by great machines, are wide enough for an expressway and tall enough for a six-story building.

Nearby is America's only "Salt Palace," a house built literally of salt blocks and housing the mine's interesting story. Grand Saline holds its Salt Festival—from street dancing to rodeo—each June.

Edgewood, 113 m., pop. 1,284, grew from a county seat feud between Wills

Point, west, and Canton, south. Now it manages nicely with its own refineries and manufacturing.

Wills Point, 121 m. (alt. 532; pop. 2,986), strings along the highway leisurely, shaded in pecan and elm and blossoming with a profusion of wild roses and honeysuckle. On the Jefferson road that your route approximates, the 1847 log cabin of first settler, William Wills, still stands downtown. North is big Lake Tawakoni, good fishing, camping and all facilities.

Terrell, 137 m. (alt. 530; pop. 12,490), seems unusually sunny after you leave the shade of East Texas woodland for blackland prairies. Here, flowered lawns edge right into the business center, and there are a number of fine old homes, toured each April. Settled in 1846, the town arrived with the railroad a quarter-century later and has grown steadily, if not flashily, since. Here is Terrell State Hospital and, close by, the Porter Farm where, in 1905, the first demonstration farm in America was established—the beginnings of the Home Demonstration Agency of the U.S. Department of Agriculture. Live buffalo and crossbred beefalo graze the ground. Terrell is home of the Silent Wings Museum, honoring WW II glider-fighters, Southwestern Christian College, the Carnegie Cultural Arts Center, and a Heritage Trail Jubilee each Spring (home tours). It's also an excellent place to eat, with more than 40 restaurants, including an array of fast-food stops, primarily west of town. Beyond, 8 m. west, is "Antique Row," a string of little dealers, the delight of nearby Dallas shoppers. Northwest is Lake Ray Hubbard; southeast, Cedar Creek Reservoir, water sports. Close in is new Terrell City Lake. Beyond Terrell, merge with I-20/Tour 3A.

Dallas, 170 m. See Tour 2A. Continue west on I-30/Turnpike.

Arlington, 186 m. (alt. 616; pop. 261,721), asprawl a once-rolling prairie, is to many the entertainment capital of Texas. Here is Six Flags family playground, 1,250 woodland acres divided into sections roughly following Texas history. Arlington Stadium is home of the American League Texas Rangers. The University of Texas at Arlington occupies a massive campus near the center of town.

At the TX 360 exit off the turnpike, Traders Village is one of Texas' biggest swap-shop flea markets—80 acres of everything from arts and crafts to antique auto parts.

The Caelum Moor Sculpture Park (I-20 between Cooper St. and Matlock Rd.) features five acres of giant granite megaliths similar to Stonehenge. The Sewing Machine Museum (804 W. Abram) has examples dating from 1858.

Arlington dates to the frontier. North 2 m. is the site of Bird's Fort where, in 1843, Sam Houston signed a treaty which drew the line "where the Indian's West begins." A downtown fountain still draws on the settlement's first well, and out at the city's golf club is the site of a sharp Indian clash, the 1839 Battle of Village Creek. An excellent historical tour is available at the C of C.

The Dallas-Fort Worth Regional Airport, largest in the world, is close by.

Fort Worth, 202 m. (alt. 670; pop. 447,619 city), is where the West begins. At a quick glance snatched from onrushing traffic, you cannot tell where this big city began and its eastern neighbor left off. Stop a minute; you are indeed where the West begins and, in the judgment of many, in the friendliest big city in the state. Fort Worth still maintains a nice disregard for haste.

Fort Worth was long called Cowtown, but it is known today for its cultural richness. Its museums, art, theater, opera, ballet, and symphony offer delights for all. The C of C has complete listings.

Leading the list of exceptional museums is the Amon Carter Museum of Western Art, featuring Remington and Russell. The Kimbell Art Museum is known not only for its Old Masters but also for the ultramodern structure designed by Louis Kahn. The Modern Art Museum features contemporary artists, while the Sid Richardson Collection of Western Art also leans toward Remington and Russell. The Stockyards Collections and Museum recalls Fort Worth's days as the stockyard and packinghouse capital of the Southwest. The Tandy Archeological Museum displays artifacts from the Holy Land. The Fort Worth Museum of Science and History/Omni Theater is a general museum that includes a curved screen theater that plunges viewers into the midst of the action.

On a smaller scale are the Cattle Raisers Museum; the Eddleman Mc-

Farland House, a Victorian residence; Fire Station No. 1; and Log Cabin Village, seven authentic pioneer homes from the 1850s. In nearby Cresson, the Pate Museum of Transportation features vehicles that roll, float, or fly; its antique car collection is outstanding. The Southwest Aerospace Museum features military aircraft.

Other attractions recall Fort Worth's western heritage: Billy Bob's Texas, the world's largest honky-tonk; the Fort Worth Championship Rodeo, held every Saturday night from April through September; and the Stockyards Historic Area, renovated western-style stores along old-fashioned boardwalks. Sundance Square is a popular area for dining, shopping, and carriage rides.

Next to the downtown convention center is the Water Garden, a cascading tumult of waterfalls, fountains, and pools into which one literally descends. Forest Park Zoo includes a Children's Zoo, Great Apes House, and a reconstructed ranch headquarters complete with animals. The Nature Center and Refuge has bison, deer, and a prairie dog town on its 3,500 acres. On to the north some 20 miles from downtown is La Buena Vida Vineyards, complete with tasting room and gift shop.

Mini-Tour Guide

Amon Carter Museum: Western art. 3501 Camp Bowie Blvd.

Botanic Gardens: 2,500 species of living plants. 3220 Botanic Dr.

Forest Park Zoo: Forest Park.

Kimbell Art Museum: 3333 Camp Bowie Blvd.

Log Cabin Village: Forest Park.

Modern Art Museum: 1309 Montgomery St.

Museum of Science and History: 1501 Montgomery St.

Sid Richardson Collection: 309 Main St.

Southwest Aerospace Museum: 300 N. Spur 341.

Stockyards Museum: 131 E. Exchange Ave.

Stockyards Historic Area: 123 E. Exchange Ave.

Sundance Square: Second and Commerce Sts.

Tandy Archeological Museum: 2001 W. Seminary Dr.

Water Garden: Downtown next to convention center.

Fort Worth is home to Texas Christian University, Texas Wesleyan College, Tarrant County Junior College, Southwestern Baptist Theological Seminary, and the

Texas College of Osteopathic Medicine.

Annual events include the Southwestern Exposition and Live Stock Show and Rodeo in late January, the Colonial National Invitational Golf Tournament in May, the Chisholm Trail Roundup in June, and Pioneer Days in September.

Immediately surrounding are many lakes—Arlington, Benbrook, Eagle Mountain, Grapevine, Joe Pool, and Worth. The city also maintains many parks.

In 1849 Brevet Major Ripley Arnold pitched Camp Worth (never a fort) on the frontier where Sam Houston agreed the West began. For a time the town showed promise: it straddled the Chisholm Trail, as little Dallas eastward, had gatewayed the Shawnee Trail (Fort Worth is still "Cowtown" to Texans). By 1870 the railroad neared—the end of the line reached only 26 miles away. Then came the Panic of '73 and the financial failure of Jay Cooke, who controlled the Texas and Pacific road. One skeptic soon wrote that Fort Worth was so dead, a panther could sleep unmolested on its streets.

The people of Fort Worth responded with their "Panther Club," marched almost en masse to the rail end—the women serving meals in shifts—and built the remainder of the line. On July 19, 1876, the first train—its whistle tied down—clanged into the city.

In its early days, Fort Worth was still a rough town with its share of gunhands and gamblers—the intersection of 12th and Main was once the center of Hell's Half Acre. Indians wandered into town all the time. One chief lay down to sleep, carefully blowing out the white man's candle: it was a gas lamp . . . and he never awoke.

The big ranches spread west, the city grew. Of the many old cattlemen's mansions once on Summit Avenue, only one remains—Thistle Hill, built in 1903. For a complete historic tour, see C of C maps.

At Fort Worth, intersect, clockwise, US 287/Tour 16; I-35W/Tour 15A; US 377/Tour 3B. Continue Tour 3 west on US 180.

Weatherford, 231 m. (alt. 1,052; 14,804), rolls across the low hills, a staunch city of handsome native rock homes and a history of many years as Texas' northwest outpost. County seat in 1856, it occupied an area exposed to intense Indian attack, particularly after nine companies of Parker County men

The public market, Weatherford.

had left for Confederate service. Here, for a time, the notable Indian-fighter, John R. Baylor, published *Whiteman*, a pamphlet attacking Indian atrocities. Weatherford's survival was assured with the arrival of rails in 1880; and she became famous when Parker County men exhibited watermelons at St. Louis' 1904 World's Fair. Twelve melons averaged 100 pounds each, and Parker County melons have been in demand ever since. The area's peaches also have gained fame. The Public Market, long a fresh produce supply center, has grown into a West Texas giant flea market with its First Monday get-togethers.

Holland Lake Park, a living nature museum and restoration center, exhibits a double log cabin, assembled and restored log by log. Dog run supporting columns are said to have come from outlaw Sam Bass' hideout in the Palo Pinto Mountains. Trail driver Oliver Loving's grave is in Greenwood Cemetery. Near the library, a bronze statue honors Weatherford's daughter, Mary Martin, in her role as Peter Pan. The old depot, now housing the C of C, will recall to old timers the 25-mile-long Weatherford-Mineral Wells and Northwestern railroad, parodying its initials into the "Water, More Water, and No Whiskey" line.

Water sports are available just east, at Lake Weatherford; and south, at Lake Granbury.

At 243 m., tiny **Millsap,** pop. 485, lies immediately south. It suffered many Indian attacks between 1850 and 1870. Just beyond and north of the highway is Lake Mineral Wells State Park (camping and all facilities), and close by its site—that of WW II Camp Wolters—is the ghost of **Rock Creek,** a 1900-1910 coal-mining boomer, reaching a population of 1,500. As veins played out the

town dwindled, but the old shafts still reach below the park.

Mineral Wells, 250 m. (alt. 925; pop. 14,870), lies within the edge of the Palo Pinto Mountains in rough, broken country long the hideout of Indians and bandits. The city came into being, almost by accident, well after the county was organized. A well-digger in 1881 found water which demonstrated medicinal qualities.

In 1885, the "Crazy Well" was discovered: its waters exhibited the effects of a tranquilizer. Within a few years, hotels and health spas were springing up—the unusual Hexagon House first, in 1897. By 1920, 400 mineral wells existed and an important health resort was assured. If the resort's medicinal appeal has lessened, its prosperity has not: the rugged hill country draws vacationers, and its city now counts a number of varied industries.

At Mineral Wells, intersect US 281/Tour 17. Beyond, enter Region IV, where your route becomes Tour 50.

☆

Tour 3A

I-20
Marshall, Canton, Terrell, 114 m.

This limited-access tour, while providing expressway travel, to a degree duplicates Tour 3/US 80, immediately north. Major points of interest along that route may be reached from appropriate exit ramps.

Marshall, 0 m. See Tour 3.

Longview, 27 m. See Tour 3.

At 45 m., intersect US 271/Tour 11. West 3 m., and northward above little Winona, near the Sabine crossing of TX 155, is the site of **Old Belzora,** head of

Sabine riverboat navigation from 1850–1870, and the dream of southerly Tyler for a great inland port, perhaps to rival then-metropolitan **Jefferson,** which shipped via the Red River. Civil War interrupted ambitious plans for a system of dams and locks; Belzora died and is now only a fisherman's haven and pretty picnic spot.

At 51 m., intersect FM 14. Immediately north is beautifully-wooded Tyler State Park, camping and all facilities. For Tyler, south, see Tour 4.

At 57 m. intersect US 69/Tour 12. At little **Lindale,** pop. 2,428, just north, is Steen's Saline where, during the Civil War, 3,000 workers—many more than the population of today's town—mined Confederate salt. Lindale lies in an area famed for roses and peaches, a riot of color and scent in spring.

Near **Van,** 72 m. (alt. 512; pop. 1,854), the headwaters of the Neches mark the site of the Cherokee nation's last stand in East Texas. In 1839 at the Battle of the Neches (see Chandler, just south), 500 Texas militia attacked 800 Indians in the last of several engagements that amounted to a protracted running fight up this river. The Cherokee defeat resulted in the virtual clearing of all East Texas for settlement by 1840.

Canton, 85 m. (alt. 540; pop. 2,949), is a quiet, shaded little county seat (Van Zandt Co.) until the first weekend of each month when "First Monday" Trades Day produces one of America's biggest combination garage sale-flea market-horsetrading extravaganzas. Most Texas towns observe a trades day or similar event, but none equals this.

The event (which actually commences each Friday preceding) began in 1873, when circuit court convened on a first Monday. Today it has grown to national prominence, covering some 100 acres of land with several thousand dealers selling or trading whatever you're looking for. Canton also hosts the Van Zandt County Fair each August.

An independent a community as you'll find anywhere, Canton took the county

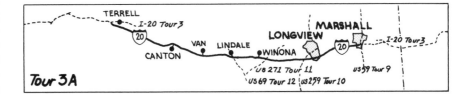

"First Monday" Trades Day at Canton.

seat in 1870 and found itself railroad-by-passed two years later. Ignoring that slight but smelling trouble, the settlement sent a posse up to Wills Point when that new railroad town threatened to take its court records. The Texas Supreme Court finally had to rule, and Canton held on to its governmental reins.

Cantonites, not about to forget Wills Point's rivalry, declined to ship their produce from that depot; instead they saw to the building of another railroad stop, Edgewood (Tour 3), east of its competitor.

During the Civil War, scarcity of slaves in this area caused a Canton editor to coin a phrase that stuck as a county epithet: "The Free State of Van Zandt."

Terrell, 114 m. Merge with Tour 3, continuing west.

☆

Tour 3B

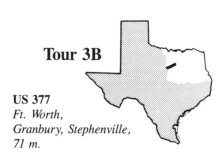

US 377
Ft. Worth,
Granbury, Stephenville,
71 m.

This brief tour climbs from the rolling prairies around Fort Worth into a barrier of low hills westward and, beyond those hills, enters the scenic valleys of the Paluxy and Brazos Rivers.

From Granbury to Stephenville, the land roughens to ranching country. For all its brevity the tour offers much scenic beauty and historic interest, particularly in the area of excellently restored Granbury.

Fort Worth, 0 m. See Tour 3.

Benbrook, 13 m. (alt. 658; pop. 19,564). Camping and all facilities are offered at Lake Benbrook, including a nature trail and horseback riding.

Cresson, 28 m. (alt. 1,047; pop. 208) has a museum of farm and ranch machinery.

Hood County Courthouse on the Town Square in Granbury.

Granbury, 41 m. (alt. 725; pop. 4,045), with its handsome courthouse and fine old rock homes, is a restoration delight and centers an area of concentrated historic and scenic interest.

The entire square has been designated as a Historic Site, the first so recognized in Texas. The old (1886) Opera House, restored handsomely in 1975, now offers good theater from March through Labor Day.

The C of C, housed in the old jail, offers tours of cell block and hanging tower. The

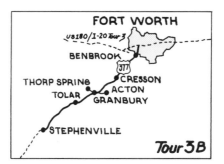

Opera House presents plays year-round. The *Granbury Queen* offers cruises on Lake Granbury. The historic Nutt House, 1893, features food and rooms.

Each July 4th, Granbury stages its biggest gala, naturally at its most proud restoration—the Square Fair. It's intriguing.

Immediately south, Lake Granbury offers water recreation, campsites.

Via FM 4 west is old **Thorp Springs,** pop. 184, settled in 1855. Still standing—"Stony Lonesome," as old-timers called them—are the ruins of the two-story rock wing of Add Ran College, founded in 1873. The Disciples of Christ successfully operated Add Ran for many years with early-day admonitions against the "love of dress," prohibition of smoking or profanity and, incidentally, gun-toting. Growing, the college moved for a time to Waco; then, as Texas Christian University, it moved to Fort Worth in 1910–1911.

Via FM 208 east 6 m. is **Acton State Park,** a tiny cemetery plot where Elizabeth Crockett, Davy's second wife, died and was buried in 1860. A handsome monument marks her grave.

South 10 m. down TX 144/FM 3210 the sweeping horseshoe of the Brazos River's DeCordova Bend contains one of the nation's largest pecan orchards, a beautiful, orderly forest. Within the bend are the rock traces of old **Kristenstad,** a Norwegian share-and-share-alike community which flourished briefly in the early 1900s and was abandoned by 1935. Below the bend, via local roads and FM 2174 is the site of **Fort Spunky,** 12 m., an 1847 Indian trading post-fort which drew its name from the number of shooting scrapes close by.

Via FM 51, due south 14 m., is scenic little **Paluxy,** pop. 76, by the clear-running stream of the same name. Established in the 1880s, it has been known by an extraordinary number of names: Goathers, Himmons, Haley's Mill, Pull Tight, Paluxyville and, finally, Paluxy. Toward Bluff Dale, on the Paluxy River, is Old Rock Church, beautifully situated and the site of camp meetings for well over a century. Its cemetery has the unusual distinction of grave-marking with coffin-shaped tombstones which rest flat against the ground.

Tolar, 50 m. (alt. 1,015; pop. 523), like Glen Rose to the south, occupies a prehistoric land, surrounded as it is by a petrified forest. Many of its buildings use the wood in place of stone.

Stephenville, 71 m. See Tour 2A. Enter Region IV—West Texas.

☆

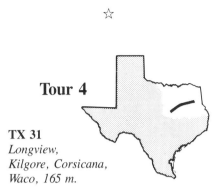

Tour 4

TX 31
Longview, Kilgore, Corsicana, Waco, 165 m.

Beginning in the middle of the East Texas pine belt, and at the center of that region's famed oilfield, your route angles south and west, from forest to prairie. As you travel, the eastern red hills level out, timber thins, and, near Corsicana, the terrain becomes rich, black, rolling countryside. This is land settled by early Anglo pioneers who founded moral, religious-minded communities, as today little white churches in occasional clearings still testify. You are also viewing much of Texas' old Confederacy, particularly as you near the Waco area, a region that sent many of Hood's famed Texas Brigade to Virginia.

Longview, 0 m.—See Tour 3/US 80.

At 9 m., veer west from US 259/Tour 10.

Kilgore, 11 m. (alt. 371; pop. 11,066). Near the center of the fabled East Texas field, this "Oil City of the World" once boasted 1,134 wells within its city limits. It was said that from the center of town you could not fire a gun in any direction without hitting a der-

rick. Most of the derricks are gone now; only the big pumps remain. The irony of this bonanza lay in the region's writeoff by major oil company geologists as worthless for exploration. But on December 19, 1930, Kilgore's Bateman No. 1 blew in and, in 24 hours, 5,000 oil men, plus followers of every persuasion, descended on the town. Production, drilling and leasing went on 24 hours daily, 7 days weekly. Oil flow was so prodigal, prices fell from $1.10 to 10¢ per barrel!

In successive steps, the National Guard, U.S. marshals, and finally the Texas Rangers moved into Gregg, Rusk, Upshur, Smith and Cherokee counties to enforce a developing proration—an orderly production of petroleum that has since distinguished Texas producers as farsighted conservationists.

Old-time Derrick on the site of "the World's Richest Acre," Kilgore.

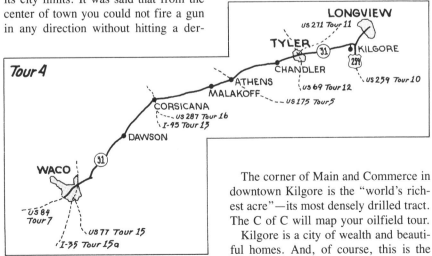

The corner of Main and Commerce in downtown Kilgore is the "world's richest acre"—its most densely drilled tract. The C of C will map your oilfield tour.

Kilgore is a city of wealth and beautiful homes. And, of course, this is the

home of Kilgore College and the nation's first and most famed formation-marching beauty corps, the Kilgore Rangerettes. The college maintains a "Showcase," reflecting the history of the Rangerettes. Also on campus, the East Texas Oil Museum depicts every aspect of the 1930 oil boom.

Nearby, see Henderson, Gladewater.

Tyler, 36 m. (alt. 558; pop. 75,450), believes itself one of America's most beautiful cities, and with some justification. This is "Rose Capital of the World," a 20-mile surrounding area producing more than *half* of America's roses! October, month of the Rose Festival (a five-day extravaganza), is also a time of blazing color—from sweetgum's scarlet to sycamore's gold—in the surrounding forests. March–April is the time of the Azalea and Spring Flower Trail—the tints are pastel, the woodland scent, that of new life.

Tyler is a pioneer town—its old-fashioned square shows this—a settlement in republic days and then, in 1846, a developing county seat growing around a log courthouse and jail. In its immediate area the Cherokee Indians, displacing the earlier Caddos (Tejas), were driven from Texas in a series of battles along the Neches to the west. Plantations followed. During the Civil War, Tyler was a Confederate stronghold, with a commissary, ammunition depot, iron foundry and, at Camp Ford (now a small city park), a prisoner-of-war camp once confining 6,000 Union soldiers from the close-by Louisiana campaigns of 1864. Rose culture was introduced in the 1880s; in the 1930s, Tyler rode the East Texas oil boom to its status today: local industry headquarters, a city of beautiful homes and of colleges (among them, the University of Texas at Tyler, and Tyler Junior College, and its precision-marching beauties, the Apache Belles).

Tyler's Municipal Rose Garden is a 27-acre work of art—some 38,000 bushes in 400 different hues—a geometry of color banked against a piney hillside. There is a handsome art museum, and the Patterson and Goodman houses are examples of fine old homes. The palatial Goodman, or LeGrand, "Bonnie Castle" houses a showplace of antebellum times.

The city boasts several other attractions including the Carnegie History Center, the Hudnall Planetarium, the

Museum of Art, the Caldwell Zoo, and the World of Wildlife Museum.

In late September Tyler hosts the week-long East Texas Fair. Just north is lovely Tyler State Park, camping and all facilities. Southeast on TX 64 is Lake Tyler; southwest on TX 155, Lake Palestine offers water sports. In the area also see Jacksonville and Mineola.

At Tyler, intersect US 271/Tour 11; US 69/Tour 12.

Just northwest of tiny **Chandler,** 48 m., pop. 1,630, the Battle of the Neches (see Van, Tour 3A) began a week-long running fight, which in 1839 ended with the expulsion of the Cherokee Indians from East Texas. Believing they had both Mexican and Texan promises of land, this Indian nation chose to fight, and lost.

Athens, 72 m. (alt. 490; pop. 10,967), rolling across low hills, is a quiet, shaded little city that grew around its square and courthouse oak. Under that giant tree, since burned, the first session of a district court was convened in 1850. The court oak is fresh in memory because a twin giant, over three centuries old, still stands a block east of the courthouse.

Here, returned to civilization, Cynthia Ann Parker spent the last few years of her "rescue" from the Comanche (see Groesbeck, Medicine Mounds). Neither she nor her Indian daughter could adjust to the white world; both died shortly and were buried here. Later her son, Quanah Parker, removed her body to Oklahoma.

Since the time of the skilled Caddo Indian craftsman, area clays have provided fine pottery. Earliest pioneers took up the craft in 1857, and today Athens con-

"Old Fiddlers Reunion," Athens.

tinues the tradition, also adding brick manufacture to its diversified industries.

Since 1931, the last May weekend is Athens' "Old Fiddlers Reunion." From everywhere they come, and the town, often swelled to 40,000, rocks to hoedowns, reels, and buck and wing. A giant square dance is the finale. In late July, Athenians observe an earthy, three-day Black-Eye Pea Jamboree, complete with cookoff and taste-in.

The city is the home of Trinity Valley Junior College. Just east via FM 2495, Lake Athens offers good fishing and water sports.

At Athens, intersect US 175/Tour 5.

Malakoff, 82 m. (alt. 377; pop. 2,038), now a brick-manufacturing town, was formerly a coal and silver-miner. Old-timers tell of a strange, carved image, the "Malakoff Man," found in an excavation at a geologic date level estimated beyond 12,000 years.

Immediately northwest, big Cedar Creek Reservoir offers water sports, good fishing.

Corsicana, 109 m. (alt. 411; pop. 22,911) is a steady, solid city centering rich farmland with handsome old homes nestled deep in planted shade. It was long known as "The Oil City." From an 1849 stage stand, it had grown substantially when, in 1894, a city-sunk water well struck oil. This sparked heated argument over the additional cost of casing through such worthless stuff . . . in the days before the automobile.

Eastern capital, however, built America's first big refinery south of town, and Magnolia Petroleum, later known as Mobil, was in business. Corsicana was first to use natural gas for cooking and lighting, and first to drive a locomotive with oil.

Near the courthouse is City Park and Pioneer Village, complete with a dog-run cabin, a log kitchen, slave quarters, store, barn, smithy and well—even to fireplace-cooked meals. This is one of the state's best pioneer restorations.

The Hartzell Store here may be particularly famous. Corsicanans believe that material came from the building at Washington-on-the-Brazos (an unfinished store owned by Noah Byars) in which the Texas Declaration of Independence was signed. Also at the park is an unusual monument—to Charlie M, an ordinary dray horse who became one of America's champion pacers at the turn of the century.

Downtown, the Collin Street Bakery first made its now world-famous fruit cake in 1896—today a holiday delicacy known everywhere. Navarro College, on the west side of town, displays an outstanding collection of Indian artifacts—some 44,000 pieces—in its Arrowhead Room, part of the Gaston C. Gooch Library.

At Corsicana, intersect I-45/Tour 13, and US 287/Tour 16. Nearby are Fairfield, Mexia and Ennis.

At 122 m. intersect FM 55. Just north is **Dresden,** once a thriving town with two-story Dresden College and its "Justice Tree," where a justice of the peace returned sentence of hanging. Today it's a near-ghost, with only 25 inhabitants.

Beyond **Dawson,** 130 m., pop. 766, Richland Creek becomes "Battle Creek." On October 8, 1838, one of East Texas' more savage Indian fights occurred when a party of 25 surveyors was hit by 300 Kickapoo Indians. All but seven of the pioneers fell, and by the time a burial party reached them, wolves had left only bones. A marble shaft marks the grave. Navarro Mills Reservoir, with camping and all facilities, lies north on FM 667.

Hubbard, 136 m. (alt. 627; pop. 1,589), was the much-loved home of one of baseball's greatest players—Tris Speaker, buried here. The Onstott-Rigsby House is a beautiful Victorian home.

680-acre Cameron Park on the Brazos River, Waco.

Waco, 165 m. (alt. 427; pop. 103,590 city). This distribution and manufacturing center—Dr. Pepper was born here—long marked by a single tall building, spreads along the Brazos now, a handsome city often called Texas' most pleasant in which to live. Its springs have always made it a favored spot, originally the site of a Waco Indian village and noted by early explorers as an exceptional location for a great city.

In the early 1800s the Wacos were pushed from the land by Cherokees in a battle near what is now Waco High School. By 1837, remote Ranger Fort Fisher was perhaps Texas' most exposed outpost, but within 12 years the new city served as the center for rich Brazos bottom plantations. Waco volunteered heavily for the Confederacy and was occupied by Federal troops for a time after the war. On the route of the cattle trails, the city began to recover, and in the 1870s the rails brought a boom.

In 1870 Waco spanned its river with what was then the nation's longest suspension bridge—475 feet—hung from Waco-built brick towers with New Jersey-built cables. It seemed so miraculous, just hanging there as it does today, that Texans called it "The Magic Bridge." At the turn of the century, determined to be an inland port, the city began its first Brazos lock and dam, but a flood changed the river course. East, near tiny **Asa,** the concrete ghost stands in a field today.

Also eastward, near little **Harrison Switch,** the long valley where Tehuacana Creek empties was site of Texas' great Indian Council Grounds. Here every major treaty took place, from Stephen F. Austin's 1824 truce with the Karankawa to Sam Houston's great council in 1845 with 20 Indian nations and more than 3,000 braves. Here also was the first U.S. treaty which pushed the Indians farther west.

Waco boasts many attractions—Fort Fisher Park, excellent in-town camping facilities and a replica of the old ranger outpost. The Texas Ranger Museum displays dramatic history in film and diorama; the Texas Ranger Hall of Fame salutes great lawmen. The Dr Pepper Museum at 300 S. Fifth St. recalls invention of the popular soft drink in surroundings of original 1906 bottling plant. Soda fountain serves visitors. Waco also opens four Southern mansions for tours twice a year (April and December) and every weekend; contact Visitor Center at Fort Fisher.

Among four other colleges, Baylor University has always been a dominant force in Texas. Quietly shaded for its proximity to the central business area, the Baptist institution, founded at little Independence in 1845, moved to this 30-acre campus in 1861. The Armstrong-Browning Library boasts the world's most complete collection of works by Robert and Elizabeth Barrett Browning, and its Texas Collection is excellent.

The original springs that made Waco such a favored site for settlement are preserved in a small park immediately adjacent to the old suspension bridge, now a pedestrian walkway.

The Heart O' Texas Fair and Rodeo entertains each October. Year-round, 36 municipal parks beautify the city, anchored by 380-acre Cameron Park in the heart of the city. The Cen-Tex Zoo, specially planned for children, includes playground, petting zoo, and hand feeding areas. On the Baylor campus, the Strecker Museum includes varied collections adjacent to a village of 14 historic buildings depicting a Texas river town of the 1800s. The Texas Sports Museum (1401 Jefferson) honors Texas high school athletes. Labor Day features the Great Raft Race, entries including anything that will float (and some that don't).

At Waco, intersect US 84/Tour 7; US 77/Tour 15; I-35/Tour 15A.

☆

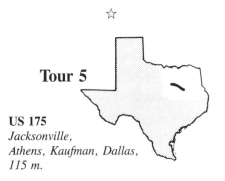

Tour 5

US 175
Jacksonville, Athens, Kaufman, Dallas, 115 m.

A northwestward route from mid and lower East Texas, US 175 provides one of the more lightly traveled accesses to Dallas, crossing from piney woods to prairie.

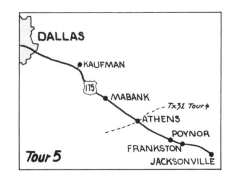

Your road begins in the forests of the Cherokee who, driven westward, had replaced the Caddoan tribes around the Jacksonville area and who, in turn, were expelled by 1839 pioneer settlers.

Near Athens, the iron-red hills begin to lower, the timber thins, and at Kaufman you are into the blackland prairies. Throughout, you traverse a region where farming is still the way of life and townfolk trace their ancestry to the lower Southern states. Beyond Kaufman you move quickly into the loom of metropolitan Dallas.

Jacksonville, 0 m. (alt. 516; pop. 12,765). A pioneer town established in 1849, this little city has grown with easy grace and today displays a handsome, ample business area with broad streets and sidewalks and a lived-in, cared-for residential section. Always proud of its educational institutions (see Old Larissa, north, Tour 12), this is home of Lon Morris College (known nationally for its Drama Dept.), Jacksonville College, and Baptist Missionary Theological Seminary.

Jacksonville is busy with festivals year round—Western Days in July, the famed Tomato Fest in September, County and Regional fairs in October, and a down-home Christmas festival in December. The public library displays regional history.

Many pretty scenic tours traverse the surrounding area, a major beauty spot being Love's Lookout Park, 5 m. north on US 69 (see Mt. Selman).

Here, too, is the center of unusual early colonization—the region's first "settlers" were Cherokee Indians who, like other homesteaders, sought and believed they received Mexican land grants. Their friend Sam Houston later upheld their claims, but they were driven from the land.

All about, the hilly red land suggests iron; the Confederacy mined it, and close by Jacksonville are several old iron-boomers—**Reklaw, Dialville** and **Ironton,** tiny survivors of the great iron rush of the 1880s. On country store porches of many little towns about, seemingly perpetual domino games go on.

Nearby are Alto and Palestine. Immediately south, Lake Jacksonville provides recreation and excellent bass fishing. Especially scenic drives around the lake are FM 747 and FM 2138.

Frankston, 18 m. (alt. 389; pop. 1,127), is an old sawmill town looking out from its hill across a checkerboard of pasture and timber. South 2 m. is the site of the Kickapoo Battlefield where, in 1838, General Thomas J. Rusk led 200 Texans to victory over a band of hostile Indians and Mexican allies. North is Lake Palestine, offering water sports.

Poynor, 24 m. Old-time Milner's Mill stone-grinds corn. Ribbon cane syrup is available, as are recipes run off on an antique printing press.

Athens, 42 m.—see Tour 4.

Mabank, 61 m. is gateway to big Cedar Creek Reservoir, all facilities, west.

Kaufman, 82 m. (alt. 439; pop. 5,238) is a quiet, somewhat withdrawn town that used a remodeled blacksmith shop for its first courthouse and presently clusters about an ornate structure built in 1885.

In the early 1840s, a party of Mississippians pushed to the three forks of the Trinity and built King's Fort, later called Kingsborough, finally renamed Kaufman for a pioneer legislator. Caddo, Kickapoo, Delaware, and Cherokee Indians living in the area when Dr. William King arrived leading the first Anglo settlers accepted the newcomers peacefully, and there was only one recorded instance of an Indian attack in the county.

Dallas, 115 m., see Tour 2A.

☆

Tour 6

US 79
Louisiana line,
Carthage, Henderson,
Jacksonville,
Palestine, Hearne, 200 m.

Angling southwest, this was for many years a principal route from Arkansas and Tennessee to South Texas. Half the trip is East Texas forest; the last half, rolling prairie. You begin in some of the earliest-settled Texas land and end in antebellum plantation countryside.

From Carthage to Palestine you traverse thick forest; beyond that point,

East Texans claim you have left their area . . . that beyond the Brazos, even the dogwood will not blossom. As the land levels into the rich Brazos bottoms, you enter a region that was cotton plantation-rich immediately prior to the Civil War, a land of "fire eaters" who made up most of Hood's Texas Brigade, Lee's Grenadier Guards. To this country one in ten returned, and only recently did the countryside itself recover, now prospering with recent oil and gas discoveries and renewed agriculture.

Louisiana line (immediately west of Shreveport), 0 m.

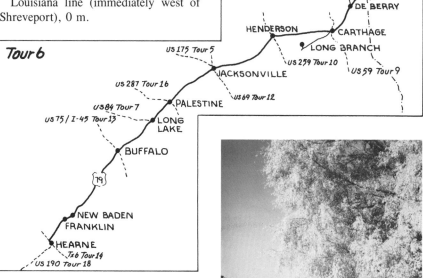

Just north of De Berry, 9 m., **Elysian Fields,** pop. 300, is an old settlement, taking its name from the enthusiasm of its pioneers. It is an area of old plantation homes.

Carthage, 24 m. (alt. 249; pop. 6,496), is a tranquil little woodland city with a reputation for good "home-cooked" restaurant meals, a holdover from early days when the gathering spot was Sam Sprauls' ginger cake and beer shop—a time when both school and worship were held in the 1848 pine-walled Masonic Hall.

Carthage was heavily involved in East Texas' Regulator-Moderator War (see Shelbyville), an upheaval that threatened the Republic of Texas until Sam Houston sent an army to put it down. The town progressed modestly until 1944, when its completely rural economy altered with the discovery of a vast condensate gas field close by. Music fans know it as birthplace of Tex Ritter and Jim Reeves, honored in Heritage Hall on the square.

At Carthage, intersect US 59/Tour 9. Lake Murvaul, southwest on FM 10, of-

fers all facilities; Toledo Bend Reservoir, heading southeast on FM 699 to US 84, is a massive, forested water recreation area. Nearby, also see Marshall, Teneha, Tatum.

At 39 m. intersect FM 1798. Here you cross Trammel's Trace, one of the earliest northbound pioneer trails and a smuggler's route prior to Texas independence.

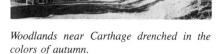

Woodlands near Carthage drenched in the colors of autumn.

Follow FM 1798 southwest 5 m. to tiny **Pinehurst.** West 4 m. on FM 2867 is Old Pine Grove Church. The Cumberland Presbyterian Church was organized in 1850, and this building, erected in 1870, is one of the area's oldest.

Henderson, 51 m. (alt. 500; pop. 11,139), dappled with redbud and magnolia, has the new look of oil prosperity but is older than its appearances. Founded in 1843, it grew with lumbering, then plantation agriculture, survived a disastrous 1860 fire and Civil War reconstruction, then just west of town in 1930 ushered in the mighty East Texas oil boom and its own solid future. With all its oil, Henderson is blessed with lignite coal reserves and

TX 64 between Henderson and Joiner-ville.

operates the world's largest lignite-fired electric power generating plant. The city also boasts the largest auto-mated face brick plant in the world.

There are several handsome old homes—the Howard-Dickinson House preeminent among them—and south of town, the site of an 1822 Shawnee Indian village. Northeast is Martin Lake with all facilities; southwest, Striker Creek Reservoir offers good fishing, campsites. Harmony Hill ghost town lies northeast on Texas 43; Depot Museum houses county history at 514 N. High St.

At Henderson, intersect US 259/Tour 10.

Via TX 64 west, 6 m. is **Joinerville,** a wayside village on the site of a Cherokee town where the East Texas field blew in. Despite geologists' conviction to the contrary, 70-year-old C. M. Joiner, who had made and lost two wildcat fortunes in Oklahoma, was certain he was drilling into an oil pool. Using a flimsy rig and battered tools, he missed twice, but on September 8, 1930, Daisy Bradford No. 3 hit. Father of 25,000 wells to follow his discovery, the oldtimer became "Dad" Joiner to the petroleum industry. A park here salutes pioneering "Joe Roughneck."

At 56 m., cross the Angelina River. Near here in 1836 Sam Houston negotiated a treaty with the Cherokee Indians, critical to Texans embattled with Mexico. The Cherokee, promised land for neutrality, kept the treaty; the Texas Legislature later overrode Houston and abrogated it.

Jacksonville, 86 m.—see Tour 5.

Palestine, 111 m. (alt. 510; pop. 18,042), is an intriguing blend of old and new: its outer, circling highways glitter with new construction; its residential area displays fine old antebellum homes. In its business district you have the compulsion to drive to the depot to watch the

train pull in, for the tracks run right through downtown, and Palestine has long been a railroad town. An interesting self-guided downtown walking tour is available. See the C of C in the old Carnegie Library, 502 N. Queen.

It is an old town, having grown out of remote Fort Houston since 1835. The old fort site lies west of town and is almost traceless today. Fort Houston provided refuge for the survivors of the 1836 Fort Parker massacre (see Groesbeck), those desperate pioneers struggling through 60 miles of wilderness to reach this outpost.

Resting atop an enormous salt dome, an early supply for Indians, Palestine offers varied enticements. Here is one terminal of the Texas State Railroad Park (also see Rusk) offering an old-fashioned train ride. Nearby are Palestine's community forest, the Engeling Wildlife Refuge, and the U.S. government's scientific balloon station which releases the enormous weather-gauges. In late March-early April the Dogwood Trails attract thousands when surrounding woodlands whiten and the city's fine old homes are on tour. Trails are mapped and marked. The scenic Davey Dogwood Park is a major Trails beauty spot. The old Pilgrim Church (see Elkhart), south of the city, is also a favorite tour landmark.

Southwest on US 79/84 is Old Magnolia Frontier Town, restored historic buildings recreating an Old West town.

In Reagan Park, named for Confederate Postmaster General, the Museum for East Texas Culture, housed in a 1915 school, includes a vintage classroom, refurbished caboose, special interest exhibits, and numerous historical exhibits.

US 79 near Palestine.

Eilenberger's Butternut Baking Co. at 512 N. St. John St. has been making fruitcakes since 1898. The Palestine Firefighters' Museum is unusually housed in a working fire station on US 287 north. Outlying are a number of lakes, and near town in June–July, you can pick your own blueberries at an unusual commercial farm. The week-long county fair is an August–September gala. At Palestine, intersect US 287/Tour 16. Merge with US 84/Tour 7 to Long Lake.

Long Lake, 124 m., is near the site of ghost riverport **Magnolia,** a mid-1800s boomer named for its huge, blossoming tree that centered the town. Veer south from US 84/Tour 7.

At **Buffalo,** 146 m. (alt. 370; pop. 1,555), a major crossroads and a farming center, intersect US 75, I-45/Tour 13. Nearby see Fairfield, Centerville.

New Baden, 184 m. (alt. 427; pop. 105), a wayside village, was founded by cultured German immigrants in the 1880s. Unable to adjust to farming, many moved away.

Franklin, 188 m. (alt. 450; pop. 1,336) has been Robertson County seat since 1874, ending a series of courthouse shifts which left several ghost towns, including Old Franklin, close by. As in early days, residences flank one side of the town square. At Mt. Pleasant Church cemetery, just southeast, is the grave of Walter Williams, Confederate soldier, who survived all Civil War veterans, both North and South.

Hearne, 200 m. Intersect US 190/Tour 18; enter Region II, Southeast Texas where your route continues as Tour 18B.

Tour 7

US 84
Logansport La.,
Rusk, Palestine, Mexia,
Waco, Gatesville, Evant, 267
m.

T his tour very nearly cuts the middle of Texas, east to west. You begin in some of the state's densest woodland, the

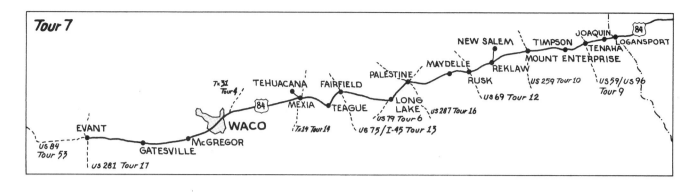

upper Sabine National Forest. Climbing gradually, you emerge beyond Palestine into more open, rolling countryside, prairies which extend a short distance beyond Waco, where the land roughens.

En route, you cross the upper edge of the old Tejas Indian nation to the land where the Tawakoni held its western ramparts around Mexia. Beyond Waco, you penetrate the eastern edge of Comancheria. As early Texans knew their land, you move from the livelihood of timbering to old plantation country. Beyond Waco, you face the embattled frontier where early Texas Rangers had to shoot their way in.

Louisiana line at the Sabine River above Toledo Bend Reservoir, 0 m.

At **Joaquin,** 1 m., pop. 805, access roads lead south to the upper reaches of vast Toledo Bend Reservoir, 1,200 miles of shoreline, flanked on the Texas side by Sabine National Forest. All recreation facilities, public and private, are offered.

Tenaha, 15 m. (alt. 351; pop. 1,072), is an area known to pioneer Texans as the Redlands, early-settled and aggressive in the Texas Revolution. Part of a region in question between early American and Spanish claims, Shelby County knew violence that extended beyond the revolution. A major power struggle between contesting vigilante groups—the 1840s Regulator-Moderator War—was finally put down by Sam Houston.

With several false-fronted buildings, Tenaha still projects an old-time look, but with the opening of Toledo Bend recreation facilities, the town is waking to tourism.

Intersect US 59-US 96/Tour 9. Merge with US 59 to Timpson. Nearby are Carthage, Center, Shelbyville.

At **Timpson,** 25 m. (alt. 394; pop. 1,029), a red-dusty lumber-shipping and

tomato-growing town, US 59 veers south into Tour 10.

Mount Enterprise, 42 m. (alt. 610; pop. 501). In 1832 this town's name projected its ambitions, and by 1860 it was site of a factory, advanced schools, sawmills, gins—a sure future. By-passed by the railroad, the town moved two miles to trackside, but its promise dwindled. Traces of the first settlement still exist. Here you intersect US 259/Tour 10.

At 53 m., FM 2753 leads north 1 m. to **Glenfawn** and the restored showplace plantation mansion, Monte Verdi, built in the mid-1800s by Julien Devereux, whose Virginia home had been near Mount Vernon and who sought to recall such a Southern Colonial home here.

Little **Reklaw,** 61 m., pop. 266, was an 1880s iron-rush boomtown.

Via FM 839 north is tiny **New Salem,** pop. 31, and a small sawmill typical of this longtime timbering area. Nearby are Lake Striker, camping and good fishing.

Rusk, 72 m. (alt. 489; pop. 4,366) is a pretty, glistening town nestled in rolling hills and tall pines. A state park marks the birthplace of Texas' first native-born governor, James Stephen Hogg. Also here is one terminus of America's narrowest state park, the **Texas State Railroad Park,** a 25-mile forest run to Palestine, beautifully scenic and filled with the bittersweet nostalgia of old railroad travel (camping and all facilities available). Close about is the site of pioneer Cook's Fort, a Confederate gun factory and ironworks. In town, the old Bonner Bank Building is a hospitality center; an interesting old footbridge—claimed to be the world's largest—is nearby. The Thomas Jefferson Rusk Hotel is a prettily-refurbished inn.

Early each October, Rusk hosts the two-day East Texas Regional Arts and Crafts Fair. It's a good one!

At Rusk intersect US 69/Tour 12. Nearby, see Jacksonville, New Birmingham, Mission Tejas State Park.

At little **Maydelle,** 81 m., pop. 250, Fairchild State Forest offers nature trails.

Palestine, 103 m.—see Tour 6. Merge with US 79 to Long Lake.

Long Lake, 116 m. Tour 6/US 79 veers south.

Fairfield, 140 m. (alt. 461; pop. 3,234), has the air of a shaded little deep-southern city miraculously removed to rolling prairie. Becoming county seat in 1851, it indeed centered a rich plantation area by 1860. The Freestone County Museum, housed in a century-old jail, preserves the region's rich history.

On the south side of the town square is an unusual cannon—one of a six-gun battery captured in the 1861 Confederate invasion of the Far West and dragged more than 1,000 miles in the ordeal of mountain retreat. As it fought through the war, the battery became famed as the

The Valverde Cannon, used in an 1861 Confederate invasion, sits on the courthouse lawn at Fairfield.

"Valverde," for the site of its capture, but one by one the guns were lost. The last surviving captain took this piece home near here and buried it, to be unearthed 15 years later in celebration of Grover Cleveland's election. The gun has guarded this square since that time. Northeast 6 m., via FM 1124, is Fairfield Lake State Recreation Area—camping and all facilities, including a good hiking trail.

At Fairfield, intersect US 75, I-45/Tour 13.

Turn-of-the-century architecture: the railroad station at Teague. (Courtesy of Genie Mims and Burlington-Rock Island Railroad Museum.)

Teague, 151 m. (alt. 499; pop. 3,268), has an early-1900s brick-built look about it; it boomed with railroad shops then, and today maintains an interesting railroad museum. Westward, the terrain flattens to sloping hills dotted with post oak. The immediate area boasts deposits of coal, oil and natural gas.

Mexia, 163 m. (alt. 534, pop. 6,933), wears the look of a city much larger than it is, the result of a spectacular 1920 oil boom. Born somewhat recently, in 1871 railroad growth, it actually occupies ancient land, long the home of the Tehuacana (Tawakoni) Indians. On nearby Tehuacana Hill is the site of an early Indian village destroyed by invading Cherokees in the early 1800s. For generations, oldtimers have sworn to the presence of a ghostly Indian lookout, on watch atop that hill.

Via FM 1633 southwest 6 m., the old Confederate Reunion Grounds are marked by a cannon and pavilion near the Navasota River. Reunions ended in the late 1930s. Nearby, between here and Groesbeck (see Tour 14), historic old Fort Parker stands restored guard. Fort Parker State Park offers all facilities and good camping, and Lake Limestone,

good fishing. At Mexia intersect TX 14/Tour 14.

At **Tehuacana,** 5 m., pop. 322, northwest on TX 171, a massive, cupola-topped early Victorian building crowns the dominant hill. Trinity University was originally housed here in 1869. The school moved to Waxahachie and finally to San Antonio's handsome campus in 1942. Since then, the old building has served various purposes. These Tehuacana Hills, highest point between Dallas and Houston, mark an area that Philip Nolan explored for President Thomas Jefferson. For Nolan details, see San Augustine (Tour 8), and Blum (Tour 15A).

West along your route, all water sports are offered at big Lake Mexia.

Waco, 203 m.—see Tour 4.

McGregor, 222 m. (alt. 713; pop. 4,683), is a brisk center of rich agriculture. Southward, in the spring, bluebonnets and paintbrush are particularly beautiful.

Via TX 317 to FM 2671 southwest, **Mother Neff State Park,** 11 m., is a 259-acre scenic woodland along the Leon River, with camping and all facilities. Given by former Governor Pat Neff, it began the Texas State Park system in 1917. Earlier, the area was a popular camp meeting site.

Gatesville, 242 m. (alt. 795; pop. 11,492), nestles behind suddenly rearing low hills as the central prairies break off into rougher country. Rambling along its main street-highway, past a weathered square, Gatesville reaches across its Leon River valley, giving the appearance of a town larger than it is. The settlement grew from old Fort Gates (today a marker only), a big establishment east of town that in 1848 lay along the earliest U.S.-built cordon of frontier forts. The Buckhorn Museum on the square and the Coryell County Historical Museum at 199 N. Eighth provide an interesting step into the past. The 1897 courthouse is one of the finest examples of the style in Texas.

Near **Pancake** in the hills north of town, a strange search for the Lost Jim Bowie Mine has proceeded for half-a-century. A well-to-do ranching family discovered a sealed cave with a rock allegedly carved with Bowie's name and, over the years, many Spanish and Indian artifacts. For the lifetime of a father, and

now a son, the search for three thousand pounds of Comanche-hidden treasure has continued.

At **Evant,** 267 m., a little crossroads town, intersect US 281/Tour 17. Enter Region IV, West Texas, where your route continues as Tour 53.

☆

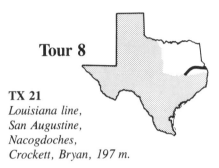

Tour 8

TX 21
Louisiana line,
San Augustine,
Nacogdoches,
Crockett, Bryan, 197 m.

This route, sloping southwest, is one of America's oldest, following the ancient trail known as Spain's Royal Road, Camino Real, blazed in 1691. Beginning at the Louisiana line, it angles down across the state, eventually to Mexico, where it becomes Highway 57 across from Eagle Pass, bound for Saltillo. Its original purpose in Spain's "New World" was to connect the outposts of upper Mexico with missions on the East Texas-Louisiana line.

You begin in red, pine-forested hills and, on this leg, end in blackland prairie. In pioneer days, the forests from San Augustine to Crockett were known as the "Redlands," seat of early Texas revolts. Beyond Madisonville, opening of the land was slower, Indian opposition stiffer. Around Bryan you reach the region of the great Brazos bottom plantations, just beginning to flourish when the Civil War brought their demise. Until recently, most Texans were descendants of the Old South.

Toledo Bend Reservoir, 0 m. You are now entering Sabine National Forest, edging this great lake and providing superb fishing and a multitude of facilities both north and south of your route. Take note also that from this national forest, all the way across to the Davy Crockett National Forest (around Crockett), your route will travel near many good hiking trails. (Inquire locally.) Near Hyland Park, immediately north, some old

Tour 8

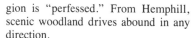
Traveling through the forest on TX 87 between Milam and Hemphill.

Toledo Bend Reservoir, an angler's paradise bordering Sabine National Forest.

homes remain from the town of Pendleton, dating from the 1812 James Gaines Ferry, which carried both the earliest invaders and settlers into Texas.

Across the Sabine here in 1806, United States and Spanish troops faced each other in a boundary confrontation which nearly resulted in war. Completely unauthorized, American General James Wilkinson agreed to a "Neutral Ground" separating the two nations along the Sabine, an act which clouded American claim to Louisiana Purchase lands westward and which would result in 15 years of freebooting expeditions to claim land that American frontiersmen believed rightfully theirs.

Milam, 7 m., pop. 177, a red-dusty forested village. Good hiking trails lie to the south.

South via TX 87 is **Hemphill** (alt. 267; pop. 1,182), a closeted little county seat (Sabine Co.) and long a lumbering center now awaking to Toledo Bend's tourism. The outlying area is still little changed from its pioneer beginnings—crops are "pitched," reli-

gion is "perfessed." From Hemphill, scenic woodland drives abound in any direction.

Eastward, largely submerged in the lake, is the ghost of **Sabinetown,** once a prosperous shipping point launching both cotton floats and logging rafts. The passing of the riverboat era brought Sabinetown's decline, but during the Civil War the expectation of Federal invasion brought heavy Confederate fortifications here, their traces still visible.

At 10 m. is **McMahon's Chapel,** the first Methodist church organized in Texas (1833), now in its third building on the same site, and still holding services.

San Augustine, 28 m. (alt. 304; pop. 2,237), situated on low red hills, is proud of its heritage, calling itself "the oldest American town in Texas"—its Anglos slipped into Spanish Texas as early as the 1790s. But civilization reached the region long before this, for in 1716 San Augustine was the site of Mission Nuestra Senora de Dolores de los Ais, and later Presidio San Agustin de Ahumada, its guardian fort. Both of these were log establishments, long since reclaimed by the forest.

Here in 1794 Philip Nolan corralled mustangs to drive into Louisiana, and from here he scouted Texas for the United States. With the establishment of the Texas Republic, San Augustine became a leading community and educational center, with the University of San Augustine and Wesleyan Male and Female College—the rivalry between them closing both prior to the Civil War.

San Augustinians are rightly proud of the historic homes in and outlying their city—the Blunt, Cartwright, Cullen and Garrett Houses, and that of Philip Sublett where Sam Houston recuperated from his San Jacinto wounds. These East Texans are quick to point out that their 1840 homes, unlike most, were no log cabin shebangs, but handsome, finished homes—Texas versions of Virginia's Williamsburg. See the C of C.

The old Town Well, slave-dug in 1860, has been restored, complete to its sweetgum roller, hand-wrought iron handle, and oaken bucket.

With national forests east and west, many hiking trails are available. Immediately south is Angelina National Forest and big Sam Rayburn Reservoir, all facilities. At San Augustine, intersect US 96/Tour 9. Nearby, also see Center and Shelbyville.

At **Chireno,** 43 m., pop. 415, a village delightful for its gingerbread houses, you'll find the Halfway House or old Stagecoach Inn, a private home and museum. Built in the early 1840s, it employs a wide center hallway flanked by rooms to either side—a style of the time.

South on FM 95, near tiny Woden, 8 m., is **Oil Springs,** claimant to Texas' first oil well. In 1866 oil appeared on the spring's surface; it was struck at a depth of 100 feet. The restored site is open to visitors.

Nacogdoches, 64 m. (alt. 283; pop. 30,872), spreading over its red, piney hills, seems more deep-southern than its Spanish heritage claims. Its beginnings were seeded in 1690 with the lodgment of Mission Tejas at nearby Weches, followed by the extension—a barrier against French Louisiana at Natchitoches—to Spain's entire East Texas establishment centering on this area. Nacogdoches was also the site of Mission Nuestra Senora de Guadalupe, two other

Restoration of Nacogdoches' Old Stone Fort built by Spanish settlers in the 1700s.

outpost missions, and a guarding presidio.

Off-and-on occupation by the Spanish—its location was fearfully remote from Mexico—resulted in the town in 1779. Spain had ordered East Texas abandoned, but in an extraordinary pilgrimage, settlers returned under resolute Antonio Gil Y'Barbo, walking from San Antonio in defiance of his king's orders.

Y'Barbo's people built the Old Stone Fort, restored today as an excellent museum (copy of the first Texas newspaper) on the handsome campus of Stephen F. Austin University; and this old red rock building has seen much of Texas history pass by. It can claim three flags in addition to Texas': the green banner of the Gutierrez-Magee Expedition (1812–13), which from here declared the First Texas Republic, and the flag of Dr. James Long (1819–21), both forays destined for failure. Here also briefly flourished the strange Fredonian Rebellion of 1826, when red men and white allied to divide Texas on a north-south basis between them. The Fredonians were short-lived.

Old Nacogdoches University, the first non-sectarian institution chartered by the Republic, is now a colonial-columned museum on the Rusk Middle School campus. Directly opposite is one of the ancient Indian temple mounds (three of them here were razed unknowingly).

North Street (US 59) is one of America's oldest thoroughfares, a village-connecting Indian trail when Spain arrived to place Mission Guadalupe on what she renamed "La Calle del Norte."

At the city's edge, up that street, is Old North Church—one of Texas' first—with its great Post Oak. Under these branches, early settlers worshipped secretly as early as 1832, when protestantism was forbidden. Immediately after San Jacinto, a log church was built. In 1852, on the same foundation stones, the present frame structure went up.

East of the city 4 m. on Melrose Road is an 1829 dwelling, one of several homes of Peter Ellis Bean, a survivor of the 1800 expedition of Philip Nolan. In town, the old Adolphus Sterne home is now the Hoya Memorial Museum: here Sam Houston was baptized into the Catholic faith (then a prerequisite to receiving Texas lands). At Millard's Crossing is one of the state's finest collections of pioneer dwellings—from a dog-run to a parsonage, where weddings still are performed. Oak Grove Cemetery, with graves dating from 1837, inters four signers of the Texas Declaration of Independence.

These Nacogdoches pioneers struck one of the first sparks in the Texas Revolution when, in 1832, they drove a substantial Mexican garrison from the little city, which thereafter remained free of occupation and served as a gateway of supplies, money and men for Texas independence. It was in representation of Nacogdoches that Sam Houston made his first real entry on the disturbed Texas scene.

West 4 m. on TX 21, then south on El Camino Real is Goyen's Hill, home of black patriot and entrepreneur William Goyens.

At Nacogdoches, intersect US 259/US 59 Tour 10. Nearby, also see Lufkin, Sam Rayburn Reservoir.

At **Cushing,** pop. 587, northwest 22 m. via US 259/TX 204, is the site of Mission San Jose de los Nazonis (1716–30). In the withdrawal of Spain's East Texas missions to San Antonio, this one was re-established there as today's Mission San Juan.

Near tiny **Douglass,** 78 m., is the site of Nuestra Senora de las Purisma Concepcion and its guarding presidio. The mission—also bound for San Antonio re-establishment in 1730—became Concepcion in that city. Here you're also close to the site of ghost town Mount Sterling, in 1837 projected as the metropolis of East Texas. Faintest traces remain. Just south is Lake Nacogdoches, with water sports.

At **Alto,** 89 m. (alt. 433; pop. 1,027), a forested village that seems to have changed little over the years, you enter an area old in pioneer history, ancient in Indian prehistory. Here stood a village of the Neches Indians, forced out of Texas in 1839. Later came a Delaware Indian village. Northwest 3 m. was the last home of Chief Bowles of the Cherokees, killed in a battle with Texan forces in 1839.

Each fall during Indian Summer the latchstring is out at Forest Hill for "Alto's Past Treasures," an authentic showing of period furnishings and craft demonstrations of the 1800s with a sparkle of entertainment features.

At 91 m. is the site of Lacy's Fort, built prior to 1835 by Indian agent Martin Lacy. For several years the fort guarded against Indian uprisings.

At 97 m. immediately south of the highway is the **Caddo Indians Mound** (state historical park) considered by archeologists to have been the temple mound of the Tejas Indian Confederacy. These advanced and hospitable farmer-weaver-potters are believed to have lived here prior to 1000 A.D., first encountering white men when survivors of Hernando de Soto's expedition penetrated this far in a vain attempt to reach Mexico overland. Westward, near the Trinity River crossing of your route, the Spaniards are believed to have turned back and escaped by way of the Mississippi River, boating to Mexico. It was the Tejas settlement throughout this area that attracted the early cluster of Spanish missions. East Texans also claim that La

Mission San Francisco De Los Tejas, Weches.

Salle was killed here. This park includes a reconstructed Caddoan dwelling, a visitors center, and an interpretive hiking trail.

At 97.8 m., cross the Neches River. On the east bank, inaccessible by road, is the site of short-lived Mission Santisimo Nombre de Maria, a 1691 companion to the installation immediately ahead.

Weches, 99 m., pop. 26. Immediately north is **Mission Tejas State Park,** one of Texas' most significant. Here, in 1690–93, Spain anchored her easternmost mission, and to reach it from far-distant Monclova, Mexico, her troops blazed the Camino Real, known as TX 21 today—the road you're on! It was Spain's dogged determination to hold this eastern front, later against France, which brought about the establishment of the Nacogdoches area. In the forested park is a faithful replica of the little log church where, toward the end of 1693, founding Father Damien Massanet mounted a cannon in the doorway to defend against Tejas Indians turned hostile. Unsupported, he finally burned the church and returned to Mexico. Spain tried the area again 23 years later but finally abandoned her installations in the 1730s and moved three of the missions to San Antonio, where they became, respectively, San Francisco, San Juan and Concepcion. A beautiful park with camping and all facilities, Mission Tejas also provides a scenic nature trail. Also located here is the restored Rice Stagecoach Inn, typical of the many that marked this pioneering thoroughfare.

At 101 m. intersect FM 227 south, into Davy Crockett National Forest. This road takes you to **Ratcliff Lake Recreational Area,** with camping, hiking trails, and other facilities as well as a lovely lake.

A nature trail through the deep woods at Ratcliff Lake Recreation Area.

Crockett, 123 m. (alt. 350; pop. 7,024), is an elegant old town, shaded by hundreds of pecan trees and assembled about its compact square much as a dignified Southern dame would carefully spread her skirts. But here you are about to leave the Old South, its soft accents and reserved old homes. The Monroe-Crook House was built by the great nephew of President James Monroe in 1854. The Downs-Aldrich House with its elaborate Victorian gingerbread, was built in 1891.

Crockett is headquarters of the Davy Crockett National Forest. Some two blocks from the downtown circle a drinking fountain near the underpass marks the old spring where, tradition insists, Davy camped en route his destiny at the Alamo (inquire at the C of C). The handsome little city also boasts a Davy Crockett Memorial Park (municipal), a Houston County Museum, and a county Cultural Center. Its World Champion Fiddlers Festival, each June, is a gala event. Northwest is Houston County Lake, offering water sports.

At Crockett, intersect US 287/Tour 16. Nearby, see Elkhart, Grapeland, Trinity.

At 145 m., cross the Trinity River. Westward, the pine forest opens to tim-

ber-patched, rolling prairies, standing principally in oak and elm. On the west bank is the site of a Spanish settlement known variously in the late 1700s and early 1800s as Bucareli, Trinidad and—to the oncoming Anglo—Spanish Bluff. The little town was razed and its inhabitants massacred by Spanish troops in retaliation for its participation in the 1812–13 Gutierrez-Magee Expedition, the first attempt to free Texas. Just upriver is the ghost site of Hall's Bluff, once a thriving riverport; downriver is a similar ghost—Navarro, which so prospered in the 1870s that it had its own race track. The railroad killed both.

At **Midway,** 149 m., the original Camino Real bent in a northward loop (followed today by TX OSR—Old San Antonio Road). This road rejoins TX 21 below Bryan.

The Madisonville Sidewalk Cattlemen's Association stages a feast and street party and rodeo here the first week in June every year. Association members have been known to dunk in the horse trough people found to be wearing cowboy boots without owning enough cows to justify them.

Madisonville, 161 m. (alt. 278; pop. 3,569), gathers quietly around its castle-like courthouse, where Sam Houston made one of his most impassioned speeches against secession. This seat of Madison County centers an area criss-crossed by early Spanish and French explorers. Outlying are several old villages, like Joyze, Laceola and Mecca, all near-ghosts. For two weeks each May-June, Madisonville is host to the down-to-earth Sidewalk Cattleman's Association, a gala complete from rodeo and trail ride to parade and street dancing. The restored 1904 Woodbine Hotel offers handsome lodging and excellent cuisine.

Built in 1904 by Russian-Jew immigrant Sarah Shapira as a hotel near downtown Madisonville, this rambling 2 1/2-story structure with octagonal turret is a registered state and national landmark.

At Madisonville, intersect US 75, I-45/Tour 13 and US 190/Tour 18. Nearby see Centerville, Huntsville.

At **North Zulch,** 174 m., a short drive north reaches **Normangee** (alt. 375; pop. 689), semi-official headquarters of the Old San Antonio Road. In 1929, the Texas Legislature designated the recently surveyed and marked route; the Daughters of the American Revolution marked it with red granite waymarks. Here the last connecting link was completed and dedicated with a large granite shaft. Near Normangee is resort-oriented Hilltop Lakes. In town is Leon County's only museum, reflecting the life and times of this area.

Camino Real was blazed in 1691 by Domingo Teran de los Rios, first provisional governor of Texas, as a direct route from Mexico to the Spanish missions of East Texas. In 1714, French chevalier Louis Juchereau de St. Denis, crossing from Louisiana outposts, followed the road to Mexico and so alarmed Spain that she decided Texas colonization was imperative (see Eagle Pass).

At 195 m., cross the site of Old Boonville. Now absorbed within growing Bryan, this town preceded the latter and held Brazos County seat as early as 1843. The railroad that developed Bryan killed Boonville. There are no traces.

At **Bryan,** 197 m., intersect TX 6/Tour 14 and US 190/Tour 18. Enter Region II, Southeast Texas, where your route continues as Tour 18A.

☆

Region I
North-South: Tours 9 through 17

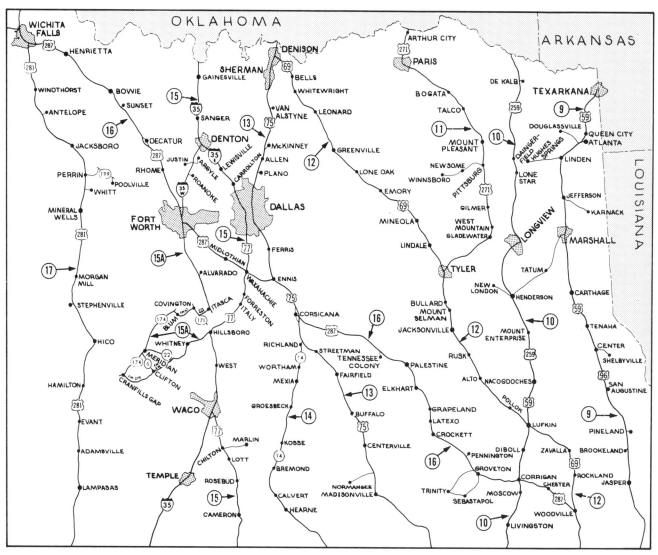

(Also see page 1)

Tour 9

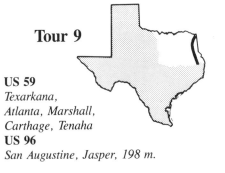

US 59
*Texarkana,
Atlanta, Marshall,
Carthage, Tenaha*
US 96
San Augustine, Jasper, 198 m.

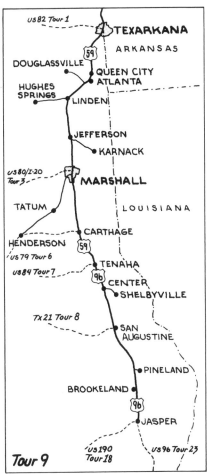

Tour 9

Your southward route parallels the eastern edge of the state and, along its lower reaches, the Sabine River, an important early-day waterway. It traverses some of Texas' most majestic forests, which deepen as you move south.

Your first leg, approximately to Marshall and Carthage, follows an ancient Indian trail, a route taken by Spanish and French explorers as early as the 1500s.

Below Tenaha your route parallels the infamous ''Neutral Ground'' (east of the Sabine) of the early 1880s, then a no-man's land between American Louisiana and Spanish Texas, a hideout for smugglers and outlaws, and a staging ground for filibusters.

In the back country along the way, old customs—Saturday night "sociables," quilting bees and coon hunts—still survive. The dialect is often early Texian and superstitions are plentiful. The towns string along, one similar to the other, but, with their new resort lakes, now showing signs of tourism awareness. For woodland scenery—dogwood snowy by spring and ablaze with fall—this tour has few peers. Many hiking trails exist throughout. Inquire locally.

Texarkana, 0 m.—see Tour 1.

Queen City, 23 m., pop. 1,748. West on FM 96 are Wright Patman Lake and Atlanta State Recreation Area, camping, good fishing, and all facilities.

Atlanta, 25 m. (alt. 264; pop. 6,118), is a handsome little city that rambles across wooded hills. Settled by Georgians in 1872, it boomed with lumbering in 1890. The surrounding Sulphur River bottoms were a longtime hideout for the Confederate renegade-deserter, Cullen Baker, who terrorized the countryside until he was killed in 1869.

The museum here displays an interesting collection of Indian artifacts. Nearby is an organic gardening demonstration farm.

Via TX 77 west 14 m. is little **Douglassville,** pop. 192, an area once occupied by great plantations and still a land knowledgeable of "ha'nts" and "sperits," of ghostly giant rattlesnakes and wraith-inhabited churchyards.

Linden, 40 m. (alt. 410; pop. 2,375). There is an Old South grace in this shaded little county seat, whose staunch native brick courthouse may be Texas' oldest in continuous use. Linden also is home of the *Cass County Sun,* a leading early-day paper which until the late 1930s was hand-set on an old George Washington Press. The press had served a paper in Shreveport and was thrown into the Red River in 1864 when Federal invasion threatened that city. Ironically, the invasion was routed, and the old press missed its biggest story. Fished out of the river, it was hauled here and put to work.

Late each April, the Linden-Avinger-Hughes Spring Wildflower Trails attract hundreds. In each of the close-neighboring towns, aside from trailing country-side beauty—afoot or saddled—a little of everything old-fashioned is offered. This ranges from horseshoe-pitching to country-store visiting and from street dancing to gospel singing.

Via TX 11 west 14 m. is **Hughes Springs,** one of the region's older towns, settled in the 1830s and recalling its heritage with a three-day Founder's celebration early in October, and with Pioneer Days late in September. It was the site of a Confederate iron foundry during the Civil War (see Daingerfield).

Jefferson, 58 m. (alt. 200; pop. 2,199). Under its iron-red, pine-plumed hills, here is an Old South jewel box and one of Texas' most fascinating little cities, with 59 showplace homes and buildings, many of them magnificently restored and displayed in the city's annual historical pilgrimage held each May. The towering old post office has been restored as a historical museum—it's one of the best.

The city's story is equally absorbing: Jefferson is supposed to be dead. Born with the Republic in 1836, the city became the primary inland port, via Caddo Lake and the Red River, for all northeast Texas. A major shipper, industrial city and plantation center, it survived the Civil War and a disastrous 1866 fire, rebuilding by 1880 to a population of 35,000, first in Texas with artificial gaslights and ice manufacture. Jefferson also boasted a brewery. In 1872 alone, no less than 226 steamboats tied up at Jefferson wharves.

In 1882, Jefferson refused right-of-way bonuses to rail baron Jay Gould, who was launching the Texas and Pacific Railroad westward. The tycoon laid a curse on the town: grass would grow in her streets. He signed the hotel register, today on display at the Excelsior House, "the end of Jefferson." The following year, Caddo Lake mysteriously lowered—its barrier "raft," a natural dam of clogged timber, blown up—and the city's wharves were useless. The town shriveled, although a 1938 oil play kept the near-ghost barely alive.

In a massive do-it-yourself restoration, the ladies of Jefferson's garden club began a town-wide restoration, borrowing money to restore what is now the classically beautiful little Excelsior House. Among other major restorations

Railroad magnate Jay Gould's private dining car, Jefferson.

are The Captain's Castle, the Culberson House, Freeman Plantation (a mile west on TX 49), the House of the Seasons, and Roseville Manor. Bed and breakfasts are housed in historic homes too many to mention. They may be seen by special arrangement or when thrown open in the spring pilgrimage. Several restorations provide unique lodging as historic inns, notable among them being the Excelsior House and the New Jefferson Inn, a remodeled warehouse. Surrey rides (arrange at the museum) will guide you through the old river port. The grand tours occur each early May in the annual Jefferson Pilgrimage. Interestingly, a primary attraction is the restored and sumptuous private dining car of Jefferson's nemesis, Jay Gould, found abandoned on a wood-laced East Texas siding.

Almost as interesting as the fine old homes is the still ghostly section of this once-metropolis: the old brick buildings—some restored—along the bayou, and back in the press of forest, the faint lines of forgotten streets and markers, and block-long foundations of Jefferson's once-limitless industrial future. A turning basin boat ride provides a narrated tour of the famed old port.

For hikers the Yellow Poplar Trail is north of the city.

Via TX 49 west 4 m., **Kellyville** is the 1848 site that promised to grow with Jefferson. An iron foundry established the Kelly Plow Company, and Kellys were an everyday word on farms throughout Texas. With Jefferson's decline, the company—a one-family operation for six generations—moved to Longview.

Farther west (via FM 729) is scenic **Lake O' The Pines,** camping, good fishing, all facilities.

Via several roads east is ghostly **Caddo Lake,** 11 m., one of the largest natural bodies of water in the South, 110 square miles of eerie wilderness water fingering a 65-mile bayou into Louisiana and, in the early days, access to the sea via the Red River. Interestingly, pearl-hunting occurred here briefly at the turn of the century. This is a labyrinth of silent, dark water, hidden lakes and sloughs, and moss-bearded cypress. Boat trails have been cut and marked, but don't venture in without a guide.

An earthquake formed the lake, it is believed. On the north side, via FM 805, is Potter's Point, site of the once-secluded mansion of Robert Potter, Texas Secretary of the Navy. Becoming embroiled in the bloody Regulator-Moderator War, he was murdered trying to escape into the swamp; his body was never found.

Mysterious and beautiful Caddo Lake, near Karnack.

On the south side, via FM 134, are **Karnack** (alt. 237; pop. 775) and Caddo Lake State Park, camping, exceptional fishing and all facilities. Nearby along the half-submerged banks are the sites of once-promising ports such as Benton, Port Caddo, Macon, and Swanson's Landing, first Texas port with a railroad terminus. Here in 1869 the steamboat *Mittie Stevens* burned, killing 60 passengers, none of whom were aware they were close to shore and the water was only waist deep. Karnack is the girlhood home of former First Lady Mrs. Lyndon B. Johnson. Via TX 43, the 1854 Taylor House—Mrs. Johnson was born

Claudia Alta Taylor—is 3 m. south of Karnack. Across the road is the sign once over her father's store: T. J. Taylor—Dealer in Everything. Bricks from the old Taylor store built Karnack's post office. Just south of the Taylor home an interesting backroad—the old "Sunken Road"—leads to Marshall (get local directions).

Marshall, 74 m.—see Tour 3).

Via TX 43 southwest is **Tatum,** 22 m. (alt. 385; pop. 1,289), an old town with its share of legend. A stopover camp on the smuggling trail, Trammel's Trace, which looped up from Nacogdoches, around Marshall, and finally to St. Louis, was at nearby Hendricks Lake. The legend persists that in 1816, pirate Jean Lafitte rushed $2 million in Spanish silver bars up this trail. Overtaken by Spanish troopers, the buccaneers dumped their loot into a mile-long, swampy lake which proved to be nearly bottomless in blue gumbo mud. The treasure has been sought by attempts to drain the lake as early as 1880, up to present-day efforts with divers and draglines—all failures. Some claim the treasure to have been Santa Anna's, from a later time; all claim the mud still holds its secret.

TX 43 continues to **Henderson** (see Tour 6), route of the "Old Wire Road." In 1854, telegraph service reached Texas from Shreveport to Marshall. Wires were strung to trees down this road, connecting the eastern fringe of Texas only, leading south through Rusk, Crockett, Montgomery, Houston and Galveston. In those days, any windstorm might force a station telegrapher to saddle up and ride out to splice the wire, snapped by the storm somewhere along this road.

Southwest of Tatum 3 m. is the ghost of **Harmony Hill,** survivor of a railroad by-pass and known by old-timers as Nip and Tuck. Virtually destroyed by a 1906 tornado, a few old homes remain.

Carthage, 105 m.—see Tour 6.
Tenaha, 121 m.—see Tour 7.
Center, 132 m. (alt. 345; pop. 4,950). This county seat (Shelby Co.) with its dignified old homes is a relative newcomer on old ground, established in 1866 when law required its central location; thus its name. Its surrounding piney hills, however, reflect a close-mouthed, closeted atmosphere inherited perhaps from the county's proximity to the old "Neutral Ground," with its lawlessness and feuds. The area was settled before 1820.

Throughout all Shelby County, that lawlessness manifested itself in the 1841–44 Regulator-Moderator conflict, a near civil war in Texas. It began with the influx of settlers from the lawless Sabine bottoms and with disputed land titles resulting from indiscriminate squatting. Law ceased; it was holstered on a man's hip, and shootouts turned to mass battles. One group formed to restore order, calling themselves "Regulators." However, power drove them to excess, and a group of "Moderators" opposed them. At one time these factions openly defied the Republic and threatened to overthrow it. Sam Houston mustered a 600-man army and put down the war.

Center has an interesting county museum, and its classic, century-old courthouse is modeled on an Irish castle, complete with its own secret passageway, said to have provided a quick exit for judges who had just tried some area bad man.

The surrounding area offers a number of scenic drives.

Via TX 87 southeast, 7 m. is tiny **Shelbyville,** pop. 215, principal town of the area in early days. It fringes the deep Sabine National Forest with many tourist facilities. Here the story is told of the first district court session in the Republic's very beginnings. Judge Robert M. Williamson ("Three-legged Willie," see Columbus) drew up a dry-goods box for his bench and called his first witness. The leader of the Shelby lawless faction stepped forward, declaring there would be no Texas court. "This," he said, driving a Bowie knife into the bench, "is the law of Shelby County." He found himself staring into the muzzle of Judge Williamson's revolver. "And this," said the judge, "is the Texas Constitution, which overrides your law." The witness was promptly called.

San Augustine, 151 m.—see Tour 8. Southward, your road winds close between Sabine and Angelina National Forests, east and west, and between Toledo Bend and Sam Rayburn Reservoirs, camping, excellent fishing, hiking trails, and all facilities in many locations.

Pineland, 172 m. (alt. 267; pop. 882, and little **Brookeland,** 181 m., pop. 220, both deeply forested, are villages in transition between the very old and the new. Gateways to two immense East Texas lakes, they are awaking to tourism, yet off your highway is an area little changed from its Anglo beginnings, reflecting an almost stylized manner of speech. Crops are still "pitched," radios are "radiators," and heated arguments can become "cuss-fightin'."

Jasper, 198 m. Enter Region II, Southeast Texas. Intersect US 190/Tour 18. To continue, see Tour 23.

☆

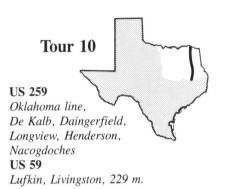

Tour 10

US 259
Oklahoma line,
De Kalb, Daingerfield,
Longview, Henderson,
Nacogdoches
US 59
Lufkin, Livingston, 229 m.

Y our southward route parallels Tour 9, immediately east; throughout, it traverses pine and hardwood forest, some of Texas' finest timberland. The terrain is rolling, hilly in the north and gradually lowering southward. As far as the scenic Daingerfield hills, the red land bespeaks its iron ore, a resource known since Civil War days and substantially mined today.

From Longview south beyond Henderson, you cross the enormous East Texas oilfield whose indiscriminate wildcatting brought on Texas' farsighted proration orders in the 1930s and established true petroleum conservation.

Farther south you enter ancient country—the Tejas Indian mound-builder forests surrounding Nacogdoches, itself one of Texas' oldest and most picturesque cities. From Lufkin to Diboll, you penetrate the state's lumbering center, and near the edge of Region I you are within the upper limits of dense, mysterious Big Thicket. For lovers of deep woodlands flavored with towns whose accents are still Old South, this is a rewarding and beautiful tour.

Okla. line, 0 m. You cross the Red River through a big-timbered area inhabited by some of Texas' earliest Anglo colonists, the Pecan Point settlers who flatboated here in the early 1800s. Their main settlement, Jonesborough (now a ghost) lies westward, just upstream (see Tour 1). Tradition insists that these

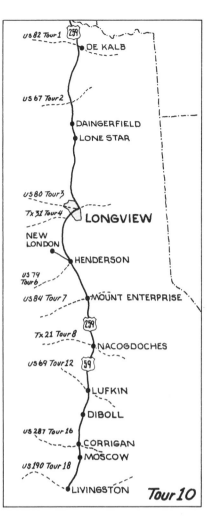

Americans were first to welcome colonizer Moses Austin and, much later, Sam Houston and Davy Crockett.

De Kalb, 13 m.—see Tour 1/US 82. At 37 m. intersect US 67, also Tour 2 as it merges with I-30 just eastward.

Daingerfield, 49 m. (alt. 403; pop. 2,572). This forested little town displays

Lake Daingerfield, Daingerfield State Park.

both scenery and industry, from chemicals to steel processing. The Morris County Museum, reflecting area history, is located in the old courthouse. Each late October, Daingerfield has fun with its Halloween Fest—parade, arts and crafts, and costume judging. Anyone not in costume is subject to "fine" or "jail." Situated in a hilly, heavily timbered area, the town is surrounded by several lakes. **Daingerfield State Park,** a few miles southeast on TX 11, offers a jewel-like, pine-banked lake with camping and all facilities. South is the head of Lake O' the Pines and north is Lake Wright Patman, both with all facilities, excellent fishing.

Lone Star, 56 m. (alt. 420; pop. 1,615), is home of Texas' steel industry. Its giant smelter borders the highway; beyond that is the ore-crushing plant. From this red land, iron ore has been mined for more than a century. On the grounds of Lone Star Steel is an old blast furnace built in 1859 at Hughes Springs to the east (Tour 9), and used to produce Confederate armament, from guns to wheel rims. The smelter remains just as Federal forces left it when seized a century ago. Special group plant tours require advance arrangements.

Just west, Lone Star Lake offers water sports, good fishing. Across your road, the lovely Chapel in the Pines is maintained by Lone Star Steel for community use. Immediately south is Lone Star Park, one of many on beautiful Lake O' the Pines, some of the best bass fishing in East Texas. FM 729 leads along its north shore to numerous excellent facilities.

Longview, 95 m.—see Tour 3. In the area also see nearby Marshall, Kilgore, Tyler, Gladewater. At 102 m., intersect I-20/Tour 3A. At 105 m. intersect TX 31/Tour 4.

Henderson, 121 m.—see Tour 6/US 79. In area see also nearby Tatum, Carthage. Northeast is Martin's Creek Lake; southwest, Lake Striker and water recreation.

Via TX 323 NW, **New London,** 10 m., pop. 926. Here March 18, 1937, one of Texas' worst disasters occurred when the handsome junior high school blew up in a gas explosion. A memorial shaft marks where 296 students and teachers died.

US 259 crosses the vast timberland and oil fields of the Longview-Henderson area.

Via FM 782 northeast is **Oak Hill,** 9 m., pop. 24. Close by is the site of old Millville, a promising little city in the mid-1800s with several industries, an academy and hotel. Railroad bypass killed the town.

Mount Enterprise, 140 m.—see Tour 7.

Nacogdoches, 162 m.—see Tour 8. In the area also see nearby Chireno, San Augustine, Oil Springs, and mission sites at Weches, near Douglass and Cushing. Southeast is big Sam Rayburn Reservoir, all facilities. At Nacogdoches, follow US 59 south.

Lufkin, 181 m. (alt. 326; pop. 30,206). Lufkin's deep forest location and handsome thoroughfares lead the traveler to overlook its role as a workingman's city. As recently as the '30s there were 275 sawmills in the immediate area; it is still the center of Texas' timber industry and is a leading manufacturer of woods and metals.

With Sam Rayburn Reservoir just east, the city is growing as a recreation center. One of its neighboring parks, Marion Ferry, is the site of Angelina county's first seat, McNeil's Landing, later renamed Marion, which in the

Sunset on Sam Rayburn Reservoir near Lufkin.

1840s was a town of some 200 buildings, now an almost traceless ghost. Two more county seats—Jonesville and Homer—would come and go before Lufkin took governmental reins in 1892. The forest has reclaimed Jonesville, and Homer is a tiny settlement east toward the lake.

Lufkin is home of Angelina College and headquarters of Angelina National Forest. Its Texas Forestry Museum reflects all phases of timbering from early times to today. The Museum of East Texas features art, science, history, East Texas artists. The Medford Collection of Western Art, housed in the City Hall, displays excellent work by contemporary artists, and the Ellen Trout Zoo is one of the finest small city installations in America. Late in May, Lufkin observes the Southern Hushpuppy Olympics.

Via TX 103, the scenic Angelina Woodland Trail is 10 m. west—a brief hike through beauty.

At Lufkin, intersect US 69/Tour 12. **Diboll,** 194 m. (alt. 232; pop. 4,341), is headquarters of Temple-Eastex, maker of wood products and successor to the Southern Pine Lumber Company. Northwest 1 m. is Ryan Chapel, dating from 1866. Its mail-order bell has called worshippers since the turn of the century. Directly west are woodland tourist facilities near both Apple Springs and Ratcliff, in Davy Crockett National Forest.

At **Corrigan,** 207 m. (alt. 226; pop. 1,764), intersect US 287/Tour 16. Just south is a scenic hiking trail.

Tiny **Moscow,** 212 m., pop. 170, was one of the earliest sawmill towns nearabouts and in 1885 boasted a mule-car from the depot to the hotel. The Moscow, Camden and San Augustine Railway is one of our shortest, a 7 m. logging track (freight only). In town, a handsome little park and picnic area honors the birthplace of William P. Hobby, former Texas governor. Dinosaur Gardens, near intersection US 59/FM 62, conceals life-size dinosaur replicas along dense forest trail. West 12 m. on FM 350 is old Bethel Baptist Church, established 1849.

On your highway, 1 m. south, is a short scenic woodland trail.

Livingston, 229 m. Enter Region II, Southeast. Intersect Tour 18/US 190. Your route continues as Tour 25.

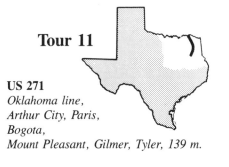

Tour 11

US 271
Oklahoma line,
Arthur City, Paris,
Bogata,
Mount Pleasant, Gilmer, Tyler, 139 m.

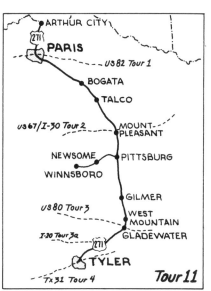

Tour 11

As the Green Carpet Route, from St. Louis and Tulsa to the Texas Gulf Coast, US 271 pursues a crescent southward through fertile blacklands into the upper East Texas forests. With the exception of a few cities toward its southern end, its countryside is rural, still a land of small farms and country folk acquainted with old customs—singing conventions, religious revivals, curative lore, sign planting, and some delightful superstitions.

Okla. line, 0 m. The Red River valley is broad, handsomely wooded.

Arthur City, 0.3 m. (alt. 426; pop. 200), in its river timber, is weathered and old-looking, believed to be the site of a 1750 French trading post—a time when not only France but England began to press inward on Spanish-claimed Texas. Here also was the early-1800s site of Fulton's Landing, where flatboats and small sternwheelers served the area developing south toward today's Paris. Big Pat Mayse Lake, just west, offers camping and all facilities.

FM 906 winds through the woodlands south of Arthur City to Pat Mayse Lake.

Paris, 18 m.—see Tour 1.

Bogata, 41 m. (alt. 420; pop. 1,421), is one of North Texas' earliest Anglo settlements, an offshoot of the Red River 1800s colonization (see Jonesborough, Tour 1). Former U.S. Vice-President John Nance Garner attended school here. The site of his boyhood home is 6 m. north up FM 410, toward Detroit.

Talco, 50 m. (alt. 350; pop. 592), seems to be resting from its 1935 oil boom, when the population shot from 140 to 5,000. Its hard-pressed single bank handled deposits by tying each billroll separately, marking its depositor on the roll—all to be balanced and credited later. Some oil activity continues.

Mount Pleasant, 67 m.—see Tour 2.

Pittsburg, 80 m. (alt. 398; pop. 4,007). In its forested hills, surrounded by many lakes (five of them), this little city lives a leisurely pace, its main street dividing to pass around a giant oak, just as pioneer paths prescribed. In an area producing both timber and iron (the old Pittsburg foundry is still intact), the city manufactures furniture, steel castings and clothing. You'll also find excellent peaches in season. Pioneer Days are observed each September.

Center Point Baptist Church, 10 m. southeast on FM 2057, anchors community founded by black freedmen in 1865. An Industrial Union aided settlers in buying farms and building homes. Cooperatively managed were brick kiln, sawmill, and cotton gin. Local school, built mostly by students, taught vocational skills on the 14-acre campus.

Here, in 1902, Pittsburg tried flying a year before the Wright Brothers. A Baptist minister determined to model an aircraft, the Ezekiel Airship, on Biblical description. Built here, the ship had large, fabric-covered wings powered by an engine that turned four sets of paddles. Late that year it was briefly airborne. En route by train to the St. Louis

World's Fair in 1904, the craft was destroyed by storm. In 1913 a second model crashed and the project was abandoned. Today a downtown restaurant displays a full-size replica; visitors welcome.

Via TX 11 west 11 m., near little **Newsome,** (pop. 100), is the Corbett log cabin, whose owners possess a quill-penned, deerskin title. Beyond is **Winnsboro,** its deep woodlands beautiful during the annual Autumn Trails Festival. Nearby, also see Daingerfield. Surrounding lakes offer all facilities.

Gilmer, 99 m. (alt. 370; pop. 4,822). This town's square boasts a handsome courthouse, but its surrounding old brick buildings admit to age, and Gilmer is an old town, having become Upshur County seat in 1846. Here, you edge the north end of the East Texas oilfields, yet the countryside remains beautifully forested. For its famed sweet potatoes, Gilmer observes its festive annual Yamboree each mid-October.

Via TX 154 east 4 m. is Indian Rock Park, site of a large early-day Indian village. Many artifacts have been found; the table rock was used for grinding corn and tanning leather.

Via TX 155 northeast 5.5 m. is Barnwell Mountain Park. Its scenic overlook provides a beautiful view of surrounding forest land.

TX 155 leading to Barnwell Mountain Park.

Just off TX 154 west is the Cherokee Trace, a historic trail marked with Cherokee roses by that retreating nation. A winding country lane still blossoms with them from May to June.

Legend also claims that San Jacinto corn came from this area. After being wounded at San Jacinto, Sam Houston lay under an oak, shelling corn on which he had subsisted for days. Looking to the future, he told his soldiers to take the corn home and plant it, for Texas croplands had been devastated. "Houston corn," the men wanted to call it. "Call it San Jacinto corn," the general is said to have replied.

Lake O' The Pines, with camping and all facilities, lies northeast. The heavily forested surrounding area offers scenic hiking trails.

Via FM 49/1795 west 8 m. are the remains of an unusual settlement, **Kelsey.** In 1902, a colony of the Church of Jesus Christ of the Latter Day Saints was established here. By 1900 all was prospering—five stores, three sawmills, a shingle mill, brick kiln, a big packing house and a two-story brick school with 12 teachers brought from Utah. In 1923 the railroad by-pass brought decline. Today Kelsey's population is 50.

At **West Mountain,** 107 m., pop. 395, see the McKay Clock Museum, a large collection of antique timepieces and wood carvings. Lake Gladewater, just west, offers water sports.

Gladewater, 113 m.—see Tour 3. Nearby also see Longview, Kilgore. At 126 m. intersect I-20/Tour 3A.

Tyler, 139 m.—see Tour 4.

☆

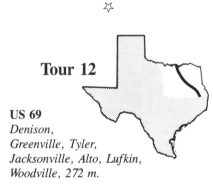

Tour 12

US 69
Denison,
Greenville, Tyler,
Jacksonville, Alto, Lufkin,
Woodville, 272 m.

Your route slopes gradually eastward as it descends from the center of North Texas' Red River Valley, aiming for our southeast corner on the Gulf Coast. You begin in the rolling post oak land around Lake Texoma on the Red River. The terrain flattens across the rich blackland near Greenville. Finally you thread through the woodlands that begin at Tyler and deepen as you travel south.

You cross a country early-settled by Anglo colonists, primarily from south-

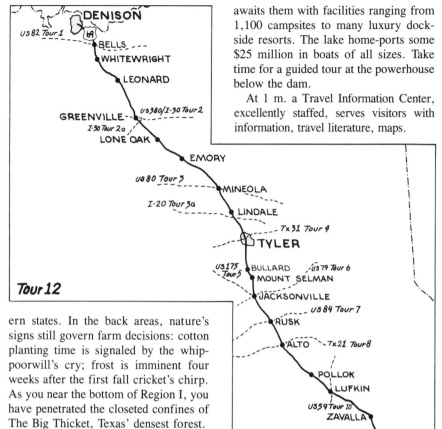

Tour 12

ern states. In the back areas, nature's signs still govern farm decisions: cotton planting time is signaled by the whippoorwill's cry; frost is imminent four weeks after the first fall cricket's chirp. As you near the bottom of Region I, you have penetrated the closeted confines of The Big Thicket, Texas' densest forest.

Okla. line, 0 m. You cross the Red River auspiciously—just below giant Lake Texoma or, via a slight westward jog, across immense Denison Dam, which is some three miles long and 165 feet high. The lake covers 140 square miles and is the tenth largest reservoir in America. Aside from **Eisenhower State Park** near the dam, an excellent installation with camping and all facilities, there are scores of well-appointed parks on both sides of the lake. The area is outstanding for fishing, hunting, or just pleasure-boating.

Approximately 11 million Americans annually visit Lake Texoma, which

The birthplace of President Dwight D. Eisenhower, Denison.

awaits them with facilities ranging from 1,100 campsites to many luxury dockside resorts. The lake home-ports some $25 million in boats of all sizes. Take time for a guided tour at the powerhouse below the dam.

At 1 m. a Travel Information Center, excellently staffed, serves visitors with information, travel literature, maps.

Denison, 5 m. (alt. 767; pop. 21,505) is a brisk, bright city of wide streets with flowered esplanades, opening the Texas gateway northward. In the early days it was a tough town, acquainted with outlaw and jayhawk trouble throughout the Civil War, but calming down with the coming of the railroads. Still a big railroad center, it is also the birthplace of President Dwight D. Eisenhower. At 208 E. Day St., the birthplace has been restored to its 1890 appearance.

Near intersection of FM 1417 and FM 691, on the west campus of Grayson County College, the Munson Vineyards recall the work of viticulture pioneer T.V. Munson. Munson saved the French wine industry by sending Texas root stock to replace French vines destroyed by disease; French wines today all have Texas roots.

Continue north on FM 1417 to sign directing you to the Hagerman National Wildlife Refuge's 11,300 acres, stopover for hundreds of migrating bird species.

Huge Lake Texoma, formed by the damming of the Red River at Denison.

Within Loy Lake Park is Grayson County Frontier Village, composed of original log cabins and structures from throughout the county, all complete with vintage furnishings.

Downtown, the original Katy Depot has been restored to its grandeur and now centers an impressive, landscaped shopping and office complex.

Via FM 120 northwest to **Preston Point,** 17 m. Here is the site of Old Preston, one of the westernmost advanced outposts in the early 1840s. Here Holland Coffee built a trading post-fort and a handsome home for his young bride, but most of the old settlement is now under Lake Texoma. Here was one of the first crossings for trail drivers northbound with Longhorn herds—the Shawnee Trail. As the land developed and barbed wire broke the routes, these crossings moved successively westward, the last and biggest of all at Doans, above Vernon, some 200 miles to the west. Preston's crossing led its herds toward Sedalia, Mo. At Denison, veer southeast from US 75/Tour 13.

At 14 m., you are just west of the site of **Dugan's Chapel,** an 1840 home-fort. Founder Daniel Dugan was killed by Indians and his sons swore vengeance, taking to the woods in an unrelenting Indian hunt. The last hostile savage was shot at Dugan's gate by his daughter, Emily, who decapitated the Indian and thrust his head on the gatepost—a warning thereafter heeded. The skull remained in the

family for years, a grim memento of frontier life.

Bells, 19 m.—see Tour 1.

Whitewright, 26 m. (alt. 746; pop. 1,713), maintains a general interest museum.

Leonard, 39 m. (alt. 704; pop. 1,744) wears a tranquil air that belies its rough-and-ready 1880 railroad founding. The town's first post office was in a saloon, its cash and stamps kept in an old cigar box under the bar. A postal inspector suggested better facilities; the postmaster slammed the cigar box onto the bar and told him to take his post office and get out. Resolute area citizens maintain that the last actual battle of the Civil War occurred here in May, 1869. Captain Robert Jackson Lee, Confederate Scouts, refused surrender and led a group of irregular volunteers until killed by a U.S. cavalry troop nearby.

Greenville, 59 m.—see Tour 2.

At 67 m., FM 1564 leads west to Cash, 8 m. Nearby is Baker No. 1, Texas' 100,000th oil well.

At **Lone Oak,** 73 m., pop. 521, take FM 513 south to Lake Tawakoni, 7 m., camping and all facilities.

This is one of Texas' best fishing lakes, many marinas dotting the 200-m. shoreline. Submerged timber provides quiet water, fish havens; limit catches are commonplace. Tawakoni stages fishing tourneys each year.

Emory, 89 m. (alt. 464; pop. 963), is the little county seat of tiny Rains County, yet for a long time it has been the center of a rich agricultural area. The town developed around a Sabine River mill and fort built in the 1840s. Farmers from as far as Dallas County brought their grains here, for an armed guard was perpetually maintained against Indians. In 1904 Emory continued as a leader in agriculture when the National Farmers Cooperative and Educational Union was begun here. Emory's region has been described as being like East Texas was before the oil boom. Descendants of the first homesteaders still comprise 90 percent of the population. Today, Emory's proximity to Lake Tawakoni is fostering growth in tourism business.

Mineola, 112 m.—see Tour 3. Also nearby are Quitman and Grand Saline.

Below **Lindale,** 127 m., intersect Tour 3A/I-20. From here to Tyler, the countryside is rich in peaches and roses,

whose bloom is something worth seeing early each spring. In late March-early April, native wildflowers and blooming azaleas add to the riot of color.

Tyler, 138 m.—see Tour 4. You are edging the great East Texas oilfield; and close by eastward are its cities, Gladewater, Longview, Kilgore and Henderson.

Bullard, 153 m. (alt. 502; pop. 890). Just southeast of here are the ruins of **Burning Bush,** a 1912 experiment in religious communal living. Midwest colonists settled on 1,500 acres of land, projecting a planned community based on common faith and share-and-share-alike agricultural production. By 1919, the experiment had failed.

West on FM 344 is Lake Palestine, water sports.

Mount Selman, 159 m. (alt. 692; pop. 200). This little village offers one of East Texas' most scenic views: Love's Lookout Park, a woodland overlook with recreation facilities, a handsome drive, and a lookout tower.

Via FM 855 west is the site of **Old Larissa,** 3 m. This was one of Texas' outstanding educational institutions from 1847 to the Civil War. Earlier here, in 1838, the Killough Massacre occurred. The Cherokee Indians were believed guilty and the killings became a primary cause for East Texans' driving that Indian nation from the territory.

Jacksonville, 165 m.—see Tour 5.

Rusk, 179 m.—see Tour 7.

Immediately south, toward Alto, is the site of **New Birmingham,** the great iron boom town which, between 1888 and 1891, grew from forest to a city of 400 buildings, electricity, schools, brick businesses, and one of Texas' handsomest hotels, the Southern. Backed by British money, New Birmingham had promise as a major iron-steel city. But passage of the Alien Land Law forbade absentee ownership in Texas and the industrial Mecca died a-borning. Some traces remain, including ruins of the old furnaces. An interesting hiking trail is close by.

Alto, 191 m.—see Tour 8. Close by are sites of early Spanish missions, and the center of the Tejas Indian moundbuilder confederacy. See Nacogdoches, Weches.

Standing Cypress in bloom along US 69 between Rusk and Alto.

Pollok, 210 m., pop. 300. TX 7 leads west into the heart of Davy Crockett National Forest at Ratcliff, offering fine wilderness camping and touring facilities.

Lufkin, 222 m.—see Tour 9. Sam Rayburn Reservoir, with camping and all facilities, is just east. Nearly a dozen marinas offer food, fuel, lodging, camping, and fishing guides. Guides provide boat, bait, and all gear needed.

Zavalla, 244 m. (alt. 228; pop. 701), itself an old town, took its name—and misspelled it doing so—from an even older 1824 settlement, now abandoned over in the Lorenzo de Zavala grant in Jasper County, to the east. A museum, "Remembering," recalls early pioneer days.

Rockland, 255 m. (alt. 128; pop. 105), lies inconspicuously just south of the Neches River and is notable for that location. At a riverside location difficult to reach is the site of 1831 Fort Teran, a Mexican establishment intended to halt early American colonization of Texas. Abandoned after the Battle of Nacogdoches in 1832, the locale still clings to the legend that gold was stuffed into a cannon muzzle and pushed into the river. Without known success, treasure hunting has persisted over the years.

Colmesneil, 263 m., pop. 569, is a wooded old sawmill town. In the "old" town below your highway, the Meadows General Store will intrigue you—operated by the same family in the same fash-

ion since 1895. Here, Lake Tejas provides water sports.

Woodville, 272 m. Enter Region II, Southeast. Intersect Tour 18/US 190. Your route continues as Tour 24.

☆

Tour 13

US 75
Denison,
Sherman, McKinney,
Dallas
US 75/I-45
Ennis, Corsicana, Fairfield, Buffalo,
Centerville, Madisonville, 223 m.

Your highway is one of the most heavily traveled in Texas, but congestion is eased by the existence of a divided highway throughout. You enter Texas on the Oklahoma City-Dallas route, crossing at big Lake Texoma. From Dallas you take aim at the metropolis of Houston.

North of Dallas the terrain is rolling prairie, farming interspersed with a growing industrialization of the pendant towns. Below that metroplex, skirting the edge of the great East Texas forests, you traverse land once rich in old plantations—a land neglected after the Civil War but awaking now with new oil and gas discoveries.

At Madisonville, where Region II begins, you have almost reached the upper edge of Southeast Texas' great coastal forests.

Okla. line, 0 m.—see Lake Texoma, Tour 12.

Denison, 5 m.—see Tour 12.

At 10 m. intersect Woodlake Road. Here, in 1901, was located the Texas Electric Railway power plant and recreation area—complete with park and pavilion—for Texas' first inter-urban railway. The line connected Denison and Sherman, directly paralleling your route—fast, convenient transportation for the turn of the century. By 1912, the line extended to Waco and Corsicana, but it was abandoned in 1948.

Sherman, 15 m.—see Tour 1.

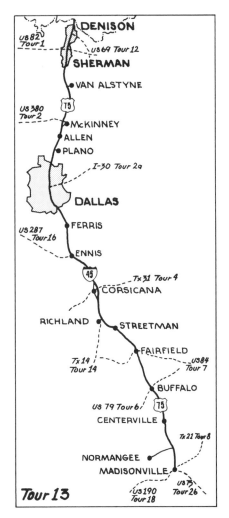

Tour 13

Van Alstyne, 31 m. (alt. 791; pop. 2,090) is an old town that grew from a still older one, Mantua, 3 m. southwest. Mantua was planned and built around an 1859 seminary for girls, and Governor J. W. Throckmorton was a leader in the project. By 1865 the town was thriving, the seminary boasted 80 pupils and eight teachers. The railroad's by-pass, however, spelled Mantua's doom and moved its residents to Van Alstyne in 1872. Van Alstyne maintains a local museum recalling these early days, and oddly featuring the antique tools of early undertakers, from old caskets to grave liners.

McKinney, 48 m.—see Tour 2.

Allen, 55 m., (alt. 637; pop. 18,309). This city, its surging population growth (nearly doubling in the last decade) fueled by Dallas sprawl, had been settled only six years when, on February 23, 1878, the Sam Bass gang robbed its bank. In the spring of that year, Bass, who ranged across North Texas, would hold up four trains within 30 miles of Dallas. By July

21, the notorious outlaw was dead of gunshot wounds in **Round Rock** (see Tour 30), trying for one more bank robbery.

Plano, 61 m. (alt. 655; pop. 128,713), rising from its blackland prairie, is an old town, founded in 1845 as Fillmore. For years it remained a quiet agricultural community. In 1881 it was almost destroyed by a fire that left it little more than a tent city. The town hung on, though, and today it's a Dallas satellite mushrooming in all directions.

In 1960, Plano counted 3,690 souls; twenty years later, the population had reached 72,331. The city considers itself "Balloon Capital of Texas," with hot-air races scheduled each September. It boasts a splendid park system with miles of hike-and-bike trails.

Plano's high school football is legendary in Texas. Successively, as the town grew, its teams have won state titles in every educational category from 2-A to 5-A.

Oddly, rural heritage is recalled at two sites, Fairview Farms (US 75 at Parker Rd., Exit 30) and Heritage Farmstead Museum (1900 W. Fifteenth St.).

Dallas, 81 m.—see Tour 2A. Follow US 75, I-45 south.

Ferris, 101 m. (alt. 468; pop. 2,095). Excellent clays here and in Palmer, 8 m. south, make both towns leading brick manufacturers.

Ennis, 115 m. (alt. 548; pop. 13,883). In 1871 the trains reached Ennis; it has been a railroad center ever since. It is also a festival town: each April the Ennis Garden Club sponsors one of the Texas' most beautiful Bluebonnet Trails. In May comes the National Polka Festival. The autumn Ellis County Fair just to the west, is one of the state's largest. Bardwell Lake, with camping and all facilities, is immediately west. Also see nearby Waxahachie and Lancaster. At Ennis intersect US 287/Tour 16.

Via TX 34 east 9 m. toward the Trinity River is little **Telico.** In 1857, a slated $200,000 expansion plan foresaw Telico as North Texas' major metropolis, perhaps exceeding that northward town, Dallas. The Civil War intervened, and the community's population today numbers 95 souls.

Corsicana, 134 m.—see Tour 4.

Richland, 145 m., (alt. 374; pop. 244). Due west of this little town runs a spur of the Tehuacana Hills, known locally as Pisgah Ridge, and best known to old-timers. These limestone cliffs are abrupt and pocked with several caves which in early days served as outlaw hideouts. One, furnished with a fireplace and make-shift furniture, bore the name of Fort Worth's most famed fast-gun saloon, "The White Elephant." John Wesley Hardin allegedly holed up here for a time, as did the notorious lady outlaw, Belle Starr. At Richland, intersect TX 14/Tour 14.

Beyond **Streetman,** pop. 260, at 157 m., intersect FM 813. East 4 m. is **Stewards Mill** (pop. 22), a delightfully sleepy wayside spot, one of the earliest area settlements and site of perhaps Texas' oldest country store, operated by the same family for well over a century; and on the sagging porch a domino game of equal duration is still in progress; on the siding by the door is a fading, handwritten almanac of weathers, hot and cold, of floods, of good times and bad. The store's interior, from its handmilled counter with its bins and spoolcases, to the old signs of a forgotten time and way of life, transport you into another century.

Fairfield, 166 m.—see Tour 7.

Via FM 1124 northeast is Fairfield Lake, 6 m., and State Recreation Area, camping and all facilities.

Buffalo, 185 m.—see Tour 6.

Centerville, 201 m. (alt. 410; pop. 812). Beneath old oaks and newer sycamores, this little town gathers around its brick courthouse, one of the state's oldest. On the square is a restoration of old pioneer Fort Boggy, an 1840 blockhouse that began and protected this area's settlements (its original site was on Boggy Creek, 5 m. south).

Southwest, toward **Normangee** is the new resort area, Hilltop Lakes. Along the Trinity, bordering to the east, are the sites of several rivertown ghosts where settlement first congregated, and shallow-draft sternwheelers could bring up supplies from Galveston. Commerce, Brookfields Bluff and Halls Bluff were such towns, offering great promise in a day that was ended by railroads; so also were Navarro, boasting a fine racetrack,

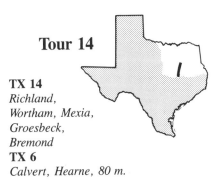

TX 7, intersecting US 75 at Centerville, offers a lovely side trip through woods and meadows to Crockett.

and inland Peeler—all settlements which the woodland has reclaimed.

At 213 m. intersect TX OSR—Old San Antonio Road (Tour 8).

Madisonville, 223 m. Enter Region II, Southeast. Intersect Tour 18/US 190. Your route continues as Tour 26.

☆

Tour 14

TX 14
*Richland,
Wortham, Mexia,
Groesbeck,
Bremond*
TX 6
Calvert, Hearne, 80 m.

This route drives straight south from I-45 below Corsicana and pursues a course generally paralleling the Brazos River—a gently-rolling land dappled with stands of post oak and elm. In early days an extraordinarily rich bottomland, this was—at the outset of Civil War—the western edge of the big established plantations, its towns substantial and promising, its spirit militantly Confederate. It suffered accordingly after the war and still has not altogether recovered.

Along the way, the careful observer can note occasional large old homes, a number in faded ruin, remembering a time when cotton was king. Today the towns remain small, the outlook is rural-farm, and many ghost settlements slumber on either side of your route.

Richland, 0 m.—see Tour 13.

Wortham, 10 m. (alt. 478; pop. 1,020), is a sleepy rural center. From Richland south to this point your road

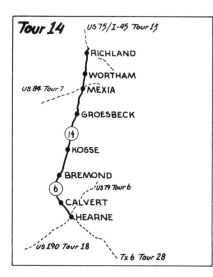

Tour 14

US 75/I-45 Tour 13
RICHLAND
WORTHAM
US 84 Tour 7 — MEXIA
GROESBECK
(14)
KOSSE
BREMOND
(6) US 79 Tour 6
CALVERT
HEARNE
US 190 Tour 18
Tx 6 Tour 28

has paralleled a ridge of the Tehuacana Hills, seemingly out of place in this otherwise rolling flatland. All this area volunteered heavily for Confederate arms, calling themselves "fire-eaters." Their casualties were high, fighting on many fronts, particularly with Hood's Texas Brigade. After the war, many remained "unreconstructed," a gunfighter breed. West of town, an elevation called Rabbit Hill served as rendezvous and hideout for their gangs.

Mexia, 19 m.—see Tour 7.

Fort Parker State Park, 24 m. is heavily-forested around Lake Mexia and offers camping and all facilities. Within the park are traces and the cemetery of ghost town **Springfield,** from 1838 the leading town and county seat of Limestone County. By-passed by the railroad, the thriving little city disappeared.

Old Fort Parker, 27 m., separate from camping-recreation facilities just

Restoration of Old Fort Parker, first destroyed by the Comanche in 1836.

north and closed in late 1992, is a log-stockade restoration of that remote outpost pushed into Comancheria in 1834. Two years later the fort was devastated, most of the founding Parker family killed, and 9-year-old Cynthia Ann Parker, together with her brother, kidnaped by the Comanche. Object of a near-lifetime search, Cynthia Ann grew to womanhood as the contented wife of Comanche Chief Peta Nocona, and when she was returned to civilization after her recapture in 1860 (see Medicine Mounds, Athens), both she and her daughter, Prairie Flower, died within five years. Her son, Quanah Parker, was one of the last fighting Comanche chieftains.

An excellent restoration, still lonely in the dense woodlands, Fort Parker graphically depicts the perilous frontier existence of these early pioneers.

According to tradition, logs from the original fort are part of the Mordecai Yale log cabin nearby. The old cabin was home to that early day circuit-riding preacher. A cemetery 2 m. northeast of Groesbeck (FM 1245) is the burial site of the fort's victims.

Groesbeck, 31 m. (alt. 477; pop. 3,185). This little county seat (Limestone Co.) occupies once-rich plantation land, an area which volunteered three-fourths of its voting-age males to Confederate service. Even earlier, it knew close-quarter warfare in Comanche raids such as that which massacred nearby Fort Parker.

Early each May, Groesbeck's county square swarms with double the town's normal population, as the annual fiddle festival runs full swing, with perhaps the liveliest of the three fiddling categories that of age 61 and up. Festivities end with an old-fashioned street dance.

The Limestone County Historical Museum salutes regional history, including memorabilia relating to Fort Parker. Nearby, Lakes Limestone, Mexia and Springfield (Ft. Parker State Park) provide camping and recreational facilities.

Kosse, 47 m. (alt. 500; pop. 505). West via TX 7, 8 m., is ghost-like **Stranger,** population 27. In the 1880s it was a booming cotton center.

Like many another small Texas town, this one—through Kosse Heritage Society—has a story to tell. Here was the pulpit of Rev. Bill Sealy, "the walkinest preacher in Texas." For 30 years Baptist

minister, Rev. Sealy shunned "gas buggies," and is believed to have walked 30,000 miles in service to his congregation. Kosse also was home to Bob Wills, "King of Country Music." A beautifully-restored, century-old home houses this tiny community's heritage society and is open for guided tours.

Bremond, 58 m. (alt. 466; pop. 1,110), settled by Poles in the 1870s, is another town that knew its heyday when cotton was king. Southwest 3 m. is the ghost of **Wooten Wells,** once a great Texas health spa. It grew up around an 1879 mineral water well and by the mid '80s was a popular resort—three hotels, a dance pavilion, a mule-drawn streetcar, and several bathhouses. Fires in the late '80s, and the emergence of Marlin to the north, faded the spa. A few traces remain today on private land. At this point, follow TX 6 south.

At 63 m., tiny **Hammond,** pop. 44, is close by the site of pioneer blockhouse Fort Welch, hit hard in one of many Comanche attacks on this area.

One of several classic Victorian era homes in Calvert.

Calvert, 71 m. (alt. 335; pop. 1,536). An air of splendor—some faded, much restored—marks this town's 1850 plantation origins. In 1871, Calvert boasted the world's largest cotton gin and, a few years later, its own opera house. Among the several historic buildings are the First Presbyterian Church and the Church of the Epiphany, as well as 1868 Cobb's Market, with its marble-top counters. At deep-shaded Virginia Field Park is the site of a post-war "tree prison"—an elevated platform confining unreconstructed Confederates. Here, a determined effort seems under way to preserve many of the fine old homes, visited area-wide in a historical pilgrimage held each April.

The Calvert Hotel, an 1872 plantation-style country inn, has been restored and provides visitors with a nostalgic glimpse of "Old South." Its town considers itself "Antique Capital of Texas." Look around.

Nashville-Port Sullivan, 79 m. Immediately north of where US 79/190 crosses the Brazos River, near Hearne, is the site of two of Texas' more famous ghost towns. The sites are close beside the Brazos crossing of FM 485. **Nashville** was headquarters of the original colony founded by Sterling Clack Robertson. A leading Texas settlement, Nashville contested closely for selection as capital of the Republic in 1836. It declined to final abandonment with the selection of nearby Cameron as county seat. A memorial park marks its site.

Almost co-existent with Nashville was **Fort** (and Port) **Sullivan,** another of the Robertson colony settlements and home of the well-regarded Port Sullivan Female Institute, 1850–77. Looking upstream from the Brazos bridge, you can detect the ruins of dam and lock that were intended to make this site a leading inland port. Brazos floods were too much for the then-fragile engineering, and the port, along with Nashville, passed away.

At 80 m. (see Hearne, below), intersect FM 391 east to **Wheelock,** 13 m., pop. 125. This village is old, growing up in 1834 around its Fort Dunn—for 10 years fighting Comanche raiders to survive. A restored log cabin dates from 1836; the Cavitt House, from 1842. Your route from Hearne is part of the region's Dogwood and Glorioso Daisy Trail, beautiful in the spring.

Hearne, 81 m. Enter Region II, Southeast. Intersect US 190/Tour 18. Your route enters Region II via US 190 as far as Bryan, where it veers south as Tour 28.

☆

Tour 15

US 77/I-35
Oklahoma line,
Gainesville, Denton,
Dallas, Waxahachie,
Hillsboro, Waco
US 77
Rosebud, Cameron, 228 m.

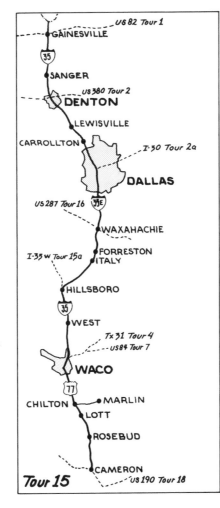

Tour 15

P erhaps more than any other, this straight-south route approximates the western edge of early Texas colonization, particularly as far as Waco. West of you lies land which at that time was still fiercely held by the Comanche, and along this frontier a man farmed with a gun at either end of his field. This route also loosely follows north-south Indian trails of dim antiquity, later the northbound route of the great Longhorn herds bound for Missouri and Kansas railheads.

The land is largely black and rich, rolling only gently. The cities—Denton, Dallas, and Waco are clean, handsome, prosperous and growing rapidly.

Okla. line, 0 m. You cross the Red River only slightly above the head of giant Lake Texoma. Upstream where the Red swings in a great horseshoe arc lies Sivell's Bend, earliest crossing of the Chisholm Trail. Later crossings would move westward to Spanish Fort and Red River Station, above Nocona. Here,

however, the great post-Civil War herds first struck out across Indian Territory. The site is best reached via FM 1201 north from Gainesville, 16 m. Along the way, Moss Lake offers water sports.

Gainesville, 7 m.—see Tour 1.

The Texas Travel Information Center of Gainesville, one of 12 around the state, offers expert counsel on traveling the roads of Texas.

At 14 m., a roadside rest area marks the site of the great Kiowa Indian raid of 1868. In early January, that year, Chief Big Tree led some 200 braves raiding settlements outlying Gainesville, and was turned back short of that town only by blizzard. The Indians burned homes, killed 13 people, captured 10 women and children—a grisly prelude to Big Tree's capture and trial at Fort Richardson (see Jacksboro) three years later.

Sanger, 26 m. (alt. 660; pop. 3,508), boasts the 1876-built Blue Mound Church. Just west on FM 455, at **Bolivar,** John Chisum ranched for a time, and Sam Bass, the ill-famed outlaw, frequented the area.

Denton, 40 m.—see Tour 2/US 380. Lake Lewisville heads immediately east; camping and all facilities are available. Take I-35E toward Dallas; I-35 w/Tour 15A leads to Fort Worth.

Lewisville, 57 m. (alt. 490; pop. 46,521), already within the outspill of the Dallas-Fort Worth metroplex, is gateway to its lake, often called Garza-Little Elm Reservoir. Lake Lewisville State Park, abundant facilities, lies on the east short of the lake. Here, archaeological findings of great antiquity were uncovered during dam construction. Here also was the 1841 land office of the Peters Colony, impresarios for much of North Texas. A few miles west, lonely on its hill is 1858 Chinn's Chapel, one of Texas' oldest protestant churches still standing. Also westward (on FM 1171 or TX 121) is Grapevine Lake, camping and all facilities.

Carrollton, 66 m. (alt. 470; pop. 82,169), absorbed Trinity Mills, a pioneer competitor to Dallas itself. Pioneer Park commemorates the area's early settlers. Here also is the site of the 1846 Union Baptist Church, the first in Dallas County.

Dallas, 78 m.—see Tour 2A.

Waxahachie, 108 m. (alt. 585; pop. 18,168), is Indian for "Buffalo Creek." An old tale claims Waxahachie is the longest city in Texas. Traveling the old highway, one end to the other, you will see most of its fine old Victorian brick homes, and its old, and highly ornamented brick and stone square surrounding Ellis County's ornate courthouse, a building unique in that many faces are carved high up in the buff sandstone—some of lovely women, some of men almost demonic in appearance. One lovely woman's face is that of a girl with whom one of the sculptors fell in love. Rejected by her, according to old story, other Waxahachie faces took on a disagreeable appearance in the sculptor's eye. He then portrayed his feelings. The pretty girl, a Miss Mabel Frame, looks down from the east entrance arch. At Getzendaner Park the 1902 octagon-shaped Chautauqua building—the only one still standing in the U.S.—has been restored as a civic center recalling old times. All the city's old buildings are part of Waxahachie's Gingerbread Trail held early each June.

Scarborough Faire, a Renaissance festival, is open mid-April—early June, and features more than 200 craftsmen and their wares in a unique theme of medieval costume and countryside.

This town is also known as the "little Hollywood of Texas," because of the 20 movies filmed here. Among the most famous are *Places in the Heart* and *Tender Mercies*.

The railroad station at Waxahachie, built in 1887. (Photo by Genie Mims)

Nearby is the planned site of the futuristic Superconducting Super Collider, a giant 52-mile oval of extremely powerful magnets designed to accelerate protons and slam them into each other for the edification of scientists. At Waxahachie, intersect US 287/Tour 16.

Forreston, 117 m. (alt. 540; pop. 300), settled in 1845, is one of North Texas' oldest communities. As Chambers Creek, it was the original county seat and the only mail station between the Falls of the Brazos and an outpost fort at today's Bonham.

Italy, 123 m. (alt. 576; pop. 1,699) is center of a rich farming area. During the Civil War its site was occupied by a Confederate hat factory.

Hillsboro, 142 m. (alt. 634; pop. 7,072), is a spread-out, crossroads little city with a quiet air of go-to-church-Sundays, come-to-town Saturdays, its big busy square filled then and on Monday trade days. Here is the home of handsomely modern Hill College, housing one of the South's most complete Confederate research centers and firearms museums. Hood's Texas Brigade Association Reunion is held here each mid-April.

The city's lofty-towered courthouse is a far cry from the elm log cabin originally erected here in 1854, an area to develop into large plantations and to furnish four companies to Confederate service. After Civil War, planting continued, but in small family farms. Just west is big, scenic Lake Whitney, camping and all facilities. Lake Aquilla, with excellent fishing, is just southeast of town. At Hillsboro, merge with I-35, continuing south as I-35.

West, 156 m. (alt. 648; pop. 2,515), is a prosperous and interesting Czech community. Its Czech paper, the statewide *Vestnik and Czechoslovak* maintains a directory of all Texas Czechs. The Church of the Assumption is beautiful, and the community is a gourmet's Mecca for Czech food—sausage, smoked bacon and delicious pastries.

Near here, in the fall of 1896, at a railroad siding appropriately called "Crush," the M.K.&T. railroad staged what was advertised for excursioners as "The Great Train Wreck." For one day, Crush was a town of 40,000. Two 35-ton locomotives, each with six boxcars hurled into collision, raining debris like shrapnel over a half-mile radius, injur-

ing several of the onlookers. The town of Crush had lived its brief life.

Today, however, the town hosts as many visitors each Labor Day weekend for its annual "Westfest," a two-day Czech festival, featuring excellent food. This successful gala has returned all funds to the community's development.

Waco, 175 m.—see Tour 4/TX 31. Follow US 77 south.

At little **Chilton,** 194 m., pop. 310, intersect TX 7.

East 12 m. on TX 7 is **Marlin** (alt. 383; pop. 6,386), with the appearance common to such spas as Atlantic City or Mineral Wells—an architecture from the period when the mineral bath was much in vogue. At Marlin, for thousands each year, it still is. In 1850, the town was ordinary Bucksnort, then, in 1891, a water well struck hot mineral water and a passing tramp claimed cure of all his ailments. The city's future direction was launched.

On the north edge of town is Highlands Mansion, a big, elegant Gay 90s home, exquisitely refurbished, with extraordinary detail in that restoration.

Investigating the promise of geothermal energy, Marlin now heats a hospital and its C of C by means of the hot spring water. In town, the Falls County Museum features regional history. Late each April, Marlin observes Festival Days, tented in its shaded city park.

Between Marlin and Lott, 3 m. west via FM 712, is the natural rock dam forming the **Falls of the Brazos,** from time immemorial a point of rendezvous for Indian and, later, pioneer. It is a natural crossing and some cars even now drive it (at considerable peril). On the west bank was the site of Sterling Robertson's land office for his 1835 colony, the settlement **Sarahville de Viesca,** and near it, Fort Milam, a frontier outpost that held off a Comanche attack similar to that which, farther east, destroyed Fort Parker. Frontier Preacher Z. N. Morrell rode alone, 220 miles in four days, to return with powder, lead, and salvation for the embattled stockade. Both the fort and Sarahville are gone now, but the falls and its park remain to remind of them.

Rosebud, 212 m. (alt. 392; pop. 1,638) is a pleasant little town with a long-standing claim that each of its homes boasts at least one rose bush. On a farm nearby, legend persists of buried treasure, believed to be part of the

Steinheimer Lode (see Belton-Little River). The site is on private land.

Cameron, 228 m. Enter Region II, Southeast. Intersect US 190/Tour 18. Your route continues as Tour 29.

☆

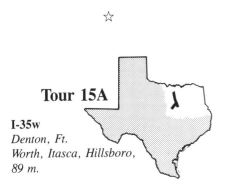

Tour 15A

I-35w
*Denton, Ft.
Worth, Itasca, Hillsboro,
89 m.*

Much of this route follows an early northern leg of the old Chisholm Trail. It also roughly skirts the line that Sam Houston drew in the 1840s— "where the Indian's West begins." Although dotted with blackjack and post oak, there is a more open feel to the rolling land here than there is on the Interstate companion just eastward: you can sense that hilly country is not far west of you.

Particularly along the northern reaches of this tour, accents are brisker: mid-westerners helped settle the land, and in the early days cattle were the staple. Today, however, small farms still patch the open country.

Toward Hillsboro, you reach beyond the line of first western forts, sidetripping into scenic Bosque County, still flavored with its early Norwegian heritage. You are also in a land not entirely wrested from the Indian until the mid-1800s.

Denton, 0 m.—see Tour 2. Junction from I-35E, bearing for Fort Worth.

Pilot Knob, 8 m. Near little Argyle, this was a favorite rendezvous for Sam Bass and his outlaw gang during the late 1870s when they terrorized the Dallas-Fort Worth-Denton area. Even then, Bass' time was running out (see Round Rock).

At 10 m., little **Justin** (pop. 1,234) is just west, via FM 410. Here in 1849 was **Icaria,** a French socialist colony (similar to La Reunion in Dallas), dedicated to unity and brotherhood. Frontier hardships prevailed; a marker alone remains.

At 17 m. is **Roanoke** (alt. 648; pop. 1,616), just east on TX 114, gateway to

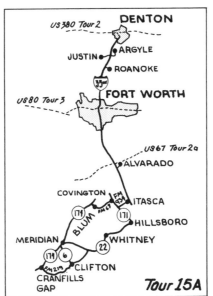

Tour 15A

Grapevine Lake, camping and all facilities. Nearby is the site of **Old Elizabethtown.** At the crossing of the Ranger Trail with the Fort Worth-Denton stage road, this was a rough-and-ready settlement boasting not only Aynes Academy and a saddle shop, but six different saloons.

Fort Worth, 37 m.—see Tour 3.

As your highway nears the Trinity River, the old Fort Worth stockyards lie just to the west. Once the world's largest cattle processing and shipping point, this is now a visitor-oriented area, the Stockyards Historic Area, the Old West recaptured in shops and restaurants.

At **Alvarado,** 61 m., intersect US 67/Tour 2A.

Itasca, 77 m. (alt. 709; pop. 1,523), with its substantial textile mills, is a weaving town. Here an interesting side trip will describe a westward circle.

Via FM 934, take TX 171 north to **Covington,** 10 m., pop. 238. This wayside village was a thriving plantation and manufacturing center—shoes, cloth, harness and brick—with its own Covington College prior to 1860. Railroad by-pass withered it. Follow FM 67 to sleepy little **Blum,** 20 m., pop. 358. Near here in 1801, Philip Nolan, first American scout into Texas and not, as the legend goes, "The Man Without a Country," was killed by Spanish cannon. Evidence is strong that Nolan scouted Texas with the knowledge, consent, and perhaps even direction of Thomas Jefferson, about to negotiate the Louisiana Purchase.

Blum was also home and winter quarters for the early Texas circus queen, Mollie Bailey. An unreconstructed rebel who, as a pretty young woman, had spied for the Confederacy, her small-town Texas circus flew three flags—Stars and Stripes, Confederate Stars and Bars, and Texas' Lone Star. Any Confederate veteran came free and her shows developed an immense following. Her husband and partner, Gus Bailey, had been bandmaster for Hood's Texas Brigade and wrote "The Old Gray Mare" on the eve of the Second Battle of Manassas (Bull Run).

From Blum take FM 67 north to TX 174 south, and see **Kimball Bend Park,** 32 m. Here is one of Texas' most haunting ghosts. Within the Lake Whitney Recreation Area (an excellent campground), **Kimball** seemed blessed in its 1854 beginnings, already possessed of the county's best school, Kimball Academy. Then, in the 70s, Chisholm Trail-bound herds crossed the Brazos here, and the little city boomed. The Brazos crossing was second in hazard only to the Red River, and more than one trailboss could tell of "Stompeads." Need for a reliable lead steer was greatest at the rivers: if the herd began any circular milling, that circle would tighten and drown the inner cattle. The good lead steer kept a straight course and crossed his fellows, but more than once a drover had to swim his mount into a maelstrom—on rare occasions even walking across those milling backs—and free the struggling animals.

In 1881, the railroad by-passed the town, and Kimball's decline set in. Today the old ruins still stand resolute against a time that has passed them by. Below Kimball is the site of another ghost, an English townsite, Kent, that withered under frontier hardships. Continue southwest on TX 174.

Meridian, 47 m. (alt. 791; pop. 1,390). This county seat (Bosque Co.), established with an 1854 log cabin, is

Enjoying a quiet moment along Bee Creek in Meridian State Recreation Area, just west of Meridian.

notable for its scenic situation: its valley walls rise sharply to the west to nestle the community. Just west in the hills is Meridian State Recreation Area, wooded, camping and all facilities, and a scenic hiking trail. Take TX 6 southeast.

Clifton, 59 m. (alt. 670; pop. 3,195), is a shaded, gracious little city situated in the Bosque valley, one of Texas' prettiest. Pin-neat, it saw Norwegian settlement in the 1850s, and its county numbers most of Texas' Norsemen—their pioneer days recalled in the interesting Bosque Memorial Museum here. The old mill and dam on the Bosque River served early industry. In 1896, Norwegians established a school that eventually would become Texas Lutheran College, now in Seguin. Surrounding, particularly westward, are tiny Norwegian settlements such as **Cranfills Gap,** pop. 269, and Norse.

Just north of town is Texas Safari Wildlife Park, an interesting 850 acres drive-through, featuring exotic and native Texas wildlife. Your youngsters will like the petting zoo.

By-passed by most travelers, **Norse** (pop. 110), 11 m. west, is the spiritual heart of Norwegian country. At nearby Norway Mill, the 1865 stone mill yet stands, and at Norse is the solid, old red brick Lutheran church, surrounded with its parishioners' homes, notably the century-old Questad home. Each November the church holds a delightful observance, centering on a giant cafeteria-style Norwegian meal—potato breads, pastries, cheeses, fish and meats. Church ladies wear colorful native costumes and serve their guests in relays. Attendance is from across the country; make arrangements in advance. Take FM 219 and TX 22 northeast.

Whitney, 82 m. (alt. 585; pop. 1,626) is gateway to sprawling, scenic Lake Whitney and its big recreation and resort areas. Tours of the big dam are available. The dam itself is not an original thought; it is close by the site of Towash community, a drowned ghost with its own dam and mill in the 1870s. At

Lake Whitney, one of Texas' most popular recreation spots, is just west of Whitney on FM 1713.

Old Fort Park (east side) is the site of Fort Graham (1849–53) established on top of a Caddoan Indian village and one of the original U.S. western outposts. The old barracks have been reconstructed. In addition to **Lake Whitney State Park,** with camping and all facilities, there are 17 excellent Corps of Engineer Parks scattered about the 225 m. shoreline. Whitney Dam is some 3 m. long and 159 feet high.

From Whitney, follow TX 22 eastward, and at 96 m. rejoin I-35, 12 m. south of where you left it.

Hillsboro, 88 m. (176 m. via Itasca-Whitney loop)—see Tour 15. Follow I-35/Tour 15 south through Waco, 121 m.—see Tour 4. Continue I-35 south to Temple, 157 m., where you enter Region II, merging with Tour 18 as far as Belton, below which I-35 becomes Tour 30.

☆

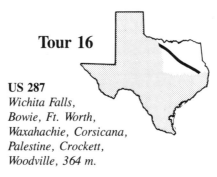

Tour 16

US 287
Wichita Falls,
Bowie, Ft. Worth,
Waxahachie, Corsicana,
Palestine, Crockett,
Woodville, 364 m.

In a great diagonal sweep southeast, this route opens two distinct areas of Texas to you. Beginning below the rough Red River country at Wichita Falls, you are on the edge of big ranch country. As you move progressively eastward, you leave that terrain behind at Fort Worth. Timber gradually gathers, the land smooths out and, by Palestine, you penetrate the forests of East Texas, which become increasingly dense as you travel.

And you travel, in the old sense, from the land of the plains Indian to that of the forest-dwelling Tejas, and his less advanced but equally sedentary neighbors southward. You also leave the land of the trail-driving cowboy for that of the buckskinned pioneer and, before him—around Crockett—that of the early Spanish explorer. Today, the early cities along the way are open, sunny, bustling. Along the latter leg, they are quieter woodland places more steeped in tradition. It is one

of the better north-south roads for exploring both West and East Texas in one drive.

Wichita Falls, 0 m.—see Tour 1. Westward in Region IV, your highway has been Tour 46.

Henrietta, 20 m.—see Tour 1. Veer southeast from US 82. From tiny Bellevue, 37 m., for a distance of some 25 miles this highway is said to be "paved with gold." The gravel from one pit was found to assay at about $1.75 per ton in gold and some silver, but its recovery cost is deemed prohibitive.

Bowie, 49 m. (alt. 1,145; pop. 4,990), named for Alamo's hero, is a bustling little city whose downtown seems as crowded as its residential area is comfortable and cared for. Immediately southwest is Lake Amon Carter, with all facilities. Jim Bowie Days, late each June, turn the years back to the time when this was a Chisholm Trail town.

Clearing the streets of downtown Bowie for the annual Jim Bowie Days festivities.

At 57 m., you might stop in at little **Sunset's** Old West Museum.

Decatur, 77 m.—see Tour 2. Along your route the Lyndon B. Johnson National Grasslands have lain to your east. Nearby are cosmopolitan Denton to the east and resort-dotted Lake Bridgeport, west.

The Wise County Courthouse, Decatur, built in 1896.

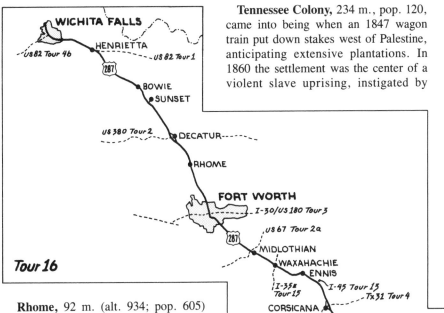

Tour 16

Tennessee Colony, 234 m., pop. 120, came into being when an 1847 wagon train put down stakes west of Palestine, anticipating extensive plantations. In 1860 the settlement was the center of a violent slave uprising, instigated by

1870s, when the International and Great Northern Railroad built through the area, naming it for the vineyards that promoters anticipated. Instead, Grapeland's produce became lumber and, later, oil. It was settled 40 years earlier than the rails' arrival when some of Daniel Parker's primitive Baptists homesteaded on San Pedro Creek, building a blockhouse—Brown's Fort—there. There is an old-fashioned air about the downtown area which parallels the railroad tracks. One of the most interesting old general merchandise stores in Texas stands, brick-fronted with great cast iron posts, on the corner. Houston County Lake offers water sports immediately west.

Latexo, 281 m., pop. 289. On the Trinity River accessible only by local

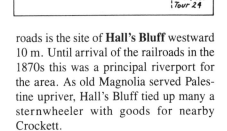

Rhome, 92 m. (alt. 934; pop. 605) was very nearly named Scuffletown for a series of fights occurring when the townsite was surveyed in 1858. Just west is little **Aurora,** which had been the promising city of early Wise County until by-passed by the railroads. Most Aurorans moved to Rhome.

Fort Worth, 116 m.—see Tour 3. Your inbound route parallels scenic Eagle Mountain Lake and enters through North Fort Worth, a major Old West restoration in the city's old stockyard area.

At **Midlothian,** 147 m., intersect US 67/Tour 2A.

Waxahachie, 158 m.—see Tour 15.

Ennis, 173 m.—see Tour 13. Merge with I-45 to Corsicana.

Corsicana, 192 m.—see Tour 4. From this point your route leaves blackland prairie and enters a long stretch of rolling blackjack and post oak prairie. For some 60 miles the towns are tiny, the countryside, small-farm-rural in nature.

Downtown Corsicana. This city was the first in America to use natural gas for cooking and heating.

white renegades who were summarily tried, convicted, and hanged.

Palestine, 251 m.—see Tour 6.

Elkhart, 262 m. (alt. 390; pop. 1,076). One mile west of this quiet, shaded town is a replica of the original Pilgrim Predestination Church, a "hard-shell Baptist" denomination moved by Rev. Daniel Parker from Illinois in 1833 and considered one of Texas' first protestant churches. The rough log walls and split-log benches arrayed before a roughhewn pulpit testify to the resolute faith of early pioneers. Interestingly, both slaves and freedmen were accepted as church members here.

A branch of this family suffered the Fort Parker massacre (see Groesbeck), and during Palestine's annual Dogwood Trails, which extend to here, the ordeal of that family is recounted.

For a time in the early 1890s, Elkhart boasted a mineral well resort complete with hotel, dancing pavilion and billiard hall. By 1907 the wells had failed.

Grapeland, 274 m. (alt. 480; pop. 1,450), did not become a town until the

roads is the site of **Hall's Bluff** westward 10 m. Until arrival of the railroads in the 1870s this was a principal riverport for the area. As old Magnolia served Palestine upriver, Hall's Bluff tied up many a sternwheeler with goods for nearby Crockett.

Crockett, 287 m.—see Tour 8. Via TX 7 eastward, recreational and camping facilities are abundant in Davy Crockett National Forest. Jewel-like Ratcliff Lake offers excellent fishing.

Groveton, 315 m. (alt. 323; pop. 1,071), seems a city off the beaten trail in the forest. Gathered about its big pink brick courthouse that more resembles a large school building, it was once a booming lumber town. However, some 2,000 inhabitants left when the mills closed in the 1930s. Now, with the beauty of its surroundings and vast Lake

Livingston's resort area southwest, this seat of Trinity County is optimistic for its future.

East 5 m. is the site of Sumpter, a ghost community marked only by its cemetery and a gully that was once the main street. This was Trinity County seat from 1850 to 1872, and the boyhood home of gunfighter John Wesley Hardin. When Sumpter's courthouse burned, **Trinity,** pop. 2,648 (via TX 94, 17 m. southwest), took it, only to lose to Pennington, northward, which in turn lost finally to Groveton.

Near Trinity, a lumbering center close on Lake Livingston and coming to life with tourism is **Sebastopol,** pop. 31, once a major riverport turned ghost, now a recreational gateway.

At **Corrigan,** 333 m., intersect Tour 9/US 59. East 9 m. at FM 62 is the Longleaf Pine Trail, a two-mile scenic hiking trail through deep forest. West 9 m., near Carmona, is equally scenic Bull Creek Trail, notable for its large magnolias, gums and oaks.

Chester, 348 m. (alt. 237; pop. 285). Close by is the site of **Peachtree Village,** a large settlement occupied by the Alabama Indians in the early 1800s, taking its name from a peach orchard planted, the story goes, from peach pits the Alabamas carried here as they retreated westward, finally to their home today near Livingston. Here also is the handsome John Henry Kirby Chapel. Kirby is recognized as father of the Texas yellow pine industry.

Woodville, 364 m. Enter Region II, Southeast. Intersect US 190/Tour 18. Your route continues south to Beaumont as Tour 24.

☆

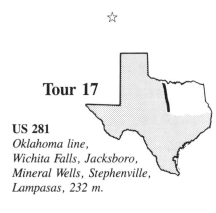

Tour 17

US 281
Oklahoma line,
Wichita Falls, Jacksboro,
Mineral Wells, Stephenville,
Lampasas, 232 m.

This southbound route borders the western edge of Region I and could easily be called the Frontier Trail, for you travel country on or beyond the barest edge of early Texas colonization. It could be known as the Battle Trail as well, for from start to finish you penetrate the east frontier of Comancheria and along your road are countless sites— a gap, a divide, a gully, a mott of trees— where savage little fights occurred and deaths were by twos and threes and, occasionally, dozens. This may be no coincidence for you are approximating one of the oldest north-south Indian trails known in recorded history.

The land is rough, originally cattle country and later, in some areas, oil. Today the towns are of medium size, solid and settled. Scrub oak and mesquite— except for bottom land—comprise the timber you'll see, with cedar increasing as the hills rise progressively southward. At Lampasas, ending Region I southward, you are close indeed to the scenic Hill Country of Texas.

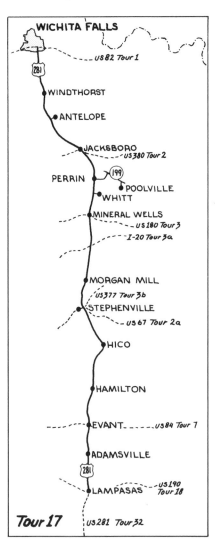

Okla. line, 0 m. Immediately west in Region IV is **Burkburnett** (Tour 46), scene of one of the biggest, wildest oil booms in Texas history.

Wichita Falls, 14 m.—see Tour 1. Just south, via FM 1954, is lovely Lake Arrowhead State Park, with camping and all facilities.

Windthorst, 39 m., pop. 367. The land rolls out to hazy rims and across it dot the neat dairy farms which German Texans built around their great red Romanesque Benedictine church in the 1890s. The church interior is beautiful in vaulting arches and pastel blues. Fronting the building is a grotto, a replica of Lourdes, and a deep sense of miracle. In the 1940s, Windthorst, with a population of 120, sent 59 sons into World War II, this church's priest among the first to go. Of them, 80 percent saw battle action. There is a bronze plaque listing the names and, in red marble, a prayer: "Our Lady of Perpetual Help, Pray For Us."

The grotto was planned by young men—before leaving—as thanks, if they might be allowed to return. Though some sustained wounds, every man came home.

Antelope, 50 m., pop. 65, was an 1860 trail camp. Until recently, this was a settlement of a century ago—log cabins with split-rail fences, a resolute frontier survivor. Some traces of the old times remain.

At 58 m., cross Camberon Creek. Just downstream in 1859 two families were massacred by Indians. A mile beyond, within **Lost Valley,** rangers in 1875 cut down a war party and found a blue-eyed, brown-haired squaw with no memory of her past.

Jacksboro, 73 m.—see Tour 2. Fort Richardson State Park, located here, is steeped in history. The park offers camping and all facilities.

Perrin, 88 m., pop. 300. On Keechie Creek, Indians killed two boys hauling water, captured two others for ransom. Immediately beyond is old Dillingham Prairie where, in 1847, a Southern family incredibly attempted an extensive plantation. Slaves were cut down; the manse, under almost constant attack, was finally abandoned.

Via FM 2210 east is the ghost of **Gibtown,** 6 m. In the 1890s here was Jack

County's cotton boomer—a dozen stores, two gins, a school and academy, Masonic Hall, and hundreds of Saturday horse-and-wagon come-to-towners. Careless of plowing, Gibtown found its fields eroding to deep gullies, its cottonboom days finished within 30 years after its original promise.

Farther east, off TX 199, little **Poolville,** pop. 230, once a thriving trail town, offers another interesting step into the past: little has changed from frontier days.

At 94 m., via FM 52 east, is the near-ghost **Whitt,** 3 m., pop. 38. This was once a thriving town on the stage road from Weatherford to Jacksboro, its Half Way House well known to travelers of the 1860s. Whitt had two schools of then "college" rank.

Salesville, 97 m., pop. 40. From Loving Valley here, the dean of Texas traildrivers, Oliver Loving, made his first cattledrive north to Chicago in 1858, his route veering east to approximate the Shawnee Trail, above Dallas. With his close friend and neighbor, Charles Goodnight, who moved into the area, he later blazed the Goodnight-Loving Trail westward (see Palo Duro).

Mineral Wells, 104 m.—see Tour 3. Lake Mineral Wells State Park has developed for overnight use.

At 118 m. intersect I-20/Tour 3A.

Morgan Mill, 134 m., pop. 206, is the site of a sawmill of the 1870s. Headwaters of the Paluxy furnished the best timber stands of this area.

Stephenville, 145 m.—see Tour 2A.

Hico, 165 m. (alt. 1,006; pop. 1,342), is a shaded little road-bend town origi-

US 281 between Stephenville and Hico.

nally located 4 m. south of Honey Creek, where rock ruins of an old mill still stand. Railroad by-pass moved the little city. Legend persists among some old-timers that Billy the Kid was not killed in New Mexico but spirited away instead—Pat Garrett was his friend—and lived to peaceful old age under an assumed name here.

Hamilton, 186 m. (alt. 1,154; pop. 2,937), is prosperous-looking around its busy square, the center of a rich farming area. Hamilton exhibits a changeless serenity, living much as it has for several decades. It was raw country, Indian contested from westward Indian Gap (Region IV) until the 1880 railroads. The Hamilton County Museum, reflecting pioneer days, is housed in the courthouse.

Evant, 202 m.—see Tour 7.

Tiny **Adamsville,** 215 m., pop. 28, looks eastward into the hilly and vast Fort Hood military reservation (see Killeen). Here train America's tank corps and attack helicopter crews; Operation Desert Storm troops learned here.

Lampasas, 232 m. Enter Region II, Southeast; or Region IV, West. Intersect US 190/Tour 18, Region II. Your route continues southward as Tour 32.

☆

Region II
East-West: Tours 18 through 22

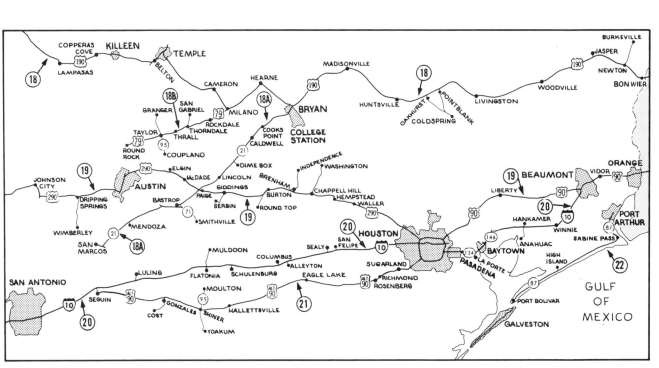

(Also see page 64)

Tour 18

US 190
*Louisiana line,
Jasper, Livingston,
Huntsville, Madisonville,
Bryan, Hearne, Cameron, Temple,
Killeen, Lampasas, 335 m.*

As with most east-to-west highways in Texas, your route climbs steadily, if imperceptibly, beginning at near sea level in Newton County, ending almost 1,000 feet higher in Lampasas.

The first third of your journey edges within the north fringe of the Big Thicket, a once near-impenetrable wilderness of secretive beauty. These woodlands offer many excellent hiking trails of varying length. Inquire locally. Beyond Madisonville you emerge into the rich Brazos River bottomlands and cross gently rolling blackland prairies until, west of Temple, you penetrate the upper Hill Country with its rugged terrain, thinner vegetation (except along streams) and its clear-running rivers.

Similarly, you cross from timbering land to a land devoted to agriculture, and you end in ranch country. Your Texans along the way are first soft-spoken Southerners, then Texas-drawling farmer-ranchers whom you'll often see with rifles strapped behind the seats of their pickup trucks. In earlier days you would have journeyed from the sedentary forest Indian country to that of the fierce Plains rovers.

The cities along this route are largely of modest size and are almost invariably neat and prospering.

La. line, 0 m. Your highway crosses the Sabine in dense pine and hardwood forest.

Bon Wier, 2 m., (alt. 60; pop. 475), rests deep in forest, long a logging, sawmill town. Via FM 1416 and local roads leading downriver are the ghosts of lumber camps and river ports, **Trotti** and **Belgrade,** and farther south, the ghost of **Old Salem.**

At 8 m., opposite a roadside park, the Sylvan Trail meanders through great loblolly pines—a brief, scenic hike.

Newton, 13 m., (alt. 172; pop. 1,885), seems a withdrawn, forest-closeted little town, its citizens descendants of earliest settlers; but its proximity to resort lakes—Steinhagen, Sam Rayburn and Toledo Bend—is fast bringing tourism. Newton is immediately adjacent to the site of an old Indian village, just west, and lies alongside the strip of Louisiana once known as "Neutral Ground," a forest land infested with smugglers and outlaws.

North 14 m. via TX 87 is **Burkeville,** pop. 515, almost isolated within its forest and with the distinction of being perhaps the most complete do-it-yourself town in Texas. Grown from an 1821 settlement and populated by its settlers' descendants, these citizens ground their own cornmeal, grew their broom corn, made their own household furnishings and generally subsisted independent of the rest of Texas.

Jasper, 28 m. (alt. 221; pop. 6,959) describes itself as "Jewel of the Forest," and has a history dating back to its 1824 career as the municipality of Bevil, its men among the leaders in the Texas Revolution 11 years later. During the Civil War, Jasper and southward Wiess Bluff were Confederate depot/strong points. An interesting record of those Civil War

Bank fishing off the Neches River near Steinhagen Lake between Jasper and Woodville.

days is displayed at the Jasper County Museum, housed in the courthouse.

With its wide streets and narrow walks, this was until recently a sawmill town, the strong scent of pine and the whine of giant saws ever present. Now, almost surrounded by lakes—Steinhagen, Sam Rayburn and Toledo Bend—and 90 percent of its area forested, Jasper is a tourist-sportsman-hunter's Mecca. Southward (see Tour 23) was once a particularly violent area known locally as Scrapping Valley for a long-time blood feud between two families. Today this whole area is pastoral.

In and around the city are many fine old homes toured each March–April when Jasper celebrates its Azalea Trail—a month-long riot of color (C of C map available).

At Jasper, intersect US 96/Tour 9 north, Tour 23 south.

At 36 m. your road crosses beautifully wooded B. A. Steinhagen Lake, flanked by **Martin Dies State Park,** both with camping, all facilities, and magnificent magnolia trees. Several old homes or sites, particularly the R. C. Doom House (1856), are close by. Off FM 1747, the Old River Trail hikes to the site of ghost **Bevilport,** a 1.5 m. walk, to

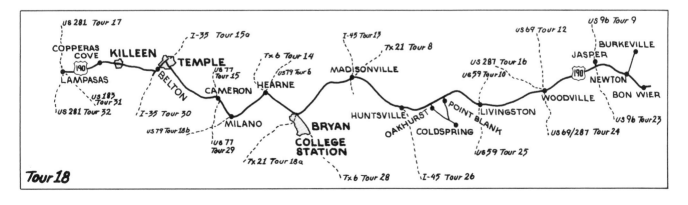

what was a major rivertown of the 1830s. It is a boat ramp and picnic area today.

At 54 m., hikers may take to the Dogwood Trail, 1.5 m., snowy-blossomed each spring.

Woodville, 57 m. (alt. 232; pop. 2,636), is a beautiful little city in its magnificent yet tranquil forest setting. The entire city has been set aside as a bird sanctuary. Housed in one of the oldest homes here, beautifully restored and furnished, is the Allan Shivers Museum and Library, with considerable memorabilia from that former governor's administration. Governor Shivers maintained a Woodville residence. South of the city is one of the state's largest magnolia trees, and also a Golden Pine, one of only two known specimens which winter turns to gold.

This is a festive town; its Dogwood Festival (late each March or early in April) is one of Texas' most showy. Each January Woodville gathers for the Neches Valley Singing Convention, and in September stages the Tyler County Fair.

At Woodville intersect US 69/Tour 12 north, US 287/Tour 16 north; US 69-287/Tour 24 south.

Just west of town are the Big Thicket Gardens.

One mile west is **Heritage Garden Village,** one of the outstanding living museums of pioneer life in Texas. Here you literally step into a past so authentic and so complete that the 30-building locale is sought for TV and films. Displays range from syrup mill to smithy, from whiskey still to jailhouse. There is an excellent dining room where you eat sumptuously in old-fashioned boarding-house style.

Alabama-Coushatta Indian Reservation, 73 m. This area's first permanent settlers migrated in 1809, moving to a reservation established by Sam Houston, steadfast Indian friend. On their 4,351 acres, while maintaining their tribal customs, the people in recent years have developed their community into a prospering tourist attraction, with authentic Indian handiwork, a museum, Indian foods, complete camping facilities and a Big Thicket Tour. Tribal dances are performed daily through the summer and on weekends spring and fall. In the Living Indian Village, tribal members make goods to sell. South of the reservation is the

Big Sandy Creek unit of the Big Thicket National Preserve, one of several such in the state, designed to maintain the integrity of this wilderness.

South 14 m. down US 287 is Kirby State Forest. Throughout this entire area of rolling, flowered countryside, many scenic drives are available, and well marked hiking trails invite exercise.

Livingston, 90 m. (alt. 194; pop. 5,019), edging the Big Thicket, is a prosperous little city thriving today in its location close by immense, resort-minded Lake Livingston (and its state park). Grown from a log cabin settlement in 1848, the town long centered its forest land where great mounds of sawdust reminded that sawmill camps had come and gone. In 1902, a fire destroyed Livingston's center: the rebuilding accounts for its more modern appearance, enhanced now by tourism. The Polk County Museum offers excellent exhibits, including early American glassware and a 1700 candelabrum from the White House. A historic log cabin has been relocated downtown.

At Livingston, intersect US 59/Tour 10 north, Tour 25 south.

At 108 m. your road crosses 82,600 acre Lake Livingston, with a multitude of recreational facilities all about.

An autumn drive through the forest near Livingston.

Among them is excellent Lake Livingston State Park, a big one with all facilities. The lake offers fine fishing. On the west bank is **Pointblank,** no guntown but a derivation from French Point Blanc, so named by an early Gallic settler. Here is the homesite of Texas' second governor, George Wood.

Via TX 156 south 13 m., **Coldspring** (alt. 356; pop. 538) has a handsome, big-columned courthouse looming over its village. The United Methodist Church (1848) is beautifully restored

and boasts a century-old bell. The old city jail is now a museum. South 2 m. is crystalline Double Lake, deep in Sam Houston National Forest, with camping, all facilities and nature trails.

East 7 m. is the site of **Swartout** beside Livingston State Park (most accessible from Livingston). In 1835 this was a major Trinity port: 86 blocks platted, with two public squares. Like other riverboat towns, railroads finished it.

From Coldspring north 16 m. via FM 946 is **Oakhurst** near Raven Hill, Sam Houston's home for a time.

Oakhurst is at 199 m. on your route.

Huntsville, 133 m. (alt. 400; pop. 27,925), rambles over its red hills, a forested city with dignified old homes. Sam Houston State University crowns one hill (12,000 students), the headquarters unit of the Texas Department of Criminal Justice, another. Several other units are located nearby. A driving tour is available from the C of C. Sam Houston State maintains a $20 million criminal justice center, a major American installation in law enforcement education. The Texas Prison Museum (south side of square) displays historical artifacts relating to the town's main industry—ball-and-chains, Bonnie and Clyde's rifles, and "Old Sparky," the state electric chair used for 40 years. Crafts produced by inmates are also available.

Founded as an Indian trading post in 1836, then a plantation center, Huntsville—despite Houston's opposition to secession—gave heavily to the Confederacy and for a time in 1871 was under martial law. Today it is a city of churches, many of them serving since the 1840s. Austin College, now in Sherman, was founded here in 1849; its original building is now on the Sam Houston State campus.

Above all, Huntsville was Sam Houston's town, the one he loved most. The Sam Houston shrine is one of Texas' finest. The grounds are beautiful; the structures include an outstanding museum, Houston's home and law office, the War and Peace House, and the Steamboat House where he died, July 26, 1863. The Sam Houston Folk Festival is held on the grounds each April. In Oakwood Cemetery a gray granite monument records Andrew Jackson's assessment of his protegé: "The world will take care of Houston's fame."

A former Tennessee militia general, congressman, governor and friend of the Indian, sometime recluse with them,

Sam Houston's outdoor kitchen, Sam Houston Memorial Park, Huntsville.

Houston came to Texas in 1832 representing President Andrew Jackson, his old friend, in an investigation of Indian conditions. He returned in 1833, and again in 1835, making his home in Nacogdoches and quickly assuming a dominant role in the Texas move for independence. Despite reversals and opposition, he led his small army through its retreat to San Jacinto and in 1836 became the Republic's first president. He was instrumental in securing annexation by the United States, and throughout a long career as U.S. Senator, then governor, he vigorously opposed Texas secession. When it came in 1860, he took the position that Texas once again became a republic and refused to swear allegiance to the Confederacy, an act which deposed him as governor. He refused the support of federal troops (see Georgetown) to hold Texas to the union and retired here to live out his life.

Huntsville State Park, big, forested, with camping and all facilities, is immediately south. Here also is access to Texas' longest backpack challenge—the 140-m. Lone Star Hiking Trail. Huntsville's C of C offers complete information, including a "Funmap." In this area also see Trinity, New Waverly.

At Huntsville, intersect I-45/Tour 26 south. Merge with I-45 north to Madisonville.

Madisonville, 162 m.—see Tour 8. Veer from I-45 and continue west on US 190.

Bryan-College Station, 198 m. (alt. 367; pop. 107,458 combined) is a fast-growing twin city spreading wide streets over the flats of the Brazos bottoms, centering an area once rich in old plantations. The town of Bryan began in 1855, anticipating the railroad's extension north from Houston, but Civil War stopped the line at little Millican to the

south. With Allen Military Academy moved up from Madisonville, and already-established Villa Maria Ursuline Academy for girls, Bryan gained additional educational prestige with Texas' first state venture into higher education, the establishment of Texas Agricultural and Mechanical College, immediately south, in 1876; and the city and university have grown together. The surrounding Brazos bottoms furnished many of Hood's Texas Brigade, regarded as Lee's most formidable troops, and Bryan for years was reunion headquarters for those surviving veterans. The Brazos Valley Museum of Natural Science, housed in the big new Brazos Center, features natural history, archaeology, and pre-history. The center is an immense multipurpose facility designed for any gathering from fairs and festivals to lectures and rodeos.

Bryan also boasts the Messina-Hof Wine Cellars, a vineyard and winery upholding Italian and German winemaking traditions.

Southward—and properly on Tour 28/ TX 6—big, handsome and proud Texas A&M University must be considered together with Bryan: the two form a virtually unbroken city. "Old Army," as this institution is known, opened its doors with a faculty of six and 40 students. First presidency was offered to Jefferson Davis; he recommended his friend Thomas Gathright, who took the post.

Coeducational today, TAMU spreads over a broad prairie with campus of some 20,000 acres (the largest in the U.S.) with an enrollment of over 40,000. It is one of America's fastest-growing institutions of higher education. Its men have served their country well: the school furnished more WW I officers than any other in America, including West Point. Twenty thousand Aggies, 14,000 of them officers, served through WW II. The school is famed for technical, scientific and agricultural studies and development. It was one of the first to teach space technology and is a leader in oceanography. Of particular interest on-campus are the 15-story Oceanography-Meteorology Building, the Space Research Center, Cyclotron Institute, Data Processing Center, Nuclear Science Center. The beautiful Memorial Student Center displays a rare antique gun collection, also an extraordinary miniature wagon display. The Evans Library

houses the Kruger Art Collection of European Masters. Arrange campus tours at the Information Center at Rudder Tower. They should include the Albritton Bell Tower, with its 49 bells cast in France, the Floral Test Garden, with hundreds of colorful varieties under study for regional practicality, and the branding iron and barbed wire collection housed in the Kleberg Center.

A major stop for any Aggie will always be 70,000-capacity Kyle Field, where Old Army's Maroon and White attacks all invaders.

Aggie tradition runs deep, from its Twelfth Man (in 1922 a student left the stands to substitute for an injured football player) symbolizing the entire corps (who stand throughout all games), to Silver Taps, final tribute to an Aggie who has died.

At Bryan, intersect TX 21/Tour 8 north, Tour 29 south; also TX 6/Tour 14 north, Tour 28 south.

Hearne, 216 m. (alt. 305; pop. 5,132), is an agricultural and trade center that rambles across junctions—railroad and highway crossroads. The Hearne C of C and Heritage League have prepared an excellent do-it-yourself tour featuring a number of historic buildings and homes, as well as Hearne's handsomely-restored depot. Just west on the Brazos is the peculiar rock formation known as Cannonball Shoals for its big, rounded rocks; here also are the abandoned river locks from the late 1800s, when attempts were made to create a navigable river all the way to Waco. Just upstream are the sites of old Nashville and Port Sullivan, pioneer colonies (see Tour 14). In this area also see Calvert, Franklin.

At **Hearne,** merge southwest with US 79. At **Milano,** 237 m., continue northwest on US 190.

Cameron, 250 m. (alt. 402; pop. 5,580), is an agricultural center and county seat (Milam Co.), whose settlers came from Kentucky, Tennessee and Louisiana. It grew from nearby Jones Prairie, settled in 1833. Its Milam County Museum is the old three-story jailhouse built in 1895, with a tower containing a hanging room.

The Magnolia House (502 N. Travis St.) is a Victorian mansion thought to be the finest of its type and size in the nation. Every piece of lumber in the 1895 home was hand-picked for rarity and beauty.

At Cameron, intersect US 77/Tour 15 north, Tour 29 south.

Temple, 282 m. (alt. 736; pop. 46,109). Neat, orderly and rapidly spreading around a compact business area, this city is a widely-known medical center, with Scott and White, among others here, one of America's leading medical institutions. Temple's total hospital installations are valued at more than $300 million. Home of Temple Junior College and an expanding industrial-business complex, it is also an important railroad hub. Together with Belton and Killeen, in 1980s its metro area was sixth fastest-growing in America, altogether a far cry from pioneer beginnings that saw savage Indian fighting.

Settlers built a blockhouse on Little River, southward, in 1836 (see Tour 30), but could not hold it. Continual fighting brought abandonment again in 1838, and only victory at Bird's Creek, on the north edge of today's Temple, began to allow settlement in 1839.

Temple has a little of everything: an outstanding shopping mall, an exceptional number of good antique shops in its immediate area, a wide range of cultural and special events. Museums are particularly interesting.

The Grove Country Life Museum, 15 m. northwest on TX 36, recalls small-town life in days gone by.

Saluting its railroad heritage, Temple's "Depot," authentic 1907 Santa Fe, is for old train buffs. Scott and White maintains a medical museum—the founder's original log cabin study. Most interesting of all is the museum at the Slavonic Benevolent Order state headquarters—coins dating to the seventh century, a 1530 Bible, and antique musical instruments such as an 1895 hand-made dulcimer. Let the curator show you the intriguing century-old "Magic Gambling Machine," whose automatic man rolls dice to determine who pays for the drinks. Just west is Temple Lake Park, with camping, fishing, swimming and all outdoor recreational facilities. Each April and October Texas Early Day Tractor and Engine Association hosts shows.

At Temple, intersect I-35/Tour 15A north, Tour 30 south. Merge with I-35 south.

Belton, 290 m. (alt. 511; pop. 12,476), first known as Nolanville, began colonization in 1850, although immediately south on Little River is the site of Smith's Fort, the 1836 blockhouse which failed. Charter Oak, where this city was organized, stands just north of Belton's city limits on old US 81. Here is the home of Mary Hardin Baylor University, until coeducational, the oldest women's college west of the Mississippi. Each spring, the student body presents a beautiful Easter pageant.

There are many fine old Victorian homes, 1860–1904, toured on the city's annual open house in late April or early May. A Chisholm Trail town, the first store was the merchant's wagon; barrel of whiskey and a tin cup under a tree were the saloon. In 1874 its county jail, now a private residence, was stormed by vigilantes, who executed in their cells several men charged with horse theft.

Camping and recreational facilities are immediately west at two lakes, Belton and Stillhouse Hollow. South on Little River, buried treasure legend (Tour 30) has persisted for a century. In the area also see Salado.

At Belton, veer from I-35 and head west on US 190.

Killeen, 307 m. (alt. 833; pop. 63,535), mushrooming beside immense Fort Hood, gives the impression of a one-street town that stretches on indefinitely. In 1940, population was 1,263, then WW II sent it booming. Fort Hood, 216,915 acres that comprise the Army's largest installation, is home to the First Cavalry and Second Armored Divisions. "First Team" Museum (General Douglas MacArthur so nicknamed the 1st Cavalry) tells that elite outfit's history from horse to copter. The Second Armored Museum displays General George Patton's famed "Hell on Wheels" fighters. At both installations the displays are excellent, the weaponry impressive, the guides informed. Second Armored shows the film "Patton" on closed-circuit TV.

Copperas Cove, 315 m. (alt. 1,086; pop. 24,079), long little more than a wayside village, grows mightily today in overflow from the military outspill of neighboring Killeen. Westward, your route continues to climb.

Lampasas, 335 m. (alt. 1,025; pop. 6,382). Settled in the mid 1850s, this town fought Indians until 1875. Its cattle trail and frontier background is reflected in broad streets and an ample courthouse square; its durability in the solidity of its rock homes, and carefully-restored downtown area, where the Keystone Square Museum reflects frontier days. Here was a rough trail town in the 1870s, when the Horrel-Higgins feud erupted.

The feud began when the Horrel family, resisting reconstruction state police, killed four of them and fled to New Mexico. Returning in 1877, they fell out over cattle with former neighbors and friends, the Higgins family. This feud was shot out twice, once at "Battle Branch," a creek 4 m. west of town, and finally in the middle of the town square, where some 50 men joined the battle. Rangers put down the feud, forcing the signature of an unusual document to regard the feud as "a by-gone thing." The truce, rare for feuds, was kept.

In 1875, the Farmer's Alliance, which grew to 3,000 lodges before merging with the Farmer's Union in 1887, was founded here. The aim of the alliance then, as today, was betterment of farm conditions through cooperative effort.

Several ghost towns, most of them traceless, are scattered in the surrounding area. Each July, Lampasas holds its Spring Ho Fest—everything from pet parades to an air show.

At Lampasas, enter Region I, Northeast, or Region IV, West. Your route continues west to Brady as Tour 54. Intersect US 281/Tour 17 north (Tour 32 south), and US 183/Tour 59 north (Tour 31 south).

☆

Tour 18A

TX 21
*Bryan, Caldwell,
Bastrop, San Marcos,
120 m.*

Your southwestward road—the extension of Tour 8, Region I—is the old Camino Real, Spain's royal road into Texas, blazed in 1690. Although the old road pressed on into Mexico near Eagle Pass (like the ancient Indian trail it followed), for today's purposes your tour breaks off at San Marcos, intersecting with I-35, San Antonio-bound.

You begin in the rich Brazos valley with its broad, unfenced fields and pas-

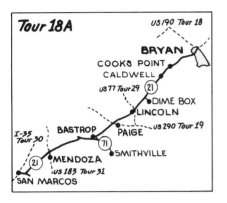

Tour 18A

tured cattle, crossing near Caldwell into rolling post oak and blackjack terrain which extends to the sudden appearance of Bastrop County's great island of pines. Across the Colorado River, these give way to scrub oak country once more, and, near San Marcos, you verge into rich black land that runs level to the abrupt line of hills against which that scenic little city stands, and where you intersect busy I-35.

Bryan, 0 m.—see Tour 18. At 9 m. merge with the Old San Antonio Road, which in old days had looped briefly north between the Brazos and Trinity rivers.

Cooks Point, 18 m., pop. 60, is the site of an early plantation.

Via FM 1362 and local roads north 9 m., near Rita, the site of **Fort Tenoxtitlan** guards the west bank of the Brazos. In 1830 this was to be a major Mexican strongpoint to check further Anglo colonization of Texas, particularly along this road from Nacogdoches, a rapidly anglicizing settlement which Mexico feared. Lt. Col. Jose Francisco Ruiz, who commanded here, shared completely the republican views of his American neighbors and in time was one of the signers of the Texas Declaration of Independence. The fort was abandoned within two years. Plans are projected for its restoration; the site is now hard to reach.

Caldwell, 25 m. (alt. 406; pop. 3,181), a pleasant little city surrounded by several showplace farms, is also an old settlement, founded in 1840 and growing up in an area of big plantations. At the Waugh Campground Oak, 4 m. northeast, one of Texas' first camp meetings was held in 1841. The old oak was used continually, at first for open-air services and later for "political speakings." In the 1880s, Caldwell was a major stop-

over for westbound travelers and boasted a fine hotel. An excellent country inn is located there today. The Burleson County Historical Museum displays pioneer relics and exhibits of old Fort Tenoxtitlan. Caldwell hosts many annual events, including an April Spring Festival, a June County Fair, a July Youth Rodeo (a big one), a September Kolache Festival, and a Christmas Home Tour in December. The town is also home of the Burleson County Opry.

Via TX 36 southeast 18 m. **Lake Somerville** (and its excellent state park) offers camping and all facilities. Nearby, the little town of Somerville maintains an interesting museum.

Old Dime Box, 39 m., pop. 313, is a quaint village named for the early settlers' practice of leaving a dime in a box at Joseph Browne's mill—postal payment for errands run in nearby Giddings. Here, in 1944, President Franklin D. Roosevelt launched the March of Dimes, a suggestion from his Texas friend, Lyndon B. Johnson.

Lincoln, 47 m. (alt. 367; pop. 276), is a pastoral village that grew from **Old Evergreen,** home of William Preston Longley, who rivaled John Wesley Hardin as a dangerous gunfighter-outlaw. Longley began his career fighting reconstruction forces, ended with an East Texas hanging and a reprieve when the rope broke. Finally, after 32 killings, he was hanged in Giddings in 1878. Legend persists that he escaped even this sentence (though his grave is in Giddings), having fitted himself with a special harness to absorb the wrench of the noose, and then disappearing. The Old Evergreen Oak, a magnificent tree, is 4 m. northeast of Giddings, an area settled by the Slavic-German Wendish people (see Giddings, Serbin).

At Lincoln, intersect US 77/Tour 29.

Near **Paige,** 61 m., pop. 275, an 1880 German settlement, intersect US 290/Tour 19.

At 69 m., **Lake Bastrop** lies just west, camping and all facilities.

Bastrop, 74 m. (alt. 374; pop. 4,044), nestles about the old Camino Real's crossing of the Colorado, where Texas' "Lost Pines" begin. It is an old town, looks it, and wears its age pridefully. Among the first settlements in an 1832 grant to Stephen Austin's friend, Dutch Baron de Bastrop, the town was first

named Mina for a Mexican patriot. Its men led in the movement for Texas Independence, 51 of them fighting at San Jacinto.

When the site for a permanent Texas capital was debated (1837–39), Bastrop was a leading contender, ultimately a close second to Waterloo (renamed Austin) in the final decision.

Many old buildings, including the homes of Governor Joseph Sayers and of Josiah Wilbarger, are excellently preserved here. Wilbarger, originally forted upriver at tiny Utley on Wilbarger Bend, had the strange distinction of surviving a Comanche scalping. The ghost of his sister, who had died in St. Louis the day before Wilbarger was scalped, directed rescuers to her stricken brother in time to save his life—or so Wilbarger and others believed for the 20 years he lived after his brush with death.

Bastrop's museum, displaying considerable Texana, is located near the site of the old Camino Real crossing, the same site chosen for a Spanish fort in 1806, Puesta del Colorado.

A self-guiding tour (maps at C of C) lets you explore the little city's historic past. The restored 1889 Opera House once again serves as Bastrop's cultural center, and Pfeiffer Inn, an antique showplace, provides weekend tourists with nostalgic quarters. Downtown, Lock's Drug also offers a glimpse of our past, while the Bastrop *Advertiser* is the state's oldest weekly newspaper.

Erhard's Drug Store, established at Bastrop in 1847, is Texas' oldest.

Above the city, the "Lost Pines"—an island of loblolly timber 80 miles west of the state's pine belt—begin and embrace the twin state parks of Bastrop and Buescher, both with camping and excellent facilities.

Via TX 71 east is **Smithville,** 12 m. (alt. 324; pop. 3,196), occupying an area that was forted as early as 1828.

The shaded, slumberous little city wears a look, within its great live oaks, more Southern than Texas. Among several beautiful old homes are the Burleson home, the Hill House, and the Yerger Hill home, shaded by a handsome magnolia tree. Just east of the city is a lofty roadside park overlook. Of Texas' 1,100 roadside parks, this was the first (1930); in fact, it introduced to America the concept of such rest areas. Just southwest, gravel pits have revealed dinosaur bones and petrified palm wood—whispers from the past of a far different terrain than that of today.

Big and handsome Buescher State Park (all facilities) lies just to the north.

At tiny **Mendoza,** 101 m., pop. 50, intersect US 183/Tour 31.

San Marcos, 120 m., see Tour 30. Intersect I-35.

☆

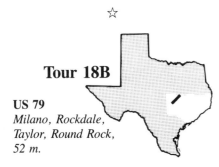

Tour 18B

US 79
Milano, Rockdale,
Taylor, Round Rock,
52 m.

Scenic only in the richness of its rolling countryside, your route—the lower extension of Tour 6, Region I—proceeds southwestward, parallel to old Camino Real just below, and the quiet San Gabriel River, just above. In earliest days it was a trail followed by Spanish explorers almost to the degree of its more famed neighboring road to the south. Later it became a principal highway from central Texas northeastward.

You cross the land of the long-ago Tonkawa Indians, a region much sought by Spain in a failing effort to establish a midway point between San Antonio and Nacogdoches missions. In pioneer days, it was subject to Comanche raids down from the westward hills. Still, plantations grew in great white seas of cotton, giving way to family farming after the

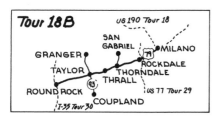

Civil War. Some of Texas' richest land, the black, waxy soils of Wiliamson County reach from Taylor westward to Round Rock, where your road intersects I-35/Tour 30.

Milano, 0 m. (alt. 485; pop. 408), was supposed to have borne its county's name, Milam, but a post office mixup determined otherwise. You veer from US 190/Tour 18 which had merged with this highway just east at Hearne.

One of Rockdale's gracious, comfortable old homes.

Rockdale, 9 m. (alt. 467; pop. 5,235), wears an air of leisurely prosperity along its wide, shaded streets and neat business area. The little city borders Texas' largest lignite coal reserves and much of the employment here accrues from Rockdale's aluminum plant. Close by is the cemetery marking the ghost of coal-mining **Witcher.**

At Rockdale intersect US 77/Tour 29.

Thorndale, 22 m. (alt. 459; pop. 1,092), boasts a cotton oil mill, tales of buried treasure haunted by the ghost of a miser murdered for his gold, and perhaps the source of that treasure—the old mission sites that lie just north.

Via FM 486 north, tiny, **San Gabriel,** 6 m., pop. 96, barely occupies a bend in the road. Along its river close by are the sites of three San Xavier missions, established 1748–55 in an ill-fated Spanish attempt to link up with her eastern church establishment around Nacogdoches. Internal disorder, murder of a priest by the military, tales of a curse—a fireball's appearance over the Spanish fort, a plague, drought, and drying up of the river followed, causing abandonment of the easward linkup and shifting of mission site to a new location near Menard (see Tour 54). Traces of the old Spanish dam remain. Historical markers locating sites (all on private land) have been proved by archeology to be in the wrong places.

Thrall, 28 m. (alt. 500; pop. 550), saw a brief oil flurry, 1925–30, but has returned quietly today to agriculture.

Taylor, billing itself as barbecue capital, holds this International Barbecue Cook-Off each August.

Taylor, 35 m. (alt. 583; pop. 11,472), is a brisk agricultural and manufacturing center with wide streets and the pin-neat quality associated with German-Czech population, settled here. Established in 1876, Taylor's growth has been steady rather than spectacular. There are several handsome old homes, and the First Christian Church, 1891, maintains its original interior. Former Governor Dan Moody's hometown has a museum of memorabilia from his administration.

Taylor's C of C provides maps guiding you through a tour of 30 sites. Claiming the title of Barbecue Capital of the World, the city boasts several establishments catering to that delicacy, and each August, Taylor hosts its International Barbecue Cookoff at big, shaded Murphy Park.

North 6 m. via TX 95 is **Circleville,** pop. 42, named for the form of the original community. The 1846 home of original settler D. H. McFadin has been restored. Granger, 12 m., is a small, neat Czech community.

TX 95 leads south to **Coupland,** 7 m., pop. 135, a village little changed from its 1887 beginnings. An old pharmacy has been restored to a pleasant inn here: barbecue is served close beside the old marble counter and rows of patent medicines.

At 51 m. you are on the outskirts of fast-growing Round Rock (see Tour 30) beside Brushy Creek. On its south bank here is the site of Kenney's Fort, a log stockade built in 1835. From here, close by the present railroad span, the 1842 Texan Santa Fe Expedition was launched, an effort to extend Texas jurisdiction over New Mexico by a 321-man military-trading party with 20 ox-drawn wagons and some $200,000 in trade goods. Expecting a New Mexico welcome, the Texans, exhausted from blazing their own trail to Santa Fe and then betrayed by one of their own, were disarmed and marched to Mexico and prison until U.S. intervention the following year.

At the little fort also occurred the "Archives War" in 1843. Fearing Mexican invasion of Austin, Sam Houston called the Texas Congress into session at Houston. Austinites, suspecting removal of their capitol, guarded its archives, and when Texas Rangers—ordered by Houston to remove the archives peacefully—made off with them, Austin innkeeper Angelina Eberly raised the alarm with a cannon shot. Pursuers caught up here and ordered the surrender of the documents; the capitol was restored to Austin the following year.

Round Rock, 52 m.—see Tour 30/I-35.

☆

Tour 19

US 90/I-10
Louisiana line, Orange, Beaumont
US 90
Liberty, Houston
US 290
Hempstead, Brenham, Austin, Johnson City, 326 m.

This tour begins in the southeast corner of Texas, aiming almost due west. As far as Houston, your route traverses dense forest, pine and hardwood, and you travel near sea level. Beyond Houston, particularly above the Brazos, the land is mottled with great live oaks and begins an almost billowing climb through farmlands—among those first colonized by Americans in Texas. At the state capital you climb abruptly into the Hill Country—rough and scenic terrain where ranching predominates.

Similarly, occupations change as you move west: the Houston leg occupied with highly industrialized, oil-based economies; the Austin leg, primarily farming and stock-raising. Within the

hills you are in ranch country. All across to those hills you have traversed "Independence Country," an area where Texas' colonial revolt began, and that which the old Republic occupied.

For much of the way this is a city-connecting route: the Texas Golden Triangle from Orange to Beaumont, then the metropolis of Houston, up to booming, handsome Austin. Around Brenham you cross some of Texas' most storied land—that of the first colonists and their Declaration of Independence, the earliest schools and churches: the cradle, in fact, from which the Texas Republic grew.

La. line, 0 m. Cross the navigable, opaque Sabine River directly into . . .

Orange, 0.2 m. (alt. 20; pop. 19,381), is a glistening city in the forest with wide streets and a clean business area, its past history predicting its future as a port. Tradition claims that Lafitte's ships used the site as a repair base in 1817–19. Earliest settlers were trappers and shingle-makers using the cypress lining the swamps. Development of rice growing was followed by lumbering; then, during WW II, Orange swelled to 60,000 population engaged in shipbuilding. Today part of the Texas Gulf Coast's metropolitan "Golden Triangle," including Port Arthur and Beaumont, this easternmost Texas city is a rice, timber, petroleum processing and shipping center.

A branch of Lamar University is maintained here. The Stark Museum of Art—Remingtons, Audubons, Russell bronzes and Steuben crystal—is notable, as is Heritage House, a period mansion of 1900, handsomely refurbished. The city also boasts a community playhouse, a big theater for the performing arts, and the Farmer's Mercantile, an intriguing display of agriculture's tools, from those used by our ancestors to our latest devices. Toward Port Arthur, the "Rainbow Bridge" lofting above inbound shipping, is one of the South's highest—high as a 20-story building. Also southward on FM 1006 is Chemical Row, an enormous concentration of modern plants producing the many products derived from petroleum.

Close to the Sabine highway crossing, the present Naval Reserve Training Station occupies a site of more recent historic importance. Here until recent years was maintained an armada of WW II's fighting ships—everything from knife-thin destroyers and sleek, fast attack

transports to ocean-liner-sized troopships, beach-ramming LST's sub-hunting destroyer escorts, sweating tugs and a sectioned drydock husky enough to hoist a battleship. They have been moved, scrapped, lease-loaned, given away, but their ghosts still tug against their mooring lines.

Vidor, 19 m. (alt. 26; pop. 10,935), reflects area growth fueled by oil booms; the prospering, wooded city is twenty times its size of hardly 40 years ago. Immediately north is the site of what was once a small but prosperous Mormon settlement, and beyond that some 10 m., is Four Oaks Ranch and its interesting 1832 cypress wood house located high above the Neches. In town, crystalline Smith Lake offers camping and all recreational facilities. Each April, Vidor stages a Barbecue Festival.

Beaumont, 28 m. (alt. 24; pop. 114,323), on the very edge of jungle-like Big Thicket, stands green-lawned and wide-avenued, a near-tropical flower garden much of the year; at the same time the center of a vast refinery and tank farm area. Begun in 1825 as a trapper's outpost, the settlement grew to a Neches river town, turned to lumbering in the mid 1800s, grew on outlying rice plantations and, in 1901, thundered into world prominence with the discovery of the Spindletop Oilfield.

As the first year of the twentieth century turned, drillers on the Lucas well had reached a depth of over 1,100 feet where sand changed to a rock formation. With no great expectations, the Lucas crew was changing bits when the well roared in, sending a 10-day column of oil 200 feet in the air.

The city ran wild, with food and lodging astronomically priced . . . when it could be found. Police warned citizens to walk in the middle of the street after sundown. All at once, here in one area was 96 percent of Texas' oil production. Gladys City, a rough-and-ready re-creation, depicts the hubbub of the world's first oil-boom town here. However, Beaumont's emergence as a metropolitan hub occurred when oil men determined to place refineries adjacent to the field. Here were born three major companies—The Texas Company, Gulf, and Magnolia, for close at hand was the age of the automobile and oil. In 1908 Beaumont began engineering that would give access to the sea, digging a channel, then

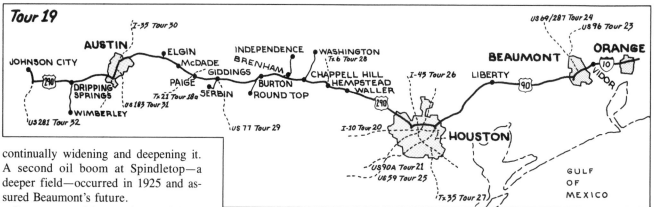

continually widening and deepening it. A second oil boom at Spindletop—a deeper field—occurred in 1925 and assured Beaumont's future.

Beaumont celebrates its week-long Neches River Festival—pageantry and water shows—early each April. In October, the 10-day South Texas State Fair is staged: from exhibit halls to a midway, one of Texas' biggest. A major rose show colors each. The Beaumont Art Museum, on beautifully landscaped grounds, is housed in a Southern Regency mansion. The 1845 French Trading Post, restored, is a historical museum. A visitors information center, on I-10 at Walden Road, will help you plan and map your visit. Your tour should include the Babe Didrickson Zaharias Memorial Museum, which salutes Beaumont's great woman athlete, the Edison Plaza Museum, honoring early American inventors; and, of course, the Texas Energy Museum (campus of Lamar University) reflecting the beginnings of our Oil Age. One stop should be the handsome woodland of Tyrrell Park where, among many attractions, the botanical gardens provide a special "touch and smell" garden for the blind. At Beaumont, intersect US 96/Tour 23, US 69-287/Tour 24. In this area also see Port Arthur, Kountze. From Beaumont, veer from I-10 and follow US 90 west.

The Beaumont Art Museum situated in its tranquil, wooded landscape.

Liberty, 72 m. (alt. 30; pop. 7,733). This quiet, well-kept, shaded town reaches north of the highway, deep in the forest. An old town, it boasts several fine old antebellum homes. It occupies an area early in contest between France and Spain; the latter established a mission fort a short distance south (Tour 20) to block French penetration of the Trinity River area in the 1750s. In 1805, Spain's eastbound Atascosito Road passed close to the site of Liberty.

In 1818, Napoleonic exiles under French General Charles Lallemand unsuccessfully attempted to establish a fort-base, Champ d'Asile, near Moss Bluff on the Trinity, just south. Disguised as a farming community, the establishment actually planned an invasion of Spanish Mexico but was broken up by Spain.

Early Anglo settlers drifted into the area prior to 1826, and the old settlement of Atascosito was renamed Liberty in 1831. With Texas independence, lumbering became a primary industry. Oil discovery followed, and by 1940 Liberty had become a substantial inland port.

Moss Bluff, an early 1830s town, for a time prospered as a Trinity River port, vying with Liberty in importance. To the north, near Moss Hill on the Trinity, is the site of ghost town Grand Cane, where Sam Houston maintained a home from 1843–45.

At Liberty, the Geraldine Humphreys Cultural Center houses a museum, library and theater and on its block-square grounds displays the Liberty Bell Tower, with the first perfect replica of Philadelphia's original. The city also boasts the new and imposing Sam Houston Regional Library and Research Center, a major state archival repository with such gems as the Jean Lafitte Journal and the original letter from Andrew Jackson introducing Tennessee Congressman Sam Houston to President Thomas Jefferson.

Just north of town is Holly Ridge Ranch, home of former Governor Price Daniel. Mexican Hill, in town, is the site of Liberty Post, where San Jacinto's prisoners were held from August 1836 to April 1837. Many chose to remain as citizens. Late each April, Liberty conducts two days of historical tours. In this area also see Saratoga, Anahuac.

Sam Houston Regional Library and Research Center, Liberty.

Houston, 117 m. (alt. 55; pop. 1,630,553, city). Largest in Texas and fourth largest in the United States, Houston's growth has spurted and sputtered with the rise and fall of oil, but its path has been ever upward. Typical of its determination, this city 50 miles from the ocean is a deep-sea port.

To see it properly, take a commercial tour; it can overwhelm you.

Mini-Tour Guide

Allen's Landing (Old Market Square): Houston's beginnings. Downtown, off Buffalo Bayou.

Astrodomain: World's first air-conditioned domed stadium. Kirby Dr. off S. Main.

Astroworld/Waterworld: Rides, slides, and fun. Loop 610 at Kirby Dr.

Bayou Bend Collection: American decorative arts, 1650–1850. No. 1 Westcott St.

Burke Baker Planetarium: Outstanding. Hermann Park.

Christ Church Cathedral: (1839) Texas Avenue.

Civic Center: Glistening downtown showplace. Includes Tranquility Park, Convention-Exhibit Center. Performing Arts Hall, Alley Theater, Coliseum and Music Hall.

Contemporary Arts Museum: 5216 Montrose.

Houston Arboretum-Nature Center: I-610—Woodway St.

Miller Outdoor Theater: Jazz to symphony, ballet to Shakespeare. Hermann Park.

Museum of Fine Arts: World-wide collections. 1001 Bissonnet.

Museum of Natural Sciences: From archaeology to space. Hermann Park.

Orange Show: Eccentric's labyrinth. Munger at Sanders.

Port of Houston: Modern sightseeing boat tours. (Reservations.)

Railroad Train Museum: 7390 Mesa Rd.

Sam Houston Historical Park: 13 acres of city's heritage. Downtown.

Texas Medical Center: One of world's greatest. Off South Main.

Visitor Information Center: Start here. Parking or drive-up. 3300 Main. Note: Area attractions include Armand Bayou Nature Center, Battleship Texas, San Jacinto Battleground (state park), near Pasadena, Lyndon B. Johnson Space Center, southeast on I-45, NASA Rd. 1, Round-up Rodeo (every Saturday, with country dance), west at Simonton.

The inner city, despite its size, is one of America's least congested and most handsome, its wide streets a fortunate holdover from days when wagon teams needed room to maneuver. Its high-rising buildings seem to shimmer in the coastal sun. Residential areas, luxuriant in year-round blossom, are among America's most beautiful.

It is a far cry from the straggling 1836 settlement that was so hidden by Buffalo Bayou "jungle" that an arriving riverboat overshot its landing by three miles without notice. Access to the sea, rails, oil, and a determination to think big have produced the metropolis.

Here is the third largest U.S. port, America's fastest-growing major city, boasting its country's space exploration center, a world-famed medical and educational establishment, and the international petroleum capital. More than 3,800 manufacturing plants base here, most along Houston's 50-mile ship chan-

nel. Aside from Astroworld and the Astrodome (the first major domed stadium, where you can watch anything from baseball to bullfights), there are scores of parks, theaters and events of all types. If you intend to explore Houston on your own, see the Greater Houston Convention and Visitor's Council for literature and maps: 3300 Main Street.

The city's many colleges and universities include Rice University's gracious, shaded campus and high academic standards, the booming University of Houston, already with a 30,000 enrollment after inclusion within the state system as recently as 1963. Also here are the University of Texas medical and research centers, and Baylor University's College of Medicine.

Houston's coastal area was recognized as strategic as early as the 1750s when Spain tried a mission-fort establishment near Wallisville, and then at Spring Creek, an effort that failed due to a location too remote from the rest of New Spain.

Present development began in 1822 above Highlands on the San Jacinto River. Boats operated on Buffalo Bayou as early as 1824, predicting things to come. Harrisburg, now within city limits, was the first town in the vicinity, and prior to being burned by Santa Anna just before the Battle of San Jacinto, that town for a time vied with newer Houston. The Allen brothers of New York, John K. and Augustus C., seeking a site for their city, found both Harrisburg and Texana overpriced (Tour 25) and platted their town here, displayed promising maps before the first Texas congress at Columbia (Tour 27), and named their city for the Texas hero. In one year the Allen's promotion already had attracted 1,200 settlers and a capitol, until it moved to Austin in 1839.

By 1840 Houston signaled her bid for Texas leadership. Fifty miles inland, she began deepening her bayou channel, at the same time projecting the first of what would become a railroad web with the motto "where 11 railroads meet the sea." Surviving great fires in 1859 and 1860, she continued her drive for a major port, widening and deepening her channel almost continually from 1869 to 1940.

In 1866 Dick Dowling, hero of the Battle of Sabine Pass (Tour 22), inaugurated oil exploration in what is now

the Woodland Heights area. In 1904, the Humble field just north (Tour 25)—at that time, Texas' largest—blew in, and the city laid claim to a title it has maintained: capital of the petroleum world.

Notable among scores of special events are the Houston Livestock Show and Rodeo, late February-early March; Houston International Festival each April celebrating performing and visual arts with ten-day outdoor festival of multi-cultural music, dance, arts and crafts, food.

In this area also see Galveston, Richmond.

At Houston, intersect I-10/Tour 20; US 75/Tour 26; TX 35/Tour 27; US 90A/Tour 21; US 59/Tour 25. Westward, follow US 290.

Beyond **Waller,** at 159 m., is Prairie View A&M University, with an enrollment of 5,000. In 1876, the institution was established as a land grant college for blacks.

Hempstead, 169 m. (alt. 251; pop. 3,551), came into being in 1857 as terminus of the Houston and Texas Central Railroad. For a time after the Civil War, this L-shaped little city—a major Confederate troop and supply center and the site where most of the Trans-Mississippi forces broke up to walk home at the war's end—became a violent place, with feud-like shootouts continuing for several years. One of the last riddled the courthouse with 75 shots, killing 4 men, wounding others and earning Hempstead (along with Kenedy and Harlingen) the title "Six-Shooter Junction." A boarding house from those days has been remodeled to become the attractive Hempstead Inn, with good lodging and excellent food.

South 4 m. is the site of Bernardo Plantation, founded by Jared Groce, wealthy Alabama planter who came here in 1821 with a 50-wagon train, carrying his own pontoon bridges for the streams en route. He planted Texas' first cotton and corn and established one of the first cotton gins. In 1836, Sam Houston's Texas army camped in this area from March 31 to April 14 and here ceased its retreat, turning on Santa Anna at San Jacinto. FM 1887 southward approximates the Texans' line of march toward freedom. The great plantation was destroyed by an 1870 flood and was not rebuilt.

Eastward some 3.5 m. is a second Groce plantation, Liendo, built in 1853 by slave labor to become one of Texas' handsomest homes and a social center of antebellum days. A Confederate mustering camp (and later a prison camp) was set up here; later reconstruction troops under George A. Custer camped on the grounds. In 1874, Liendo became the home of famed sculptress Elizabet Ney and her noted husband, Dr. Edmund Montgomery, both of whom are buried here. Liendo is now a restored private home shown only by appointment.

In this area also see Navasota, Anderson, San Felipe. At Hempstead, intersect TX 6/159/Tour 28.

Chappell Hill, 180 m. (alt. 317; pop. 310), established in 1847, was Texas' educational center for a time with its Male and Female Institute, as well as Soule University. This tiny village, with its fine old antebellum homes set on large grounds, boasts more than 25 historically-cited structures, several interesting antique shops, and a former hotel, the Stagecoach Inn, built in 1847. The Chappell Hill (accepted spelling then) Historical Museum is housed in an old institute building. Patrons have individual keys to their 1893 library. Here is one of the better locales to envision Texas of more than a century ago. Each October the little village becomes suddenly populated with "stuffed" citizens in every conceivable enterprise, as Chappell Hill observes a charming "Scarecrow Festival." It's worth your visit.

Via FM 1155 north is **Washington-on-the-Brazos,** 18 m. pop. 265, sprawling along its river bluff where Andrew Robinson, first of Stephen F. Austin's colonists set up a ferry in 1822. The town followed in 1835; and here on March 2, 1836 Texas' Declaration of Independence was drawn. The interim government fled Washington before Santa Anna's advance, but the town served as capital briefly in 1842, when Mexico again invaded Texas. The railroad by-pass in 1858 relegated its promise to the status of village.

A state park now encloses Washington and features a star-shaped museum and film presentation, and a replica (see Corsicana) of the Independence Hall where the declaration was drawn. Several old structures are still in place; additional restoration will enhance the park with early homes, shops and stores—Old Washington come back to life.

Brenham, 190 m. (alt. 350; pop. 11,952) is a city of fine old mid-Victorian residences, deeply shaded, once a rich plantation town prior to the Civil War. Brenham suffered during reconstruction, was partially burned in one riot, and endured military rule until 1868. With its surrounding countryside a riot of color each spring, Brenham observes an area-wide historical heritage tour early each April, an annual Maifest, and a county fair in September.

Just southeast of town is Blue Bell Creamery, nationally famous for its ice cream. Plant tours and ice cream samples are offered. Northeast 9 m. is St. Claire Monastery Horse Ranch, providing daily tours. East on US 90 is the restored "town" of Winkelmann, with several authentic buildings, from emporium to saloon. An elegant restaurant occupies the 1850 plantation house. Several ghost towns have faded away nearby—Union Hill, Mt. Vernon, and Zionsville among them.

Heritage Belles (and escorts) at Brenham's annual Washington County Heritage Tour.

Via FM 50 north 11 m., little **Independence,** pop. 140, was established in 1824. Stop first at the Baptist Historical Museum for all information on the area. Here Sam Houston was baptized in 1853, and across the road are the graves of Nancy Moffette Lea and her daughter, Margaret, who was Houston's wife. Dead of yellow fever four years after her husband's death, she had lived in the house close by the ruins of the old Blanton Hotel, where many delegates had met before going on to Washington to sign their independence declaration.

Just west are the imposing ruins of old Baylor College (Female Department), founded here in 1846. Note that the square at Independence was laid out for its county courthouse, taken instead by Brenham by a margin of two votes. Still, this was a booming little city until the 1880s, when railroad by-pass, following on reconstruction, very nearly finished it. FM 390 will lead you west to Burton, through an area of beautifully maintained farmlands, close by Lake Somerville State Park, camping and all facilities, and Old Gay Hill, home of Scotsman Thomas Affleck, who pioneered advanced farming in 1832. Gay Hill also housed Live Oak Female Seminary, 1853–1888.

From **Burton,** 203 m., pop. 311, follow TX 237 southwest 8 m. to **Round Top,** pop. 81, a jewel-box restoration within itself. The Bethlehem Lutheran Church has a century-old, hand-built cedar organ. Restored Moore's Fort is an information center for the extraordinary little town square, bounded by its own split-rail fence and many exceptional restorations. Immediately north is Festival Hill and its James Dick Institute, where serious music is studied and outstanding summer concerts are presented.

The plantation house at Winedale Outdoor Museum, Round Top.

Winedale Outdoor Museum (Winedale Inn) is also superbly restored: its big plantation home surrounded by its farm, barns, and kitchen—all in authentic pioneer style.

Giddings, 225 m. (alt. 520; pop. 4,093), marches along the railroad which founded the town in 1872, and centers an area of predominantly Ger-

History comes alive at Washington-on-the-Brazos, where this young "Texian" learns musket skills from a modern-day soldier of the Texas Army.

man and Slavic extraction. The Lee County Museum, housed in a century-old dwelling, reflects the contributions of those cultures, and the *Giddings Star* has the only type fonts for printing in the Wendish language—that of early colonists close by.

Via FM 2239 south 6 m., **Serbin,** pop. 90, virtually a ghost now, was settled in 1854 by a colony of 500 Wendish people (Slavs from eastern Germany). For religious freedom, the Wend emigration sought two asylums—Australia and Texas—and old rock St. Paul's Church, with its towering steeple, is mother church of those who came to this state. Old World customs—such as orally notifying all household domestic animals at the death of a family member—are fading. Texas Wendish Heritage Museum (at cemetery) displays Wendish and Slavic artifacts and photos.

Loebau, a tiny village northeast of Giddings, rests in the midst of a petrified forest showing traces of a primitive race: fragments of pottery and weapons have been found.

In this area also see La Grange.

At Giddings, intersect US 77/Tour 29. At Paige, 235 m., intersect TX 21/Tour 18A.

McDade, 246 m. (alt. 568; pop. 345), was once an important freighting center, its quietness of today belying a violent past. In the 1880s the town was a haven for outlaws and gunfighters who terrorized stages and meetings until vigilantes struck back and on Christmas Day, 1883, hanged 11 of them in one wholesale lynching.

Elgin, 254 m. (alt. 579; pop. 4,846), a century-old, sunny little city, was first known as Glasscock, then Hogeye (for a favorite fiddling song). Beginning with hand-pressing, Elgin has made bricks since the 1880s. Nearby, also see Taylor, Bastrop.

Austin, 279 m. (alt. 550; pop. 465,622). Designated one of America's top places to live, this handsome city nestled against its purple western hills, is Texas' governmental center, a city of educational institutions. It seems to mushroom because people who have seen it—particularly students of the now enormous University of Texas—come back to live here.

Two old bridges mark the sites of Austin's founding—Congress Avenue and old Montopolis—where the early frontier sites of Waterloo and Montopolis preceded Austin in the 1830s. Originally part of Stephen F. Austin's second grant, the Waterloo site was chosen by Republic President Mirabeau Lamar when he buffalo-hunted the area in 1837–38. Lamar wanted a western capital site because he envisioned (and tried for) a Texas reaching across New Mexico, conceivably to the Pacific. Though for years on frontier's edge and literally fighting Comanche in its streets, Austin became capital in 1839 and, in a struggle from 1842–45 known as the Archives War, held the seat of government from Houston. Arrival of railroads in the 1870s and establishment of the University of Texas in 1883 speeded its growth. Today, Austin has diversified its economic base by attracting "21st Century" industries, such as those dealing with computers and semi-conductors.

Here are located all state buildings, including the towering Capitol (replacing one that burned in 1881), completed in 1888 at a cost of 3 million West Texas acres, which became the great XIT Ranch. Rich only in land, Texas struck a deal to pay for its capitol construction with an immense land grant—most of some 10 Panhandle counties today—and the XIT grew from that grant, one of the largest ranches the world has ever seen (see Dalhart). Granite was quarried at Marble Falls (Tour 32). Among capitols, the building is second in size only to Washington's national capitol. From the floor to the star in the inner dome, it is 314 feet high. The shaded grounds are heroically statued, depicting the march of Lone Star history. The Texas Department of Transportation's Visitor Center, in the Capitol, has all information on Austin as well as Texas tourism. The Capitol complex includes the State Li-

FM 2222 winding through the hills west of Austin.

brary, Museums of the Daughters of the Republic of Texas, Daughters of the Confederacy, and the stately 1856 Governor's Mansion.

Mini-Tour Guide

Capitol Building: Head of Congress Avenue.

Discovery Hall: Hands-on science. Congress Ave. at 4th St.

Elizabet Ney Museum: Famed sculptures. 304 E. 44th.

Fiesta Gardens: Exotic flora. Town Lake.

French Legation: Classic architecture, restored. 802 San Marcos.

Governor's Mansion: Public tours. 1010 Colorado.

Harry Ransom Center: Art. U.T. campus.

Laguna Gloria: Art museum. 35th at Old Bull Creek Rd.

Lyndon B. Johnson Library and Museum: 2313 Red River.

McKinney Falls State Park: All facilities. Visitors center. Off US 183 south 13 m.

Metropolitan Park: Swimming, fishing, camping. Lake Austin, west.

Nature Center. 301 Nature Center Dr.

Neill Cochran House: (Colonial Dames of America in Texas). 1853 Greek Revival. 2310 San Gabriel.

O. Henry Home: 409 E. 5th.

Old Bakery & Emporium: Handicrafts, baked goods. 1006 Congress.

Old Pecan Street: Former town center. Shops, galleries, restorations. 6th, east of Congress.

State Cemetery: The Texas Arlington. E. 7th at Comal.

Texas Memorial Museum: Outstanding exhibits, dioramas. 2400 Trinity.

Town Lake Riverboat: Lake tours. At Hyatt Regency on lake, downtown.

University Art Museum: 23rd at San Jacinto.

University of Texas (at Austin) campus: Just north of Capitol.

Wild Basin Preserve: Hill Country wilderness. Loop 360 west of town.

Zilker Park: Theater, garden center, Barton Springs Pool. Barton Spgs. Rd.

Equally imposing in a different sense is the campus of The University of Texas, whose some 50 thousand students refuse to add to its title "at Austin." One of America's most handsome campuses, U.T.A. became oil-rich when grazing leases in West Texas blew in and educational lands became oilfields. Notable is the University Tower, housing the school's library, the impressive Lyndon

B. Johnson Presidential Library, with use of motion pictures, closed-circuit television and mobile techniques relating not only to the LBJ administration but to the office of the presidency itself.

Also on campus are the outstanding Texas Memorial Museum and the immense sports complex where the Texas Longhorns mobilize.

Other Austin educational institutions include St. Edward's University, Concordia College, Huston-Tillotson College and Austin Theological Seminary. The city boasts museums, both art and natural history, the old home of O. Henry, Treaty Oak, its famed 165-foot-tall "Moonlight Towers"—each of the 27 illuminating with mercury vapor lamps a 4-square block area. The Austin C of C provides an excellent self-guiding "Downtown Stroll," plus complete tourist data on the Central Texas area.

Shaded Zilker Park is worth a visit, with its famed Barton Springs, near where, in 1730, San Antonio's Missions Concepcion, San Francisco and San Juan lodged for one year. Close by is Bergstrom Air Force Base.

Like great beads on a string, the beautiful Highland Lakes descend from westernmost Lake Buchanan, to Inks, Lake LBJ (formerly Granite Shoals), Marble Falls, to resort-centering Travis, then Austin, and finally, at the city's foot, pretty Town Lake.

Not far from the Capitol is the restored French Legation, Texas' only foreign-built edifice during Republic days.

East on FM 973 is the National Wildflower Research Center, site of experiments in wildflower propagation.

Manor Downs, US 290 east, offers quarter horse racing, pari-mutuel betting during spring and fall races.

Each July and August Austin celebrates its Aqua Festival, climaxed by a lighted nighttime water parade. The Laguna Gloria Art Festival each May is one of Texas' most prestigious arts and crafts fairs. In early April the Texas Relays are run at Memorial Stadium. Under Congress Ave. bridge is nation's largest urban bat colony, emerging nightly at dusk during summer. In the area, also see Round Rock, Lockhart, San Marcos.

At Austin intersect I-35/Tour 30 and US 183/Tour 31.

Dripping Springs, 308 m. (alt. 1,190; pop. 1,033). Immediately west of Austin you climb into the scenic Texas Hill Country; at this village you've already ascended some 600 feet. Nearabouts are several headsprings feeding eventually to the Colorado. Just north is scenic Hamilton Pool, a small, shaded lake within a cavelike depression.

South 15 m. via FM 12 is **Wimberley** (alt. 967; pop. 2,403), centering this area of dude ranches, youth camps and resort homes. On the quaint town square you may explore many rustic buildings for arts and crafts, also antique shops. Pioneer Town, a re-created Western village nearby, features an old-time saloon, general store, post office, hotel, opera house and log fort. Medicine shows and melodramas are the bill of fare. There is also an antique narrow-gauge railroad. Wimberley hosts several galas annually, including a "Funfest," along with a "Hillaceous 10 K Run" each April, a moving sunrise service each Easter, a rodeo each July, and a Gospel Music Festival in October. The little city also stages a series of plays throughout the fall, and a concert series, fall and winter. A major attraction falls the first Saturday of each month from March through November, when "Market Days" assemble more than 200 vendors selling everything from "art to junk." The views around these Blanco River hills are spectacular.

At 316 m., via FM 3232 6 m. north, Pedernales Falls State Park, with camping and all facilities, displays its crystalline river in a stairstep of sliding-board falls and pools.

The upper cascade of the three-tiered waterfall at Pedernales Falls State Park, off FM 3232 between Dripping Springs and Johnson City.

At 326 m. intersect US 281/Tour 32 south of **Johnson City,** where you enter Region IV, West Texas. US 290 continues west as Tour 55 through LBJ country. US 281 is Tour 32, north-south.

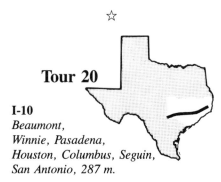

☆

Tour 20

I-10
*Beaumont,
Winnie, Pasadena,
Houston, Columbus, Seguin,
San Antonio, 287 m.*

This east-west interstate route begins crossing Texas at its greatest width—Orange to El Paso, 855 m. Through Region II, you travel as far as San Antonio.

Vegetation changes perceptibly as you move westward, beginning with the deep pine forests at the Sabine, modifying to pine and hardwoods as far as Houston, where you emerge onto the rich, level coastal plain. Beyond the Brazos at Sealy, the land begins a rolling climb, and around Columbus you cut through a belt of great, moss-draped live oaks. These gradually thin to scrub and mesquite as, near San Antonio, you begin to edge the southward brush country.

Across to Houston you traverse an industrial region—oil and petrochemicals. Westward lie some of Texas' handsomest agricultural lands, a countryside particularly beautiful with Spring's cloak of bluebonnet and paintbrush.

Throughout, you travel old land, the eastern coastal region in early contest between Spain and France. Between the Brazos and Colorado—from Sealy to Columbus—you are within the heart of Stephen F. Austin's first American colonization. At San Antonio, you have reached the mission and military capital of old Spanish Texas.

Beaumont, 0 m.—see Tour 19. Veer southwest from US 90.

Winnie, 24 m. (alt. 25; pop. 2,238), is a new-looking, prospering center of rice-farming. Here your route turns due west to cross just above the head of Galveston Bay.

At **Hankamer,** 39 m., pop. 189, intersect TX 61.

Anahuac, 7 m. south (alt. 24; pop. 1,993), weathered and secluded, has the look and feel of age. On Perry Point, named for an American filibuster, Mexico established Fort Anahuac in 1830. The fort was intended to check

American colonization: colonists had used the settlement here as a port of entry since 1821–22. Anahuac has been called the site of Texas' Boston Tea Party for difficulties between colonists and Mexican officials enforcing restrictive laws. The jailing of William Barret Travis and others here precipitated the Battle of Velasco, 1832, when Brazorians tried to come to the aid of their fellow colonists.

As a result of these disturbances, colonists drafted the Turtle Bayou Resolutions, protesting autocratic Mexican rule; the resolutions are considered a forerunner to a final declaration of independence, three years later.

Chambersea, the 1845 home of Texas Revolutionist Thomas Jefferson Chambers, for whom the county is named, is here. Chambers, who had recruited volunteers in the United States and who later ran unsuccessfully for the governorship, was assassinated in 1865 in an upstairs room of this home. His murderer was never apprehended.

Tradition adds two interesting stories. The circular outside staircase was supposedly constructed so that only one person could approach Chamber's quarters at a time. A more bizarre legend persists that the bullet which pierced his body lodged in a portrait across the room—at exactly the same spot as the real wound!

Traces of the old fort remain at Fort Anahuac Park, where scenic camping facilities are provided. In town, the Chambers County Museum displays area history and archaeology. Southeast, big Anahuac National Wildlife Refuge provides excellent bird-watching.

At 42 m., via FM 563, 3 m. west, is **Wallisville,** pop. 25, a tiny village resting on an old site. Close by in 1756, Spain established Mission Nuestra Senora de la Luz and Presidio San Agustin de Ahumada—the establishment to be known as El Orcoquisac—designed to check French pressure from Louisiana. The remote location and hurricanes

forced abandonment ten years later. Anglo settlement occurred in 1825, first known as Wallis Hill, the Wallis home being a principal stopover for travelers and, according to story, an overnight prison for Santa Anna immediately after San Jacinto. Wallisville Heritage Park, on the Trinity, displays artifacts from the old mission and presidio.

Between this area and close by Anahuac, the first recorded cattle drives in Texas pushed eastward for Louisiana in the late 1830s, opening what was to be known as the Opelousas Route. For much of the way, the trail followed the route of US 90/I-10. At 55 m. intersect TX 146.

Southward, **Baytown,** 8 m. (alt. 20; pop. 63,850), is an industrial complex which has absorbed earlier towns of Goose Creek and Pelly, all of which grew from the 1822 settlement at Lynch's Ferry (there has been a ferry here since that date). Oil discovery in 1916 brought massive industrialization. The Baytown Historical Museum reflects rich area history. The big Exxon Refinery provides tours on Fridays (reservations). Follow TX 146 through the Baytown Tunnel. Just south of the intersection with TX 225 lie **La Porte** (alt. 28; pop. 27,910) and **Sylvan Beach,** which during the Big Band era boasted one of the country's finest dance floors. The old pavilion has been replaced by a county park. Follow FM 225 west 4 m. to **Deer Park** (alt. 33; pop. 27,652), a pleasant satellite community of Houston. Follow TX 134 north 4 m.

San Jacinto Battleground: With an excellent regional museum at the base of a 570-foot, four-inch memorial shaft, the world's tallest masonry monument dominates this now tranquil, once bloody battlefield. Here, April 21, 1836, 783 Texas volunteers under General Sam Houston routed 1,600 troops under General Santa Anna, ending the Texas Revolution and effectually winning freedom for the Republic

of Texas. The beautifully landscaped park is well marked. The museum depicts this region's history in a chronological line from the Indian to Texas as a State in the Union. Here also are a reference library and archives.

Moored alongside, in the Houston Ship Channel (Buffalo Bayou) is Battleship Texas, a WW I dreadnought forced to serve through WW II. From her decks came General Dwight Eisenhower's first war message at Casablanca. Off Omaha Beach and Cherbourg, Texas shot it out with massive shore batteries and won. At Cherbourg, she took 87 hits or "near misses" and kept fighting. The State of Texas was the first to save its namesake battleship from the scrap heap. North Carolina, Alabama, and Massachusetts have followed, in that order.

Pasadena, (alt. 35; pop. 119,363), 6 m. west, was envisioned in 1895 as the center of a lush fruit- and vegetable-producing area. Houston's ship channel changed these fields to a booming industrial complex today. With neighboring Deer Park, Pasadena claims San Jacinto's battleground for its own. From here, proceed to Houston via TX 225 or, via the battleground road, TX 134 over the Lynchburg ferry to I-10, then west. If you take the Federal Road route to I-10, due north, near the entrance to the tunnel under the ship channel, you pass the site of Santa Anna's capture, the day following the battle. Disguised in a private's uniform, he was brought before the wounded Houston, where his own men recognized him. On the western edge of Pasadena is Vince's Bayou, where Deaf Smith, following Houston's orders, burned the bridge and left the two armies cut off, to fight it out. Nearby also see NASA, Seabrook, Galveston, and the Armand Bayou Nature Center, a pre-

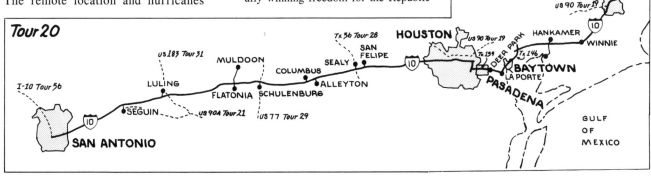

served wilderness area, with canoeing and hiking trails.

Houston, 86 m.—see Tour 19. Follow I-10 west. In March–April, the countryside across to San Antonio is a pastel blanket of bluebonnet and paintbrush.

A replica of Stephen F. Austin's log cabin home at Stephen F. Austin State Park near San Felipe.

San Felipe, 132 m. (alt. 155; pop. 618), north of your highway, is at first glance a collection of new and old homes wandering along the approaches to **Stephen F. Austin State Park** (camping and all facilities, including golf). Here, however, is the cornerstone of Anglo Texas, the site of Stephen F. Austin's colonial capital. In July 1823, Austin chose this high prairie, above a Brazos River bend where the old Atascosito Road crossed, as location for colony headquarters—San Felipe de Austin. By 1828, there were four plazas, beginning at the riverbank "Boat Landing Cottonwood," also some 30 log cabins and five stores.

Here were held the Consultations of 1832–35, as Texas colonists moved nearer to a fight for freedom. Here was the capital of the republic's provisional government until burned in April 1836, during Houston's retreat. Partly rebuilt in 1837, the town never recovered and for years in the early 1900s narrowly missed abandonment.

Much restoration has accompanied the state park (two areas—camping and historical): a replica of Austin's cabin, the hand-dug well, site of the old town hall, a bronzed memorial statue of the "Father of Texas," as well as the location of the first Sunday School in Texas, taught by Thomas J. Pilgrim in 1829. San Felipe, known and visited by every important Texan of pre-war time, also published the state's first real newspaper, the *Texas Gazette,* as well as the *Telegraph and Texas Register,* edited by Gail Borden. The J. J. Josey Store, 1847, is an intriguing museum displaying merchandise of its era. The recreation portion of

this beautifully wooded park has all facilities.

The old ferry crossing, where Captain Mosely Baker blocked Santa Anna's troops, forcing them downriver, is within the park, the old wagon ruts still visible.

Immediately south of the highway is Frydek, pop. 150—"peaceful corner" to its Czech settlers. On the grounds of its church is a grotto built by the thankful families and friends of 67 men and women of the Frydek Parish who served in WW II and came home safely (see Windthorst).

Sealy, 134 m. (alt. 203; pop. 4,541), grew up with the arrival of the railroad in 1875 and today is merging agribusiness with manufacturing. Sealy has a picturesque downtown area, with several interesting old homes and buildings. To its north via TX 36 (see Tour 28) are a number of intriguing little German villages, their first settlements in Texas.

At Sealy intersect TX 36/Tour 28. Nearby also see Bellville, Hempstead, Richmond.

Alleyton, 157 m., pop. 65, was for a time during the Civil War, end of the westward rail line. As such it became a key point on the supply line of the Confederacy. Here began the great "Cotton Road," a route to the Rio Grande. Cotton was brought here from Texas, Louisiana, and Arkansas and shipped by wagon to Mexico, where it was traded for supplies desperately needed by the blockaded South.

Columbus, 159 m. (alt. 201; pop. 3,367). Within the great bend of the Colorado and shaded by giant live oaks, the handsome old homes of this little city seem to ignore traffic pouring along your interstate route, just south. Columbus is old, occupying an area crossed many times by early Spanish explorers and by La Salle, seeking escape to the Mississippi. As early as 1819, some of Moses Austin's colonists settled on the site of an old Indian town known to Spain as Montezuma. Stephen F. Austin's Old Three Hundred found their way to settlements along the river to here and beyond, into Fayette County.

Austin selected this site first as capital-to-be of his colony, later transferring to San Felipe on the more navigable Brazos River. Just below the highway bridge Sam Houston very nearly fought his decisive battle in March, 1836, but, buying time, burned the city and fell back to San Jacinto instead.

The Old Water Tower, built in 1883, at Columbus. Known today as the Confederate Memorial Hall Museum, the tower houses history and lore of Stephen F. Austin's original colony in this area.

On the east side of the courthouse square a stump, with its plaque, remains of the Columbus Court Oak. In 1839, with the city still struggling from ruins, Judge Robert M. Williamson convened First District Court under these now-gnarled branches (see Shelbyville). Known as Three-Legged Willie because of a childhood withering of one leg, Williamson was a firebrand revolutionist who later helped establish the Republic's judicial branch.

Many old homes are toured in Columbus' Magnolia Homes Tour (one of Texas' finest—there are 48 historical markers here) the third weekend each May. There are buggy and surrey rides, sausage suppers, a sidewalk cafe and beer garden and then the homes, ranging from the 1836 Alley Cabin to the magnificent Senftenberg-Brandon and Cone-Glueck Houses, and from the old Stafford Opera House to the Confederate Museum. Downtown, the historic Brunson Building now houses the Live Oak Art Club, showing many exhibits each month.

The First and Third Thursday Walking Tour, self-paced, features many historic homes and buildings normally closed to the public as well as businesses, antique shops, tearooms, and restaurants.

Borden, 169 m., a virtual ghost today, was home of Gail Borden, newspaperman, scientist, surveyor and early revolutionary. Borden moved here from San Felipe and in 1870 erected America's first canned meat packery, later a condensed milk plant.

Schulenburg, 181 m. (alt. 344; pop. 2,455), around its proper square, is a comfortable community of pretty homes. Settled by Germans, Czechs, and Austrians in 1875, the town made history with one of America's first cottonseed crushing plants and developed a particularly nutritive flour. A musical-minded community, the town probably boasts more bands per capita than any community in Texas. The town remains a favorite eating-stopover for tourists, and the Schulenburg Festival, with everything from a rodeo to "oom-pa" bands and good German-Czech cooking, is a three-day tourist delight each August. The Schulenburg Historical Museum depicts early life; C of C supplies maps for driving tour of painted churches in nearby communities. At Schulenburg, intersect US 77/Tour 29. Nearby also see La Grange, Hallettsville.

Flatonia, 196 m. (alt. 458; pop. 1,295), like its neighbor, Schulenburg, was German-Czech settled with the railroad's passage in 1875.

Via FM 1295 east 3 m., **Praha,** pop. 25, was among the first Czech settlements in Texas in 1856, and the great church here serves as homecoming center for Czechs throughout the country. Each August, Praha homecoming attracts thousands.

Via FM 154 north, tiny **Muldoon,** pop. 98, takes its name from the homesite of an extraordinary Texan, Father Miguel Muldoon, the priest who guided Stephen F. Austin to a colony, then became its resident priest, later rescuing both Austin and William Wharton from Mexican prison, then disappearing from history's pages. A nearby monument calls him "The Forgotten Man of Texas."

Luling, 230 m. (alt. 419; pop. 4,661), is a railroad-side town that has lived three lives. In 1874, it began as a rail-end camp and was a hard-bitten guntown roamed by men like John Wesley Hardin and Ben Thomson. The relative peace of cattle-driving giving way to farms brought a quiet period, followed by a 1922 oil boom. The nearby oilfield was developed by Edgar B. Davis, an unusual philanthropist who, when selling his interest, gave over $1 million in bonuses to his management officials, the same amount to his employees, then established the Luling Foundation Farm

close by with another million. The field, still producing, centers an area noted for fine watermelons. The last weekend of each June, Luling holds its three-day festival—a Watermelon Thump. At Luling, intersect US 183/Tour 31. Nearby also see Lockhart, Gonzales.

Scenic Palmetto State Park, camping and all facilities, is 7 m. southeast.

Seguin, 252 m. (alt. 520; pop. 18,853), is neat and shaded, with pretty homes, many of historic note. Sebastopol, built in 1850 with an inverted V-shaped cistern roof, is a museum. The Los Nogales Museum, adobe-built during the mission period, was a known trail stop in 1765, a post office in 1825, and a pioneer home in 1840. Today it serves as an unusual museum, inside and out. The Fiedler Museum displays minerals and archaeology on the Texas Lutheran College campus. South of town, Max Starcke Park, deep-shaded on the Guadalupe, is one of the nation's finest for a city of this size.

The city's namesake, staunch Texas patriot Juan Seguin, commanded a detachment of Texas-born Mexicans at the Battle of San Jacinto. The city, however, was settled to a great extent in the massive German immigration of the 1840s. Discipline of early days is evidenced in the "Whipping Oak," opposite the courthouse on the square, a three-inch iron ring, still embedded, secured thieves and wifebeaters for public lashing. Nearby are Seguin's Ranger Oaks, which sheltered early Indian fighters' campgrounds. Outlying little settlements such as New Berlin, Barbarosa, and Zuehl testify to the area's genealogy. Nearby is Lake McQueeney, water sports.

At Seguin, merge with US 90A/Tour 21, proceeding west. In this area also see New Braunfels, San Marcos.

The spillway on the Guadalupe River, Seguin.

San Antonio, 287 m. Enter Region III, South Texas. For city and route intersections, see Tour 33. Following I-10 westward, your route becomes Tour 56.

☆

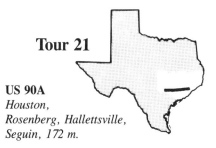

Tour 21

US 90A
Houston, Rosenberg, Hallettsville, Seguin, 172 m.

Following old east-west trails blazed by Indians and widened by Spain, your route edges along Texas' upper coastal plain. You emerge from Houston's pines into level, open prairie which, with the exception of timbered Brazos and Colorado bottoms, extends about to Hallettsville. Gradually the terrain becomes rolling and you cross a heavy live oak belt extending beyond Gonzales. As you near Seguin, open prairie reappears. Rich throughout, this countryside is beautiful with spring wildflowers.

While the land shows little change, the genealogy of its Texans varies considerably along your route. Old South plantation country at Richmond merges quickly into Czech-German stock at Rosenberg, this same stock dominant around Halletsville and again at Seguin. The cities, none large, reflect their settlers' backgrounds: Richmond's reserved antebellum grandeur as compared with the tidy bustle of Rosenberg or Seguin.

Throughout, although you cross heavy oil-producing areas, particularly near Houston, the towns you pass are agribusiness-oriented, and their Texans—of whatever occupation—are mindful of their basic dependence on the surrounding land.

Your entire route lies within the area first colonized by Americans, and the last leg—from Gonzales to Seguin—approximates the route of march of the handful of Texans who in 1836 sought to relieve the Alamo.

Houston, 0 m.—see Tour 19.

Stafford, 16 m. (alt. 92; pop. 8,397), to all intents within today's outreaching Houston, was in 1853 the west terminus of Texas' first railroad: the 20-mile Buffalo Bayou, Brazos and Colorado.

Sugar Land, 21 m. (alt. 82; pop. 24,529), adjoining Stafford, was originally the site of a large 1828 plantation. Now, booming like other Houston satellites, Sugar Land's recent growth is prodigal, as reflected in substantial new

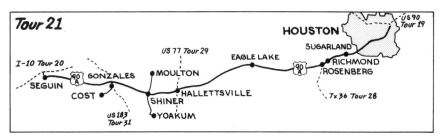

The Bozka House, a charming landmark on US 90A in Hallettsville.

construction everywhere. South, toward Galveston, some of the state's handsomest housing developments—whole villages of homes and condominiums—spread over the green coastal plain. The town came into being after the Civil War when purchased for the location of a sugar refinery, Texas' first—now the home of Imperial Sugar, one of the world's leading producers. There are weekday tours at 10 a.m. and 2 p.m. Texas prison farms are located nearby. At Sugar Land intersect US 59/Tour 25.

Richmond, 30 m. (alt. 104; pop. 9,801). Almost embraced within Greater Houston now, this historic little city remains Old South in feeling—fine old homes on deep lawns shaded by oak and magnolia trees. Richmond is different: it even seems cooler than its cosmopolitan neighbor, an island of tranquility in the rush that surrounds it.

The original settlement, by Stephen F. Austin's "Old Three Hundred" in 1821, was a pioneer blockhouse in a bend of the Brazos here—Fort Bend, later to become a village named by Virginia colonists. Santa Anna crossed his army here, believing he faced only mop-up operations eastward, not San Jacinto.

The area grew in plantation homes, and after the Civil War it saw considerable reconstruction trouble, culminating in the Jaybird-Woodpecker War, one of Texas' bloodiest feuds. Jaybirds constituted the old-line settlers; Woodpeckers, reconstructionists, controlled the black vote. A number of shootings occurred through the 1870s, climaxing in August 1889 in a pitched battle around the Courthouse square. State militia put down the war, with Democratic Party Jaybirds in control of the county once more.

Buried at Richmond's cemetery are several famous Texans, including second Republic President Mirabeau Lamar; Erastus "Deaf" Smith, San Jacinto Scout; and Mrs. Jane Long, pioneer (see Port Bolivar).

Near the square is the site of the old Nation Hotel, operated by saloon-smashing Carry A. Nation and her husband, prior to her descent on Kansas barrooms and national prominence. A deeply religious woman, Carry astounded Richmond in 1887 when she prayed for a drought-ending rain, kneeling in the street under a bright blue sky. A three-day rain followed. Decker Park, in town, contains a replica of original log-walled Fort Bend. Nearby, the old Sunset Saloon has been restored as an interesting Confederate Museum, while the county historical museum, a good one, reflects this area's deep-rooted past. South 20 m. on FM 762 is big, handsomely-wooded and watered Brazos Bend State Park, camping and all facilities, including good hiking trails.

George Ranch Historical Park is a 470-acre working ranch where visitors can learn forgotten crafts. Visitor center, an 1882 Victorian mansion, played a role in the Jaybird-Woodpecker War.

Rosenberg, 33 m. (alt. 106; pop. 20,183), although a Brazos River shipping point since 1823, became a town only with the arrival of its railroad. In 1881, headquarters were established for building the New York, Texas and Mexico Railroad, a line ultimately to run from here to Victoria (see Tour 25). Fort Bend County Fair is early each October.

At Rosenberg intersect TX 36/Tour 28. In this area also see West Columbia, Wharton, San Felipe.

Eagle Lake, 66 m. (alt. 174; pop. 3,551), is a prairie town spread around its square, and a railroad shipping point for a rice-growing area. Downtown, the Farris (1912) is a beautifully-restored little hotel, serving excellent meals.

Hallettsville, 105 m. (alt. 232; pop. 2,718), beside the wooded Lavaca River, is old, settled in 1836, and has an antique look in the homes spreading from the courthouse square. One, the 1879 gingerbread Lay-Bozka House (the Wedding Cake House) is listed on the National Register of Historic Places, as is the courthouse.

There is a comfortable feel in the old-fashioned downtown area—old stone and brickfronts, outside iron stairways, and an intriguing old general merchandise store. This is Czech and German country, as the names of surrounding villages testify: Vsetin and Moravia, Henkhaus and Koerth. The area gathers in an annual Fiddler's Frolic late each April (a Fiddlers Hall of Fame is maintained here), and an annual State Domino Championship Tournament, the fourth Sunday each January, and a High School Championship Rodeo in June.

The area grew slowly for lack of roads, until rails came in 1887. The early days saw violence before and after the Civil War. Having won its county seat (Lavaca Co.) from Petersburg (now a ghost 8 m. downriver) in 1852, this town had to mount a 100-man posse and take its records by force. Like other towns of this area, Hallettsville has its "hanging tree."

Here you intersect US 77/Tour 29. In this area also see Schulenburg, La Grange, Columbus.

Shiner, 120 m. (alt. 350; pop. 2,074), calls itself the "cleanest little city in Texas," undoubtedly spruced up for a year-long (1987) centennial celebration. Dominated by German/Czech citizenry, Shiner boasts a purely Texas brewery (Spoetzl), offering daily tours and a museum. Here also is the Edwin Wolters Memorial Museum, which features local history as well as an interesting country store. The town boasts many beautiful churches, a number of good restaurants, interesting antique shops, and an intriguing gaslight theater.

Via TX 95 north 10 m. is **Moulton** (alt. 384; pop. 923). Just west is the ghost of the original settlement—Old Moulton, which by the 1870s was called "Queen of the Prairies" and noted statewide for its school. Bypassed by rails, the town moved bodily to New Moulton, where it again prospers with manufacturing, including electronic and oilfield equipment. A German-Czech Polka and Waltz Celebration brings some six area bands for continual music early each April.

Via TX 95 south 10 m. is **Yoakum** (alt. 322; pop. 5,611), founded in 1887 with the railroads. The city occupies the once main gathering grounds for northbound cattle drives "up the Chisholm Trail." With that background it is a leather goods capital; chances are 9 in 10 your leather belt was made here. Tours of one of the many leather factories are available each second Tuesday through the C of C. The Heritage Museum (312 Simpson St.) recalls history of area and its railroad. Its Leather Room contains examples of fine hand tooling from local craftspeople and factories.

Gonzales, 138 m. (alt. 292; pop. 6,527), is the oak- and magnolia-shaded "Lexington of Texas" where, on the banks of the Guadalupe, October 2, 1835, Texans fired the first shot in their revolution from Mexico. One of Texas' earliest Anglo settlements in the 1825 Green DeWitt colony, Gonzales survived a ferocious Indian attack the following year. In 1835, Mexican cavalry rode on the town, demanding a cannon which had been used to defend against the Indians. Instead, Texans hoisted a flag inscribed "Come and Take It," and attacked, driving the Mexican forces back on San Antonio—in turn beseiged and captured.

Gonzales was first to learn the fate of the Alamo, and she was alone in Texas in answering Travis' call for aid, sending 32 volunteers who would stand and die within the walls of that doomed fortress early in 1836.

Here Sam Houston—in the act of mobilizing an army—learned of the disaster at the Alamo and, burning the town, began his retreat to San Jacinto and the Texan flight described as the Runaway Scrape.

In a block-long park near the town's center is the Texas Heroes Monument, red and gray granite shafts, and a museum housing Texan and Mexican relics, notably the "Come and Take It" cannon. Nearby is the old Eggleston dog-run cabin, 1840. In all, there are 86 historic homes or site markers in this proud little city. The C of C can provide an excellent "Come and Take It" driving tour as well as details on the story of this city. Its growing Pioneer Village displays several staunch old structures, all carefully reconstructed.

The two downtown plazas are Confederate Square and Texas Heroes Square.

This mosaic on a municipal building in Gonzales recalls the first clash in the Texas Revolution, which began here in 1835.

The Old Jail Museum is a notable stop: constructed in 1887 and in use until 1975. All is complete, from cells, dungeon, gallows and jailer's quarters, to the legend of a condemned man who—counting his last minutes—predicted that the courthouse clock would prove his innocence. After his hanging, despite repairs, none of the four faces have kept the same time. Start your tour here: Gonzales C of C offices are in the building.

Gonzales observes "Come and Take It Days" the weekend closest to October 2 each year—from parade and rodeo to historic tour, a complete celebration. Services mark the close, memorializing the Gonzales fighters, and the battle itself is reenacted.

South of town, handsomely-shaded on the Guadalupe River banks, Independence Park offers campsites and all recreational facilities. North 10 m. on US 183 is secluded and heavily-timbered Palmetto State Park, a nature-study wonderland with camping and full facilities (see Luling).

FM 466, west of the city, is the old Capote Road, route of the Gonzales men who marched on San Antonio—to take it

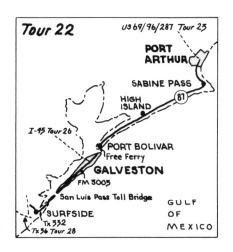

and later, to try to relieve the Alamo. **Cost,** pop. 62, at the road head is the site of the "Come and Take It" battle.

At Gonzales, intersect US 183/Tour 31. In this area also see Cuero, Luling. Follow US 90A west.

Seguin, 172 m.—see Tour 20. Merge with I-10 west for San Antonio.

☆

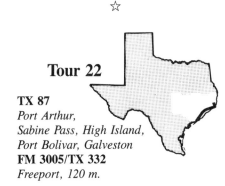

Tour 22

TX 87
Port Arthur,
Sabine Pass, High Island,
Port Bolivar, Galveston
FM 3005/TX 332
Freeport, 120 m.

Your hug-the-coast route provides a fine release for those whose concept of Texas is limited by expressway speeds, hurried cities, or vast western distances.

This is a leisurely tour, offering frequent listening-watching stops: you will be rewarded by the gathering cry of wild geese overhead and the sudden, whirling descent of thousands of birds, feeding on the marshes or rice fields just inland. Even a casual birdwatcher will be startled with the varieties of wildfowl, for you cross the overlapping of flyways from north, south, east and west.

Historically, you traverse what was a cannibal coast: the Attakapa Indians, or people-eaters, lived eastward; the dreaded giant Karankawa, from Galveston west. You cross the last coastal stand of piracy in the U.S.—Jean Lafitte's havens just up the Sabine or within sheltered Galveston Bay. Your tour ends at the site of old Velasco (today's Surfside, the coastal edge of Brazosport's mighty industrial complex) where Stephen F. Austin's first colonists came ashore.

In today's context, you travel from the industrial center of Port Arthur to that of Brazosport, with a hundred beckoning miles of beachfront between, and the resort of Galveston halfway along.

Port Arthur, 0 m. (alt. 18; pop. 58,724 city). Site of 1840 town Aurora, in 1895 a wealthy New Yorker, Arthur E. Stillwell, "dreamed" this city, envisioning a great metropolitan center beside saltwater Lake Sabine. A believer in the supernatural, he laid out the city and began a 12 mile canal to reach from lake to sea, while extending a railroad to link with inland America. In 1901, just north, Spindletop proved his vision: within a year, tankerloads of oil were moving across the first docks of Gulf and Texaco. Over the years, the "dream" has become Energy City, USA, its port today among America's ten busiest. There is a visitor's deck where a favorite pastime is watching Big Arthur, the 75-ton gantry crane, at work with the great ships.

The city itself has become one of the world's largest oil refining and petrochemical centers. Guided tours are available at the big Gulf and Texaco refineries.

Today's Port Arthur is a mixture: in some areas, handsome old homes of turn-of-the-century vintage, in others, typical seaworn dwellings; elsewhere, handsome modern structures like the big new Civic Center. The city offers a resort-seeker wide choice: 3,500 acre Pleasure Island, edging Sabine Lake, with its big marina, camping facilities, nature trails, excellent fishing from boat or 11 miles of levee, and all water sports, particularly sailboating. Fresh and deepwater fishing are good and close at hand. The surrounding area, in the central flyway for bird migration, provides exceptional hunting—ducks, geese, coots. Sidney Island, at the top of the lake, is an extraordinary Audubon bird sanctuary—one of the Gulf's largest nesting grounds for varieties of egrets, herons, ibis, and the distinctive and endangered roseate spoonbill. Some 29,000 nests are estimated. South, along the coast, are two national wildlife refuges, Texas Point and McFaddin, the former counting an enormous number of migratory fowl, while the latter domiciles Texas' largest concentration of alligators.

Port Arthur showcases its history in a variety of places. The Museum of the Gulf Coast (in Gates Memorial Library, 317 Stilwell Blvd.) includes relics from the Battle of Sabine Pass (see below). Listed

Sailboats moored at Pleasant Island Marina, Port Arthur.

on the National Register, Pompeiian Villa (1953 Lakeshore Dr.) was built for Isaac Ellwood of barbed wire fame and later traded for 10 percent of a new business—Texaco. That stock is now worth near $1 billion. Historic Rainbow Bridge's 177-foot height was due to requirement that any U.S. Navy ship could pass unhindered. New bridge to its east is first cable-stayed bridge built on a Texas highway.

At the Southeast Texas Musical Heritage Museum, Port Arthur recalls career of native Janis Joplin and others such as "The Big Bopper," Richie Valens, and Tex Ritter.

Lamar University maintains a branch here, as in Beaumont. At Port Arthur, intersect US 69-96-287/Tour 23.

Sabine Pass, 14 m. (alt. 8; pop. 1,500), is a land's-end village where, amid some oleanders and wind-bent trees, a 56-acre state park marks the site of an extraordinary battle in which Confederate Lieutenant Dick Dowling blocked a sea-borne invasion of Texas, September 5, 1863. Dowling had a small earthwork, six cannon and 42 Irish dockwallopers from Houston who called themselves Davis Guards. Against them were four Federal gunboats and a fleet of 18 transports with some 5,000 troops. Dowling literally bushwhacked the incoming fleet, sinking two gunboats, inflicting almost 200 casualties and capturing 315 men, all without losing one of his own. In the 45 minute engagement, Dowling and his men earned the Confederate medal of honor. The park, a recreational area today, is marked by four mounds—ammunition bunkers in WW II. Close by are the ruins of Confederate Fort Manhassett, built immediately after this battle. Across the narrows on the Louisiana marshland is the old Sabine Pass lighthouse, decommissioned in 1952.

At Sabine Pass, your road turns southwest to edge the Gulf's waters.

Sea Rim State Park, 24 m., spreads over 5.2 miles of coastline and 15,109 acres. Two units are maintained, a beachfront and a nearby marshland where you can enter by boat or nature trail. Back of the marshland is the J. D. Murphree Wildlife Management Reserve. Some 300 species of birds have been identified: checklists are available.

High Island, 47 m., pop. 500, is the highest point between Sabine Pass and Port Bolivar and is notable for an unusual railroad delay. On September 8, 1900, Train No. One of the Gulf and Interstate line smashed into the terrible

Statue of Richard Dowling commemorates the Confederate Lieutenant's rout of Federal invasion forces at Sabine Pass, September 5, 1863.

Galveston hurricane and was nearly buried in sand here. Three years later, the resolute line dug out its engine, validated its issued tickets, and Train No. One chugged into Galveston, 3 years, 16 days, and 10 minutes late.

Port Bolivar, 70 m. (alt. 17; pop. 1,200), strings out along the eastward beach in a stilt-legged parade of resort homes. Directly across Bolivar Roads, by free ferry, looms Galveston. Near the ferry entrance on this side is the weathered 115-foot tower of Bolivar Lighthouse, built in 1852. At its foot is the site of the mud fort of Dr. James Long, last of the filibuster-invaders of Texas. His wife, Jane Wilkinson Long waited here from the fall of 1821 to July 1822 for her husband, not knowing that he was already dead in Mexico. With her small daughter and a black servant girl, Kiamata, Jane Long survived the severe winter, using the fort's cannon to frighten off roving bands of Karankawa Indians.

Long remained in Texas and became a hotel keeper, hosting most of the leading men of the day and apparently enjoying the attentions of Mirabeau B. Lamar for a time.

The free ferry trip across the roads is an exhilarating, 20-minute sea cruise.

Galveston, 77 m. (alt. 20; pop. 59,070 city). This historic town, a major tourist, recreation and shipping center,

The lighthouse at Port Boliver, built in 1852.

splashed with the color of its oleanders and boasting scores of weathered, historic buildings, occupies the eastern end of the island first visited by Alvar Nunez Cabeza de Vaca in 1528. He knew the island as "Malhado" (bad luck) for his shipwreck and captivity at Karankawa hands. Spanish exploration was spotty thereafter, the harbor coming into prominence with the 1810–20 decade of freebooters and pirates. Jean Lafitte's Maison Rouge—red house—was near the site of the University of Texas Medical Branch. During the Texas Revolution, the ad interim government took refuge here and the valiant little Texas Navy for 10 years made Galveston its home port. During the Civil War, Galveston was occupied by Federal forces for a time but was recaptured by Confederates in a combined land-sea assault, January 1, 1863.

Until well into the 1800s, Galveston was "Queen City of Texas," but the vicious hurricane of 1900, perhaps America's worst natural disaster, killed an estimated 6,000. From that grew the massive 11-mile-long, 17-foot-high granite sea wall, an enormous engineering feat, and the invention here of the commission form of city government. To its cultured, historic past, Galveston today has added sun and fun.

Mini-Tour Guide

The Colonel Paddlewheeler: Triple-deck bay excursions. Buffet, music, dancing on weekends (moonlight cruises). 22nd St. Wharf.

Classic Car Museum: Convertibles and sports cars only. 1918 Mechanic St.

Elissa: 1877 square-rigger, a sailing museum 8 yrs in restoration. 22nd St. Wharf.

Fishing: Free jetties along seawall at 10th, 17th, 30th, 37th, and 61st Sts. Charter boats available at Piers 18, 19, and Yacht Basin.

Garten Verein: 1870 octagonal structure—now recreation building. 27th at Ave. O.

Historical Museum: County. 2219 Market.

Lone Star Flight Museum: Vintage aircraft from WWII. Scholes Field.

Seawolf Park: WWII submarine, other ships, vehicles. Commercial fishing pier. Pelican Island.

Texas Limited: Antique train ride to Houston. 25th and Strand.

Transportation and Commerce Center: Graphic story, city's development. Rosenberg, at foot of Strand.

Yacht Basin: Big, busy, elegant. 2nd to 6th, foot of Strand.

Most immediately impressive are the immense seawall and its wide boulevard where the city's resort establishments, phalanxes of handsome condominiums, and fine restaurants look seaward. You can rent bikes. Usually visible offshore are big ships making for this port.

Toward the seawall's east end is the city's medical center, one of the South's most important, building around the University of Texas Medical Branch.

In the preservation of its historic homes, churches and buildings—whole areas of them—Galveston ranks behind few American cities. Perhaps the most unique grouping is The Strand, the old business center once the "Wall Street of the Southwest." Here is a superb concentration of nineteenth-century iron fronts in restoration—street corner gaslights, galleries, studios, restaurants, shops and pubs. The Strand Theater presents good drama. There are guided or self-guiding tours. Close by is the interesting Galveston County Historical Museum.

The city's fine old homes are concentrated in two historic preserves—the East End and Silk Stocking Row historic districts. Outstanding are Ashton Villa (2328 Broadway), Bishop's Palace (1402 Broadway), Grand Opera House (2020 Post Office Rd.), Powhatan House (3427 Ave. O), Samuel May Williams home (3601 Ave. P.).

Also notable are the Rosenberg Library with its rare collection and the 72-foot-tall Texas Heroes Monument, recollecting Texas' struggle for independence. On the north edge of town is the white, airy building housing the *Galves-*

Bishop's Palace (former home of the Bishop of Galveston-Houston diocese) in Galveston is on the American Institute of Architects' list of the 100 most outstanding buildings in the United States.

ton News Tribune, Texas' oldest daily newspaper and claimant not only to the state's first telephone but one of the first 1,000 installed anywhere.

Galveston's entertainment facilities are almost unlimited. Every kind of salt-water fishing—pier, surf, deepsea—is at hand. The 32-mile-long beach offers surfing to beachcombing, scuba diving to chartered sailing. Visitor Centers are in Moody Civic Center, Seawall Blvd. at 21st St. and at 2016 Strand, where you can see a free film on Galveston Island. Stewart Beach Park (Seawall Blvd. at Broadway) has bath houses, restaurants, mini-golf, water slides, bumper boats, and beach access.

Festivals are frequent, including April's Blessing of the (Shrimp) Fleet, May's Historic Home Tour, August's Saltwater Hall of Fame Fishing Tourney, September's Oleander Festival. In December, Dickens' Evening on the Strand puts you in Christmas a century ago. For complete information, check the Visitors Information Center, Beach (Seawall) Boulevard at 21st. At Galveston, intersect I-45/Tour 26. Continue west via FM 3005 or, beyond the seawall, for a time drive the beach itself.

At 88 m. (Stewart Road) is Lafitte's Grove, where legend claims treasure is buried and history records a battle between pirates and Karankawa. Lafitte's men stole an Indian squaw; the Karankawa countered by devouring four pirates.

Galveston Island State Park, 90 m., offers all facilities—from campsites to nature trails and bird observation platforms amid the salt marshes between Gulf and bay. Musicals are presented nightly except Sunday during summer months at 1,700-seat Mary Moody Northen Amphitheater. Dinner is available. Six miles south on FM 3005 at 13 Mile Rd.

San Luis Pass, 104 m. (toll bridge), is the site of an 1832 village port that for a time vied with Galveston in ship traffic. Shifting tidal currents sanded San Luis' harbor and, by 1844, killed the town. Follow TX 332 west.

At 117 m., pass below Brazoria National Wildlife Refuge. Brazoria County provides a seafront park for fishing, picnicking and birdwatching (95 percent of the North American shorebird species have been sighted in this area).

Surfside, 120 m., is site of historic Old Velasco and part of today's Brazosport complex—see Tour 28/TX 36.

Region II
North-South: Tours 23 through 32

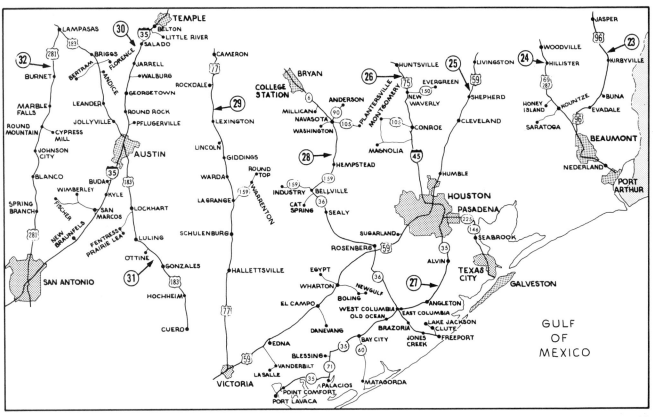

(Also see page 44)

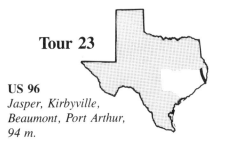
Y our southward route, a continuation of Tour 9, Region I, crosses from forest to seacoast. From Jasper to Kirbyville you travel lumbering country—dense pine woodland here and there revealing the sawdust ghosts of abandoned lumber camps. Near Silsbee you cut the east edge of jungle-like Big Thicket, then, at Beaumont, you emerge suddenly onto coastal plains and marshland that extend to Port Arthur and the Gulf, beyond.

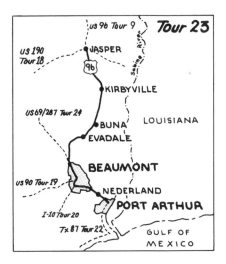

Long ago, you would have moved from the lower edge of old Tejas country, where the relatively advanced Caddo Indian first welcomed Spain, into the region of the coastal cannibal Indians, the Attakapans. Throughout, you parallel the old Sabine border which Spain tried to defend against France, England, and finally, America.

In today's 94 miles you cross from a timbering economy to one solidly based on oil. As you travel south you can note the gradual penetration of oil exploration: silvery tanks in isolated clearings, the straight forest slashes for pipelines. At Beaumont and on to Port Arthur, oil is king: here is where the mighty

Spindletop gusher introduced the twentieth century to the Oil Age. Your forests have become the steel scaffolding of oil refineries and the petrochemical industry.

Jasper, 0 m.—see Tour 18. Continue south from Tour 9/Region I.

Southward you penetrate forests long known locally as Scrapping Valley for an 1870 blood feud between two enemy families and allied relatives. Before rangers could put it down, isolated shootings had erupted into one shootout that took 11 lives. Today, Scrapping Valley is scenic, tranquil woodland.

At 6 m., FM 1005 loops southwest. Down it 4 m. is the homesite of George Washington Smyth, one of the signers of the Texas Declaration of Independence. Just beyond was old Pinetucky, an early settlement, now a ghost in the forest.

Kirbyville, 21 m. (alt. 101; pop. 1,871), is a major lumbering center named for John Henry Kirby, father of the Texas timber industry and a moving force in establishing American lumber standards. At the peak of his development of these southeastern forests he kept 12 mills in operation, five logging camps and five "fronts"; and his employees numbered some 16,500. It was Kirby who extended railroads into this area, finally opening hitherto impenetrable forest and allowing communities to develop.

Buna, 37 m. (alt. 76; pop. 2,127), is a sawmill community in a pioneer area. The Antioch Primitive Church (Baptist) was organized nearby in 1841.

Evadale, 46 m. (alt. 42; pop. 1,422) is another lumbertown on old ground. Richardson's Bluff on the Neches was the 1830 site of a ferry. During the 1836 Runaway Scrape when Texas families—mostly the women and children of embattled men—fled before Santa Anna, East Texas rivers were at flood stage. Benjamin Richardson, operating his ferry in dangerous waters, is credited with saving many lives.

Via FM 1131 south 6 m., **Wiess Bluff** was the head of tidewater navigation on the Neches and during the Civil War, a major Confederate shipping point and supply depot. For a time afterwards it prospered with lumbering, floating logs downriver. Railroad penetration finished the town and only traces remain.

At 62 m., merge with US 69/287/ Tour 24, continuing south.

Beaumont, 72 m.—see Tour 19. Nearby also see Orange, Liberty.

At 76 m. on the city's south edge is **Gladys City,** a boomtown reconstructed to show life in the Spindletop oilfield days.

Reminiscent of its Dutch heritage, Nederland's Windmill Museum houses early-day memorabilia.

Nederland, 87 m. (alt. 25; pop. 16,192), came to be settled through Dutch backing of Arthur Stillwell's port, immediately below. Stillwell platted this city for colonists from Holland, who came over in 1898. These in turn were joined by a number of South Louisianans, and though that village has grown into a big residential area within today's Golden Triangle, it has not forgotten its heritage. In 1969 Nederlanders built a 40-foot-tall Dutch Windmill—a museum for early-day memorabilia. Shortly thereafter, the co-founding Louisianans were memorialized in an adjacent building, "La Maison des Acadiens," a replica, inside and out, of a southern Louisiana home. The third week of each March, Nederlanders celebrate their Dutch and French heritage. Both museum buildings are located in Tex Ritter Park. Ritter, who was born in Panola County, grew up in Nederland

and has always considered it his home. A plaque at the park entrance salutes the city's country-western pioneer.

Port Arthur, 94 m.—see Tour 22.

☆

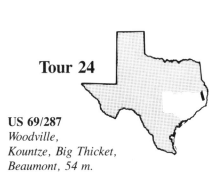

Tour 24

US 69/287
Woodville,
Kountze, Big Thicket,
Beaumont, 54 m.

This southward continuation of Tour 12, Region I, is the shortest and in some respects the most haunting journey in Texas, for it takes you closest to the heart of wilderness long known as The Big Thicket.

From Woodville all the way to Beaumont you travel forest—the Big Thicket is more woodland than swamp. This is a land of perpetual twilight, where beneath the big timber, myrtles, dogwood and yaupon bloom, where flowering woodbine, Virginia creeper and yellow jasmine interlace growth into a near impenetrable tangle. Throughout, you are still in logging country: particularly on side roads, you will encounter the lumber trucks, peaked with loads to the teeter-point.

Along this route, do not venture far from your car—even the Indian knew not to leave the trail. The Big Thicket regards you as an intruder.

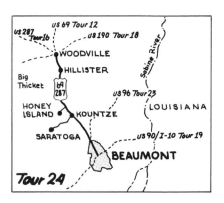

Woodville, 0 m.—see Tour 18. Continue south from Tours 12 and 16.

Hillister, 8 m., pop. 200, is a tiny and old logging village. West of here some 15 m. and south of the Alabama-Coushatta Indian Reservation is the Big Sandy Unit of the Big Thicket National Preserve. Tradition claims that wilderness to be the site of the legendary Kaiser Burnout. During the Civil War, men who wanted no part of Confederate or Federal arms disappeared into the forest, and old story insists that they were burned out and shot down as they ran from conflagration. As with legends, there are other versions, one insisting that not only they, but their descendants, remained in the wilderness.

Kountze, 31 m. (alt. 85; pop. 2,056), is the governmental seat of Hardin County, a withdrawn little town secluded in some of the Thicket's deepest woods. In 1881 it became a sawmill and railroad shipping center for the area.

Early morning mists on a swamp pond in the Big Thicket near Kountze.

West of here is a land of on-and-on wilderness, of exotic beauty, and mysterious legend. To the naturalist, most of all, the Thicket is a botanical treasure house, with every kind of hardwood known to these latitudes, with six-foot ferns, giant palmettos, blossoming creepers and shrubs, sudden ponds and bogs fringed with lilies, hyacinth, flags and iris. Eleven varieties of orchids have been discovered, and birdwatchers have identified species thought to be extinct. Kountze likes to term itself "the Big Light in the Big Thicket." Just north of

town on FM 420, an information station provides considerable data on the wilderness all around you, including the hiking trails. Undertake them with proper precaution.

Via FM 1293 west 8 m., **Honey Island,** pop. 401, is the village closest to the Thicket's densest region. Northwest some 3 m. is the tangled growth of Bad Luck Creek and Panther Den's swamps, all so interlaced that to penetrate it, as the late naturalist Lance Rosier did when surveying the Thicket, it was necessary to *crawl* at least a mile! There is a Lost Creek near here which drops suddenly into a hole at the foot of a large tree, only to reappear 5 m. distant, and just as suddenly, from under a bank of ferns northeast of Saratoga.

Via FM 770 west, **Saratoga,** 15 m. (alt. 83; pop. 1,000), is Big Thicket's acknowledged "capital." The very loneliness of this closeted little village had made it a Thicket tourist center for many years. Several area medicinal springs attracted settlers in the early 1850s. By 1880, cabins were erected for a health spa. In 1901, oil discovery destroyed Saratoga's health spa claims, along with most of its springs, but brought growth. Oil, in fact, had been known here since 1865, when John F. Cotton hammered a shallow well with a piledriver. At the edge of town is the old puddled-iron well casing for Cotton's well, one of America's oldest.

Saratoga's Thicket domain lies dense all about—you can lose yourself a thousand yards from your car. Originally the name applied to all the area between the San Antonio-Nacogdoches trail, far to the north, down to the coastal prairies, and west as far as the Brazos. Now diminished to some two million acres and criss-crossed with roads, the Thicket yet remains unyielding. Old-timers in Saratoga can recall a lifetime resident's getting lost for eight days within a mile from his home.

The Big Thicket Museum here reflects—along with its biological wonders—some of this wilderness' legend: of men hidden out, men suddenly disappearing, men killed. There are ghosts, too: perhaps the most formidable one is a light variously hunted and equally elusive—which haunts the old abandoned railroad siding, Bragg Road, that once led to a nearby lumber town. The light, a kind of luminous, pulsating ectoplasm, restlessly patrols that lonely byway. The unimaginative refer to it as a fireball or foxfire; the old-timers know better. The museum can arrange small group tours or guided canoe floats. (Arrangements in advance.)

___

At 44 m. merge with US 96/Tour 23. East of you, principally along the Neches, lies the Beaumont Unit, one of several in the Big Thicket National Preserve—each set apart to reflect a different face of this wilderness. This one, most marshy of all, is similar in nature to Georgia's Okefenokee Swamp.

Of those units established now—forerunners of more to come—the most notable are Big Sandy Creek, below the Alabama-Coushatta Reservation (Tour 18), for hiking and birdwatching; Turkey Creek, above Kountze, where not only orchids occur but also four of the five known species of carnivorous plants found in North America.

Beach Creek Unit, below Martin Dies State Park (Tour 18), mixes a wide variety of big trees and allows for camping, hiking and backpacking. North of Evadale (Tour 23) the Neches Bottom Unit is best explored by canoe or small boat. The Lance Rosier Unit at Saratoga is a canopied wilderness providing an extraordinary biological crossroads. When exploring a preserve, the National Park Service warns you not to assume that you are on federal land as yet, but to treat all property as private.

Beaumont, 54 m.—see Tour 19.

☆

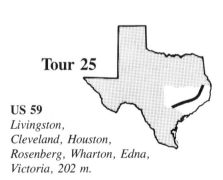

Tour 25

US 59
*Livingston,
Cleveland, Houston,
Rosenberg, Wharton, Edna,
Victoria, 202 m.*

Y our route, a southward continuation of Tour 10, Region I, cuts the western edge of the Big Thicket and—below Lake Livingston—skirts the eastern flank of Sam Houston National Forest, as far as Cleveland. There, timber

thins to a degree as you cross the big oilfields north of Houston, then that metropolis itself.

At Houston you veer southwest into the coastal prairies, and the open terrain flattens all the way to Victoria. Throughout you cross a region rich in mineral resources—oil and, near Wharton, extensive sulfur deposits; the land is devoted to cattle and rice production.

North of Houston the forests were relatively empty prior to the white man, and not heavily settled for some time after his coming—a remoteness that must have attracted Sam Houston, for this is the part of Texas he loved best.

Below Houston you enter the domain of the vicious Karankawa Indian and, as early pioneers displaced him, you travel across the center of early Texan colonization and Republic that followed.

Livingston, 0 m.—see Tour 18. Continue south from Tour 10. To the west lies lower Lake Livingston, a new 82,600 acre reservoir with all recreational and resort facilities along its forested shores.

At 2 m., FM 1988 leads west to Lake Livingston State Park, camping and all facilities.

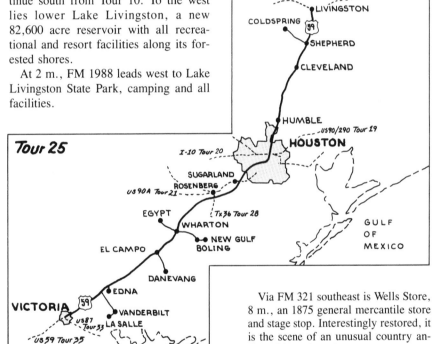

At 12 m., cross the deeply wooded Trinity River. Just west is the site of ghost **Marianna,** settled in 1838 as Drew's Landing and, by Civil War times, a major Confederate riverport and supply depot. As with so many river towns, Marianna fell victim to by-passing railroads.

At **Shepherd,** 17 m. (alt. 143; pop. 1,812), TX 150 leads west into Sam Houston National Forest. Remotely tranquil little **Coldspring** (Tour 18), at the

lower end of Lake Livingston and just above Double Lake and Big Thicket Recreation Areas, provides all recreational facilities, including scenic trails.

Cleveland, 29 m. (alt. 160; pop. 7,124), grew in 1880 as a lumber-shipping rail point. Oil discovery southward aided its growth.

___

Via TX 105 east 14 m. is tiny **Dolen** and Plantation Ranch, where former Governor of Guam Bill Daniel reconstructed a typical Texas "river town," now located at the Strecker Museum in Waco. One building, a huge barn, was moved with an open pint of water sitting inside; not a drop was spilled. Farther eastward on TX 146 is the site of Grand Cane, home of Sam Houston during his second term as president of the Republic of Texas. In this area also see Conroe, Liberty.

___

Via FM 321 southeast is Wells Store, 8 m., an 1875 general mercantile store and stage stop. Interestingly restored, it is the scene of an unusual country antique fair each spring.

___

Humble, 55 m. (alt. 65; pop. 12,060), was not named for Humble Oil and Refining Company, parent of giant Exxon; it's the other way around. In 1865, Pleasant Humble operated a ferry across the San Jacinto here, and at the turn of the century this sleek, handsome little city was a sleepy sawmill town. A 1904 gusher brought in a big new field. Here, in 1909, Ross Sterling and Jesse Jones, with others, founded the Humble company . . . the rest is history. Humble citizens happily show visitors the tumbleddown frame building on an otherwise modern Main Street. Under its rusty sheet metal roof today's industrial colossus was born. The Humble Historical Museum recollects oil-boom days. Near town is the Mercer Aboretum and Botanical Gardens, with self-guiding nature trails.

Just west of the city is big Houston Intercontinental Airport.

Houston, 76 m.—see Tour 19. For your southwestward route from here, spring is the season of beauty—the countryside remains blanketed with wildflowers from mid-March to late May. In fall and winter, however, you are close enough to the sea to glimpse great flights of coast-bound migratory birds. Follow US 59 southwest.

At **Sugar Land,** 97 m. veer from US 90A/Tour 21. Here your route swings south of both Richmond and Rosenberg (Tour 21); watch for appropriate exits. Intersect TX 36/Tour 28.

Wharton, 136 m. (alt. 111; pop. 9,011), spreads leisurely along the Colorado River and, like neighboring Richmond on the Brazos, more resembles a town of the Old South—its handsome homes set off by large lawns and moss-draped oaks. Established in 1846, it was named for the Tennesseean brothers, William H. and John Austin Wharton, leaders in the Texas Revolution. John was Sam Houston's adjutant general at San Jacinto, and his brother William was the first Texas minister to the United States, seeking annexation. This was also the last home of Robert M. Williamson—"Three-Legged Willie" (see Columbus), one of the earliest Texans to declare for independence. In town, a granite shaft honors a famed local sheriff, killed in the line of duty. Also located here is Wharton County Museum, housed in the old jail, and reflecting the area's rich history. The little city is also home to Wharton County Junior College and the Gulf Coast Medical Center.

Via FM 1301 southeast 11 m., **Boling** (pop. 1,119) and **Newgulf,** pop. 963, just beyond, are headquarters and mining center for Texas Gulf Sulphur. The sulfur is extracted by pumping superheated water into the wells, later evaporating the liquid in huge vats,

leaving small mountains of the "powdered gold." Over the years, Texas has produced more than half of the world's sulfur.

Via FM 102 northwest, **Egypt** was a plantation settlement in 1830 and took its name during a severe drought when its fields supplied corn to surrounding settlements. The fine old Northington-Heard home has been preserved as an outstanding museum. Nearby is Spanish Camp, a ghost community that was the site of one of Santa Anna's last camps prior to San Jacinto. You can note a peculiar formation of trees in this region: they interlace overhead like a canopy while their trunks, free of underbrush, allow unimpeded vision—making an endless series of arches.

El Campo, 150 m. (alt. 110; pop. 10,511), is as open, sunny and brisk as neighboring Wharton is shaded and leisurely. Originally range land within the big Shanghai Pierce ranches (see Tour 27), the town came into being as an 1880 construction camp on the New York-Texas and Mexico Railroad, projected from New York City to Matamoros Mexico, but in actuality extending only from Rosenberg to Victoria. Its leading promoter was Italian Count C. J. Telferner, who imported some 2,000 Italian laborers for the work, earning his project the title of "Macaroni Line." Telferner named towns along the way for himself and his family—Edna, Inez and Louise, his daughters. El Campo simply meant "the camp." El Campo today is a center of oil and gas production and rich rice fields; Czech population is a predominant social and cultural factor. For hunters, the El Campo museum will prove interesting, featuring big game trophies from five continents, displayed in carefully re-created natural settings.

Via TX 71 south, tiny **Danevang,** 11 m., pop. 61, is a 1904 farm community settled by Danes, whose descendants still observe some Old World customs. In 1920 Danevang pioneered many cooperative enterprises, ranging from group insurance to a co-op telephone service.

Edna, 177 m. (alt. 90; pop. 5,343), clustered about its modern courthouse,

is a glistening little city, reflecting the prosperity of surrounding oil production and solid agriculture. In 1883, Edna took the Jackson County seat from old Texana, to the south, and today maintains an intriguing museum for this historic area. Each October the town hosts the Jackson County Fair.

Just south is the site of Camp Independence, mustering point for the Texas army in the uneasy days immediately following San Jacinto. Nearby is the site of William Milligan's Gin House, where 1835 colonists passed a July 17 resolution calling for Texas independence, a preamble to the formal declaration almost a year later.

Via TX 111 south 6 m., **Texana** is the ghost of the county seat that Edna replaced. Founded in 1832 at the confluence of the Lavaca and Navidad Rivers, the pioneer settlement was named Santa Anna, for Texans then thought that general a friend of democracy. Renamed four years later, the port town was burned by its namesake en route to San Jacinto. For a time Texana was considered by New York's Allen Brothers as a site for the city they later placed at Houston. But Texanans, complacent with their natural port, priced the land too high. For a time Texana continued to show shipping promise, then was bypassed northward by the railroad. Edna became the county seat and Texana died. What was center of town lies beneath today's microwave tower atop a slight hill; other traces remain. The Lavaca-Navidad confluence is now dammed, forming big Lake Texana, with its beautiful state park (camping and all facilities), where, much like big, friendly dogs, tame deer will visit your campground.

From nearby Vanderbilt, pop. 665, follow FM 616 west 5 m. to La Salle, pop. 160. Just across Garcitas Creek and a mile south (on private land) is the generally accepted location of Fort St. Louis, the ill-fated log outpost of Rene Robert Cavelier Sieur de La Salle. The fort was built in 1685 to lodge French claim to this land and to base expeditions against Spanish Mexico. Object of a four-year Spanish search, it was the immediate cause of Spain's subsequent occupation of Texas. The French colony fell victim to starvation, disease, anarchy—the murder of La Salle by his own men (see Navasota)—and finally Indian massacre.

Victoria, 202 m. Enter Region III, South Texas. See Tour 33. US 59 continues southwest as Tour 35.

☆

Tour 26

US 75/I-45
Huntsville,
Conroe, Houston,
Galveston, 120 m.

This tour is half woodland, half coastal plain. As Tour 25 approaches Houston from the eastern upper corner of Sam Houston National Forest, similarly Tour 26 descends through the western edge of that handsome timberland—a continuation of the Dallas-Houston interstate, Tour 13, Region I.

Your route begins at Huntsville, Sam Houston's last and most-loved home, cuts through forest to below Conroe and approaches the Texas metropolis through a gradually clearing and lowering prairie. Beyond Houston you catch the brisk scent of salt air as you continue over a flat plain. Your road roughly parallels Galveston Bay, 10 to 20 m. eastward, and all along you pass the big industrial and technical installations that reach all the way to the island resort.

Your upper leg was secluded forest in Republic days; the coastal leg is storied land: you pass San Jacinto's historic battleground (Tour 20), and then the great NASA complex between Clear Lake City and Seabrook, where you can ponder the journeys of other, more distant-bound travelers.

Huntsville, 0 m.—see Tour 18. Continue south from Tour 13, Region I.

On the east side of the highway, between Huntsville and New Waverly, one of Texas' finest fences braces a two-mile perimeter of the immaculate McDermott Ranch.

New Waverly, 14 m. (alt. 362; pop. 936) is a wooded village settled in 1870 by Polish farmers. It occupies an area where earlier pioneers pushed back the forest for big 1840s cotton plantations. Old Waverly, 2 m. east, was Alabaman-settled, with well-regarded Waverly Institute segregating its boy students from girls at the time of the Civil War. Afterwards, occupying Federal troops camped Soldiers Hill, centering the settlement, and the old town gave way to the new. Tales of ghosts from those old days abound in the deep-shadowed woods all about.

Beyond, TX 150 leads into the heart of Sam Houston National Forest to **Evergreen,** pop. 50, 14 m. east. South of here, Big Thicket and Little Thicket recreation areas provide all facilities, including scenic trails in a secluded setting.

Willis, 23 m. (alt. 381; pop. 2,764) is a tidy, forested town, once famed for a booming industry based on fine tobaccos grown nearabouts. Its seven cigar factories faded years ago, when tariffs on Cuban tobacco were lifted. Today Willis looks to a combination of agribusiness and a dawning high-tech manufacturing base.

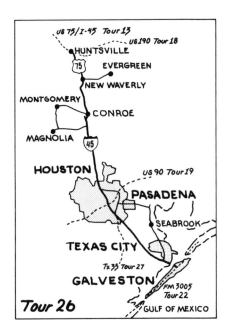

Conroe, 30 m. (alt. 213; pop. 27,610), is a handsome city, its forest seeming almost landscaped. Originally a sawmill junction, it now centers one of America's fastest-growing regions and today functions primarily as a satellite to Houston.

A recently-built covered bridge just off I-45 six miles south of Conroe.

Conroe began to boom with oil in 1930; now it looks increasingly toward woodland recreation and breathing room. There are many fine homes of Houstonians who have retired or are commuting from this more tranquil setting. This lake and forest area projects the immediate accommodation of some 50,000 people. Downtown a simulated railroad depot serves as a tourist information center for surrounding Montgomery County, one of the state's fastest-growing.

Eastward 12 m. via TX 105, **Cut and Shoot** (pop. 903) is one of Big Thicket's little strung-along settlements. The hamlet's unusual name allegedly came from a long-ago disagreement over the pattern for a new church steeple.

Via TX 105 west, Lake Conroe, close by its namesake, is resort-oriented with many recreational areas: several youth camps are located here, as are plush resorts and camping facilities. Beyond the lake is **Montgomery,** 15 m. (alt. 286; pop. 356), which seems to have changed little since its 1837 founding as seat of the county that would take its name. Texas' third-oldest, the county originally embraced several of those that surround it today. At that time it was the only settlement in this then-remote woodland, yet it was an important link on the Old Wire Road (see Henderson), route of the state's first telegraph, linking East Texas—from Marshall to Galveston—with primitive communication. Loss of its county seat to Conroe accentuated a decline that is being offset today by the picturesque town's proximity to Lake Conroe resorts, and the diligent work of the Montgomery Historical Society. Several fine old homes are opened for a spring tour each April, and for "Christmas in Old Montgomery" each mid-December. An excellent county-wide tourguide with map is available at the jewel-box city hall, itself an 1845 home, handsomely restored. County-wide special tours are available on advance request here.

From Montgomery south via FM 149, then west on FM 1488 is **Magnolia,** 16 m. (alt. 271; pop. 940), a quaint turn-of-the-century railroad town and site of Texas Renaissance Festival, each weekend through October and early November.

From Magnolia return to I-45 east via FM 1488 through W. G. Jones State Forest, a present recreation area projected for immediate, extensive enlargement. You will pass just above **The Woodlands** (pop. 29,205) 25,000 acres projecting six model villages, eventually to domicile more than 150,000 inhabitants—a bold project now underway after 10 years of planning. Rejoin your original route below Conroe at 36 m.

Houston, 69 m.—see Tour 19. From here south you travel storied land—in colonization, the struggle for independence, the days of the Republic, then of Civil War, and finally massive industrial growth. Follow I-45 southeast.

At 76 m., Pasadena and San Jacinto Battleground lie eastward (Tour 20). TX 35/Tour 27 veers south and east here. En route to Galveston you may proceed via Red Bluff Road and TX 146, edging Galveston Bay and a series of interesting, overlapping cities and towns; or you may continue via this expressway noting the appropriate exits.

At 91 m. NASA Road 1 jets east from Webster (alt. 22; pop. 4,678) through Nassau Bay (pop. 4,320), leading to NASA headquarters and the LBJ Manned Spacecraft Center. There are daily self-guided tours (Visitor Orientation Center) which let you see Mission Control (central brain for the space missions) and the space shuttle program of the 1980s. You will also see spacecraft that have journeyed to the moon, a full-scale Skylab, photos from Mars, lunar rocks, actual space movies (from rendezvous-docking to lunar exploration), and examples of space technology spinoff.

Beyond NASA is **Seabrook** (alt. 20; pop. 6,685), a quiet little fishing village until the space age. Seabrook still blesses its shrimp fleet each August, and parades Christmas at sea with a decorated boat lane each December.

At 98 m., FM 517 leads east 15 m. to once-tiny **San Leon,** swelled by newcomers to 30 times its 100 population of a decade ago. A century ago it was a thriving port with 2,000 inhabitants. San Leon boasted a block-square hotel, factories, railroad round-houses and—from an earlier time—a slave landing and trading dock. The Galveston hurricane of 1900 simply erased that city. On TX 146, between Kemah above you and Texas City below, the Houston Lighting and Power Company displays an immense, raised outdoor map, done in terrazo, of this coastal area.

Texas City, 112 m. (alt. 12; pop. 40,822), knows itself as "Port of Industrial Opportunity." An industrial city indeed—a mass of giant plants—it also provides fishermen an excellent 5 m. jetty extending into Galveston Bay, with municipal piers, picnic ground, boat ramps and camps. The city is home of the College of the Mainland, and a handsomely-restored home, which serves as a museum displaying artifacts that date back to the pirate days of Jean Lafitte and the Karankawa Indian.

I-45 becomes the Galveston causeway between Texas City and Galveston.

At Texas City on April 16, 1947, a harbor explosion disaster killed 576 people. Most of these are interred at Disaster Cemetery.

Galveston, 120 m.—see Tour 22.

☆

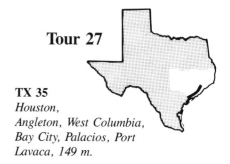

Tour 27

TX 35
*Houston,
Angleton, West Columbia,
Bay City, Palacios, Port
Lavaca, 149 m.*

Beginning at Houston and angling southwest, just in from the coast, your route traverses some of Texas' most historic early-day countryside. You cross an expanse of plain, shimmering with nearness to the sea and dappled with motts of oak that deepen to dense stands along the succession of river bottoms. This is the region where Stephen F. Austin's first colonists came up from river-mouth landings to lay the foundations of Texas today.

The majority of little cities and towns—beyond Houston you encounter no metropolitan areas—are old, dating from the 1830s. Those along the rivers came first—boat landings for the easiest means of colonial transportation. It is a land that developed from crude dog-run cabins to one of broad plantations centered by spacious homes. The Varner-Hogg mansion in West Columbia is Texas' best example of the style of living these early Texans finally achieved.

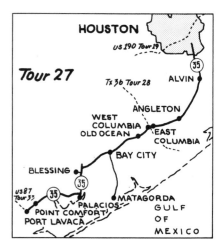

Quiescent for some time after the Civil War—this was Confederate country—this coast is blossoming again, a byproduct of the industrialization that spans all its length, from Houston through Brazosport to Port Lavaca, terminal for this tour.

Houston, 0 m.—see Tour 19.

Alvin, 26 m. (alt. 51, pop. 19,220), has an air of spaciousness; it is a fast-growing center for the rice-farming and chemical industries. Its area was settled early, but the town itself was not founded until 1876, taking the first name of a man sent by the Santa Fe Railroad to supervise cattle loading. Alvin Morgan built the community's first dwelling, its first general store, and saloon, and would later become its first postmaster. Since their founder's surname already graced a Bosque County town, these townfolk settled for Alvin. Alvin survived yellow fever epidemics, a disastrous turn-of-the-century fire, and the Galveston hurricane. Some idea of that storm's fury resides in little Algoa, 4 m. south on TX 6: here, some 18 miles from the sea, a British ship was hurled inland to lodge for 16 months. This town took its name from that ship.

Immediately west of Alvin is Chocolate Bayou, an inland waterway for early colonists.

Angleton, 50 m. (alt. 31; pop. 17,140), became Brazoria County seat in 1897 and now claims itself home of the largest county fair in Texas each October. This, too, is early-settled country: at the ghost of Chenango, immediately north, was one of Texas' first sugar mills. Farther north on TX 6, near Bonney, is the site of China Grove, the 1843 plantation home of Texas' famed Confederate general, Albert Sidney Johnston, who was killed at Shiloh. Little remains except a few hedges of Cherokee roses which legend says Johnston planted. Oyster Creek, immediately west of Angleton, was the site of many original Austin colony plantations. The Brazoria County Museum traces a pioneering story to the early 1800s. The county seat also is headquarters for two national wildlife refuges, southward toward the coast—Brazoria and San Bernard (see Freeport). Nearby also see Brazoria, Freeport.

Bailey's Prairie, 57 m., lies just beyond the Brazos and was settled in 1821 by James B. (Brit) Bailey. Something of a maverick, Brit willed that he be buried erect, rifle on his shoulder, a full whiskey jug at his feet. His wife, facing the preacher, at the last moment banned the jug; and on dark nights now, Bailey's ghost armed with a dim light, may be seen searching the prairie for his jug.

East Columbia, 62 m., pop. 95, was originally Bell's Landing, a little Brazos River port put in by Stephen Austin's close friend, Josiah Bell, in 1824. A center for cotton and sugar plantations, it declined after the Civil War, while its founder's cross-river settlement hung on. The historic Amman-Underwood House (1836) is here.

West Columbia, 65 m. (alt. 40; pop. 4,372), came into being when, in 1826, Bell cleared a 2 m. avenue onto the prairie west of the Brazos, calling his city Columbia. This became the first actual capital of the Republic. A replica of Columbia's capitol, a story-and-a-half store, has been restored. Here in late 1836 the first Texas congress accomplished much—a constitution, provision for army and navy, a judiciary, postal department, land office and a financial system. Here Sam Houston was elected president, and from here the capital was moved to Houston in November 1836. Stephen F. Austin died the same year in Columbia, having contracted pneumonia in the exertions of forming the new government. Under the Masonic Oak, Texas' first freemasonry chapter was petitioned in 1835, and close by, the Orozimbo Oak marks the site of the plantation where Santa Anna was held prisoner after San Jacinto.

Columbia also claims the Varner-Hogg Plantation, a state historic park, and this state's finest example of a massively columned, two-story colonial mansion of antebellum days. Governor James Stephen Hogg (see Quitman, Rusk) acquired the home in 1901, seeking to recall the plantation from which he was orphaned as a 13-year-old East Texas youth. In 1920 his children completed the restoration, and his daughter, Miss Ima Hogg, gave it to Texas 38 years later. At W. Columbia, intersect TX 36/Tour 28.

At **Old Ocean,** 73 m. (alt. 36; pop. 915), you pass close beside a large refinery. The round tanks store volatile fuel; the tall, scaffold-like structures provide the cracking process that through heat separates crude oil into usable components.

Bay City, 89 m. (alt. 55; pop. 18,170), has an open, clean and prosper-

ing look, and rightly so, having been first blessed with rich rice land, then railroads, oil discovery and finally petrochemical activity. The Matagorda County Historical Museum carefully displays the early days of this pioneering area, and Matagorda agriculture is saluted each October with Bay City's annual Rice Festival. In this area also see Wharton, Newgulf.

South 12 m. via FM 521 is the South Texas Project, a big nuclear-powered electrical generating plant. Displays explain the process of power generation.

Via TX 60 south, **Matagorda,** 22 m. (alt. 15; pop. 605), little, old and timeworn, was the second Texas port (Velasco, just east, was first) for Austin's colonists in 1822. The town was active during the Texas Revolution, furnishing many men to the ill-fated Fannin expedition. With 52 founding families, from New York and New England, Matagorda seemed destined for a major Texas role, with an 1832 population of over 1,200. Continued threat of hurricane slowed its growth, however, and Bay City's railroad took the county seat in 1894. A 20-mile beach, open for camping, awaits you here.

Blessing, 105 m. (alt. 44; pop. 571). Near this little town was the headquarters of an extraordinary early Texas rancher, Abel Head (Shanghai) Pierce. A Rhode Islander stowaway for Texas in 1854, he built the Matagorda Ranch to cover more than a million acres all along this coast. Old-timers claimed Pierce's holdings reached "from the Gulf to the North Pole." He is credited with helping introduce Brahman cattle to Texas ranges. Pierce also created what is now a delightful country inn in Hotel Blessing (1906), being restored by a local historical foundation. The food is inexpensive and delicious. Five years before his death he had a life-size statue of himself mounted on an immense granite monument. He was fond of looking at it and would remark, "There stands old Pierce!" Old-timers also claim he spent much time having bullet scars erased from his memorial. Pierce's grave is at Hawley's Cemetery, nearby. At Blessing your route bears due south for the coast.

At 112 m. intersect FM 521. Just east is the Yeamans-Stallard House, home of Horace Yeamans, one of Austin's 1829 colony, who received the land for service with the Army of the Republic.

Palacios, 118 m. (alt. 17; pop. 4,418), is a drowsy seashore tourist resort catering to those less in search of neon and "action." Its Gulf exposure has given it a look of age greater than deserved, for the town was founded at the turn of the century. Its surrounding land is old, however—known to French explorers in the 1600s and Austin colonists in the 1820s. The beachfront Luther Hotel is a landmark. Built in 1903, it served as a social and cultural center during the town's growth. Said to have had the longest front porch in Texas, the hotel in its heyday had a permanent orchestra for mealtimes and Sunday afternoons. Across from it are free fishing piers, boat ramps and camping areas.

Palacios counts a big shrimp fleet and houses the Marine Fisheries Research Station, where tours will interest those attracted to marine biology.

Point Comfort, 141 m. (alt. 18; pop. 956), with its glittering aluminum plant, stands at the eastern end of the Port Lavaca Causeway. The 1850 lighthouse was moved here from its location on a bombing range near Palacios.

The new Lavaca Bay causeway replaces one destroyed by Hurricane Carla in 1961. One section of the old bridge, alongside, makes up a 3,200-foot fishing pier, state park operated, with all facilities, including lights for night fishing. In this area also see La Salle, Texana, Edna.

Port Lavaca, 149 m. Enter Region III, South Texas. Intersect US 87/Tour 33. Your route continues southwestward as Tour 36.

☆

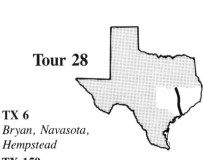

Tour 28

TX 6
*Bryan, Navasota,
Hempstead*

TX 159
Bellville

TX 36
*Sealy, Rosenberg, West Columbia,
Brazoria, Freeport, 164 m.*

As Tour 27 cuts east to west across the old Stephen F. Austin land grant, this route bisects these colonial beginnings of Texas from north to south. Throughout, you closely parallel the Brazos River, the early major waterway, and the heavy timber of that bottomland follows you across an otherwise open coastal plain.

The road is old, approximating that followed on horseback by Austin in conducting the affairs of his colony; and Austin, in fact, was following an ancient Indian trail—one used by both La Salle and later Spanish explorers. Just below your starting point, the Navasota region marked the upper colonial limits. The road then drops through San Felipe and on toward Velasco (Brazosport) at the Brazos' mouth.

The entire tour traverses a rich agricultural area, principally stockfarming northward, rice culture south. Since the bicentennial, considerable historic restoration has been undertaken both in the Navasota region and around West Columbia and Brazoria. Midway along, near Bellville, you cross a sprinkling of interesting old German settlements, their first in Texas.

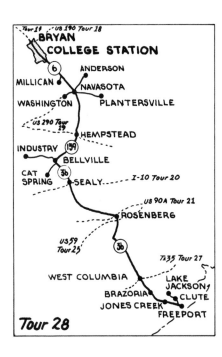

Bryan-College Station, 0 m.—see Tour 18. Continue south from Tour 14, Region I.

At 13 m. the Texas World Speedway lies just east. There is a 2-m. banked

track and a 3-m. Grand Prix road course. The big stand allows 26,000 to watch major races staged in April, July and August.

Millican, 14 m., pop. 100, just west of your highway, is a road-bend village that was the 1860 terminus of the Houston and Texas Central railroad, a major shipping point for all East Texas, and the embarkation site for eastbound Confederate troops. Throughout the war, Millican was an important Texas city; continuation of the road afterwards—to Dallas—then fire and yellow fever brought an end to its promise.

Navasota, 26 m. (alt. 215; pop. 6,296) grew from great plantations across this bottomland, and today its fine old homes stand back from the highway or ramble alongside into the little city. On the main highway esplanade, near downtown, is a statue of the great French explorer La Salle (see Edna). His isolated 1685 outpost on Matagorda Bay in desperate straits, La Salle was trying to reach French aid on the lower Mississippi when his mutinous men murdered him. Many historians believe he died near here.

Statue of French explorer, La Salle, on TX 6 in Navasota.

Its picturesque downtown area now listed on the National Historic Register, Navasota has defied disaster. The center of an area which gave heavily to the Confederacy, the town suffered in reconstruction—almost burned in 1865 by unpaid Confederate soldiers, and rebuilt only to be nearly wiped out by yellow fever in 1867. The city's C of C can route you to several interesting sites in this area. Nearby also see Brenham, Independence.

Via TX 90 north 10 m., **Anderson Fanthorp Inn State Historic Structure,** famed Fanthorp Inn (restored, private), one of Texas' earliest stage stops. Set back in moss-draped oaks, the inn hosted such distinguished guests as Sam Houston, Robert E. Lee, U. S. Grant, and Jefferson Davis. The old courthouse, third on this site, contains the original vault which has survived the years and two fires. Here the 1930s Clyde Barrow gang was arraigned. Close by is an old drug store that serves homemade ice cream across its marble counter; and among many historic homes and buildings, the Steinhagen log cabin and 1855 Baptist Church are close by. Just southwest is the cabin of Tapley Holland, first man to cross the line when Travis asked who would stay with him in the Alamo. Established in 1834, this was a major town prior to the Civil War, boasting St. Paul's College and a Confederate munitions plant, as well as a population almost 10 times its present size. During their Texas Trek, each April, Anderson citizens open their homes for visits, hosting them in costumes from an earlier time.

Via TX 105 northwest is **Washington on the Brazos,** 7 m., revolutionary capital (Tour 19).

TX 105 near Washington-on-the-Brazos.

Via TX 105 east 10 m., near the village of **Yarboro,** is the site of **Groce's**

Retreat, a plantation home of Jared Groce, pioneer Texas agriculturist (see Hempstead). Now a ghost, the site still can claim three days—March 18-21, 1836—when it was capital of the Republic of Texas. Here President David G. Burnet and his cabinet, fleeing Washington for Harrisburg, stayed until Santa Anna's approach drove them eastward. Beyond, **Plantersville,** 18 m., is the site of 1858 Markey's Seminary, a typical early school that combined the elementary, high school and college courses, with emphasis on "finishing" for girls.

Just south (FM 1774) on 6 weekends each October–November, the Texas Renaissance Festival converts 237 wooded acres to 16th century Europe, complete with minstrels, jesters, jousting knights, and ladies fair, all authentically costumed.

Hempstead, 47 m.—see Tour 19. Follow TX 159 southwest.

Bellville, 63 m. (alt. 220; pop. 3,378), grew from an 1838 settlement, becoming county seat 8 years later. During the 1830s–40s it centered an area of earliest German immigration. From spring to fall, every little community, in old custom, is busy with some celebration, usually including a barbecue, which is excellent here. A 1906 Victorian mansion has been remodeled as High Cotton Inn, handsome lodging for weekend tourists.

Via TX 159 east 16 m., **Industry,** pop. 475, is Texas' oldest German community, established in 1831–33. Industry was an early-day cigar manufacturer, and the county's first post office, a small rock building, still stands. **Welcome,** pop. 150, just north, is another early village, its 1850 Hackfield home now restored.

Via local roads south, **Cat Spring,** pop. 76, is a typical area settlement where Texas' first agricultural society was organized. Immediately west is **New Ulm,** pop. 650, another quaint village in this neat and prospering Texas German area.

At Bellville follow TX 36 south.

Sealy, 78 m.—see Tour 20. Continue south on TX 36.

Rosenberg, 106 m.—see Tour 21. At 108 m. intersect US 59/Tour 25.

West Columbia, 139 m.—see Tour 27.

Brazoria, 147 m. (alt. 32; pop. 2,717), occupies the north edge of the nine-city industrial complex of Brazosport, reaching from here all the way to Freeport on the coast. Deep shaded and quiet, the ghost of Old Brazoria lies along the Brazos, its main street fronting that river. From here, with a downriver boat attack, Brazorians opened Texas fighting in the 1832 Battle of Velasco. In this little city and all about are a number of old homes and historic homesites.

Via FM 521 west 4 m. was the plantation of James Walker Fannin, Goliad commander. Across Churchill Bridge, FM 2918 leads south to the San Bernard National Wildlife Refuge. Beside a little tavern, 1 m. from the deep-running rivermouth, is Fiddler's Island, where old story recalls pirate gold, violent murder, and supernatural music rising from the water on dark nights. Those who stay, according to legend, risk insanity.

From Brazoria southward, your road is heavily lined with live oaks.

Jones Creek (community), pop. 2,160, 157 m., is the site of Peach Point Plantation, just west, the handsomely preserved home of Stephen F. Austin's only sister, Mrs. Emily Perry, who built a special room for her brother. Austin claimed this as his only real home and his room contains much memorabilia. Visit by advance arrangement only.

At 160 m., cross Jones Creek. Near the roadside park grove, Austin colonists overwhelmed a Karankawa village.

Freeport, 164 m. (alt. 15; pop. 11,389), is a new city, a 1912 miner and shipper of sulfur, and has spread to become Brazosport, world's largest basic chemical complex. At closeby, neighboring Surfside Beach is original **Velasco,** first landfall for Austin's colonists in 1821. The Brazos River port saw 25,000 colonists pass through before Republic days. Near today's stilt-legged Coast Guard Station was the Mexican Fort Velasco, attacked June 25, 1832 by Texans outraged at blockade here and at Anahuac (Tour 20) across Galveston Bay. After 11 hours of fighting, the Mexican garrison surrendered—the first bloodshed in what would become the

Texas Revolution. Strangely, that conflict ended here as well, when the peace treaty was signed by Texas Interim President David G. Burnet and General Santa Anna, May 14, 1836. Old Velasco was almost completely destroyed in an 1875 hurricane. Toward the Brazos River mouth stretches Bryan Beach State Recreation Area (primitive camping allowed). Surfside's annual Sandcastle Festival each June brings the young in heart here to display their seaside artistry.

Just offshore, the wreck of the Confederate Blockade Runner *Acadia* (boilers only) is visible. Just inshore stretches the Gulf Intracoastal Waterway—America's major water artery—reaching 1,066 m. from Brownsville at Texas' tip, to Florida.

Northward, along TX 288, Freeport joins **Clute** and **Lake Jackson,** handsome, shaded little cities that are part of the Brazosport complex. Clute boasts the handsome Brazosport Center for Arts and Sciences (aquarium and enormous shell collection) and each late July, with resolute tongue-in-cheek, stages its "Great Texas Mosquito Festival." There's plenty of fun, but this town isn't kidding about its winged little devils, even positioning a 25-foot statue parody of the creature as the festival mascot. To the east, inshore from the Gulf, is Brazoria National Wildlife Refuge, a haven for vast numbers of migratory birds. To the west on the Gulf shore was an early Republic port and resort, **Quintana,** pop. 51, promising prior to Civil War days, but storm-battered like Velasco. A small fishing village remains. At Freeport you intersect TX 332/Tour 22, eastbound up the coast.

☆

Tour 29

US 77
*Cameron,
Rockdale, Giddings,
Schulenburg, Hallettsville,
Victoria, 153 m.*

A continuation of Tour 15, Region I, your route drops due south close to the western fringe of early Anglo settlement—the colonial grant of Tennesseean Sterling Robertson on the north to the frontier of Austin's settlements, finally to the colony of Martin de Leon at Victoria.

You begin in rolling, sparsely timbered blackland prairie at Cameron, cross a handsome belt of great live oaks around La Grange, and emerge south of Hallettsville on the Texas coastal prairies. Throughout, you will encounter an interesting blend of Texas cultures—Polish, east of Cameron; the Slavic Wends around Giddings; and a continuing mixture of Texas Czechs and Germans almost to Victoria.

Since their pioneer forebears were largely countryfolk, you see only small towns along the way: this is a rural countryside dotted with little farm-oriented villages.

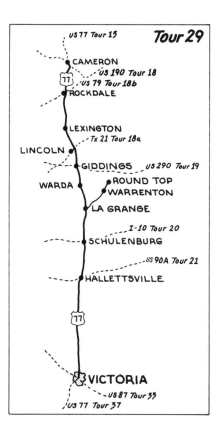

Cameron, 0 m.—see Tour 18. Continue south from Tour 15, Region I.

Rockdale, 16 m.—see Tour 18B.

Lexington, 36 m. (alt. 456; pop. 953), wanders over rolling land, the

oldest town in this area. Nearby **String Prairie,** along Yegua Creek, was settled in the 1840s, its farmers gradually converging to form Lexington. The founders, who were nearly all San Jacinto veterans, saluted another revolution in their town's name. In the area also see Dime Box, McDade.

Lincoln, 45 m.—see Tour 18A.

Giddings, 54 m.—see Tour 19.

Warda, 63 m., pop. 67, the faintest wayside scatter of dwellings, was a Wendish outgrowth of Giddings, above. The Wends, from a Slavic island in the middle of Prussia, came to Texas for religious freedom, bringing some quaint Old World customs. Easter and Christmas lasted three days, as did wedding celebrations. Wendish curatives were intriguing: a dog bite healed by dissolving, then drinking a burnt hair of the dog; carrying a black cloth cured cramps. A hazel nut filled with quicksilver prevented most diseases. Animals were protected by circling them on the run, praying all the while, and finishing with a stout jerk on the tail.

Close by Warda is a scenic park of "lost pines"—like those at Bastrop, isolated well west of the Texas pine belt.

La Grange, 74 m. (alt. 272; pop. 3,951), a tidy, big-shaded town slumbering deep in history, is one of the state's most interesting. It grew from the 1819 cabin of Virginia-born Aylett (Strap) Buckner, A Bunyanesque giant of a man who arrived before Stephen Austin's colony, of which this town was frontier. With fists like oak stumps, Buckner became a legend, dropping a wild bull with one blow, skinning a wildcat in mid air. Over-reaching, goes the legend, Strap finally challenged no less than the Devil to a bare-knucks duel, in which—due to Satan's cheating—Strap managed only a draw. The fight lasted three days, conveniently clearing land for the later settlement, but it finished Strap. Leading Texan in the first battle of revolution-to-come, Buckner—vengefully marked by the Devil—was killed in the first Mexican volley at Velasco in 1832.

Just east is Monument Hill State Historic Site, a small, oak-clustered overlook high above the winding Colorado River. There is a great shellstone shaft and granite crypt where are buried men of the ill-fated 1842 Dawson Expedition, together with those executed in the black-bean drawing after Texans, in retaliation, invaded Ciudad Mier, Mexico, the same year.

Monument Hill State Park near La Grange.

Below the hill but part of the historic site is the restoration of one of Texas' first breweries and the home of its founder (1846) Henry Kreische. An interpretive trail with scenic overlooks—the views are beautiful—leads to Kreische's installation, where guided tours are available. On the town square is Muster Oak, a living shrine to Fayette County's fighting men. Here they have mustered to serve in every war since 1842, when Dawson's men rode out to reinforce San Antonio against Mexican invasion—most of them caught in the Mexican retreat, and cut down.

Aside from excellent bakeries and restaurants, and an interesting antique shop, La Grange boasts a number of historic structures—notable among them the 1841 Faison Home Museum, with original furnishings, two century-old churches, and an 1852 German fachwerk house. C of C has information on four-county Texas Pioneer Trail and a number of painted churches (decorated inside) in rural countryside surrounding.

East 4 m. via local roads is the site of Rutersville College, the first Protestant college in Texas (see Georgetown). Founded in 1840, it was perhaps the first institution of higher education in the state.

Via TX 159/237 east, **Warrenton,** pop. 50, 12 m. exhibits the restored 1869 solid-rock Neece Home, its entire second floor originally a ballroom. There is a large antique shop, as well as a century-old meeting hall, and the 1850 Legal Tender Saloon. Close by is

what has been called the "Smallest Catholic Church in the World." Just beyond, at Florida Chapel Cemetery is the original grave of Joel W. Robison (since reinterred in the State Cemetery in Austin), one of the men who captured Santa Anna after San Jacinto. Farther east is Round Top (see Tour 19).

Via FM 609 southwest 6 m., at **Hostyn,** is a beautiful old church with a garden-like cemetery. A plaque announces the village's claim as the oldest Czech settlement in Texas. In this area also see Smithville, Columbus.

South of La Grange your road travels scenic country, climbing from the Colorado River through great live oaks.

Schulenburg, 91 m.—see Tour 20.
Hallettsville, 108 m.—see Tour 21.
Victoria, 153 m. Enter Region III, South Texas. See Tour 33. Your road continues south as Tour 37.

☆

Tour 30

I-35
Temple-Belton, Salado, Austin, San Antonio, 149 m.

Your southward interstate route continues on its way from the Red River and the metroplex of Dallas-Fort Worth, eventually to Laredo's Mexican border—this leg being the most scenic of that journey. From Temple to San Antonio you run along the foot of Texas "Hill Country"—that low, gray-green wall rising abruptly west is an old fault-line; and your road parallels it. The hilly wall is particularly noticeable from Austin through New Braunfels, for those cities nestle against their hills.

In pioneer days, these ramparts marked the edge of Comancheria, and down from them those horsemen loosed bloody raids on the settlements along this route. Later, the level going below

the hills directed a natural route for the first northbound cattle trails. Today, as you did coming down I-35 from the north, you travel from city to city.

Between the cities lies a gracious countryside, the terrain rolling like billows as you proceed south. At San Antonio you enter Region III, the level reach of South Texas prairie.

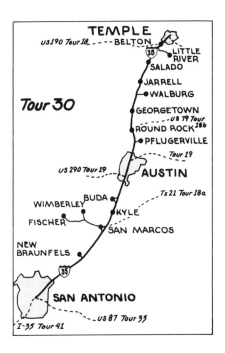

Temple, 0 m.—see Tour 18. Here your road briefly merges with US 190.
Belton, 8 m.—see Tour 18. Veer south from US 190.

Via FM 436 south is **Little River,** pop. 1,390, 7 m. Close by is the site of Smith's Fort, or Fort Griffin, which in 1836 failed to hold this area under continual Indian pressure and the threat of Santa Anna's Texas invasion. In this general region, tradition insists that 10 jackloads of silver bullion are buried. In 1838, a shadowy figure, Karl Steinheimer, left Mexico with treasure from his successful mining venture. Just before he was overtaken by renegades in these wooded bottoms he buried his lode, marked it and disappeared from history. He had managed a letter, however, to his sweetheart in St. Louis, together with a last-minute, hurried map. The courier got through, for in due time the St. Louis treasure hunters appeared, yet after a long search, rode away empty-handed. Over the years to recent times, the Steinheimer treasure has been hunted without known success.

At 12 m. FM 2786 leads to Stillhouse Hollow Lake which, with Lake Belton just north, offers camping and all recreational facilities. Close by Dana Peak Park on the north shore is Comanche Gap, regular route of early Indian raiders.

Salado, 17 m. (alt. 695; pop. 1,216). Old and weathered, this tiny village is a delightful stopover. Laid out by colonizer Sterling C. Robertson in 1838, it was considered as a site for the Texas capital; and much of its story is reflected in the Central Texas Area Museum, where you should begin your tour. Just across, beside shaded Salado Creek where old mills once operated, is Stagecoach Inn dining room. Built around 1838, and famed for its cuisine then as now, it is part of a modern motel today. Almost every illustrious name in Texas history has stopped here, including the infamous Sam Bass. The outlaw allegedly spent the night in a small cave on the grounds just prior to his fatal attempt to rob the Round Rock bank, south of here. Along the Salado banks today is a pretty picnic park.

Salado boasts many historic homes, the most notable being the 22-room, 1854 Sterling C. Robertson House, occupied by the same family for more than a century. Built by the colonizer's son, this is perhaps the only complete plantation unit still standing in Texas—with outbuildings, slave quarters, and cemetery.

Among several other historic homes are Twelve Oaks and the Baines House (that of the grandfather of President Lyndon Baines Johnson). Today, Salado is becoming an arts and crafts center, with an intriguing array of shops and galleries to invite your inspection. Each November, honoring their Central Texas forebears, Salado folks stage their "Gathering of the Scottish Clans of Texas."

Jarrell, 27 m., is a little Czech farming community. Through here, FM 487 follows the approximate route of the old Bartlett (eastward) to Florence (westward) Railroad, abandoned in 1935. Four stations along the line were Matthew, Mark, Luke and John.

At 34 m. intersect FM 972. East 4 m., near Walburg, pop. 250, is the imposing

Holy Trinity Church at a ghost village called New Corn Hill. The lofty twin spires, built in 1913, are visible from your road.

Subterranean stalactites, stalagmites and flow-stones in Inner Space Caverns, Georgetown.

Georgetown, 41 m. (alt. 750; pop. 14,842), centers an area explored early by Spaniards, particularly in the mid-1700s' founding of the San Xavier missions to the east (see Thorndale). The city has an old look around its close-crowding, interestingly Victorian square. East of there is the quiet campus of Southwestern University (Methodist), which in 1877 combined four pioneer Texas Schools—Rutersville (1840), McKenzie (1841), Wesleyan (1844) Colleges, and Soule University (1856), its direct forerunner at Chappell Hill. Georgetown has some 20 handsome old homes and historic buildings dating to the latter 1800s; the pioneer log cabin on Austin Avenue was built in the early 1850s. Just off the square on Church Street is the site of the Elias Talbot home which had an underground tunnel used by slaves escaping the South during the Civil War. Here, immediately prior to Texas secession, representatives of President Lincoln met with those of Sam Houston, offering Federal troops to hold Texas in the Union. Although he bitterly opposed secession and relinquished his governor's seat refusing the Confederate

oath of allegiance, Houston rejected Lincoln's offer on the ground that it would bring additional bloodshed into Texas. At the end he held the position that with dissolution of the Union, Texas returned to her status as a republic, independent of North and South alike. However, he was overridden and retired to Huntsville.

San Gabriel Park, which has seen everything from a Tonkawa Indian village to political speakings as well as hangings, is on the river. Beautiful Inner Space Cavern, recently discovered, is on the south edge of town, and the Mood Heritage Museum, on the university campus, reflects area history back to the Indian. The 16 m. Goodwater Trail for hikers begins at Georgetown Lake, 4 m. west on FM 2338. In this area also see Taylor, San Gabriel.

Round Rock, 51 m. (alt. 720; pop. 30,923), is an old town with a shiny new look, resulting from the booming outspill of Austin population. The general area was colonized in the 1830s with Tumlinson's Fort, just west above Cedar Park (Tour 31), and the 1838 Kenney's Fort (Tour 18B) on the east edge of town. Here occurred both the staging of the Texan Santa Fe Expedition and the Archives War of the 1840s. In the center of 1878 Round Rock, the Sam Bass shootout exploded, the notorious outlaw having led his gang against a bank here. Tipped, Texas Rangers waited and a wild ambushing crossfire killed one outlaw and mortally wounded Bass. He is buried in the old cemetery near the creek—his grave a bizarre tourist attraction. Take Chisholm Trail Road to the source of the city's name—a round tabular rock marking a safe ford.

Round Rock displays many historic old buildings dating to the mid and latter 1800s, and much restoration has been done. Notable are the Chisholm Trail Stage Stop and the Brushy Creek Inn, both immediately east of your road.

The first weekend after July Fourth, the city celebrates Frontier Days, a townwide gala from parades and street dancing to the reenactment of the Sam Bass shootout. In town, the Palm House Museum reflects early Swedish influence in the area. Close by to the west is big, resort-dotted Lake Travis, one of the chain of beautiful Highland Lakes.

At Round Rock, intersect US 79/Tour 18B.

At 56 m., just east via FM 1825, is Pflugerville, pop. 4,444, settled by Germans in 1849 and tiny until swelled by spreading Austin. Beyond 8 m. is New Sweden's beautiful Gothic Lutheran Church with its soaring steeple.

Austin, 69 m.—see Tour 19.

Buda, 84 m. (alt. 716; pop. 1,795), settled in the 1840s, straddles the Old San Antonio road, just west. In rough country beyond, along Onion Creek, legend insists that a spectral Lady in White guards buried treasure, cached in pioneer days.

Kyle, 91 m. (alt. 714; pop. 2,225), is close by the ghost settlement of 1850 Nance's Mill.

San Marcos, 99 m. (alt. 581; pop. 28,743), shaded about its crystalline river, spreads from the foot of the Balcones hills to perch along their rims. Anglo-settled in 1846, its site is much older, being occupied 40 years earlier by a Spanish outpost, San Marcos de Neve, and prior to that in the mid-1700s by temporary Spanish missions, moved from the San Gabriel River (see Thorndale).

Today this sparkling city is home to Southwest Texas State University (20,000). Here also is a beautiful family park at Aquarena Springs, where you can skyride, watch underwater ballets, or tour a crystalline lake in glass-bottom boats. A simulated Indian Village is here and nearby is tourist-oriented Wonder Cave. Downtown, a river walkway connects three parks along the limpid San Marcos River. Aquarena Springs Inn and Crystal River Inn offer attractive lodging.

San Marcos counts a number of historic homes and stately turn-of-the-century mansions—the Merriman and Burleson cabins at Aquarena Springs and, in town, several elegant restorations in the historic district along Belvin, San Antonio, and Hopkins Streets—the focus of an early May heritage tour each year. A River Arts Festival is staged simultaneously with the tour; and in late September San Marcos hosts scores of thousands in its three-day Chilympiad, the state's biggest chili cookoff. At San Marcos intersect TX 21/Tour 18A.

Southeast 2 m. via TX 80 is the wooded river crossing of Camino Real, Spanish-blazed in 1690. Westward, FM 12/32 penetrates delightful Blanco River hill country. At 10 m. FM 12 turns north over a beautiful valley for scenic Wimberley (Tour 19). At 20 m. the Devil's Backbone provides a spectacular panorama of surrounding hills and valleys. Just beyond is Fischer and an intriguing old-time general store. From Fischer via local roads south is one of Texas' most beautifully situated resort-recreation areas—hill-girded Canyon Lake, offering camping and all facilities.

Hunter, 106 m., pop. 30, is a secluded, shady near-ghost on the old highway just west. Along here is the site of an even older ghost—Stringtown, settled in 1847 by Georgians who came in a strung-out wagon train, settling along Camino Real in the same strung-out fashion from the San Marcos to the Guadalupe River at New Braunfels.

New Braunfels, 116 m. (alt. 620; pop. 27,334), is one of Texas' most fascinating little cities, an exceptional blending of the historic and traditional with the handsome new. The city was settled by Prince Carl Solms Braunfels in 1845, heading an aristocratic society of German immigrants. That settlement meant ordeal for the new Texans: arriving during the Mexican War, these colonists were badly supplied on the coast (see Indianola); many had to walk here. Along the way, "pestilent disease" killed them to an estimated number between 1,000 and 3,000. Nevertheless, the city dug in and provided a funnel for all the Hill Country colonization westward, immediately to follow.

Many fascinating old homes, in various Germanic styles, lie along San Antonio and Mill Streets. Sophienburg, Solms Braunfels' "castle," has been preserved as a pioneer museum, and from the Main Plaza, downtown, you should experience the interesting "walking tour" of the old town (C of C maps).

Special events are commonplace here where *Ist das Leben Schoen* (living is beautiful), as New Braunfels' billboards proclaim. Each May the traditional Kindermasken Ball, a children's masquerade since 1864, decks the city with fanciful little costumes and climaxes with a masked ball. In September, the big Comal Country Fair claims status as Texas' second oldest. However, the giant of all is early November's 10-day Wurst-fest, internationally known and attracting a half-million annually.

The Sausage Festival, not without accompaniment of foaming beer, German pastries and dancing to oompah bands, turns New Braunfels into a city-wide German Mardi Gras. It centers on beautifully wooded Landa Park, where immense headsprings form Texas' shortest river, the crystalline Comal—4 m. to its junction with the Guadalupe within the city. This is a water-fun city, with Schlitterbahn (slippery road) Park, an exceptional water-slide for kids of any age. Nearby is another, the Tube Chute. Up the Guadalupe River and along its wooded banks are camps and float-trip facilities. Farther north, by Canyon Lake, an extraordinary number of dinosaur tracks have been discovered. Should you put over in this tourist-oriented city, you might enjoy one of its two historic hostelries, the Faust Hotel or Prince Solms Inn.

Wurstfest *(sausage festival) draws thousands each year to New Braunfels.*

The Museum of Texas Handmade Furniture, the Alamo Classic Car Museum, the Lindheimer home, and a drive-through wildlife ranch round out a multitude of things to see. North, tiny German village of Gruene is restored, with art gallery, winery, restaurants, ice cream parlor, and beer hall, many in historic buildings.

Due west, off FM 1863, is Natural Bridge Caverns, opened in comparatively recent years and massively beautiful in bronze and golds, with many rich formations.

San Antonio, 149 m. Enter Region III, South Texas. See Tour 33. Your route continues south as Tour 41.

☆

Tour 31

US 183

Lampasas, Austin,
Lockhart, Luling,
Gonzales, Cuero, 163 m.

Your tour begins on the eastern edge of the Texas Hill Country and, angling just east of south, descends through rough, rolling terrain to emerge on prairie land at Austin. From there, through Lockhart and Luling, you travel an old northbound leg of the Chisholm Trail and end at one of the early herd gathering grounds at Cuero. From Austin to Luling, the gently rolling countryside is relatively open, its timber standing in motts. However, the last part of your journey descends the San Marcos and Guadalupe valleys and is accordingly wooded.

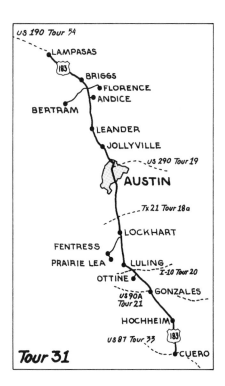

From Austin southward you follow also a trail of unusual and early violence. In 1840, the Comanche launched their most audacious strike against Texas—a

raid following your road from the hills all the way to coastal Port Lavaca (Region III). Their return by the same route met disaster at the Battle of Plum Creek, near Lockhart.

US 183 continues Tour 54 from Region IV, or Tour 17 from Region I.

Lampasas, 0 m.—see Tour 18.

Below Briggs at 25 m., FM 243 leads south to **Bertram,** 13 m. (alt. 1,268; pop. 849), a ranching center. Close by, the Oatmeal schoolhouse marks the site of that community's ghost which, in 1852, vied closely with Burnet for county seat. Each September, the town holds a fun-filled "Oatmeal Festival." Here also was the location of 1851 Black's Fort, a stone and wood stockade defending against the Comanche. In the area, dinosaur tracks may be found along the San Gabriel River.

Via TX 195 east, **Florence,** 6 m. (alt. 980; pop. 829), has an understandably time-worn look: it survived the 1848 Indian frontier. Several interesting old rock homes still stand; and to the east on Salado Creek, a gold mill operated for a time in 1883. Florence once boasted an interesting railroad (see Bartlett).

Andice, 31 m. is immediately east of Mt. Gabriel, the area's highest elevation and a longtime trailmarker as "Pilot's Knob." The knob is a small volcanic extrusion.

Leander, 45 m. (alt. 983; pop. 3,398), grew in the late 1800s from one of the region's earliest colonization efforts, Fort Tumlinson, which held on briefly in 1836. This area was hit hard several times by the Comanche, an entire pioneer family massacred close by.

Above **Jollyville,** 52 m., pop. 15,206, FM 620 leads southwest to big, hill-walled Lake Travis, 20 m., one of the major scenic Highland Lakes, and to handsome resort areas all about. At the west end of massive Mansfield Dam, an overlook provides a view of the Colorado gorge and an idea of the depth of this blue expanse of water. On the lake side is the Mansfield Recreation Area, with all facilities. Just beyond is the plush resort of Lakeway and the Lakeway World of Tennis, site of many national tourneys.

Austin, 68 m.—see Tour 19.

At 75 m., Pilot Knob, a low elevation westward is a long-extinct volcano with a three-quarter-mile crater—difficult to distinguish in the surrounding farmland.

FM 620 rolling through the hills between Lakes Austin and Travis.

At 78 m., McKinney Falls State Park, just west, provides camping and all recreational facilities. Ruins of an early gristmill and an Indian rock shelter add interest. At Mendoza, 88 m., intersect TX 21/Tour 18A.

Lockhart, 98 m. (alt. 518; pop. 9,205), centers its quaint downtown square about a flamboyant 1893 courthouse. Buildings around the square are being preserved.

On rich, rolling land, the little city which calls itself "the seedbin of Texas" began as Plum Creek, an 1840 settlement. It was destined to witness a major Indian battle but also, from the beginning, to grow from the rich land. Post Civil War days saw this become a principal trail convergence for the great Chisholm-bound cattle herds. So much a trail town, it was Emerson Hough's site for his novel, *North of Thirty-Six.*

Today the city claims the oldest continually used library in Texas in its Italian-styled, red brick Eugene Clark Library (1900). The beautifully maintained Emmanuel Episcopal Church (1854–56) is believed to be Texas' oldest protestant church still in unaltered use. The Caldwell County Museum, in old jail, reflects the city's colorful history. One story relates to famed Methodist circuit rider, Andrew Jackson Potter, who taught himself to read with the Bible and changed from a gambler-gunhand to the minister for pioneer West Texas. For his fearlessness known as the "Fighting Parson," Potter preached—pistol by his Book—in every frontier fort, cow camp and saloon on the Texas frontier. At age 65 in a Lockhart pulpit, he finished his last sermon quietly, closed his Bible, sat down and died.

Just southwest are the rolling hills of Lockhart State Park (camping and all recreational facilities) near where, in the summer of 1840, the decisive Battle of Plum Creek was fought. In that summer, retaliating for their losses at San Antonio's Council House Fight, the Comanche swept some 1,000 horsemen in a lightning strike from the hills above Austin all the way to coastal Port Lavaca. Retreating, the Comanche were hit hard and were badly defeated here. The battle broke the back of Comanche domination in South Texas, driving those warriors toward the High Plains.

Early each May, Lockhart celebrates Chisholm Trail Roundup and climaxes festivities with a reenactment of the Plum Creek battle.

Via FM 20 south 11 m., **Fentress,** pop. 85, and neighboring **Prairie Lea,** pop. 100, are tiny, drowsy villages beautifully situated along the timbered San Marcos River. Prior to the Civil War, this area was rich in handsome plantations; it was devastated during the reconstruction period and never quite recovered.

Luling, 113 m.—see Tour 20. Via TX 80 immediately south on the San Marcos River is the historic old Zedler Mill and home.

At 121 m., near tiny **Ottine,** pop. 90, is heavily timbered Palmetto State Park (camping and all facilities), a strange swampland for this temperate-zone prairie. The park is notable for palmetto palms and bubbling mineral springs. Known since Spanish days, legend holds the jungle-like area haunted by the ghosts of a fleeing Indian band who tried

to cross the bogs near the river and were sucked under to their deaths. Today, the park is crossed by excellent scenic trails. At Ottine is the Gonzales Warm Springs Foundation, or Texas Rehabilitation Center. Visitors are welcome.

Gonzales, 130 m.—see Tour 21.

Hochheim, 147 m., pop. 70, is a tiny old German community, known locally in early days as "Dutchtown." At the turn of the century, Hochheim boasted a flourishing school, an athletic building, and its own fire insurance company.

Concrete, 154 m., pop. 46, is a near ghost that was once a prospering community close by the Guadalupe River. It took its name from early-day concrete houses and at its peak, Concrete College (Baptist), with dormitories for boys and for girls, was Texas' largest boarding school, and offered—along with strict discipline—a wide range of courses. Railroad by-pass, at Cuero, caused the town's decline.

Cuero, 163 m. Enter Region III, South Texas—see Tour 33.

☆

Tour 32

US 281
*Lampasas,
Burnet, Marble Falls,
Johnson City, Blanco, San
Antonio, 124 m.*

Your southward route, a continuation of Tour 17, Region I, is one of Texas' most scenic—more inspiring than spectacular, for it unfolds vista after vista of hill-rimmed distance. From Lampasas to Burnet the terrain billows in long, sweeping slopes. From there through Marble Falls to Johnson City, wide valleys enfold crystalline streams and their clear, deep Highland Lakes.

This is Texas' Central Mineral Region, geologically the oldest, and a trea-

sure trove for rock and mineral collectors—granites, marbles, azurite, galena, quartz and agate. Traces of precious metals have been found.

Below Johnson City you leave the granite hills behind and the terrain becomes gentler toward Blanco. There you descend gradually from the Hill Country to San Antonio and the prairies southward.

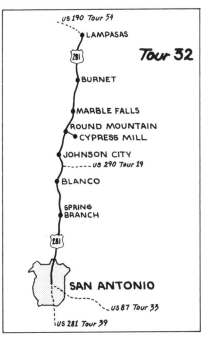

Lampasas, 0 m.—see Tour 18.

Burnet, 22 m. (alt. 1,319; pop. 3,423), is a gateway to the Highland Lakes, resting as it does just east of broad, blue Lake Buchanan and smaller Roy Inks Lake. A resort center, Burnet presents a fresh, clean look, but it is old, growing up around frontier Fort Croghan in 1849–55, when outpost-guarding Texas Rangers were replaced by U.S. dragoons. In early years this was a region of Indian trouble, one story relating a battle between rangers and the Comanche in the pitch dark of a cave.

The region's handsome granite and marble have long been known. Just south of the city, the old Holland quarries supplied a block of marble in the 1880s for Texas' contribution to the Washington Monument.

Today, Burnet maintains a museum at the Fort Croghan site featuring restored log and stone buildings, old guns, carriages, and furniture. Early each April, when

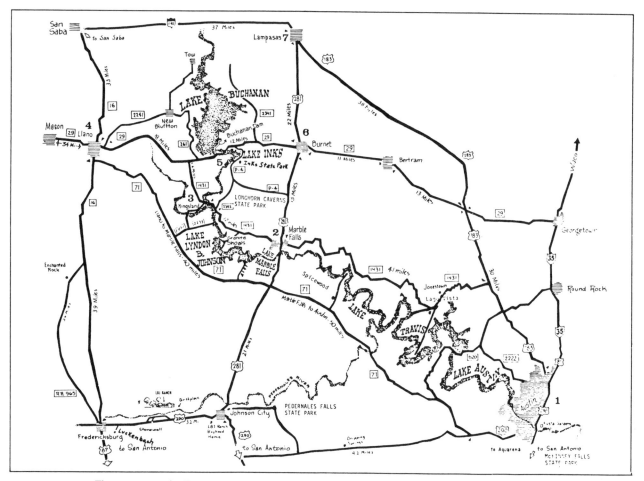

The stage is set for Texas at the peak of perfection during the bluebonnet season in the Hill Country.

wildflowers blanket its countryside, the city is a host for the two-weekend Highland Lakes Bluebonnet Trails. Late July sees the Burnet County Fair; and mid-August, the Texas Old Time Fiddlers Association Contest.

Toward Llano on TX 29 10 m. lies the beautiful blue expanse of Lake Buchanan (first of the Highland chain). Two parks—Black Rock and Burnet County—offer facilities for camping, fishing, swimming, and boating. Here also is Vanishing Texas River Cruises—a 60-foot enclosed boat that explores the upper lake and allows a view of Hill Country wildlife and scenery, including the winter nesting grounds of the American Bald Eagle.

Just below Buchanan is smaller but pretty Inks Lake and a fine state park, with every facility for camping, as well as a sporty 9-hole golf course and a 7 m. hiking trail. Some of Texas' most scenic drives (R.M. 2341, 2342) explore the

granite-girt lake country, and are spectacular in the flowering spring.

A scenic drive on Park Road 4 at Inks Lake near Burnet.

West of your road at 27 m. is Longhorn Caverns State Park. The caverns, handsome with milky-white walls and many formations, are extensive—

more than 11 miles known. Only a portion, well-lighted and easy-graded, is toured. Signs of occupation by primitive man have been found, and Sam Bass, the outlaw, is believed to have used the cave for a hideout.

At 30 m., immediately east is the pretty site of Mormon Mills, a secluded valley and waterfall on Hamilton Creek. The colony was founded by Lyman Wight, who split from Utah-bound cavalcades to seek Zion in Texas. His people stopped briefly on the Red River near Denison, and again near Austin, then close by neighboring Fredericksburg, where a flood wiped out their settlement in 1850. They then moved here for two years—their cemetery remains—finally settling near Bandera, to the south. Their journeys left a strong foundation for their church in the Texas Hill Country.

Marble Falls, 36 m. (alt. 764; pop. 4,007), nestles beside its lake in the steep Colorado River Valley—a mid-point in the chain of scenic Highland Lakes that extend along this river down to Austin. Immediately above is Lake Lyndon B. Johnson (formerly Granite Shoals), then Roy Inks and Buchanan. Below are big Lake Travis, Lake Austin and Town Lake.

Here rockhounds join hunters, fishermen, boating enthusiasts and campers to make this a year-round outdoor resort; many camps and resorts dot the shores of the neighboring lakes. The restored (circa 1880) Roper House is an intriguing country restaurant, handsomely-turned out.

Just west looms Granite Mountain, a huge dome covering 180 acres. From here in the 1880s the red granite for the Texas capitol, and later for the Galveston seawall, was quarried.

South of town your road climbs steeply from the valley, and a scenic overlook yields an impressive view of the city below and the hilly country all about. There is a memorial here to Oscar J. Fox who, gazing from these heights, was inspired to compose his classic "Hills of Home." For spectacular scenery, FM 1431 offers some breathtaking views both northwest and southeast.

At **Round Mountain,** 47 m. FM 962 leads east to **Cypress Mill,** 7 m., pop. 56, secluded on scenic Cypress Creek. Once Blanco County's largest community, Cypress Mill lost its contest for county seat and today remains almost unchanged.

Johnson City, 59 m. (alt. 1,197; pop. 932), occupying a sweeping reach of the Pedernales Valley, took its name from the pioneer Johnson family, ancestors of late President Lyndon B. Johnson.

The family home, where young Lyndon lived while attending public school, is maintained by the National Park Service as the Lyndon B. Johnson National Historic Site, scene of daily guided tours. Home is furnished with Johnson family items, period furniture. Nearby is the Johnson Settlement, original farmstead of the President's grandfather. Living history activities interpret farm life of the 1870s. West of here is the President's ranch, heart of LBJ Country (Tour 55).

President Lyndon B. Johnson's grandfather settled in this log house in Johnson City.

At 65 m., intersect US 290/Tour 19.

Blanco, 73 m. (alt. 1,350; pop. 1,238), is a quiet little town of white-washed stone that seems pleased not only with its scenic setting but also with the paradox of its small size despite nearness to metropolitan San Antonio and Austin. The town grew in 1858 from the settlement of Pittsburg, absorbing that cross-river settlement. Its square and old courthouse still stand, doing other than county business after Johnson City—in its third attempt—captured the seat.

The clear-running Blanco River, Blanco State Park.

Immediately south, on sparkling Blanco River, small but pretty Blanco State Park offers camping and all recreational facilities. Toward San Marcos, southeast on TX 32 and 12, lie some beautiful scenic views, particularly those reaching from spectacular Devil's Backbone, south of Wimberley.

Spring Branch, 89 m. At this village, FM 311 leads eastward to the upper end of hill-flanked Canyon Lake, with all recreational facilities.

Just west where Comal and Kendall Counties adjoin is scenic Guadalupe River State Park, 1,900 acres along the wooded Guadalupe River, offering camping and all facilities.

San Antonio, 124 m. Enter Region III, South Texas. See Tour 33. Your route continues south as Tour 39.

☆

Region III
Tours 33 through 43

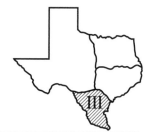

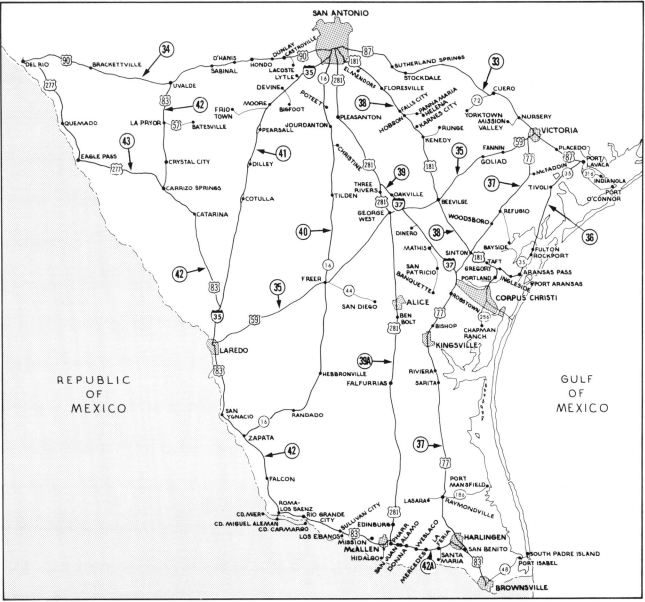

Tour 33

US 87
Port Lavaca, Victoria,
Cuero, San Antonio, 141 m.

Climbing from the coast to San Antonio, this brief tour is more pastoral than scenic. It crosses a gentle land, one that is more wooded than forested, dappled with small farms and, for the most part, small towns. It is spectacular only when spring carpets the countryside with bluebonnets and paintbrush.

The road is storied, though, connecting, as it does, two of the earliest Spanish settlements in Texas. You begin at Spain's early 1700s Matagorda Bay beachhead, close by Port Lavaca (later to become fortress La Bahia at Goliad), and travel to the mission outpost of San Antonio. The general route is almost as old as more famed Camino Real to the northeast.

In the 1840s, the road again assumed importance. Up from Indianola came the great flood of immigrants—Germans, Czechs, Poles—most of them walking to new homes within the interior. Along this road, deaths were by hundreds—poor supplies, illness, hunger, exhaustion—but the new Texans settled the river valleys, pushed on to San Antonio and beyond into the Texas Hill Country.

Port Lavaca, 0 m. (alt. 19; pop. 10,886), on the upper reaches (Lavaca Bay) of broad Matagorda Bay, is an old seaport that today is as much a fisherman's resort as it is an industrial center and shipper, with its nearby Alcoa and Union Carbide plants.

The town occupies a site almost identical to earlier Linnville. That tiny pioneer port, founded in 1831, was destroyed nine years later in a sweeping Comanche raid that drove from the hills above Austin all the way to this coast. Inhabitants were either cut down or escaped by clinging to boats offshore, watching Linnville burn. The Comanche later were routed near Lockhart (Tour 31).

Port Lavaca was built the following year and enjoyed substantial shipping until tides in Matagorda Bay clogged its channel. Today with its long beaches southward, its bay for saltwater fishing, a

solid industrial base and rich rice farming inland, the city reflects a glistening, prospering atmosphere, and a leisurely pace in living. There are excellent seafood restaurants. The old (1858) Halfmoon Reef Lighthouse, once on Matagorda Bay, has been moved to stand watch beside the city's C of C.

On Memorial Day weekend, in their Annual Texas Sea Fest, Port Lavacans simmer shrimp gumbo, bless the fleet, windsurf, water ski and dance on broad Magnolia Beach. In late September, the Calhoun County Fair sets up shop. In town near courthouse, Calhoun County Museum reflects this coast's history. Nearby is a long, lighted state park fishing pier (Tour 27). Just west, Green Lake is a haven for birdwatchers, and the site of Old Indianola southward (Tour 36) is an intriguing if tragic ghost from the past. At Port Lavaca, intersect TX 35/Tour 27 east; Tour 36 west.

Placedo, 14 m. pop. 515 is a rambling crossroads town. Via FM 616 east is the site (private land) of the lost French fort, founded in 1685 by La Salle (Tour 27).

Victoria, 25 m. (alt. 93; pop. 55,076 city), set away from its busy, bisecting highways, displays grace and beauty in homes and churches where age has worn well, and in a business center where considerable wealth makes no attempt at showiness. The city occupies one of Texas' most historic areas.

Long crisscrossed by Spanish explorers, Victoria grew from an 1824 colony grant to Don Martin de Leon, his settlement later augmented by German, Irish and Anglo American colonists. The little town survived partial burning in the Texan retreat from nearby Goliad, occupation by Mexican forces after the massacre of Fannin's men at Goliad, a savage 1840 Indian attack, and an even more deadly 1846 cholera epidemic. Later the town became a major stop on the old Indianola-San Antonio road, and

in its area are some of Texas' earliest cattle ranches.

Victoria's Memorial Square, with its picturesque old courthouse, its old bandstand and ornamental lamp posts, adds charm to the downtown area. The square includes graves of pioneers and a historic wind-driven gristmill which ground corn for German farmers before the Civil War.

Along Liberty and Glass Streets are a number of elegant old homes. The McNamara Museum, a handsome 1870 house, recollects the city's history and displays fine arts. Alongside the Guadalupe, Riverside Park is spacious and wooded and houses the Texas Zoo, native animals, birds and reptiles. The Nave Museum holds works of Texas artist of the 1920s Royston Nave, who included many area scenes in his canvases.

The *Victoria Advocate,* founded in 1846, is Texas' second oldest paper.

Nearby, also see Edna, La Salle, Goliad. At Victoria intersect US 59/-Tour 25, east, Tour 35, west; US 77/-Tour 29, north, Tour 37, south.

At **Nursery,** 35 m., pop. 106, FM 447/236 leads west to **Mission Valley,** pop. 208, a secluded village on old land. Close by are the faint ruins (private land) of mission-fortress La Bahia's second location. La Bahia was originally located on Matagorda Bay, where, in 1689, Spain found the ruined outpost of La Salle and built her own, the La Bahia establishment—Mission Nuestra Senora del Espiritu Santo de Zuniga and its guarding Presidio Nuestra Senora de Loreto de la Bahia. The mission-fort was moved here 36 years later and remained almost a quarter century, attempting to cope with the savage Karankawa Indians while at the same time blocking French coastal pressure. Finally it was permanently based at the site of present-day Goliad.

Cuero, 53 m. (alt. 177; pop. 6,700), is a clean, handsome town, with broad streets and great, moss-hung trees. Founded in 1846, it began to prosper as an assembly ground for northbound cattle drives. Since 1912 it has become famed as home of the Cuero Turkey Trot, a festival observing the town's claim as "Turkey Capital of the World." A highlight of the gala, when Cuero literally takes to the streets, is the turkey race, with Cuero's Texas speedster, "Ruby Begonia," challenging any comer and, most particularly, the Worthington, Minnesota entry, "Paycheck."

Turkey Trot time in Cuero.

St. Marks Lutheran Church, downtown, is a favorite for photos. One of its three bells once rang above the old seaport town of Indianola (Tour 36). Stolen by Federal troops, it was recovered and buried by Confederates, finally to be disinterred and moved here.

The De Witt County Historic Museum reflects Cuero's past, some of it violent.

Southwest 3 m. on the Guadalupe River is the ghost of **Clinton,** county seat before Cuero and principal site of Texas' bloodiest feud—the Taylor-Sutton blood-letting responsible for scores of deaths—by shootout, ambush or lynching. Beginning in 1869 with the killing of two Taylors, the feud essentially aligned unreconstructed Southern Taylors against reconstruction forces backing the Suttons; and it took its toll until

1876. There is little trace of Clinton today.

Via TX 72 west 17 m., **Yorktown** (alt. 266; pop. 2,207) is a town of homes, churches and big oaks. German-settled, it is notable for building around a long meadow-like commons rather than a typical Texas plaza or square. There is a historical museum and the third weekend of each October, Yorktown observes Western Days, including a carnival and a pig scramble, and climaxing with a western dance.

Stockdale, 100 m. (alt. 430; pop. 1,268), is an agricultural center originally settled by Germans and Czechs. Its area produces excellent watermelons. Nearby, Panna Maria and Helena are interesting.

Sutherland Springs, 107 m. (alt. 423; pop. 114), is a drowsy little village resting beside the ghost of its earlier days. Settled in the 1860s by plantation owners, this was a popular spa in horse-and-buggy days, moved to its present location by railroad by-pass in 1893. Nearby is handsome cutstone two-story Polley Mansion, built in 1854. Robert E. Lee was entertained in the great home's heyday, and wrote his last letter from Texas here.

San Antonio, 141 m. (alt. 701; pop. 935,933 city). Rightly termed by Will Rogers one of America's four unique cities, this old Spanish town meanders leisurely to the foot of hill country northwestward, clustering its downtown about the extraordinarily pretty and winding San Antonio River ("Drunk old man going home at night," to Indians), showcased with a beautiful riverwalk.

Founded in 1718 as a way station on the road to east Texas missions near Nacogdoches, its original Mission San Antonio de Valero and guarding presidio were located near San Pedro Springs, today a park. Moved twice, the first adobe and thatch church became world-famed in 1836 as the Alamo. Four other missions gradually developed along the river southward, while downtown Military and Main Plaza, with San Fernando Church between them, centered colonization by Spanish Canary Islanders.

From this grew the later little village, La Villita, and on the plaza was finally built the Governor's Palace, handsomely restored today.

Probably more embattled than any other American city, San Antonio fought

The Alamo, San Antonio, scene of one of history's most heroic battles, Feb. 23–March 6, 1836.

long for existence: against Apache and Comanche, then—to remain Spanish—against Mexican and American filibusters in 1812–13. In 1836 came the Texas Revolution—capture by Texans and subsequent storming of the Alamo by Santa Anna. On the plaza opposite San Fernando Cathedral, a plaque notes the site of the bloody Council House Fight which in 1840 began a 35-year war with the Comanche. From 1841–42, the city saw Mexican counter-attack but was recaptured by Texans at the Battle of Salado. Other minor fights encompassed San Antonio.

Today the city maintains a military posture—its Fort Sam Houston is one of America's largest military installations (the first Army Air Corps flights began here); Fort Sam's old quadrangle and belltower are scenic and storied—Geronimo and the remnant of his Apache braves were confined here; and here, on Dec. 7, 1941, Brigadier General Dwight D. Eisenhower learned that the United States was at war. Nearly every American flyer has known Kelly and Brooks Fields, and World War II's aces trained at outlying Randolph Field. Lackland Field is today's Air Force Basic Training Center.

A city of many celebrations, its best-known is the late April Fiesta of San Antonio, which began with an 1891 Battle of Flowers and has grown to a 10-day Texas version of Mardi Gras. Each Easter the Starving Artists Show is held at La Villita and along the riverwalk, a center of tourism. Early August brings the Texas Folklife Festival. The big Livestock Show and Rodeo, in February, converges trail riders from across all south and central Texas. Other notable festivals include the Great Country River Festival in September, the San Antonio Festival in June and the Holiday River Festival in December.

In and around downtown (C of C maps available) are scores of historic buildings, including the Cos House and the Navarro State Historic Site, the Yturri-Edmunds Historic Site, San Fernando Cathedral, the Majestic Theatre, and the shrine of Texas liberty, the Alamo. The King William Historic District, first such in the state, contains homes of some of the city's early movers and shakers.

Perhaps San Antonio's most intriguing attraction lies one level below its downtown streets. El Paseo del Rio (The River Walk) meanders beneath graceful palms and big cypress trees, past tropical greenery and under arched bridges. Here are gift shops and boutiques, pubs, sidewalk cafes and cantinas; or you can dine on a barge cruising the river. The walk leads to La Villita, one of the most exceptional preservations in America: The Village literally whisks you into the Mexico of another century.

The River Walk in San Antonio.

Second in tourist interest only to the Alamo is Mission Trail, beginning with Mission Concepcion, with its twin towers and extraordinary construction (little restoration has been needed), moved here from East Texas in 1731. Next is San Jose, 1720, "Queen of New Spain's Missions," with its magnificent doorway and rose window, its cloisters, mill, circular oak-hewn belfry stairway, all surrounded by a quarter-mile fortress wall lined with Indian dwellings and threaded by an excellent self-guiding tour. All four missions are part of the San Antonio Missions National Historical Park. Two, San

Francisco and San Juan, are active churches today, many of their parishioners descendants of the first Indian converts. Close by San Francisco is the old, still functioning Spanish Aqueduct—the only one in America—which long ago irrigated mission fields. Remarkable engineering leads river water high over a nearby creek.

San Antonio's downtown skyline is dominated by the Tower of the Americas, topped by an observation deck and revolving restaurant, and centering the grounds of HemisFair, now the city's primary civic center. On the plaza is the excellent Institute of Texan Cultures, portraying this state's varied ethnology.

Brackenridge Park is big and scenic. The Botanical Center reflects the entire Texas landscape. The Hertzberg Circus Collection contains some 20,000 items of rare big-top memorabilia; while Hangar Nine at Brooks Air Field displays the story of manned flight. At the Lone Star Brewery, famed old Buckhorn Saloon is remindful of San Antonio's early cattledrive and guntown days. El Mercado and Market Square offer shopping for imports and fine dining.

Mini-Tour Guide

Alamo Cenotaph: Pompeo Coppini monument to Alamo heroes. Opposite, on plaza.

Brackenridge Park and Zoo: Enter from Broadway or N. St. Marys.

Buckhorn Hall of Horns: Lone Star Brewery, 600 Lone Star Blvd.

Botanical Gardens: 555 Funston.

Eastside Cemeteries: Resting place of many famous Texans. E. Commerce St.

Fiesta Texas: Musical show park. I-10 W. at Loop 1604.

Hall of Texas History & Wax Museum: 600 Lone Star Blvd.

HemisFair Plaza: East edge, downtown.

Hertzberg Circus Collection: 210 W. Market.

Institute of Texan Cultures: HemisFair Plaza.

King William District: 19th Century homes. Durango and S. St. Marys.

La Villita: Classic restored Mexican village. S. Alamo and Nueva.

McNay Art Institute: 6000 N. New Braunfels.

El Mercado: Intriguing Mexican market. Commerce and Santa Rosa.

Mexican Cultural Institute: Contemporary artistry. HemisFair Plaza.

Military Bases: Among America's larg-

est. Include Ft. Sam Houston, Brooks Air Force Base, Kelly Air Force Base, Lackland Air Force Base, Randolph Air Force Base. See Visitor Information Center, below.

Missions: Include Concepcion, San Jose, San Francisco, San Juan. See Mission Trail, Visitor Information Center, below.

Museum of Art: 200 W. Jones Ave.

Museum of Transportation: HemisFair Plaza.

Navarro State Historic Site: 228 S. Laredo.

River Walk: Beautiful. Many street accesses include Alamo Plaza.

Sea World: Marine park. Off TX 151 northwest of downtown.

Southwest Craft Center: 300 Augusta

Spanish Governor's Palace: 1749 seat of Spanish government in Texas. Military Plaza.

Witte Museum: Natural history, science. 3801 Broadway.

Visitor Information Center: Start here. Good maps. 317 Alamo Plaza.

Trinity and St. Mary's Universities and the University of Texas at San Antonio top the city's array of educational institutions, offering all cultural and athletic events.

At the convergence of Regions II, III, and IV, San Antonio is a point of intersection for many routes. In Region II, Southeast Texas, intersect US 281/Tour 32; I-35/Tour 30; I-10/Tour 20. In Region III, South Texas, intersect US 181/Tour 38; US 281/Tour 39; TX 16/Tour 40; I-35 south/Tour 41; US 90 west/Tour 34. In Region IV, West Texas, intersect I-10 west/Tour 56.

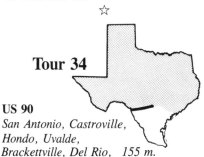

Tour 34

US 90
San Antonio, Castroville, Hondo, Uvalde, Brackettville, Del Rio, 155 m.

West of San Antonio, as far as Del Rio and the Devil's River beyond, your route follows that of the mid-1800s military road, the most southerly protected route of America's California-bound Forty-Niners. However, as with most of our highways, you actually follow an old Indian trail. This one was put to use by Spain and, later, Mexico, as the eastern leg of the Chihuahua Trail, a wide-looping road to bring treasure from the central Mexican mountains to Gulf ports, via San Antonio.

Throughout, the terrain is laced with mesquite, while heavy bottom timber flanks the clear-running or dry-bed streams along your way. From San Antonio to Uvalde, the land is gently rolling while low hills appear here and there. Beyond Uvalde, those hills grow to mesas, and to the southwest the gray mountains of Mexico loom in the distance. You can sense that shortly they will reach northward to confront you.

This is the country of the easternmost Apache—the early-1700s Lipan. It is also a land flavored with descendants of the early Spaniards who sought to subdue it. Your way is dotted with farms across to Uvalde; it is ranchland beyond.

San Antonio, 0 m.—see Tour 33. Continue west on US 90.

Castroville, 25 m. (alt. 787; pop. 2,159), is a visiting "must," the delightful "Little Alsace of Texas." In an area crossed by 1689 Spanish explorers who named its clear green river Medina, this pecan-shaded, Old-World town goes its own quiet way as it has ever since ignoring a railroad in 1880. Alsatian-settled in 1844 by Henri Castro, a French colonizer-philanthropist, the settlement was then the westernmost in Texas and fought for survival through drought, plague (cholera), and unrelenting Indian warfare, its sturdy farmers plowing with a gun ready at either end of their fields. Today it is a jewel box of old buildings, tall-steepled churches and peak-roofed homes, a village little changed since its beginnings.

Most interesting are the beautifully-restored Landmark Inn (state park operated), the St. Louis Catholic Church, Henri Castro Homestead, Carle House and Store, and the great arched galleries of the Moye Retreat Center. Landmark Inn,

Alsatian music and dancing at the Landmark Inn, Castroville.

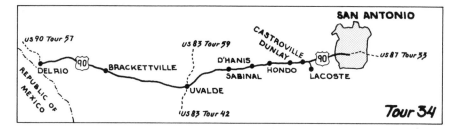

SAN ANTONIO

US 90 Tour 57

DEL RIO

BRACKETTVILLE

US 83 Tour 59

D'HANIS

CASTROVILLE
DUNLAY

US 87 Tour 33

SABINAL   HONDO

REPUBLIC OF MEXICO

UVALDE

LACOSTE

US 83 Tour 42

Tour 34

a frontier stage stop, was luxurious with its lead-lined bathtub; and the 1869 church is directly beside its original little stone chapel built by Castroville's first settlers. Virtually every corner of this village displays a quaint original or handsome restoration.

Home pilgrimages occur on even-numbered years, but Castroville's big event is the St. Louis Parish Homecoming, the Sunday nearest each August 25, when population here leaps above 20,000 and more than six tons of barbecue and sausage disappear. A pretty park, all facilities including camping, flanks the big-shaded and clear Medina River.

South 6 m. via FM 471, the village of **La Coste,** pop. 1,021, displays Our Lady of Grace Catholic Church with great Gothic arches and stained glass. Keller's Place is an oldtime tavern with a thousand odds and ends in collection.

Via FM 471 north 28 m. (Region IV), scenic **Medina Lake** is one of Texas' oldest and provides all facilities, good fishing.

Immediately west of Castroville, Cross Hill offers a fine panoramic overlook.

Just north of Dunlay, 31 m., are the tiny villages of **Quihi,** pop. 96, and ghostly **New Fountain,** Alsatian settlements that closely followed Castroville's establishment. The restored Metzger Stage Stop is a private home. Here also are many old rock homes and stately Bethlehem Lutheran Church.

Hondo, 41 m. (alt. 901; pop. 6,018), is a thriving little city in the midst of fertile farmland. Since 1930, a city limits sign has greeted travelers: "This is God's Country, Please Don't Drive Through It Like Hell." The old Southern Pacific depot is now an exceptional Medina County Historical Museum, and an alert C of C has mapped four intriguing tours of the historic county—this is the place to begin any exploration of the old Alsatian countryside. Early each May, Medina County Museum Day is cele-

brated, along with Hondo's World Champion Corn Shucking Contest. Just southwest (4.5 m.) is the 777 Exotic Game Ranch, while to the north on FM 462 23 m., the rocky bed of Hondo Creek shows clear indentations of once larger game—40-foot dinosaurs.

D'Hanis, 50 m. (alt. 881; pop. 506), founded in 1847, is known to old-timers as "New D'Hanis," for the original ghost lies a mile east, the town having moved to the railroad. Interestingly, even "New D'Hanis" has an old look. Just on the north side of town is a famous old brick plant; a city street divides huge beehive kilns from stacks of fired bricks.

Sabinal, 61 m. (alt. 956; pop. 1,584), grew up in weathered stone buildings around the site of an 1850 army post and hung on after the troopers left. North via FM 187 (Region IV) the Lost Maples of Sabinal Canyon (now a pretty state park with all facilities, its maples flaming red each fall) occupy spectacular hill country.

Uvalde, 83 m. (alt. 913; pop. 14,729), is a brisk little city, distinguished by a broad plaza landscaped with palm trees and spreading out under great pecan shade. Settled in 1853 under the protective guns of Fort Inge (1849–69), Uvalde was an Indian-fighter prior to the Civil War and a gunfighter afterwards. Just south was the home of John King Fisher, a fast gun who put up a road-fork sign: "This is King Fisher's Road; take the other." For a time, famed lawman Pat Garrett lived here.

Here also is the home and museum of former vice President John Nance (Cactus Jack) Garner, whose collection of gavels is unusual and whose suggestion of the cactus rose as Texas' state flower earned his nickname. More recently, Uvalde is home of former Governor Dolph Briscoe. The town takes its name from a Spanish Captain Juan de Ugalde, who defeated Indians in 1790 in a series of engagements in the Nueces canyons to the north. Uvalde is southern gateway to secnic Tri Canyon vacationland in the hills above (Sabinal, Nueces and Frio—see Leakey/Tour 60). It also considers itself "Honey Capital of the World." Its restored Grand Opera House (1890) is open for tours. Performances there are turn-of-the-century oriented.

At Fort Inge, just south, General Lew Wallace worked at a first draft of his famed novel, *Ben Hur.* Only a site marker remains.

Each May, Uvalde stages quarter horse races, and each June, a barbecue cookoff. At Uvalde is the intersection of US 90 and US 83, nation's two longest highways. At Uvalde intersect US 83/Tour 42 south, Tour 59 north.

Brackettville, 123 m. (alt. 1,110; pop. 1,740), lies beside green Las Moras Springs, an oasis in western brush country. This saucer-shaped valley saw early Spanish exploration during Spain's search for La Salle. Here, in 1688, Spain found one French survivor living as an Indian king. The presence of the big springs brought Fort Clark, a cavalry post in 1852, and this town shortly thereafter, as a stage stop. In town, St. Mary Magdalene Church dates from 1878 and the Masonic Lodge Building, a year later.

Fort Clark, on the hill above the deeply shaded Las Moras, knew a long career as an active and distinguished cavalry post, serving as recently as WW II, finally deactivated in 1946. One of its more famous episodes involved America's most relentless Indian fighter, Col. Ranald S. Mackenzie. In 1871, ordered to follow his own judgment but to destroy raiding Lipan and Kickapoo warriors, Mackenzie located their villages 80 miles deep into Mexico. On his own initiative, he drove into Mexico, destroyed the villages and returned, his men never leaving the saddle and unaware they had "invaded" foreign soil. "Suppose we had refused?" asked one outraged officer. "I would have had you shot," Mackenzie retorted.

In excellent preservation today, the fort and surrounding grounds function as a retirement and vacation community privately owned by its members.

The Seminole Indian Scout Cemetery, 3 m. south, is historic. These Seminoles were descended from slaves stolen by Florida Indians; in the west they performed distinguished service as scouts. Here are buried some Congressional Medal of Honor winners.

Northwest 6 m. is **Alamo Village,** built as a set for the John Wayne movie depicting the Battle of the Alamo and site now for many other movies. Completely authentic, the setting includes the fortress-mission, cantina, restaurant, trading post, Wells Fargo station and saddle shop, plus several other Old West buildings. Shootouts and stagecoach rides are featured each day. The cantina stages regular Western-style entertainment, open daily.

The western-style family recreation center at Alamo Village, Brackettville.

South via FM 693, near the Las Moras confluence with Rio Grande, is the traceless site of **Dolores,** the doomed 1834 English colony of John Charles Beales. Too remote, drought- and Indian-beset, the colony disintegrated, its last settlers fleeing before Santa Anna's advance. At Lake Espantosa, east on the old San Antonio road (Tour 42), the men were killed; the women and children were taken prisoner by the Comanche, some later ransomed at Santa Fe.

Beyond Brackettville, your road crosses empty country dotted here an there with a windmill and an occasional field; you are into ranch country. You enter Del Rio by the ancient trail routes, making directly for historic San Felipe Springs (Tour 57).

Del Rio, 155 m. Enter Region IV, West Texas. See Tour 57, a continuation of your route westward.

☆

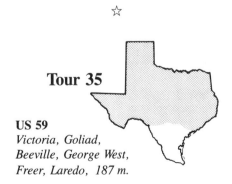

Tour 35

US 59
*Victoria, Goliad,
Beeville, George West,
Freer, Laredo, 187 m.*

Your southwestward route continues Tour 25 (Region II) in a sweeping diagonal from Victoria to Laredo, for the main part crossing ranchland on the way. The first leg, as far as Beeville, traverses a rolling, oak-studded terrain where early cattle kings grew richer with the discovery of oil. Beyond Beeville you penetrate *chaparral* country, where the profusion of thorny brush created the cowboy's need for protective leather "chaps," and where a hardy breed of cattle developed and became known as the trail-driving Texas Longhorn.

The second leg, paralleling or cutting the old trails from Laredo and Mexico beyond, crosses land rich in treasure legend—hidden loot, obscure maps, elusive way-markers. Its most visible treasures, however, are the oilfields around Freer and the new gas wells in Laredo's vicinity.

This is a sparsely-settled region, particularly along its western leg; the towns are small and the distances considerable. Historically you travel a route almost the reverse of that marched in 1836 by Santa Anna's right wing, coastal-sweeping troops under General Jose de Urrea, en route to collision with Fannin's at Goliad.

Victoria, 0 m.—see Tour 33. Continue southwest from Tour 25, Region II.

Fannin, 16 m., pop. 94. A state park marks the site of the Battle of Coleto Creek, March 19–20, 1836. After indecisive delay at his Goliad fortress, Col. James W. Fannin's eastward retreat was overtaken here by superior forces under General Urrea. Surrounded on an open plain, Fannin's 275 men—most of them newly-arrived American volunteers—fought off day-long assaults. But continued Mexican reinforcement and lack of water and food brought Fannin's surrender to four-to-one odds. Wounded, he was returned with his men to Goliad, where they were massacred.

There are no camping facilities, but a picnic pavilion, water, and restrooms are provided.

Goliad, 25 m. (alt. 167, pop. 1,946), on the lower San Antonio River, is a quiet little city clustered with big oaks and centering one of Texas' most historic regions, one with a long and violent past. Originally the site of an Indian village, it was selected as location for Mission Nuestra Senora del Espiritu Santo de Zuniga, and the Presidio Nuestra Senora

Presidio La Bahia, Goliad.

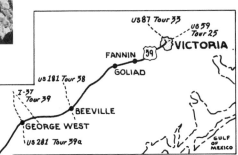

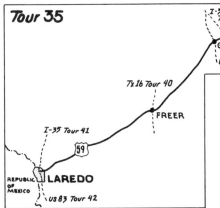

tion against Matamoros, Mexico, and ignoring Sam Houston's orders to fall back on the main Texan forces—began an eastward retreat, too late. Here on Palm Sunday, 1836, Fannin and some 342 men were massacred; and "Remember Goliad" became part of the Texan battle cry at San Jacinto. On the grounds, a large monument marks the common grave.

Within the presidio an excellent museum traces this installation's long history. Across the river, just north, is Mission Espiritu Santo, a scenic state park (camping and all facilities) and an interesting museum.

Opposite the presidio is a small, restored adobe building, the Texas birthplace of Mexico's hero of Cinco de Mayo. The Texas-born Mexican patriot was General Ignacio Zaragoza, who defeated the French at Puebla, near Mexico City, May 5, 1862.

On the old courthouse square in Goliad is located the giant Cart War Oak. It was used as a hanging tree for murderers convicted—often by Judge Lynch—during the brief but bloody Cart War of 1857, when Mexican and Anglo freighters struggled for inbound coast trade.

Fannin Plaza, in town, displays an 1885 memorial to the Texan commander, together with a revolutionary cannon. Opposite is the interesting Market House Museum. Built in 1870 for vendors, it was converted in 1886 to a fire house and in 1967, to a museum. Here, Goliad's C of C can provide all tourist information. Nearby, also see Mission Valley, Refugio.

Beeville, 54 m. (alt. 214; pop. 13,547), once known as the town where every house boasted a windmill, has been modernized by oil wealth. Since 1894, Texas A&M University has operated Substation No. 1, oldest in the Texas Agricultural Experiment Station System, just east. Now-closed Naval Air Station, Chase Field, trained seagoing flyers.

Beeville centers an area settled by Irish colonists as early as 1826 and, in pioneering days, it knew a turbulent career. In 1877, one outlaw awaiting his hanging willed that his skin be stretched over a drum which was to be beaten each anniversary of his hanging as a warning to others. Near here, to the east, the Anglo-Mexican Cart War saw its origins and on Bee County's eastern edge on Blanco Creek, via TX 202, 10 m., is the site of Blanconia or, as generally known, "Dark Corner," the home and headquarters of Sally Scull, supposedly a well-born woman who became head of a desperado gang that ran guns out of Mexico during the Civil War. Sally, who could handle a team with any man and outshoot most, finally disappeared, believed killed by her third husband. At Beeville intersect US 181/Tour 38.

At 72 m. intersect I-37/Tour 39.

George West, 77 m. (alt. 162; pop. 2,586), is Live Oak County seat, largely built—its first streets, public buildings, and schools—by a South Texas rancher by that name. It took the seat of government from neighboring Oakville, just north, in 1919. The Live Oak County Museum, in the courthouse, features artifacts and documents regarding early Live Oak County history. At George West, your route intersects US 281/Tour 39A.

West of here, the terrain roughens and treasure tales abound. Somewhere along the Nueces is the site of Rock Pens where, in 1873, 31 mule-loads of Mexican treasure were cached so they wouldn't be stolen by an overtaking Comanche war party. The search for this lode began J. Frank Dobie's famed quest for hidden silver and gold. Somewhere near the Seven Sisters oilfield, west some 15 m. is another cache at the hillock, Loma Alto (see Tilden).

Freer, 122 m. (alt. 510; pop. 3,271), came into being with the 1907 discovery of oil and, with a steady producer thereafter, has polished itself into a brisk little community. Freer rounds up coyotes in February and rattlesnakes in April. To boast of its rattlers, the town displays a statue of one, as big as the one-story C of C building it graces. In this area deer hunting is good. Nearby, also see San Diego. At Freer intersect TX 16/Tour 40.

At 151 m. via FM 2895 south, **Aguilares,** pop. 25, is near the site of a treasure tale hard to debate. A cowboy

de Loreto, moved there—after two previous locations nearer the coast (see Edna, Mission Valley)—in 1749. Both mission and presidio became known as La Bahia for their original location on Matagorda Bay, and both—overlooking the San Antonio River south of town—have been exceptionally well restored. With its block-square, great stone walls and corner bastions, the presidio particularly takes its viewers back to a long ago and sterner time. West 4 m., Mission Rosario, in ruins today, was later erected to complete the establishment.

The fortress became Spain's eastern anchor in its defense of Texas and saw much violence, beginning with Mexican-American filibustering expeditions in 1812, 1817 and 1821. In 1835, Texas Revolutionaries under Ben Milam captured the then Mexican-occupied fort and in December of that year issued a Declaration of Independence that preceded the later action at Washington-on-the-Brazos.

The following March, Col. James W. Fannin, Jr.—contemplating an expedion the Shipp Ranch was riding line when his horse stepped into a hole which proved to be a rotted, large box of Spanish doubloons. He filled his saddlebags, pockets and hat and rode to the ranch house with his find. All hands joined in returning for the major part of the treasure but on that empty sameness of range, the cowboy could not again find his lode. For years search for those golden coins has continued without known success.

Laredo, 187 m. (alt. 438; pop. 122,899), was founded in 1755, one of Texas' oldest cities. Its founding came during the great Spanish colonization of the Rio Grande line, accomplished by Jose de Escandon. Significantly, Laredo was—of some 20 towns and villages established—one of only two placed north of the river and at the time was considered unlikely to succeed.

Today, richly border-flavored Laredo is America's major gateway to Mexico, an intriguing city, with its houses close-crowding on narrow streets, and its central downtown beautified by parklike San Agustin Plaza.

Interesting old buildings surround San Agustin—its church, Laredo's oldest, was originally built in 1767. Casa Ortiz, on the corner, dates from 1830. However, the small white-plastered adobe and rock building with seven—not six—flags is most interesting of all—the Republic of the Rio Grande Museum. Some date the house from the 1760s and believe it housed that republic's capitol. That effort, in 1840, sought to split off Northern Mexico and much of today's western United States as a separate nation. After a number of battles within Mexico, the republic dissolved.

Fort McIntosh, west of downtown, was established in 1848, after the Mexican War. Laredo Junior College and Texas A&I at Laredo now share the grounds; several old buildings are now used to house museum exhibits.

Annually each February since 1898, both Laredo and Nuevo Laredo (pop. 350,000) observe the birthday of George Washington with a gala ten-day festival. Parties, dances, athletic events and parades salute the first Western Hemisphere leader to free a New World country from European domination.

A Texas Travel Information Center is on I-35 north of town. Bilingual tourist information is available here, at the C of

C, and—for Mexico—at Sanborns. A crossover to Nuevo Laredo, but not into the interior, requires no permit; and that border city provides an exciting tour of shops, restaurants, and El Mercado, a traditional Mexican market just two blocks from the international bridge. The Turf Club offers off-track betting. At Laredo intersect US 63/Tour 42; I-35/Tour 41.

☆

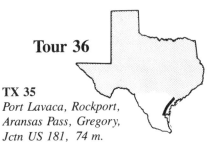

Tour 36

TX 35
Port Lavaca, Rockport, Aransas Pass, Gregory, Jctn US 181, 74 m.

This last brief leg of your hug-the-coast route, continuing from Tour 27, Region II, is a sunny, fresh and pretty one, traversing a rich coastal plain, interspersed with occasional marshland, and timbered in large oak motts. Along the seashore, many of these great trees are twisted and lean inland, having grown into the steady onshore Gulf breeze.

In earliest days this comparative Eden—abounding with game and fish—was home to the Karankawa Indians, much maligned as ritual cannibals, who paradoxically tenderly cared for the shipwrecked Spaniards of the Cabeza de Vaca party, mourned greatly at the Europeans' discomfort, and shared their meager food and homes with them.

Spain sought to establish her first ports in shallow Matagorda and Copano Bays, and during Republic days names like Indianola, Copano and Aransas City were commonplace shipping destinations.

Hurricanes and tidal sanding finished them.

The towns—you find no large cities—have a clean, fresh-scrubbed look, as though the steady sea breeze washes them daily.

Port Lavaca, 0 m.—see Tour 33. Continue west from Tour 27.

Via TX 316 south, **Indianola,** 14 m., fronting an outthrust point into broad Matagorda Bay, is perhaps Texas' most famed and tragic ghost. Founded in 1844 to land German immigrants, the port was first known as Carlshafen. As Indianola it developed rapidly, becoming a port of entry for most Texas immigration from Europe, for a camel corps from Arabia (see Camp Verde), and ice from the Great Lakes. With a population reaching 6,000, the town vied with Galveston as a Texas leader, oblivious to its flat coast, with a bay close behind; then an 1875 hurricane, pushing a tidal wave, crushed it. Attempts were made to rebuild, but a second hurricane in 1886 caused its abandonment. Only a few foundations, largely awash, remain. In a beachfront park on Indianola's site is a giant statue of La Salle, who was forced ashore inside this bay (see Edna) when his supply ship ran aground off Pass Cavallo, opposite Port O'Connor.

Via FM 1289/TX 185 south 25 m., **Port O'Connor** (alt. 15; pop. 810), at land's end, is a jaunty little resort with a phoenix-like quality, having risen from several storms and almost total destruction from Hurricane Carla in 1961. Across on Matagorda Island, visible from the seaward tip of this town, is the 1852 Matagorda lighthouse and Coast guard station. Near the station and almost awash is the 1847 site of what was planned as Texas' most luxurious resort—Saluria, conceived by Texas leaders but doomed by storms. On its site was later erected Confederate Fort Esperanza (Hope) which for a time bluffed Federal warships off the pass with timber imitating big guns. The fort was abandoned and burned in 1863.

Carla was not Port O'Connor's first brush with disaster. In the late 1800s this was an ambitious resort with its grand seaside Hotel La Salle and an immense pleasure pavilion, both victims of earlier storms. Today this community offers one of Texas' best chances for solitude with a visit to Matagorda Island State Park, 7 m. south. Separated from the mainland by two bays, its primitive camping and picnicking facilities are accessible only by boat.

At **Tivoli,** 19 m., pop. 540, TX 239 leads south 14 m. to Aransas National Wildlife Refuge, winter home of the great white whooping crane. Summering within the Arctic Circle they unerringly fly thousands of miles to arrive promptly each October, and remain until March. For a time, this giant bird seemed near extinction, but, though still a rare species, its numbers are increasing (well over 100 now) under watchful protection. Many other birds inhabit this 47,000-acre wooded sanctuary (more than 300 species have been observed). Observation platforms allow wildlife study, and a boat cruise from Rockport provides a closer look at the whoopers, nesting in offshore flats. Near the visitors center, a special pond displays big specimens of the American alligator. The refuge offers an excellent opportunity for wildlife observation in a 7 m. nature trail.

At 43 m., Copano Bay curls above the old community of **Lamar,** pop. 150. Immediately south is Goose Island State Park (big and shaded, with camping and all facilities). Here is the "Big Tree," national co-champion live oak, estimated more than 1,000 years old, and a one-time council tree for the Karankawa. It measures 422 inches in circumference, is 44 feet tall with an 89-foot crown. The park provides a 1,600 foot night-lighted fishing pier. A second state fishing pier—the old causeway—extends 1.5 m. across Copano Bay. Close by the park, is Villa Stella Maris, Our Lady Star of the Sea Chapel, built of oystershell tabby concrete. This was the place of worship for old Lamar, later a missionary school. During the Civil War it was shelled by Union vessels, which made several appearances off Lamar.

Fulton, 49 m. (alt. 19; pop. 763), was founded as Aransas City in 1837. The palatial Fulton Mansion was built in the 1870s (with a form of air conditioning) by Col. George W. Fulton, an early cattle baron and cousin of the steamboat's inventor. Beautifully restored today, the mansion is a state historic site. Across on St. Joseph's Island is the ghost of Aransas, which prospered as a port of entry from 1845 until the Civil War, when Federal blockade and occupation razed the city.

Rockport, 52 m. (alt. 20; pop. 4,753), growing from 1868 hide-shipping plants, today curves around a pretty boat-dotted harbor, its wind-twisted trees lining the seafront. The Zachary Taylor Oak marks the first Texas campsite of American forces marching on the Rio Grande and the Mexican War—Taylor's troops having landed from sea, July 23, 1845.

This is a seaside recreational haven and houses a substantial artist's colony. There is an excellent swimming beach and skiing basin, and outlying are handsome leisure home developments like Key Allegro, where homeowners dock at their back doors. Here, the Texas Maritime Museum details the state's water related development, including river steamboats. This, too, is a bird watcher's paradise, more than 200 species having been identified in a single day. And while you fish for pleasure—surf, jetty or pier—Rockport fishes commercially, its fleets of shrimp trawlers in constant evidence. Rockport's oysters are winter delicacies, and seafood restaurants are very good.

The city is festive as well, with a two-day outdoor art festival during the July 4 weekend. The SeaFair Festival, each mid-October, attracts thousands to a "county fair, church supper and family reunion, rolled into one," with virtually every known seafood.

Between Rockport and Aransas Pass, you cross coastal marshland and patches of wood, yielding occasional close-by glimpses of blue Gulf waters.

Aransas Pass, 63 m. (alt. 20; pop. 7,180), calls itself the gateway city for its passageway between St. Joseph and Mustang Islands. With wide palm-lined streets, it is a sparkling port city, concentrating on commercial fishing and leaving most resort functions to its Mustang Island counterpart, Port Aransas. Some 400 large shrimp trawlers base near the Seaman's Memorial Tower, a silent monument to fishermen lost at sea.

Via TX 361 7 m. (causeway and free ferry), **Port Aransas** (alt. 20; pop. 2,233) is a carefree, many-colored vacation center, a longtime tarpon fishing capital, excellently turned out with lodging facilities and restaurants. Tarpon scales on the lobby wall of Tarpon Inn have been signed by such famed fishermen as Franklin D. Roosevelt. Various fishing tourneys are scheduled through the year.

The University of Texas Marine Science Institute displays specimens of Gulf plants and animals: visitors are welcome to a layman's introduction to oceanography. For handy reference see *Beachcomber's Guide to Gulf Coast Marine Life,* 2nd Ed.(Gulf Publishing Co., 1989).

One of a fleet of free ferries linking Aransas Pass with Port Aransas on the north end of Mustang Island.

Nearby Harbor Island stations the Aransas Pass Lighthouse, more than a century old. At Mustang Island's northern tip, a beachfront county park provides all facilities, and southward the island stretches out in a dunefronting array of stilt-legged resort homes, its beaches similar to neighboring Padre Island, with which it connects. The best of seaside camping—two miles of fine beach—lies southward at Mustang Island State Park (all facilities).

Via TX 361 west from Aransas Pass, **Ingleside** 68 m. (alt. 18; pop. 5,696) was an early cattle ranching town, mounting a Kansas drive in 1859, later a turn-of-the-century resort with an elegant bluffside hotel. In 1927, with installation of the Humble Oil refinery, industrialization began, and has continued. Nearby is Ingleside Cove Wildlife Sanctuary.

Gregory, 74 m. merge with US 181/Tour 38, en route to Corpus Christi. In the area also see Bayside, Sinton.

☆

Tour 37

US 77
Victoria, Refugio, Robstown, Kingsville, Raymondville, Harlingen, 210 m.

From Victoria to the Rio Grande Valley, your route, continuing from Tour 29, Region II, follows the contours of Texas' south-bending coastline, some 30 m. inland. The terrain is virtually flat throughout, fertile across to the Robstown-Kingsville region, then becoming a long and seemingly deserted reach of chaparral southward. This, in turn, gives way suddenly to the lush tropical growth of the Valley, where this tour ends.

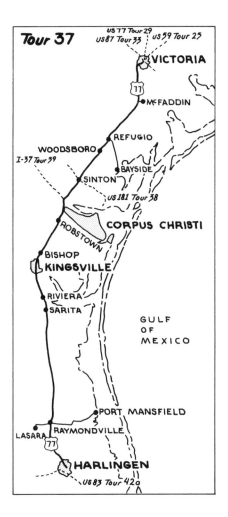

From Kingsville south, you travel within the vast King Ranch, one of America's largest—a land that seems to have defied taming since its first settlement some three centuries ago. From the edge of this brush country, progressively southward, you can sense another change—you begin to sense the flavor of Old Mexico.

Long a land where traditional ways held sway, even here modern cattle ranching methods are winning out. Today helicopters are the preferred method of herding cattle, and cowhands are more likely to mount a pickup truck than a fleet-footed steed. Still, cattle are king in this vast grassland; memories remain of past glory.

Victoria, 0 m.—see Tour 33. Continue west from Tour 29, Region II.

McFaddin, 19 m., pop. 320. Near this tiny village, in the San Antonio River bottoms, is the site of Anaqua, a placename perhaps oldest in Texas, persisting from the days of an Anaqua Indian village here. From these Indians, Cabeza de Vaca, after long captivity, made his westward escape in 1534, finally to reach the Mexican Pacific coast. His tales of this northern land began Spain's attempt to colonize in the mid-1500s—both Coronado's and DeSoto's explorations coming as a result. Nearby also see Aransas National Wildlife Refuge.

Refugio, 43 m. (alt. 49; pop. 3,158), mixes the dignity of age with broad streets and the brisk activity of oil production—heavy in this area. The town was founded in 1790 when Franciscan monks established Nuestra Senora del Refugio, the last mission to be built in Texas. Comanche-Karankawa warfare destroyed the first building; 1836 Mexican bombardment, the second. Our Lady of Refuge Church now stands on the ruins of the old mission.

Here, in March, 1836, part of the Goliad forces of Col. James W. Fannin were trapped and overwhelmed, dying either in battle here or with their comrades in the Goliad Massacre. A block-square park by the courthouse displays a 30-foot monument, an eight-sided memorial above a star-shaped garden of flowers, to the Texans and Georgians under Col. William Ward and Captain Amon King.

On the church grounds is a large anaqua tree, largest of its species in America, where Sam Houston pleaded with newly-arrived U.S. volunteers not to join Fannin in an expedition against Matamoros. However, the bickering Texas provisional government was embroiled in a power struggle and Houston found himself relieved of command (temporarily), his mission a failure, as most of the young volunteers stayed with Fannin to the end. Subsequent desperate fighting was in and around this mission. A county museum displays some of the area's rich history.

Via FM 2678 south, **Bayside,** 17 m., pop. 400, spreads its little community along a bluff over Copano Bay. Close by, on private land, is the ghost of old Copano (best seen by boat), which Spain established in the mid 1700s as port of supply for the mission-presidio La Bahia, north at Goliad. The area was long known, having been explored by sea captain Alonzo Alvarez de Pineda in 1519. For a time the haven for pirates and filibusters, Copano in the 1820s became port of entry for Irish immigrants who settled this coast. During the Texas Revolution it experienced the "Horse Marine" incident, when a group of mounted rangers captured three ships and cargo bound for Santa Anna. The Texans lured the ship captains ashore, seized them and then their ships; for those Texans an intrigued U.S. newspaper coined the term, "Horse Marines."

Close by, also on the bay, is the later ghost of St. Mary's of Aransas, once Refugio County seat and "metropolis," 1850–1866. Hurricane-damaged and by-passed by the railroad, St. Mary's lost her government seat to Rockport, and faded. Only faint traces remain.

Woodsboro, 48 m. (alt. 47; pop. 1,731), centers a rich agricultural area settled in the early 1900s by Czechs. Southeast toward the mouth of Mission River at the head of Copano Bay is a popular water skiing area. Somewhere near that mouth, tradition insists that a treasure-laden pirate sloop was driven ashore by storm, its booty still awaiting recovery.

At 58 m., the **Welder Wildlife Refuge** is the world's largest privately-endowed sanctuary, its 7,800 acres occupying a portion of the old Robert E. Welder Ranch. Species of more than 1,300 plants, 450 birds, and some 50 mammals have been identified here. Make visiting arrangements in advance through the Sinton C of C; the refuge normally opens to visitors only at 3 p.m. each Thursday. The big, handsome museum displays wildlife dioramas and Karankawa Indian exhibits.

Sinton, 66 m. (alt. 43; pop. 5,549), is a bright, breeze-whipped little city of parks that seems to shimmer with the promise of nearby Gulf waters. With the railroad's coming in 1885, it captured the San Patricio county seat from historic, once-flourishing San Patricio (Tour 39) to the south. Sinton stages livestock and agricultural shows; and its Old

Fiddlers Contest, the last weekend each October, draws attendance from across Texas. At Sinton, intersect US 181/Tour 38. In the area also see Rockport, Aransas Pass, Port Aransas, Corpus Christi.

At 82 m. intersect I-37/Tour 39.

Robstown, 88 m. (alt. 85; pop. 12,849), is an open, sunny and new little city, established in 1903. On its rich black Nueces County soil, it prospered with the development of a superior strain of cotton. Throughout this area, the presence of numerous gins emphasizes that cotton is still a major cash crop on this coast.

Bishop, 106 m. (alt. 59; pop. 3,337), is a trim, prospering town that was totally pre-planned. In 1910, a complete power and sewerage system was installed, all streets graded and waiting with sidewalks before the first town lot was offered for sale. Today Bishop centers a rich cotton- and grain-producing region and has added a number of neighboring petrochemical plants.

Kingsville, 111 m. (alt. 66; pop. 25,276), just west of your route, is to most Texans synonymous with the giant King Ranch, stretching southward here. It is also home of burgeoning Texas A&I University, handsome in Spanish architecture (6,000 enrollment), considerable industry, and a Naval Air Station, many parks, with Loyola and Riviera Beaches nearby. On the university campus, the John E. Conner Museum displays collections reflecting prehistoric, Spanish, and pioneer Texas. Also here is the Graves Peeler collection of mounted trophy heads from around the world. Downtown, in a restored ice plant, the King Ranch Museum and Archives displays Toni Frissell photographs of the ranch and historic ranch items. The King Ranch Saddle Shop, also downtown, offers saddles, purses, luggage, and other leather goods. Nearby Sellers Market is craft shop and tearoom.

Via TX 141, immediately west is entrance to the headquarters of King Ranch, where a visitor center anchors guided tours aboard air-conditioned buses of cattle pens, ranch headquarters, horse stables, and more. Special tours are offered to any part of the ranch.

The 825,000-acre ranch was begun in 1853 by a one-time Rio Grande steamboat captain, Richard King. Its foundation stock was the Texas Longhorn. A crossbreed of Brahman with Shorthorn cattle resulted in the famed Santa Gertrudis strain. In various working sections, the ranch spreads over four South Texas counties, is contained behind some 1,500 m. of fence, counts 75 artesian wells and more than 200 windmills. At one time it also counted some 390 producing oil wells. From the time you enter Kleberg County driving south, you reach almost into the Rio Grande Valley before leaving King Ranch country.

Windmills are still used to supply water for livestock at the King Ranch, Kingsville.

The ranch is also notable for having developed two Kentucky Derby winners, Assault and Middleground.

South of Kingsville you cross 73 m. of brush country—land of the big South Texas ranches—before reaching the upper valley at Raymondville. Check your automotive needs before leaving Kingsville.

Riviera, 127 m., pop. 550, is a village at the head of Baffin Bay. Here in the fall of 1568 three English sailors, survivors of Sir John Hawkins' raiders trapped in Vera Cruz, supposedly walked northward to ultimate rescue aboard an English ship in Canadian waters. Their disputed report noted vegetation at the Rio Grande, as well as this indented coastline. The bay, 9 m. east, is not extensively developed but offers fishing and camping.

Sarita, 133 m., pop. 185, a wayside spot, is more ranch headquarters than town; yet it is seat of government for one of the state's emptiest counties, Kenedy County—in all directions southward, a thousand square miles of mesquite-studded ranchland. Just east of the highway is the headquarters of the Kenedy La-Parra Ranch, its founder an early shipmate and partner of the King Ranch's founder.

Armstrong, 153 m., pop. 20, is headquarters for the Armstrong Ranch, founded in 1882 by a famed Texas Ranger. Before retiring to ranching, Ranger John B. Armstrong had arrested not only King Fisher (Uvalde), but even more dangerous John Wesley Hardin.

Raymondville, 182 m. (alt. 40; pop. 8,880), a gateway both to the Rio Grande Valley below and to the fishing haven of Port Mansfield eastward, more resembles a friendly, brisk Texas plains town than it does its neighbors. Occupying an area penetrated by Spanish exploration in the 1700s, Raymondville was established in 1904 and today leans more to livestock and row crops than to the citrus of its southerly neighbors. A historical center reflects the regional story, and each January the city stages its Willacy County Livestock Show. Many municipal recreation facilities are provided in planned tourist programs for winter visitors, October through March. Close by, Delta Lake provides freshwater fishing and water skiing.

Via TX 186 west 10 m. above La Sara, **La Sal Vieja** is a salt lake used by man since antiquity. Earliest Spanish chronicles report harvesting salt here, and on one of the lake's islands a 6,000 year-old Indian skeleton was found.

Via TX 186 east, **Port Mansfield,** 24 m., pop. 731, facing Laguna Madre, attracts fishermen from everywhere, for the Mansfield channel cuts through Padre Island, with access to deep water. Beachcombers take the trip to the lonely foot of North Padre Island, difficult for Corpus Christi vehicles to reach (Tour 38), and a treasure trove of sea shells, fishing floats, driftwoods, and other flotsam.

Below Raymondville, great citrus groves and stately palms become much in evidence as you approach Harlingen, entering the Rio Grande Valley.

Harlingen, 210 m. Intersect US 83— see Tour 42A, Rio Grande Valley.

Tour 38

US 181
San Antonio, Floresville,
Karnes City, Beeville,
Corpus Christi, 145 m.

B earing south-southeast, Tour 38 descends gradually from the foot of the Hill Country at San Antonio to the flat coastal plain at Corpus Christi. The land is rich throughout, originally devoted to ranching and more recently to stockfarming, yielding a wide variety of produce. Timber thins as you progress southward, but each of several stream crossings is flanked with woodland, generally big pecan trees.

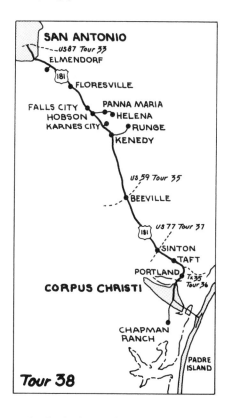

As Spain knew the land, your route crosses from the southern edge of Lipan Apache country to that of the coastal cannibal, the Karankawa. As the countryside was settled, a mixture of racial heritage developed—Germans below San Antonio, Poles around Karnes City. Below that are the Irish from Beeville south and all along the way, our heritage from Spain, the Texas Mexican.

En route, you pass a number of interesting sites, ranging from early Spanish ghost towns to modern-day uranium mines. You cross America's first Polish settlement and a promising town that was killed by the will of one man. You end at one of the Gulf Coast's most beautiful cities and major ports—a site, ironically, that Spain rejected for early settlement.

San Antonio, 0 m.—see Tour 33. Along your outward route, San Antonio's four southerly missions—Concepcion, San Jose, San Juan and San Francisco—lie close to this road (see mission tour road signs).

Elmendorf, 15 m. (alt. 506; pop. 568), is a sleepy village whose excellent clays have long occupied it with pottery-making and brick manufacture.

Floresville, 29 m. (alt. 389; pop. 5,247), with its sandy loam, harvests some 30 million pounds of peanuts annually. It is an oak-shaded community which dates far back—growing in the 1820s around Spanish haciendas. The area is older than that, however. On the city's northeast edge (FM 536) is the ancient Canary Islander cemetery of Las Islitas settlers. That community, almost as old as San Antonio, was established in the 1730s, many of its inhabitants fleeing to Mexico during the Texas Revolution.

The Islanders, who put Spain's stamp on San Antonio, were originally projected to colonize all of Texas, but Spain's king shortly cancelled the undertaking because of expense. Many of San Antonio's most distinguished families trace their lineage directly to these first settlers.

Former Texas governor and U.S. Treasury Secretary John B. Connally once made Floresville his ranch home. Nearby also see Sutherland Springs, Pleasanton.

Via FM 536 west 3 m. is the site of the cattle ranch of San Jose Mission. The missions ran thousands of cattle and sheep on outlying rangeland, and the San Jose ranch was one of their largest. Close by tiny Labatt, 6 m., is the Francisco Flores hacienda. The adobe part of this structure, once the home of a Spanish grandee, is believed to date to the 1700s.

Falls City, 42 m. (alt. 307; pop. 478), an 1884 railroad-born town, is the site of

Texas' first uranium discovery, and a nearby processing plant.

Hobson, 46 m., pop. 125. Just east is an ancient ford crossing the San Antonio River, one very likely used by Alamo's gallant courier, Col. James B. Bonham, on his mission to seek aid from Fannin's men at Goliad.

Via FM 81 east, **Panna Maria,** 6 m., pop. 96, is notable for its tall-steepled church and mighty oak, and the history they signify. Here on December 24, 1854, America's first colony of Poles arrived, most having walked 200 m. from Galveston. Nothing awaited them; the big oak sheltered their bitter-cold midnight mass that Christmas Eve. Living literally in grass-lined mud dug-outs, these pioneers suffered terribly in that first year, but they held on, later building their church in testimony to faith that sustained them.

A historical museum is housed in an old school building. In 1963, as Poland neared her millenium, Panna Maria's Texas bells, ringing the Angelus on Christmas Eve, were broadcast to Poland by Radio Free Europe.

Helena, 11 m., pop. 35, a ghost in restoration, was a promising town with a violent past. Founded in 1852 on the site of an earlier Mexican settlement, Alamita, it straddled the Chihuahua and Indianola roads and was the scene of bloodshed during the Cart War, when Anglo and Mexican teamsters fought for freighting trade. Here was conceived the grisly "Helena Duel," where two antagonists, each man's wrist lashed to the other's, fought it out with knives whose blades were too short to inflict a mortal wound. The result was a slashing bloodletting that continued until one man collapsed.

Helena's death, according to old story, came about from violence of a different nature. The son of a prominent rancher was killed here, and the father rode Helena's main street challenging the killer to come out. When no one appeared he vowed to kill the town itself and granted railroad right-of-way across his land, to the west. The rail by-pass effectually finished Helena.

A somber two-story courthouse has been restored as a museum, as have been an old store and post office, a barn, a farmhouse, and one of the original jail cells. Open on Tuesdays only.

Karnes City 53 m. (alt. 404; pop. 2,916), with its broad streets topping a low hill, prospers as a farming center—flax is grown in the terraced fields—enriched by mineral discoveries close by, both oil and uranium.

Taking the county seat from Helena in 1894, Karnes citizens, fearing violence in securing the records, removed them by night and avoided using the local roads. The road they cut remains today as TX 80. The little city observes Town and Country Days each September, and in October, treks over to old Helena for Indian Summer Festival.

Kenedy, 60 m. (alt. 271; pop. 3,763), is a quietly prospering L-shaped town today but in the past was a valid claimant to the Texas title of "Six Shooter Junction." Early-day excursion trains from San Antonio to Corpus Christi announced the station stop in that fashion. Often passengers dropped to the floor while celebrating cowboys made targets of the train windows.

Growing up on the site of an early cow camp, Kenedy had a grimmer side to its six-gun heritage—there were numerous feuds, and the brush country attracted outlaws. Nearby, John Wesley Hardin was beginning to notch his gun. At little neighboring Daileyville, one 1886 election shootout—over in a few seconds— killed five men and wounded another.

Entirely tranquil today—its major observance is Bluebonnet Days early each April—Kenedy recalls its gunsmoke past with its new "Sixshooter Junction Museum." In the area also see Yorktown, Goliad.

Via TX 72, east 10 m., **Runge,** pop. 1,139, is an old, staunch Polish settlement with a heritage museum. Under the old San Antonio River bridge, about midway, a "ghost light" is said to have inhabited the bottom pastures for more than a generation.

Beeville, 88 m.—see Tour 35.
Sinton, 118 m.—see Tour 37.

Taft, 126 m. (alt. 34; pop. 3,222), trails coast-weathered homes and business houses along a highway lined by windwhipped palms. Once center of the million-acre Taft Ranch, owned by the half-brother of President William Howard Taft, this area boasts some of Texas' richest land, once devoted almost entirely to cotton production, days recalled by exhibits in the Blackland Museum.

Gregory, 133 m.—merge with TX 35/Tour 36.

Portland, 37 m. (alt. 21; pop. 12,224), on its bluff overlooks the gray-blue waters of Corpus Christi Bay. On a clear day you can see the long thin line of Mustang Island opposite. Long projected as a resort, Portland booms today with the substantial addition of industry; the result is a glistening, new-looking city that has grown by several hundred percent in the last 40 years.

Corpus Christi, 145 m. (alt. 35; pop. 257,453, city). This two-level city—spread along its bayfront and back from its overlooking bluff—is a major resort area and port. The city spreads about its bay in a glittering crescent, particularly noticeable at night. To the south it is gateway to Padre Island National Seashore. The city is also home to a Naval Air Station, an Army Depot, Corpus Christi State University and Del Mar College, and several exceptional museums. The beaches, both on the bay and on Mustang and Padre Islands, are excellent. Dominating North Beach are the Texas State Aquarium, which showcases the environment of the Gulf of Mexico, and the USS *Lexington,* WWII aircraft carrier.

Corpus Christi and its bay.

The bay was first explored by Spain's Alonzo Alvarez de Pineda in 1519, among the earliest American landfalls. Settlement of the area, Villa de Vedoya, was considered in 1747 when Spanish colonization centered on the Rio Grande area. Actual city beginnings occurred with the arrival of Zachary Taylor's Mexico-bound army in 1845 and the assured permanence of then-isolated Kinney's Trading Post. The Civil War saw the little town bombarded by Federal gunboats twice and finally occupied in 1864. Since 1900, first with cotton, then natural gas in 1922, growth has been rapid. Corpus Christi arrived as a major port in 1926.

You entered the city via the 235-foot-high Harbor Bridge—a magnificent pan-oramic view of this entire coast; thereafter, to see the city best, stop at the Corpus Christi Area Tourist Bureau on Shoreline Boulevard—literature, maps and information are available.

Mini-Tour Guide

Art Museum of South Texas: 1902 N. Shoreline.

Art Center of Corpus Christi: Local artists. 100 N. Shoreline Blvd.

Bayfront Plaza Auditorium: (Corpus Christi Symphony) N. end, Shoreline Blvd.

Centennial House (1849): 411 N. Broadway.

Corpus Christi Museum: Natural history. Spanish galleon artifacts. 1900 N. Chaparral.

Dolphin rides: Meet dolphins up close. US 181/TX 35 east at Nueces Bay.

Greyhound Race Track: I-37 at Navigation Blvd.

Harbor Playhouse: Community theater. 1 Bayfront Plaza.

Heritage Park: Turn of century homes. 1600 N. Chaparral.

Marina: Foot of downtown.

Museum of Oriental Cultures: 418 Peoples.

Mustang Island State Park: Opposite bay (Port Aransas).

Padre Island National Seashore: Via John F. Kennedy Causeway.

Paddlewheeler *Flagship:* Bay cruises. Peoples St. T-head.

Port of Corpus Christi: (Observation platform). Below 235-foot-high Harbor Bridge.

Texas State Aquarium: 2710 N. Shoreline Blvd.

USS *Lexington:* "Blue Ghost" of WWII fame. Next to Texas State Aquarium.

Unique in all of Texas is the chance to meet, feed, and pet wild dolphins. Daily April to October, boat trips take visitors from a bait shop on Nueces Bay. Take Surfside Exit off US 181 and turnaround under the bridge.

Perhaps showiest of all the city's attractions is Shoreline Blvd/Ocean Drive itself, a splendid seafront-hugging avenue curling from the city's yacht basin below Harbor Bridge and fronting the downtown area.

The Bayfront Arts and Sciences Park, at the north end of Shoreline, houses the pure white Art Museum of South Texas, the Bayfront Plaza Convention Center, and its auditorium, the Harbor Playhouse, Heritage Park, and the Corpus Christi Museum, which displays natural history, seashell collections and some fascinating treasure artifacts. This park offers your best view—close up—of the big ships in- or outbound from the Gulf Coast's deepest port.

Padre Island, 166 m. The great white island—Spain's Isla Blanca—reaches from its northern tip opposite the city through a handsome developing resort area to the primitive domain of Padre Island National Seashore, and on to its tip opposite Brownsville, a distance of 116 miles—one of the world's longest barrier islands. On the map it appears pencil-thin; in reality it is a broad, seemingly endless expanse of shifting, cream-colored dunes, its shoreline dotted with occasional shrimper hulks or rusting carcasses of automobiles caught in the treacherous banks of Big and Little Shell. This dangerous driving area begins some 20 m. down the island, where only 4-wheel drive vehicles are recommended.

The island was first known to some 300 shipwrecked survivors of a 1553 Spanish treasure fleet smashed by a hurricane. Of the survivors, only two reached safety, the rest being cut down by cannibal Karankawa Indians in a macabre pursuit down the long shoreline. Padre Island was variously explored by Spain in the 1700s, occupied for many years by a Spanish priest in the 1800s—thus its name—and has known several ranching attempts. On the whole it has resisted subjugation and, particularly along its mid-reaches, remains remote and mysterious.

For the nature-loving beachcruiser there are some 600 different plants—sea oats, wild morning glories, beach primroses, and rare, tiny oak trees. The sea has lavished its cargo on these beaches—some 265 varieties of shells, rare glass fishing floats, and driftwood. Federal law forbids using metal detectors or collecting items more than 100 years old.

Inquire at National Seashore headquarters before attempting island-long travel; it is hazardous.

Via TX 286 south, **Chapman Ranch,** 16 m., on rich, black soil, was one of the world's first completely mechanized farming operations, employing in 1920 some 200 tractors alone. Under one roof was headquarters for everything from general store to barber shop and auto sales.

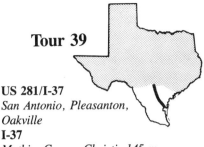

Tour 39

US 281/I-37
San Antonio, Pleasanton, Oakville
I-37
Mathis, Corpus Christi, 145 m.

Continuing southward from Tour 32, Region II, this is a fast interstate route connecting San Antonio and Corpus Christi. Except for a brief oak-timbered region extending to Pleasanton, it traverses sparsely-populated countryside, a mesquite and scrub-studded land known to the vaquero as *chaparral.* From Pleasanton south to Mathis, you travel some 70 miles of it with no town of any consequence along the way. To those who are part of the land, there is still a raw beauty in the sweeping vistas of empty distance.

In earliest days, Spain knew this for the domain of her dreaded adversary, the Lipan Apache. As that bloody man faded under pioneer pressures, the lonely expanses of scrub provided a convenient hideout for outlaws. Until well into the early 1900s, bandits—road-agents, they called themselves—operated along then little-traveled roads. Today, the land sustains a blend of ranching and stock farm-

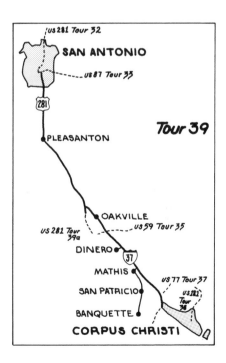

ing, with moderate to substantial oil production as you progress southward.

San Antonio, 0 m.—see Tour 33. Continue south from Tour 32, Region II.

Losoya, 14 m., pop. 322. Just east, along that river bottom is the site of the decisive Battle of Medina. In 1813, Americans and Mexicans, allied in what has become known as the Gutierrez-Magee Expedition, had declared for independence from Spain. With the tacit approval of fledgling United States—seeking to clear the continent of European domination—they had fought their way from Nacogdoches to Goliad and across to San Antonio, successfully holding that little capital in two stiff battles, Rosalia and Alazan.

However, heavily engaged in her War of 1812, America could offer little support, and a Spanish army of some 4,000 men drew the insurgent allies into an ambush here. The battle was bloody—little-known Medina engaged more men and inflicted more casualties than any other ever fought on Texas soil. Finally shattered, the revolutionary survivors fled the province, ending the first effort to free Texas.

Pleasanton, 33 m. (alt. 374; pop. 7,678), as its name implies, is a pleasant, liveoak-shaded little city. Settled in the 1850s, it grew up as a gathering ground for cattle drives up the Dodge and Western Trails—Pleasanton knows itself as "Birthplace of the Cowboy," with a statue and marker on its city hall square. There is merit to the claim: old records report that in the first three months of 1873 alone, 43,000 head of Longhorns, "native to the manor born" went up the trail from here.

The city used to own a "cowboy tree." In early days, poker-playing riders "raised so much dust" that one harassed saloon keeper built a treehouse for their games to continue, with less disturbance for his emporium. It was a satisfactory arrangement until one drunk waddy fell and broke his neck; the treehouse then was removed. Some years ago, the tree died.

A Longhorn Museum is located on TX 97, west toward Jourdanton, and late each August, Pleasanton hooks bootheels on the corral rail and stages three days of Cowboy Homecoming—featuring everything from parade and rodeo to old fiddlers contests and the naming of Texas' Cowboy of the Year. In the area also see Floresville, Christine, Poteet, Jourdanton.

Below Pleasanton, your road leaves the liveoak belt and strikes across rolling, mesquite-laced terrain. Campbellton and Whitsett are quick-passed villages. At 70 m. you veer eastward from US 281 (Tour 39A), holding to I-37 south. Choke Canyon Lake is just west.

Oakville, 78 m., pop. 260, is a lean, wayside near-ghost, dominated by a stern two-story building, now a residence, that for a time served as Live Oak County's courthouse. Once a lively town, Oakville became a hangout for brush country hardcases—its dusty street shot up each Saturday night, even its jail windows serving for target practice. Rangers finally cleaned up the place in 1876, but with George West's (Tour 39A) ascension to power as county seat, steady decline set in here.

At 87 m. intersect US 59/Tour 35.

At 97 m. FM 534 leads west across the Nueces River/head of Lake Corpus Christi to **Dinero,** 3 m., pop. 35. Close by is the site of 1850–55 **Fort Merrill,** which lived a brief life guarding the dangerous old San Antonio-Corpus Christi road.

Mathis, 108 m. (alt. 161; pop. 5,423), is a once-secluded old cowtown that, with its new interstate highway location and proximity to big Lake Corpus Christi, prospers today. Old-timers, remembering when in 1913 the first Mathis C of C needed a vote to remove fences from the city limits, eye the resort growth spilling out from Corpus Christi with something of wonder.

The broad lake's shoreline is dotted with many leisure home developments and close by is Lake Corpus Christi State Park, a 350-acre installation with camping and all facilities.

Down the Nueces River, the area toward Corpus Christi was thoroughly explored by Spain as early as 1747, when the very site of that port city was actually recommended—and rejected as too Indian-infested—for settlement.

Via TX 666 south 11 m., near-ghost **San Patricio,** pop. 369, was settled by Irish colonists in 1830. For a time, this southwesternmost Texas colony thrived; then during the Texas Revolution it became headquarters for the ill-conceived Matamoros Expedition under Francis W. Johnson and James Grant (see Goliad). On February 27, 1836, some 36 men of that command were surprised here by forces under General Jose de Urrea and, in a battle fought in these old streets, most were killed. The town was burned but later rebuilt, although continuing Mexican pressure, then the Mexican and Civil Wars, slowed resettlement. In 1893, the old town, beginning to show promise once more, missed the railroad, and Sinton took its county seat.

The home of colonizer James McGloin, built in 1855, still stands 1 m. from town, close by the 1876 St. Paul's Academy for Boys. The academy itself has been restored as a handsome private home. As might be expected, San Patricio observes St. Patrick's Day, reunion time for all Irish descendants.

The countryside here abounds with several tales of the supernatural, from the ghost of the first woman ever hanged in Texas (Chipita Rodriguez) to that of a headless horseman.

South, then west 9 m. via FM 624 is the site of historic Lipantitlan (no remains or facilities open). Here, in 1831, Mexico garrisoned Fort Lipantitlan, one of a chain designed to halt further Anglo colonization of Texas. The fort was captured by Irish Texans in late 1835, then lost to Santa Anna's invading army. On lonely dark nights, the ghost of a lovely "Lady in Green" wanders through the old trees, awaiting the return of her lover, who commanded here.

South 1 m. is the Knolle Jersey Dairy Farm, the world's largest jersey herd. Visitors are welcome.

South of San Patricio 9 m. on FM 666 is **Banquette,** pop. 449, an old site which drew its name from a gala celebration held for 1830 Irish colonists when Mexico, at first, welcomed them here.

At 130 m. intersect US 77/Tour 37. Nearby, see Sinton, Robstown.

Corpus Christi, 145 m.—see Tour 38.

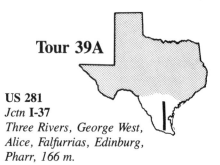

Tour 39A

US 281
Jctn **I-37**
Three Rivers, George West, Alice, Falfurrias, Edinburg, Pharr, 166 m.

Your route veers just west of I-37 to drop straight for southward Rio Grande Valley. Briefly, above Alice, you roll across long, lowering hills; and from there traverse the flat coastal plain the rest of the way. Almost entirely, you travel across South Texas brush country all at once—at Edinburg—bursting into the lush colors and tropical vegetation known to Texans as their citrus-producing "Valley," and to Midwesterners as a favorite winter resort.

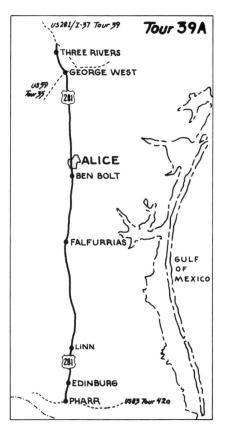

Along the way, below Falfurrias, you cross the big South Texas ranches— King, Kenedy and others (Tour 37). Throughout, you are well within a region heavily populated by Mexican Texans—a land of old custom and of

An overlook in Lake Corpus Christi State Park, near Mathis.

marvelous legend. This is a land of buried Mexican treasure, a region where on dark nights apparitions come from the shadows. Sometimes these are dreadful monsters, quite as often lovely and sad ladies awaiting lost lovers.

At Pharr, end of your journey, you intersect US 83, the east-west Valley route (Tour 42A).

At 0 m., veer west from I-37. Follow US 281 south.

Three Rivers, 5 m. (alt. 155; pop. 1,889), takes its name from the wooded junction of the Nueces, Atascosa and Frio rivers. An oil refinery sustains this little retail center. South of town, Tips State Park, along the river, offers limited facilities. Big Choke Canyon State Park, camping and all water sports lies 15 m. west on TX 72. Westward, along the great loop of the Nueces, old story claims several treasure caches (see Tours 35, 40). In the area also see Oakville, Tilden.

George West, 15 m.—see Tour 35. Southeast via local roads 6 m. is the site of old Gussettville (cemetery only), and its mighty Charter Oak, where Live Oak Citizens organized their county separate from San Patricio in 1856.

At 31 m. via FM 3162 east 10 m., the ghost of **Lagarto,** pop. 80, once this region's most promising community, occupies the west bank of Lake Corpus Christi. Lagarto—suggesting that early Spaniards saw alligators along the Nueces' lower reaches—in 1880 boasted a population exceeding 500 and a college with nine instructors, one from England, one from Washington, D.C. The railroad by-pass eastward across-river killed the town and gave Mathis life (Tour 39). Not only is the old town a ghost, but it is inhabited by ghosts—on dark nights the drum-beat . of a horseman can be heard by the old ones, but the rider is never seen.

Alice, 56 m. (alt. 205; pop. 19,788), is a heavily-trafficked north-south, east-west crossroads and, in addition, a dividing line between hilly brush country and borderland. Originally, Alice was no more than a 1911 railroad shipping point for cattle, and Mexican ranchers comprised its early population; but oil discovery in 1928 changed its area from South Texas' last frontier to a thriving regional center.

Prominent among exhibits at the annual Jim Wells County Fair each October

are beefmaster cattle, the hardy breed developed for sometimes harsh, arid South Texas range conditions. At nearby Alice Reservoir, birdwatchers can identify scores of species, and in this area, hunting—bird, deer and javelina—is good. For its Mexican heritage, Alice also celebrates Fiesta Bandana early each May, to coincide with the Mexican national holiday, Cinco de Mayo. The South Texas Museum reflects regional history.

Ben Bolt, 63 m., pop. 110, originally a settlement of Mexican herders, perhaps was named for a now-forgotten settler. Buried in an old cemetery nearby is the legendary Headless Horseman, a phantom-like figure that terrorized South Texas in the mid 1800s, its head dangling from its saddlehorn. Actually, the man was a rustler who was trailed, killed and beheaded by Bigfoot Wallace and Creede Taylor, Texas Rangers. He was tied in the saddle of a wild mustang as a warning and in this macabre fashion roamed the countryside for years.

Falfurrias, 92 m. (alt. 109; pop. 5,788). In planted downtown shade, this county seat (Brooks Co.) occupies an area that for a time in the early 1800s was ranched out of Mexico; the outposts, however, failed under Indian attack. Arrival of rails in the early 1900s brought mail, which prior to then had come in by horseback. By 1908 a large creamery was introduced and grew to such an extent that by the 1920s Falfurrias, for its fine butter, was a household name. In town is the Texas Ranger Museum, and in nearby countryside is preserved a small shrine and the grave of Don Pedrito Jaramillo, famed curandero (healer). Hundreds still visit this site. Just north, up US 281, the phantom Lady in Black is supposed to manifest her presence to passersby.

At 140 m. TX 186 leads east 4 m. to **El Sal de Rey,** a salt source for Spain in 1687. Confederate saltworks here were destroyed by Union forces during the Civil War.

Edinburg, 158 m. (alt. 91; pop. 29,885), fringed with stately palms and splashed with the color and fragrance of citrus, opens your gateway to the Rio Grande Valley. Moved in 1908 from the site of present-day Hidalgo on the Rio Grande (Tour 42A), the city almost immediately became center of a burgeoning

citrus industry. The All American City (1969) is home of handsome, internationally minded Univ. of Texas Pan American. Housed formidably in the old county jail, the Hidalgo County Historical Museum displays regional history and interesting collections of dresses fashioned entirely of citrus products and worn by past citrus queens. Fiesta Hidalgo is staged each Columbus Day. In mid-April, Pan American Days salutes the 22 republics of this hemisphere.

Visitors to Hidalgo County Historical Museum viewing turn-of-the-century memorabilia through the store windows in the "Old Town" walk-in exhibit.

Cactusland, 6 m. north on US 281, boasts 20 acres devoted to all forms of cactus and other succulents. Aloe vera is grown commercially. There are self-guiding walkways.

Pharr, 166 m. Intersect US 83/Tour 42A.

☆

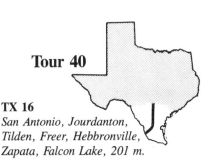

Tour 40

TX 16
San Antonio, Jourdanton, Tilden, Freer, Hebbronville, Zapata, Falcon Lake, 201 m.

Your route, due south from San Antonio, finally veering southwest to reach big, international Falcon Lake, crosses one of Texas' loneliest regions. Still, the combination of good highway and light traffic makes it a good alternate route for the Rio Grande Valley.

Below Jourdanton, an early belt of timber thins out and you penetrate the heart of South Texas brush country, remaining in it for the balance of your journey. As far as Tilden, you travel a

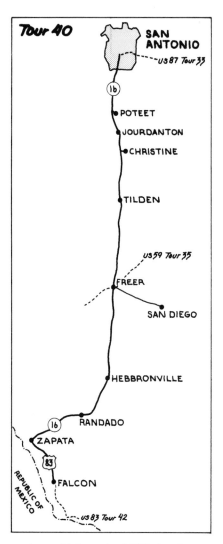

Tour 40

region which early 1900 developers failed to open for winter-garden agriculture—the land is rich, but water remains the problem.

At its lower end, your trip crosses land that bore great Spanish ranches pushed out from the Rio Grande during the 1700s. The Lipan Apache drove them back, but here and there in the brush traces of old haciendas remain.

Midway—from Tilden to Freer—you cut across early northeastbound trails from old Laredo, a region rich in tantalizing legends of buried treasure.

San Antonio, 0 m.—see Tour 33.

Poteet, 27 m. (alt. 525; pop. 3,206), is a quiet and pretty little city, shaded by big oaks and pecans, and claiming title as "Strawberry Capital of Texas." Each mid-April, Poteet holds its gala Strawberry Festival to prove that claim, which it bolsters with a "statue" of the world's largest strawberry—7 feet tall, weighing 1,600 pounds. In earlier days the town

was a miner of lignite coal, and a legend persists that the braying of a ghost mule, buried in one abandoned shaft, can be heard when nights are still. Nearby, also see Pleasanton, Bigfoot.

Jourdanton, 36 m. (alt. 490; pop. 3,220), with broad, sunny streets, and an interesting old courthouse, is a trade center for a rich agricultural area. South of here your road follows a long, straight cut through dense chaparral.

At 45 m., FM 140 leads east to **Christine,** 3 m., pop. 368, a little farming community and seat of one of Texas' most grisly mysteries—Dead Man's Tank. In 1928, Rancher Dick Wiley dug a tank on his south pasture, close to town, cutting into what appeared to be a natural dam. He found it an embankment for a massacred Spanish outpost, its charred ruins still visible then, and a count of 68 skeletons, some with arrowheads imbedded in open, screaming mouths. Scientists dated the find to the time of San Antonio's founding, yet no official explanation or name for the place has been discovered.

Tilden, 68 m. (alt. 270; pop. 500), a small, mesquite-shaded town, for a long time off the main roads and deep in inaccessible brush, has found development slow in coming. Settlement attempted in the 1860s was abandoned because of violent banditry throughout the brush country. Vigilantes finally cleared the area; and today, if few people come to live, many come to poke around. An old smugglers' trail from Laredo to San Antonio came this way, and operations of the outlaws gave rise to many stories of buried treasure. Tilden has based its share of searches for the legendary Rock Pens treasure (see George West, Cotulla), somewhere in this lonely reach of land.

At 78 m. the pyramid shape of San Caja (hill) looms to the east. Legend claims treasure is buried in a cave midway up the side—from gold candelabrum to silver bullion, all looted from Mexico. The hill has been pried at, dug into, cross-lateraled for perhaps a century without yielding its secret. Lending credence to the treasure's presence is the fact that the most formidable search ever undertaken here was backed by a banker.

East on TX 72 about 7 m. is Choke Canyon State Park, with camping and facilities for all water sports.

At 100 m., a long, flat-topped hill lies east along FM 2359 in the area of the Seven Sisters oilfield. This is Loma Alto, where a treasure was once marked with seven rocks placed along the base of the elevation. The line of rocks pointed to a muletrain of buried riches.

Freer, 109 m.—see Tour 35.

Via TX 44 southeast 24 m., **San Diego,** (alt. 312; pop. 4,983), a sunbaked little town, was political headquarters for a long-time powerful family who for years managed to successfully vote more than 90 percent of its county for any favored candidate. Here also, in 1914, was uncovered an extraordinary scheme known as the "Plan of San Diego." It called for a general uprising, scheduled for February 20, 1915, and the assassination of every non-Latin male over 16 years of age—the strike area to include all of South Texas. Interestingly, Germans were excluded from the killings, and shortly thereafter the infamous Zimmerman Note disclosed German efforts to involve Mexico and America in war, thereby diverting American aid to the allies. The San Diego Plan was one part of the plot, which collapsed immediately on discovery.

Hebbronville, 148 m. (alt. 550; pop. 4,465), in 1881 became a rail shipping point for cattle from the vast South Texas ranches. At one time it was credited with more cattle shipped than any other U.S. depot. Oil discovery in the 1930s has dressed up this little city, but it still retains the air of a brush country range town. The area south of here was crisscrossed by early Spanish explorers, as testified to in such old placenames as tiny **Alta Vista** (30 m. south via FM 1017) and **Agua Nueva,** 5 m. beyond—named, respectively, for a prominent elevation and the discovery of a good spring in otherwise arid land.

Don Scotus College, Hebbronville, once a seminary of the Franciscan Order. The interesting walkway on the third story is visible as you approach town.

South of tiny **Randado,** 169 m., pop. 15, via FM 649, is even tinier **Cuevitas,** 18 m., pop. 12, where interesting old ruins may be found. These date back to 1775 ranches, pushed out from Rio Grande bases but beaten down and abandoned under unrelenting Indian attack and confiscation by hostile Anglos following the Texas Revolution and the Mexican War.

Zapata, 201 m. (alt. 311; pop. 7,119), is a very old settlement disguised now with turista trappings for Falcon Lake vacationers and fishermen. Originally this was Carrizo, an outgrowth of cross-river Revilla (later named Guerrero and now submerged by Falcon). Carrizo was part of the great Rio Grande colonization in the mid-1700s directed by Jose de Escandon, who strung his outpost cities at river edge from Matamoros to Laredo. Today the descendants of these first settlers occupy this burgeoning resort gateway to the big lake. In 1839, Zapata was the first headquarters of the short-lived Republic of the Rio Grande. The Republic, conceived by Col. Antonio Zapata here, would have combined the states of northern Mexico with much of today's western United States (see Laredo), an area bigger than the United States. The effort collapsed in 1840, and Zapata was executed.

At **Falcon Lake,** 23 m. southeast (Tour 42), the State Park offers camping, water sports, and all facilities.

☆

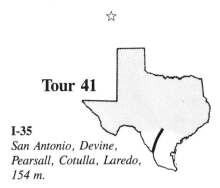

Tour 41

I-35
San Antonio, Devine, Pearsall, Cotulla, Laredo, 154 m.

Perhaps more than any other, this handsome interstate is the broad road to Mexico—you begin in old Spain's major Texas outpost, San Antonio; and end in another early town, Laredo, today America's major gateway to Mexico.

There are a few ghost towns along the way, and near Cotulla you cross a land originally home to the wild, free-run-

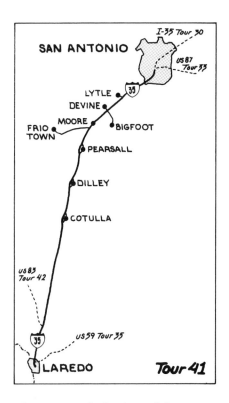

Tour 41

ning mustang. In the tiny outlying towns, particularly beyond Cotulla, you can sense the flavor of Mexico more sharply than anywhere else in Texas. You are in the realm of wondrous superstitions, of ghosts and magic cures—these healings attributable to the *curandero,* a doctor whose skill with herbal medicine is derived from ancient Indian ancestors.

Historically, you reverse the general route of Santa Anna's 1836 invasion—Alamo-bound and later crushed at San Jacinto. Throughout, the terrain is rough South Texas brush country. Cleared and watered, as you see it occasionally, this is exceptionally rich land. The little cities—none are large—without exception are neat, bright, and prospering.

San Antonio, 0 m.—see Tour 33. Continue south from Tour 30/Region II.

Lytle, 23 m. (alt. 745; pop. 2,255), a neat little town grown from an early ranch, then 1912 rails, today occupies an area of irrigated farming, producing excellent vegetables. Close by is the site of old Benton, a boomer in the 1870s, its Benton Institute offering degrees in law. Like others, it died of railroad by-pass; some traces remain. Immediately west are coal mines on private land.

Devine, 32 m. (alt. 670; pop. 3,928), spreads green-lawned homes and planted shade over a wide area, looking larger than it is. A memento of its earlier days

can be found at Stroud Blacksmith Shop, a creator of branding irons in operation since 1903. The red soil is peanut-growing countryside. In the area also see Hondo, Castroville, Poteet.

Via TX 173/FM 472 southeast 8 m., **Bigfoot,** pop. 75, took its name from Texas' most famous ranger, William A. A. (Bigfoot) Wallace who, outliving a multitude of scrapes from 1840 Texas onward, spent his declining years here. After the ill-advised Mier Expedition (Tour 42), Wallace survived the Black Beans drawing and more than one Indian ambush. One of his forays provided this area and nearly all South Texas with the "Headless Horseman" (see Ben Bolt). A little museum preserves relics of his life and times.

Below Moore at 44 m., US 57 and FM 140 lead west 19 m. to **Frio Town,** pop. 38, a ghost whose skeletal ruins rise from a field today. First Frio County seat, this was a lively town, experiencing Indian raids and the thundering evangelism of circuit riders like Andrew Jackson Potter, the Fighting Parson (see Lockhart). O. Henry supposedly came to a dance here, as did John Wesley Hardin, the gunfighter. Ruins of the courthouse remain; the jail museum, now moved to Pearsall (below), contains interesting pioneer memorabilia.

Pearsall, 54 m. (alt. 646; pop. 6,924), occupies an area traversed by La Salle, searching for Spanish Rio Grande outposts in 1685. The town was established in 1880 with the arrival of rails, and took Frio County's seat in 1883. A prosperous, growing little city with new oil and gas fields nearby, Pearsall also displays the "world's largest peanut," located on South Oak Street to advise of the area's 55 million pounds of peanuts harvested annually. Years ago Pearsall demonstrated unusual innkeeping in the operation of the Mercantile Hotel, run on self-serve room selection, no desk clerk, and an honor system in leaving lodging payment. A $5 annual loss was experienced. Hunting is generally excellent in the surrounding brush country.

Dilley, 70 m. (alt. 586; pop. 2,632), another town born of the railroad, has long been famed for its watermelons.

Cotulla, 86 m. (alt. 442; pop. 3,694), shows a fresh, wide-street look, still with the feel of a brush country ranchtown, centering, as it does, an area where the cattleman is more vaquero than cowboy and must equip himself against every type of thorn, from cactus to catclaw and mesquite to Spanish dagger. For this range riding, chaps of leather or heavy canvas, or denim jumpers, and gloves are worn.

In early days Cotulla knew gunplay, particularly during elections, when one or the other side held armed guard over the polls. A toll count at one time listed three sheriffs and 19 "citizens." An old story claims the biggest roundup of wild mustangs ever attempted was once mounted here. A giant, open-ended corral was used and more than 1,000 of the hardy mounts filled an Argentine contract.

Two distinguished Americans resided here for a time—the school where late President Lyndon B. Johnson once taught is open to visitors; and O. Henry lived for a time on a neighboring ranch.

FM 624 leads southeast 24 m. to the approximate site of Fort Ewell, 1852–54 (inaccessible across the Nueces). The fort was established to guard the then-dangerous San Antonio-Laredo road, and was abandoned for unhealthy location. A settlement, La Salle, hung on as county seat until Cotulla took the reins in 1882. Somewhere in the close, dense brush is the site of the Rock Pens treasure. According to story, 31 mule loads of silver looted from Mexico were buried inside rock barricades thrown up when the looters were overtaken and most of them killed. The 1873 treasure apparently still eludes its searchers.

At 135 m., merge with US 83/Tour 42. **Laredo,** 154 m.—see Tour 35.

At Laredo, FM 1472 parallels the Rio Grande northwest 25 m. to the ghost site of mining town **Dolores,** or **Minera.** The town dated from 1880 when cannel coal was mined in shafts back from the river. On dark nights now, a lantern-carrying ghost may be seen wandering the lonely, low hills. According to legend, it may be Dolores, a beautiful girl who threw herself down a mineshaft after a tragic love affair. Other accounts believe the wanderer to be the spirit of a murderous bandit who hid treasure in the shafts below. Ruins of the old mine works are on a private ranch.

Upriver, via local roads toward Eagle Pass, are the ruins of **Villa de Palafox,** established in 1810 but abandoned within a decade under incessant Indian

attacks. In 1829 the Indians almost completely destroyed the little town. Here, too, the ghosts of its dead wander about, awaiting aid. The ruins lie on private land.

☆

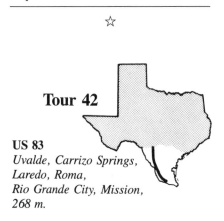

Tour 42

US 83
Uvalde, Carrizo Springs, Laredo, Roma, Rio Grande City, Mission, 268 m.

Continuing Tour 59 (Region IV), this southerly route describes a sweeping curve from Uvalde through Laredo,

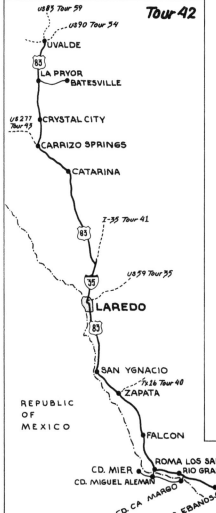

to bend eastward, following the Rio Grande toward its mouth. From the foot of the hills at Uvalde, you descend through a variety of terrains: first, the rich, flat Winter Garden with its irrigated truck farming; then the rolling, rough ranchlands around Laredo; finally—at Mission—the tropical garden of the lower Rio Grande Valley.

Historically, you follow a great procession—the Rio Grande's banks had been trail worn for centuries before Anglos arrived. Beginning in 1519, Spain pushed tentative exploration up from the river's mouth, a search to continue over three centuries. From Laredo southeast, you follow the route of Spain's great colonizer, Jose de Escandon, who in the mid-1700s established most of the border cities between Laredo and Matamoros. Throughout, the flavor is richly that of Old Mexico.

Along the way, a number of crossings allow a quick look into that southerly neighbor. The most impressive crosses mighty Falcon Dam, below Zapata. The most intriguing is the old hand-pulled ferry at Los Ebanos, near the end of this tour.

Uvalde, 0 m.—see Tour 34. Continue south from Tour 59, Region IV.

At La Pryor, 20 m., US 57 leads east to **Batesville,** 15 m., pop. 1,313, a sleepy village in timber along the Leona River. Here in the mid-1800s, famed Texas Ranger Ed Westfall trapped and hunted alone. His picket cabin attacked by Comanche, he was left for dead, shot through the neck. After three days he regained consciousness and, although blind and without food, crawled for a week—feeling his way along the Leona banks—30 m. to frontier Fort Inge (see Uvalde). To the amazement of the fort's doctor, he recovered his eyesight and health.

Crystal City, 38 m. (alt. 581; pop. 8,263). This spinach capital of America, with its statue of Popeye, is a relatively new town in old land, lying as it does on the route of Camino Real. From Spanish Mission San Juan Bautista, near Eagle

Who else would Crystal City, the spinach capital of America, honor but Popeye?

Pass in Mexico (Tour 43), the Old San Antonio Road was blazed in 1691 and was the main thoroughfare into Texas until well into the 1800s. Settlement here was delayed until the 1860s because of Indian menace.

Via FM 1433 south 4 m., **Lake Espantosa** is a strange, listless, jungle-like oxbow or *resaca* from the ancient Nueces River, out of place in this brush country. In the 1700s it was the best campsite—both wood and water—between San Juan Bautista and outpost San Antonio. A 1750 wagon train camped here and one woman was dragged into the lake by a monster "much larger than an alligator." Tales grew that a later treasure train with Spanish payroll for the San Antonio garrison was sucked into the lake—some old-timers believe that on dark nights the rumble of that wagon train, and the screams of its drivers, can be heard. Later, refugees fleeing the 1830s English colony of Dolores, nearby (Tour 34), camped here and were massacred. Thereafter, the lake itself was deemed the killer, and its name, loosely translated, became "Lake of Terror."

Carrizo Springs, 50 m. (alt. 602; pop. 5,745), is a vegetable processing center occupying an area long known to history but late in development. Camino Real crosses from southwest to northeast, nearby. Apparent lack of water limited the region to ranching, and this city was first settled in 1865 as a range town. At the turn of the century, artesian wells were discovered and the Winter Garden boom was on. Date palms abound through town. At Carrizo Springs intersect US 277/Tour 43.

Catarina, 69 m., pop. 45, is being retaken by the brushland it edges. It blossomed in the early 1900s as a promising resort, with wide, palm-bordered streets and flowering esplanades. The area failed to develop as its promoters had hoped and the tiny village has faded steadily. Some handsome old homes watch Catarina's decline.

At 112 m., merge with I-35/Tour 41.

Laredo, 131 m.—see Tours 35 and 41.

At 147 m., cross **Arroyo Dolores.** Briefly south, where the arroyo empties into the Rio Grande, is the stark, rock and adobe ghost of Dolores (not to be confused with another ghost of the same name just north), desolate around its weedblown plaza. Simultaneously with upriver Laredo, the town was founded in 1750; with a ferry here, it promised for a time to outstrip its struggling neighbor. Indian attacks, however, were unrelenting, and the northbound road chose Laredo's better crossing, relegating this ranching center to oblivion. A number of old ruins huddle on the bluff over the river (on private ranch).

San Ygnacio, 166 m. (alt. 324; pop. 895), founded in 1790, with its ancient fort, old church on the plaza and homes of early Mexican design—the Jesus Trevino house dates from 1830—is so typically Mexican it was chosen for many scenes of the Marlon Brando film, "Viva Zapata." The quaint little village rests in a road bend just south of the highway. Most of the town is on the National Register of Historic Places. The La Paz Museum is located in a 200-year-old Mexican home on the campus of Benavides Elementary School.

The sundial topping the old fort recalls 1815 perils. Jose Villareal, a boy of 15, and his cousin were captured by Indians near downriver Guerrero. The boys managed to escape just short of the hill country and, through Jose's knowledge of the stars, were able to find their way home after great ordeal. Grown to manhood, Jose settled here and fashioned the sundial, setting it at midnight, aligned on the North Star. The ancient time piece—a gesture of gratitude—keeps accurate sidereal time.

Zapata, 180 m.—see Tour 40.

Falcon, 203 m., pop. 50, is a lakeside tourist stop opposite one of the most fully-equipped Texas state parks. The 60-m. long, 78,000-acre lake, popular for all water sports, is known as "Black

Bass Kingdom." Also abounding are white bass, crappie, walleye, and big catfish.

Falcon Dam, 206 m., is a 5-m.-long earth and rockfill structure constructed by the U.S. and Mexico, an outstanding example of practical cooperation between neighboring countries in the utilization of natural resources. Simple metal shafts bearing the seals of both countries mark the international boundary line. Fine views are available from the concrete spillway. When dammed to form this lake, the river submerged four old towns—Zapata (Revilla), Ramireno, Lopeno and Falcon, all dating to the 1700s.

You can cross the dam into Mexico and circle back via **Ciudad Mier,** site of the 1842 Texan invasion of Mexico, an ill-advised venture that ended with surrender in the still bullet-scarred plaza, and the subsequent drawing—by Santa Anna's orders—of black or white beans—a lottery whose stakes were life or death. Deep in Mexico, the drawing executed one man in ten (see Monument Hill, La Grange). Mier, and **Camargo** just below it, are fascinating old Mexican towns, original settlements and once at the head of riverboat navigation of the Rio Grande. The Mexico tour approximates 40 m., recrossing from Ciudad Miguel Aleman to Roma or from Camargo to Rio Grande City.

U.S.-Mexico international boundary marker on Falcon Dam near Falcon, Texas.

Roma Los Saenz, 220 m. (alt. 200; pop. 8,059). This river town, one of our oldest, seems like a bit of Spanish Morocco, with its tucked-away streets, its blocky houses with iron-barred windows and overhanging balconies. Founded in 1751, an outgrowth of Ciudad Mier, across-river, it housed an early Indian mission, grew into a riverport, then seems to have skipped two centuries to today. A mission chapel still stands. Some of Viva Zapata was filmed in Roma. The Roma Historical Museum reflects the area's rich story.

Rio Grande City, 234 m. (alt. 190; pop. 9,891), with a broad approaching esplanade, clusters a tight little downtown on the river opposite Camargo, having grown out from that Escandon settlement. Originally, this was Carnestolendas. In 1847–48, Henry Clay Davis settled here and began what was to become an American riverport. In 1848, Zachary Taylor established Fort Ringgold on the east edge of the city, an outpost that saw considerable bandit activity in 1875. The old Davis landing where sternwheelers tied up has been preserved, and the La Borde House, adjacent, is an interior-patioed landmark, as well as a picturesque little inn. Across from the courthouse is a replica of the grotto at Lourdes.

Fort Ringgold, in excellent preservation, is now used by the Rio Grande City School District. Among those who served here are such distinguished names as Robert E. Lee, U.S. Grant, Stonewall Jackson, Jefferson Davis, and John J. (Blackjack) Pershing.

At little **Sullivan City,** 250 m., pop. 2,371, a gradual change begins to alter the landscape—the upriver brush country giving way to fertile cropland.

Immediately south via FM 886 is **Los Ebanos,** pop. 100, a tiny riverbank village boasting the only government-licensed hand-operated ferry in Texas. Slated to be replaced by a private toll bridge, ferry operates on cables. The two-car raft, leading to tiny Diaz Ordaz in Mexico, anchors its U.S. side to a big ebony tree, source of the village name.

At 259 m., via FM 1427, little **Penitas,** pop. 1,077, slumbers just south, its sprawl of frame buildings belying great age—it could be one of our nation's oldest towns. An Indian village was known here in 1625, a settlement of Spaniards in 1682. Legend persists that 12 surviving shipmates of Cabeza de

Birdwatchers in Bentsen-Rio Grande Valley State Park, Mission.

Vaca actually settled among the Indians in the 1530s at this site.

At 263 m., FM 2062 leads south to **Bentsen-Rio Grande Valley State Park,** alongside the Rio Grande, with camping and all facilities, including two interesting hiking trails. This is an excellent bird-watching area—many of the species sighted are common only to Mexico. You may see the green jay, chachalaca, kiskadee and Lichtenstein's oriole.

Mission, 268 m. Enter Rio Grande Valley—see Tour 42A.

☆

Tour 42A

US 83
(Rio Grande Valley)
Mission, McAllen, Weslaco,
Harlingen, San Benito,
Brownsville, 73 m.

Your route is the central one of three traversing the Rio Grande Valley, beginning at Mission's palm-lined citrus orchards and ending at Brownsville's Tip of Texas, with glittering South Padre Island just opposite.

The impact of the Valley is color—bougainvillea's lavender in spring and poinsettia's crimson in winter, the many shades of green in citrus orchards lined divisionally with towering palms and splashed with yellow and orange globes of fruit. In all this, the green-lawned

homes seem even more dazzling white in their low, rambling Monterrey architecture.

Today the Valley is winter home for the "Snow Birds," thousands from the North who, more than Texans, have discovered this vacationland. Before 1904, few travelers penetrated this region—it was a forbidding sea of thorny brush. Northern farmers, excited with year-round planting, brought about the transformation.

Eastward to Harlingen, the string of close-marching cities comprises what Valley residents term "the longest Main Street in the World"—43 miles of it on US 83 business route; and you could lengthen it by allowing one road bend southeast for Brownsville. North of US 83, TX 107 runs east from Edinburg (Tour 39A), offering a different landscape—it cuts across the great agricultural area, free of the cities. Also varied is the lower of the three routes, US 281, closely paralleling the river between Reynosa, Mex. and Brownsville, the route of Zachary Taylor's old military road. Here the atmosphere is of Mexico; the villages are old—many, like Progresso and Hidalgo, dating back to the 1700s. Your route follows the town-to-town middleground of US 83, business route. If you prefer the paralleling expressway, watch for appropriate exits.

Mission, 0 m. (alt. 134; pop. 28,653). Home of the Texas Ruby Red grapefruit, this palm-flanked capital of Valley citrus orchards was established in 1824 by Oblate Fathers at La Lomita Chapel, south. Their experiments with growing oranges were forerunners of today's industry.

The city is a continuing splash of color—the American Poinsettia Association, headquartered here, each December stages its brilliant Poinsettia Show. Following that, late each January the 10-day Texas Citrus Festival is held, with a style show where all costumes are made of citrus or vegetable materials. Throughout the winter, Valley visitors are treated to a succession of festivals, each boasting one city's contribution to a varied economy.

FM 1016 leads south to **La Lomita,** 3 m., a mission of the Oblate Fathers built as early as 1820. The little 12-by-25-foot chapel has been restored and surrounded by a park and picnic area. Anzalduas Park, 100 acres of big shade trees with a boat-launching dock, is immediately south on the Rio Grande.

Adjacent to the chapel is Pepe's on the River, popular with tourists who dine and dance in a patio-like setting on the bank of the Rio Grande. Sunsets over Mexico here are said to be the prettiest in Texas.

McAllen, 7 m. (alt. 122; pop. 84,021), the major city of this upper valley, is a gateway to Old Mexico, just south, and a principal winter resort for midwesterners. From January through March, McAllen hosts special state picnics honoring its visitors. Like most of its sisters, this city of palms, bougainvillea and poinsettias came into being in the early 1900s.

The McAllen International Museum features Mexican folk art, masks, and regional costumes in its Ethnography Gallery; traveling exhibits are varied. Mexican city of Reynosa, south, maintains a Zona Rosa for *turistas* with shopping for handicrafts from across Mexico, fine dining, and a traditional Mexican market as well as bullfights on occasion.

Via FM 115 south 8 m. is old **Hidalgo,** pop. 3,292, a combination of the very old—Hidalgo was an outgrowth of

Tropical palms bespeak McAllen's gentle year-round climate, which attracts thousands each winter.

mid-1700 Rio Grande colonization—and the very new: the bridge across to Reynosa, Mexico, is a busy one, making Hidalgo an international trade city with many fruit and vegetable brokers, customhouse brokers, and duty-free stores. Several ancient buildings such as the first post office and the old Rodriguez General Store are scattered about, and the old courthouse and jail are interesting. Each March, Hidalgo hosts "Borderfest," a four-day celebration of friendship with Mexico. Across the river are the shops and cabarets of Reynosa, a big border city spread around its fascinating, block-square Mercado Zaragoza, the market. You can park on the U.S. side and walk across, or you will find excellent facilities (and a good road beyond) for entry and an extended Mexico visit.

Eastward on US 83, **Pharr-San Juan-Alamo,** 10 m. (alt. 107; pop. 51,946), follow so closely they appear as one city. Pharr—biggest, and designating itself as "Crossroads of the Rio Grande Valley" for its northward access via US 281/Tour 39A—is a busy commercial center, and each December hosts the All-Valley Winter Vegetable Show. A leather factory producing custom garments is open to visitors at 904 E. US Business 83. A tourist information center at 308 W. Park has information on historic buildings and other points of interest, such as the Old Clock Museum (929 E. Preston St.), with its collection of 450 antique clocks dating from 1690 on.

At San Juan, tidy in its slender palms, is the Church of Our Lady of the Valley, a massive miracle shrine to which pilgrims journey—often long distances afoot—from throughout the U.S. Note the many crutches discarded here in silent testimony. The San Juan Hotel, charmingly remodeled, is a delightful border inn.

Alamo offers fruits as well as tours of Sunderland's Cactus Garden (north on FM 907), a nursery featuring acres of native and exotic cacti and other plants.

Via FM 907 south 7 m. is Santa Ana National Wildlife Refuge, a beautiful 2,000-acre sanctuary for birds and animal life. Species not common elsewhere in America may be found here. There are several interesting hiking trails.

Donna, 18 m. (alt. 88; pop. 12,652), is a big produce shipper and brisk agribusi-

ness center, hosting the South Texas Lamb and Sheep Exhibition each January. The American Legion Hall houses a museum reflecting Donna's early days.

Weslaco, 22 m. (alt. 70; pop. 21,877), with an interesting downtown area in Spanish-Moorish architecture, is a Mexico gateway via Progreso, 7 m. south. Progreso is another old offshoot of the 1700s Rio Grande colonization.

A winter visitors center is maintained at Weslaco, close by the city's Nature Garden with plants and birds native to the Valley. Name of the town was taken from the initials of W. E. Stewart Land Co., its developer. Center of a large citrus-growing area, the world's largest grapefruit juice canning plant is here. A Bicultural Museum (515 S. Kansas Ave.) showcases both Hispanic and Anglo cultures.

Llano Grande Lake, offering water sports, is 1 m. south. Between Weslaco and Mercedes, look for the Lower Rio Grande Valley C of C—all Valley information.

Mercedes, 27 m. (alt. 61; pop. 12,694), was one of the first Valley cities built, after engineers determined that gravity flow irrigation was feasible from the Rio Grande. Each March, 4-H queens reign over the annual Rio Grande Valley Livestock Show.

La Feria, 33 m. (alt. 56; pop. 4,360), centers the valley east-west and was settled by Spanish ranchers in the 1780s, taking its name from rodeos and festivals held here. Anglo settlement did not occur until 1910.

Immediately south is **Santa Maria,** pop. 210, also an early settlement, with an interesting mid-1800s Gothic-style church.

Harlingen, 43 m. (alt. 36; pop. 48,735). At the crossroads of two of the Valley's entering highways, here is its metropolitan center, handsome with wide, palm-lined streets and a broad, clean downtown area. It was one of the Valley's first Anglo settlements, founded in 1901 by Lon C. Hill, who foresaw the area's rich future. By 1915, with border difficulties along the Rio Grande, Harlingen stationed both Texas Rangers and National Guardsmen and was known as Six Shooter Junction.

In its way, stationing of the guardsmen boomed the Valley, for after W.W. I the men—from their various homes across the U.S.—recalled the mild year-round climate here, and Valley development was under way. A barge channel (fishing is good) has made Harlingen an inland port.

A Texas Travel Information Center at the intersection of US 77/US 83 features bilingual travel counselors, maps, and videos to help you plan your Valley stay.

Hill Park contains the plantation home of Harlingen founder Lon C. Hill. Numerous RV parks cater to "Winter Texans"; many have recreation centers far outstripping public facilities.

The Rio Grande Valley Museum and Hospital Museum (Boxwood and Raintree Sts.) features historical and cultural items, rock and shell displays, and a Valley map with lights to pinpoint locations, as well as original Harlingen Hospital and a Garden for the Blind.

The Marine Military Academy, America's only college prep school that maintains customs and traditions of the U.S. Marine Corps, is near the Industrial Air Park. Featured is the plaster model for the Iwo Jima War Memorial at Arlington National Cemetery. The huge figures, 32 feet tall, honor the soldiers who raised the U.S. flag over Iwo Jima to signal its WWII capture.

Valley Greyhound Park, south on Ed Carey Dr., features racing. At Harlingen, merge with US 77/Tour 37.

Via FM 106 and local roads northeast, Laguna Atascosa National Wildlife Refuge, 20 m., shelters thousands of ducks and geese from October through January.

San Benito, 55 m. (alt. 33; pop. 20,125), is one of the Valley's prettiest cities, one of palms and *resacas*—serene oxbows from the ancient Rio Grande. The homes are handsome; the streets, broad. The city has a Spanish look, and merits it—its area was settled with outpost ranches as early as 1770. Anglo settlement began in 1880. San Benito stages the Cameron County Fair each January.

Brownsville, 76 m. (alt. 35; pop. 98,962), parlayed southmost location in Texas into a major winter resort and retirement center, and a primary international gateway to Mexico, via Matamoros. Seaward opposite is the resort-sparkling tip of South Padre Island. Brownsville is a mixture of old and new, with much to see—a local tour is best started at the Brownsville Information Center on the north side of the city.

Historic old Fort Brown is well preserved, with its buildings used by Texas Southmost College.

At the southmost bend of the Rio Grande (just below the city via FM 1419) are the remains of a natural palm forest such as that seen by 1519 Spaniards, when Rio Grande received an early name: River of Palms. The Gladys Porter Zoo is an excellent zoological park without bars or cages—a number of small "islands" in a *resaca* house the animals. The International Friendship Gardens are located nearby at the bridge; across is the major city of Matamoros, steeped in historic sites and with every tourist facility—see it with a guide.

The old Stillman House Museum, dating from 1850, recalls much early history, while the Brownsville Art League Museum displays regional works. The city began with the Mexican War, when Zachary Taylor established Fort Brown as a base, his beachhead from the sea lying at Point (now Port) Isabel to the east. Mexican troops from Matamoros attacked the fort and brought on the war's two opening battles—at Palo Alto, 9 m. north, and Resaca de la Palma, 3 m. north. In these, Taylor drove the attackers back across the Rio Grande, relieved Fort Brown, and shortly thereafter occupied Matamoros before moving on to Monterey.

The shallow-draft steamboats he left behind opened a brisk river trade for the port near the Rio Grande's mouth. Forty-Niners rode them to the head of navigation at Rio Grande City before hitting the California Trail. During the Civil War, the area experienced intense activity as a shipping outlet for the Confederacy, across-river through Mexico. The Confederates lost and burned the city, then retook it, and finally fought and won the war's last battle just east at

The Children's Parade during Charro Days, Brownsville.

Palmito Hill (TX 4, toward Brazos Santiago Island). After the war, a large U.S. army was rushed here to end the French occupation of Mexico under Maximilian. A period of extreme isolation followed, one of the last stage lines in Texas—from Brownsville to Alice—operating as late as 1904, when railroad and rapid growth overtook the area.

Today the port city is a mixture of tight, narrow streets and adobe dwellings, in contrast with sweeping boulevards and handsome homes. However, of all the Valley, Brownsville carries the sharpest flavor of Old Mexico, and with four days of pre-Lenten festivities, stages Charro Days late each February to enrich that flavor.

Eastward, TX 4 ends on the broad beaches of **Brazos Island,** 30 m., a developing state park (beach camping allowed anywhere). Beach-running, you can reach the Rio Grande's mouth, 4 m. south, once a great roadstead for shipping but now bypassed by Brownsville's ship channel. At the mouth, the deep sand hides two ghost towns, Clarksville, a collection of shacks left from army occupation during and after the Civil War, and Bagdad, across in Mexico. During the Civil War, Bagdad was a city of 35,000 engaged in gun-running and any other profitable war-time trade. Legend claims a Spanish resort preceded this city in the 1700s—both destroyed in time by hurricane.

Upriver toward Brownsville at a yet-undetermined site near the city, was Spain's first colonial attempt north of the Rio Grande, the settlement in 1519–20 of Garay, at one time supported by some 750 troops with cannon. The savage Karankawa Indian, together with Spain's failure to find treasure—as Cortes had done, only months earlier in Mexico City—forced abandonment.

Via TX 48 northeast, **Port Isabel,** 25 m. (alt. 15; pop. 4,467), opposite the tip of South Padre Island, occupies an area ranched by Spaniards as early as 1770, their descendants moving with Padre Nicolas Balli to escape Mexican revolutionists in 1820—hence the Island's name. In 1846, the point based Zachary Taylor's Mexico-bound army. Today it is gateway to the handsome resorts of South Padre Island, across Queen Isabella Causeway. The 1852 lighthouse, now a state historic site, offers an excellent view of this southernmost tip of Texas. Dry-cradled and fully restored, the 54-foot shrimpboat,

A beached shrimp boat near the north end of Park Road 100, South Padre Island.

Lady Bea, is open for inspection nearby. The Spanish-style Yacht Club Hotel offers handsome lodging and excellent cuisine, particularly seafood.

Across Queen Isabella Causeway, at more than 2 m. one of the Gulf Coast's longest (the old causeway now serves as a fishing pier), is glistening **South Padre Island,** 29 m., pop. 1,677, with its handsome resorts, excellent fishing—jetty, surf, pier or charter—exceptional beaches and beachcombing. Isla Blanca and Andy Bowie Parks offer all seafront facilities. Pan American University's Marine Biology Laboratories display oceanic flora and fauna. Together with Port Isabel, South Padre stages an International Fishing Tournament early each August, and the fun festival of Queen Isabella Days each mid-October.

Known around the world for her efforts to save the sea turtle is Ila Loetscher. A museum at 5805 Gulf Blvd. showcases her work. Many of the beachfront condos can be rented by the day or week; inquire at C of C (600 Padre Blvd.) for information.

☆

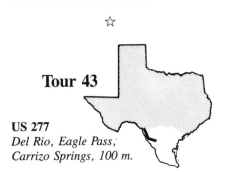

Tour 43

US 277
Del Rio, Eagle Pass,
Carrizo Springs, 100 m.

This brief trip, a continuation of Tour 58 (Region IV), parallels the Rio Grande from Del Rio to Eagle Pass, a hilly, rough land of brush and thorn, one with a feel of great isolation, yet with a kind of austere beauty in its very solitude. At Eagle Pass, your road angles eastward through lowering brush coun-

try to Carrizo Springs, and a junction with southbound US 83/Tour 42. The cut-across at Del Rio allows travelers from western states to veer directly toward the Lower Rio Grande Valley.

Until comparatively recent times this was the dangerous land of the border Apache, the Lipan; and you may likely encounter some of his descendants in tiny and isolated dwellings along the way. It is also a land of relatively recent American settlement, although it was among the very first areas of Texas known to Imperial Spain. Driving north from Mexico City, Spaniards crossed the Rio Grande at the site of Del Rio and Eagle Pass in the 1600s. La Salle, in all probability, traversed much of your route in his 1685 search for Spanish outposts along the Rio Grande; and the last leg of your journey—northeast from Eagle Pass—approximates the beginnings of Camino Real, Spain's 1691 royal road into Texas.

Del Rio, 0 m.—see Tour 57 (Region IV). Continue southeast from Tour 58, US 277.

At 20 m., FM 693 leads northeast 8 m. to the ill-fated ghost settlement of **Dolores,** 8 m., founded in 1834 by English colonists. See Brackettville.

Quemado, 36 m. (alt. 790; pop. 426), is an isolated little community centering an area of rich, irrigated farms. Its name derived from early Spanish explorers who misread the arid land with its traces of petrified wood as an area of volcanic activity and called this the "Burned Valley." In the early 1900s, gravity irrigation was found feasible here with water canalized 40 m. from upriver Rio Grande, a project which has yielded farmers three crops yearly. Much of the

television production "Lonesome Dove" was filmed along Rio Grande near here.

Eagle Pass, 56 m. (alt. 726; pop. 20,651). The narrow streets of this little city wander down to the Rio Grande gateway to Mexico at Piedras Negras (Black Rocks), across-river. Both cities are growing with increasing traffic bound south for Saltillo, San Luis Potosi and Mexico City. Piedras Negras is an intriguing border town, not too "turista," yet with good restaurants, cabarets, shops and a big market.

Both cities sprang from one of Mexico's earliest crossings into Texas, at Presidio San Juan Bautista, 30 m. downriver at tiny, secluded Guerrero, Mexico. In 1849, Eagle Pass came into being as a military camp in the Mexican War, strengthened later by the founding of Fort Duncan, outpost guard on the California Trail. Fort Duncan was involved in Indian campaiging; then, as the fort became an active Confederate base, Eagle Pass became a trade outpost for shipments via Mexico.

Eagle Pass saw the burial—100 yards downstream from today's international bridge—of the last Confederate battleflag as, on July 4, 1865, General Joseph Shelby's Missouri cavalry crossed into Mexico without surrendering. This spot has been called the grave of the Confederacy.

Fort Duncan served periodically until 1940, when its grounds became a city park. Many of its old buildings still in good preservation, the fort is a historical museum today. Early each May, Eagle Pass observes Pioneer Heritage Week.

The brief trip across the river to Guerrero and San Juan Bautista is well worth your time—a 45-minute run over paved road. The 1700 establishment—three missions and a fortress—served as Spain's launchpad for the occupation of Texas, including the founding of San Antonio and the East Texas missions around Nacogdoches. For more than a century the presidio marked the beginning of Imperial Spain's Camino Real in Texas. Much of the old Mexican town is built from the rock of the ancient complex; however, the ruins of Mission San Bernardo, largest of the three missions and alone still standing, are formidable.

Eight miles south is the Kickapoo Indian Reservation, one of three such in Texas.

Carrizo Springs, 100 m.—see Tour 42.

Region IV
Tours 44 through 62

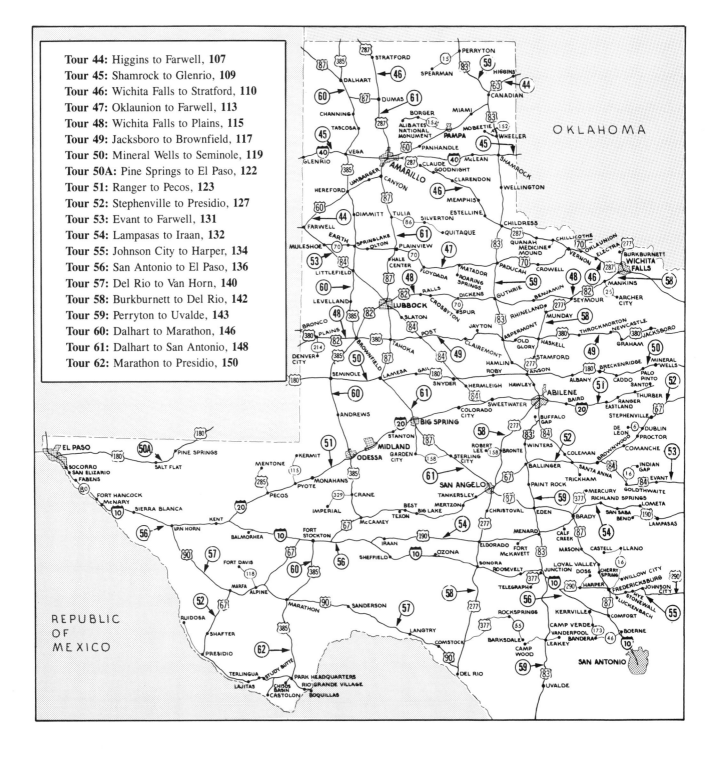

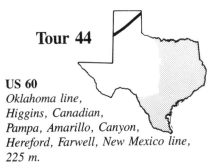

Tour 44

US 60

Oklahoma line, Higgins, Canadian, Pampa, Amarillo, Canyon, Hereford, Farwell, New Mexico line, 225 m.

This road, crossing the continent from Norfolk, Va. to Los Angeles, Calif., takes the High Plains route through Texas, starting near the northeast corner of the Panhandle at Higgins and slanting southward to exit in New Mexico southwest of Amarillo.

Your first few miles traverse sparsely-timbered rolling plains, dotted with occasional low mesas, but beyond the Canadian River breaks—deeply eroded to near-canyon proportions—the terrain flattens to a level sweep of land that early settlers could cross, treeless as it was, only with a saddlehorn compass. Today it is a land of rich fields, of cattle, and of oil; and its towns rise from the horizon with skyscraper skylines that, upon approach, become towering grain elevators. On the western leg of your tour, where shallow-well irrigation is common, it is nothing to drive through a manmade rain drenching green fields in which oil well pumps bow and nod at their work.

golden cities of Cibola and Quivira, returned to minister to pueblo Indians in 1542 and two years later died at their hands.

Higgins is in an area once disputed between Texas and Oklahoma due to surveying errors in locating the 100th meridian. A strip 134 miles long and between 3,600 feet and 3,700 feet wide was involved. A 1927 survey placed the new line in its present location, and the Supreme Court awarded the land to Texas. A few Sooners became instant Texans. Westward from Higgins, for half your journey you reverse the approximate route followed by Coronado immediately before he turned his long-suffering force back in disillusionment. This tour takes you to his last few camps—among the pueblo dwellings along the Canadian breaks, the flint quarries above Amarillo, and the great gorge of Palo Duro Canyon, immediately south of there, where the Spaniards celebrated a Thanksgiving Day in 1541.

Northwest of Higgins 3 m., via TX 213, is the site of old **Timm City,** once an overnight trail stop for cattle drives into Indian Territory.

Canadian, 27 m. (alt. 2,339; pop. 2,417), within a timbered bend of that river, grew from a crossroads settlement of soldiers, railroaders and cowhands. With a hardbitten beginning, the place was alternately known as Hogtown or

ber of old homes and buildings, the most unusual being the Public Library—the only one in America built and owned by a local chapter of the Women's Christian Temperance Union. In 1910, the WCTU financed that building through contributions—the more substantial ones made by Canadian's then-numerous saloons!

Each late October the city stages its Fall Foliage Festival, with everything from team roping and a chili cookoff to a show of arts and crafts and antique autos. Occasion is the reddening of the great trees banking the Canadian River.

At Canadian merge briefly with US 83/Tour 59.

FM 2266 leads east through the Gene Howe Wildlife Management Area (largest game preserve in the Panhandle) to Lake Marvin, 11 m., with good fishing, cabins and camping facilities.

A fine, tree-lined road: FM 2266 en route to Lake Marvin, near Canadian.

Southeast of the city, near tiny **Gem,** are the sites of the Lyman Wagon Train Battleground, and of the Buffalo Wallow Fight (see Tour 59). In the area, also see Mobeetie.

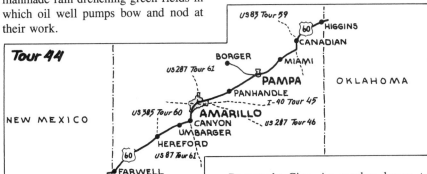

Okla. line, 0 m. You cross into Texas 50 m. southwest of Woodward, Okla.

Higgins, 2 m. (alt. 2,569; pop. 464), a little oasis of planted shade in the deep grasslands of these High Plains, is a retail center for this agricultural region. Northwest some 15 m. via TX 213/305, near Lipscomb, is the site where America's first priest, Fray Juan Padilla, was martyred. The priest, who had accompanied Coronado on his search for the

Desperado City. As ranches began to move in, Canadian laid claim to one of America's first rodeos, when cowhands used its main (and only) street to prove their prowess at bronc riding. That claim is recalled each July Fourth with Hemphill County's Old timers Reunion and Rodeo (see Pecos, Seymour).

Canadian settled down, growing slowly with wheat farming; however, in recent years, extensive oil and gas discoveries have produced a mild boom. The early days are recollected in a num-

Miami, 50 m. (alt. 2,744; pop. 675), the solitary town in Roberts County, lies pinched between deep-cut Red Deer Creek and a steep hill—all its streets running uphill. The surrounding broken red land, scoured by Coronado's treasure-searchers, is rich in prehistoric Indian ruins; and this village came into being, more than three centuries later, as a staging area for Fort Elliott (see Mobeetie), last outpost in the drive to clear Indians finally from the region. Occupy-

REGION IV

ing cattle country today, Miami holds a two-day festival climaxing with its National Cow-Calling Contest the first weekend each June. The Roberts County Museum here reflects both local history and the extensive archaeology of the region.

Toward Pampa the land climbs, then flattens to a level plain. Along the way are *playas,* small lakes formed when rainfall simply has no place to drain. They are numerous throughout the Panhandle, usually shallow, and in times of drought, completely dry.

Pampa, 74 m. (alt. 3,234; pop. 19,959), spreads tidy residential areas and gracious parks outward from a downtown area notable for extremely wide streets and the look of 1930s' prosperity. Long in wheat and cattle country, the city centered a major oil play in 1928 and, over the years, has balanced its agriculture with substantial industry—from petrochemicals to giant gun barrel manufacture. Here the C of C will route tours of industries like the big Celanese plant, where space age technology is demonstrated. Pampa recollects its early days the last week in July with the rough-and-tumble Top o' Texas Rodeo and—throughout the year—with its White Deer Land Museum. Occupying the original 1916 building, the museum harks back to a time when whole townsite areas were sold.

Via TX 152 west, **Borger,** 29 m. (alt. 3,116; pop. 15,675) is a new city, oil booming into existence in 1926 and within eight months counting some 35,000 inhabitants toughing it out in frame shacks or tents. Borger was rough—3 m. of oilfield shanties strung across broken red land: by 1929, state guardsmen moved in to clear out undesirables. Then, after years of labor, Borger's business men redesigned and landscaped the entire downtown, put in 16 parks and —42 years after springing raw from the Canadian River breaks—won the All-American City title in 1968. Today a tranquil city prospers with its still-producing oilfield. Each June, Borger feeds some 5,000 people at its "World's Largest Fish Fry," a salute to its big recreational neighbor, Lake Meredith. Here also, exhibits at the county historical museum recall the land's story, from Coronado's time to that of the boisterous Borger oil boom.

TX 136 leads west 8 m. to **Lake Meredith National Recreation Area.**

The 16,500-acre lake extends 110 m. up the Canadian River and provides camping and all facilities.

At 15 m. the prehistoric **Alibates Flint Quarries** gives Texas an intriguing National Historic Monument. For 12,000 years these rainbow-tinted flint cliffs were the site of the American Indian's Pittsburgh, source of the "steel"—flint is a very hard stone—for his weapons and tools. In the deadly age of the fierce-tusked mammoth and the giant bison, Indians came here from across all of America 7,000 years before the pyramids. In the "yesterday" of 1542, Coronado saw Alibates' Indian treasure and shortly despaired of finding what he considered precious stones, giving up his two-year search for the treasures of Cibola and Quivira. Today, summer tours are conducted daily by National Park Service rangers, with demonstrations of flint chipping as done here for so many centuries. In the area, also see Adobe Walls.

Panhandle, 101 m. (alt. 3,451; pop. 2,353), announces itself in the loom of tall grain elevators and appears—with handsome homes and churches—larger than it is. The town grew from the old Four Sixes Ranch and preserves its heritage in one of Texas' more interesting museums, the Square House, located in Pioneer Park. The little complex includes dioramas in the wildlife building; a complete ranch spread, from half-dug-out dwelling to windmill and cowboy workshed; a cattle company headquarters—the Square House; and Freedom Hall, where you may reflect on how much freedom meant to these pioneers. There are literally thousands of artifacts.

Two of the town's institutions are High Plains' firsts—the *Panhandle Herald,* oldest newspaper in the region—printed in 1887 in a tent; and the First National Bank, first on the plains.

At 106 m. a marker and protective fence on the south edge of the highway guard the stump of a small bois d'arc tree. Of all the countless planted shade across the Panhandle, this was the first, put down in 1888 by Thomas Cree. Trees grew only by scattered streams; settlers longed just for the sight of one. Cree hauled the sapling from east of the Cap Rock, and nurtured it. Legend relates that when the early going was hardest—winter blizzard, summer drought—the first settlers would watch the little tree each spring: if it survived, so could they.

Ironically, in 1969 an agricultural chemical killed the tree, but natural seedlings grow on.

Amarillo, 130 m. (alt, 3,676; pop. 157,615 city), Texas' northernmost city, today displays a casually brisk grace for a city grown from a collection of railroaders, cowboys and buffalo hunters. In 1887 the Fort Worth and Denver Railroad pitched a construction camp at what was then known as Ragtown—for its appearance. The town selected the more acceptable name Oneida for a time, but when its developer, Henry Sanborn, swapped town lots for cowboy county seat votes, Amarillo—named for the color of its yellow creek banks—came into being. For a time, Sanborn kept all his own buildings painted yellow.

Today Amarillo is capital of the Panhandle oil and gas region, with many adjacent fields pipelining as far as the East Coast. The city also rests atop the world's largest helium field and has commemorated the 1868 discovery of that element with a six-story stainless steel monument, containing time capsule documents relating to this odorless, colorless gas. A museum at its foot features exhibits on helium's uses in industry, medicine, defense and other fields.

The city's handsome Discovery Center houses an exceptional planetarium and exhibits relating to man and his development. The big new civic center accommodates the Amarillo Symphony and Civic Ballet and handles gatherings that range from circuses to politics. West of the city, the Garden Center displays flower shows throughout the year. Harrington House (1600 S. Polk) offers guided tours of 1914 mansion. Wonderland Park (off US 287 north) is 4th largest amusement park in Texas.

Each Memorial Day weekend, Amarillo stages a family "Funfest," and each September hosts the big, weeklong Tri-State Fair. Most unique of its observances is Cowboy Morning (or Evening), from mid-April to mid-October, opportunity to enjoy a group chuck wagon breakfast or dinner on rim of Palo Duro Canyon, go for wagon rides, or watch real cowboys at their daily work.

Not forgetting its western heritage, Amarillo stages the world's largest cattle auction, selling some 600,000 head annually for more than $130 million. Also here you may tour the national headquarters for the American Quarter Horse Association, where more than 200 people computerize records on some two million horses. A bizarre exhibit is "Cadillac Ranch" on the western edge of the city where a millionaire half-buried 10 Cadillacs, their tail fins in the air—avant garde art, according to the California architects who designed it. At Amarillo intersect I-40/Tour 45, US 287/Tour 46. Merge southward with US 87/Tour 61 to Canyon. In the area, also see Tascosa.

Canyon, 146 m. (alt. 3,566; pop. 11,365), beginning as an old range headquarters, has developed into a smart little city that is both a recreational and educational center. Here on a shaded 130-acre campus is West Texas State University with an enrollment of 7,000; and on that campus is the big Panhandle-Plains Museum, called one of America's finest by UN scientists. The city expands toward the western edge of the great gorge of Palo Duro, from which it took its name. To the west is Buffalo Lake and its National Wildlife Refuge.

WTSU, the oldest state-assisted higher educational institution west of Fort Worth, devotes 3,900 acres of rich land to ranching, dairying, cattle-feeding, and farming—a substantial contribution to Panhandle growth.

On campus, the big museum—with its facade of cattle brands—houses an exceptional collection of articles reviewing the culture and progress of the Great Plains. Artifacts and exhibits show primitive Indian life. The cattle industry is pictured from open-range days onward. An excellent display is the Pioneer Village, with full-size indoor restorations of streets, stores and shops of a western frontier town. An art collection emphasizing the west includes some 3,000 paintings. On the museum grounds is the log cabin headquarters (1877) of the huge T-Anchor Ranch, from which Canyon grew. The cabin is the oldest surviving house in the Panhandle. In 1986, a new $6 million Petroleum Wing was added to the museum complex.

Via TX 217 east, **Palo Duro Canyon,** 18 m., is a quick, sheer gorge, 1,000 feet deep and more than 100 miles long. There is no hint of anything but rolling prairie as you drive eastward until suddenly the canyon yawns up at you. On the rim, an interpretive center tells its story in a series of graphic exhibits. Below, down a scenic

Palo Duro Canyon, a spectacular slash in the high plains of the Panhandle.

cliff-clinger and within the state park (one of Texas' biggest), saddle horses provide the best means of exploration. And whether it be the canyon's geologic story or its startling rock formation—purple-spined Devil's Slide, the Lighthouse or the minarets in Big Sunday Canyon—Palo Duro is for exploring. There are 15 m. of scenic drive, 20 m. of bridle paths and 30 m. of hiking trails. Campgrounds are spacious and fully equipped, and the Goodnight Trading Post is an in-canyon concessionaire.

Palo Duro's newest feature is the Pioneer Outdoor Amphitheater, featuring its annual production of the award-winning drama, Texas. The setting, at the foot of a 600-foot bluff, is spectacular; the production is too.

So is the Canyon's story. Down the east face of the rockslide opposite the entrance, Col. Charles Goodnight brought his first wagon train in 1876 to found, within shelter here, the plains' first ranch—the J. A. Only two years before, Col. Ranald Mackenzie, America's best Indian fighter, led his Fourth Cavalry down the canyon cliffs to attack the last Comanche stronghold in Texas. Mackenzie's strike wisely was directed against the Indian's horses, not the braves—for the Comanche afoot was finished. Cavalrymen drove some 1,500 mounts down the canyon, then up the walls, killing nearly all of them at Tule Canyon just south. This effectually ended a bitter 35-year struggle with the most formidable of all Plains Indians (see Lockhart). From Canyon, follow US 60 west.

Umbarger, 158 m., pop. 327. Immediately south is Buffalo Lake National Wildlife Refuge. In the fall, more than one million ducks and geese stop over here on their way to winter grounds. The lake offers fishing and water sports.

Hereford, 178 m. (alt. 3,806; pop. 14,745), under its towering grain elevators, is a pin-neat, thriving little city centered primarily on agribusiness, but

known widely as "The Town Without a Toothache" because of fluorides in the soil and water. Hereford took its name from the whitefaced cattle introduced from England by Col. Charles Goodnight and John G. Adair in neighboring Palo Duro Canyon in 1883. The section headquarters of famed XIT Ranch once were located at Buffalo Lake.

Hereford is home of the National Cowgirl Hall of Fame, and the Deaf Smith County Historical Museum reflects early plains life. A full-sized pioneer sitting room is reproduced. Center of an immense cattle-feeding industry—three million head a year—the city bears a second name: Beef Headquarters, USA.

West of Hereford you traverse some of Texas' richest agricultural lands, much of them blessed not only with shallow well water, but with oil. Quite often across the lush green fields you will see oil and waterwell pumps working almost side by side. At Hereford intersect US 385/Tour 60.

Farwell, 225 m. (alt. 4,375; pop. 1,373) is Parmer County seat, resting squarely on the New Mexico line. The town was named for the Farwell brothers of Illinois, whose Capitol Syndicate built the Texas capitol in 1881 and were paid with 3,000,000 acres of plains land, for a time functioning as the gigantic XIT Ranch.

At Farwell merge with US 84/Tour 53 and enter New Mexico 9 m. east of Clovis.

☆

Tour 45

US 66/I-40
Oklahoma line, Shamrock, McLean, Amarillo, Vega, New Mexico line, 177 m.

This tour crosses from Oklahoma to New Mexico through the center of the Texas Panhandle—these High Plains once considered the Great American Desert. This was the country of the Comanche and his buffalo, and for a time—perhaps the late 1700s—before the coming of other white men, it was a

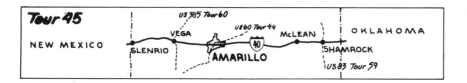

Tour 45

NEW MEXICO · GLENRIO · VEGA · US 385 Tour 60 · US 60 Tour 44 · AMARILLO · 40 · McLEAN · SHAMROCK · US 83 Tour 59 · OKLAHOMA

land inhabited by the Pastores and Indian-trading Comancheros of New Mexico. Scattered ruins of their adobe and rock settlements lie along the western leg of this tour, for as ranchers moved into the region, the sheepherders and traders gave way, some returning to New Mexico, those who remained turning to ranching.

You cross an almost level plain, rich in nearly all that land can yield: oil, gas, wheat, small grains, cattle pasture. Once believed suitable only for ranching, this soil has seen the deep gouge of the plowshare, furrow on furrow, mile upon mile. Weather here is taken in good-humored stride: if a norther rolls down in a wall of dust, plainsmen will sight a prairie dog trying to dig his way out, 200 feet up in the air. A day can begin warm and sunny and end with snow: old-timers will recall the horse whose head almost died of heat exhaustion while his hindquarters were nipped with frostbite.

Okla. line, 0 m. Cross into Texas 28 m. west of Elk City.

Shamrock, 14 m. (alt. 2,310; pop. 2,286), sprang from the 1890 post office in the half-dugout home of an Irish sheep rancher, 6 m. north of today's town, the present site arriving with 1903 rails. A petrochemical town principally, Shamrock's population swells to more than 40,000 each St. Patrick's Day when, as it has since 1938, the town lets go in celebration.

Shamrock has its own Blarney Stone, originally the deadman for a hitching post but now legitimately from County

Shamrock's Irish Rose, named each St. Patrick's Day, pays respects to the town's Blarney Stone, brought all the way from Ireland.

Cork. It also has a tongue-in-cheek legend that the greenest spot in Texas was to receive St. Patrick's blessing and the name it bears. Here any visitor would observe a people wise as New Englanders, cordial as Kentucky Colonels, and with all the other natural graces of a true son of the old sod. On St. Patrick's Day, Shamrock wears the green along with true Donegal beards, parades and dances and selects the year's Irish Rose.

The Pioneer West Museum, the town's old hotel, has rooms depicting the institutions of Shamrock's early life. There is the first barber shop, complete with tub, the first dentist's office, and the post office room duplicates the original half dugout where the little city began. In keeping with its Blarney Stone atmosphere, Shamrock claims the "tallest water in Texas," its 50,000 gal. tank rearing 181 feet into the air. At Shamrock intersect US 83/Tour 59. In the area also see Mobeetie, Wellington.

At **McLean,** 34 m. (alt. 2,812; pop. 849), TX 273 leads north to the site of the **Battle of McClellan's Creek,** 7 m. Here on a November day in 1874, as last-ditch plains Indian fighting neared climax in scattered engagements, Lt. Frank D. Baldwin was routinely leading empty supply wagons back for replenishing. He topped a small rise, unexpectedly confronting some 300 Cheyenne warriors, their mounts at hand. Baldwin had one company of weary foot soldiers: if he tried to hold the ground he could be cut to pieces.

To his wagon skinners he gave the command to charge and their empty wagons responded so spectacularly that in moments, the Cheyenne broke and fled—Baldwin's bluff had worked, and he had recovered two captured white girls. The Alanreed-McLean Area Museum preserves community history; the Devil's Rope Museum features a large barbed wire collection and Route 66 memorabilia.

At 57 m., TX 70/FM 2477 leads north to Lake McClellan National Grasslands Park, fishing and water sports.

Amarillo, 107 m.—see Tour 44. At the eastern city limits on I-40, a Texas

Travel Information Center provides highly trained travel counselors and a wide selection of literature and maps. West of the city, you pass one of America's largest helium plants; beyond, you travel across immense fields of hybrid grain.

Vega, 140 m. (alt. 4,030; pop. 840), in cottonwood shade, is the town that killed Texas' deadliest guntown, Old Tascosa, north on the Canadian (see Tour 60). In 1900, Vega arrived with railroads and by 1915 had taken the Oldham County seat from Tascosa. In this expanse of ranch and grain-growing country, a surprise awaits you—five acres of tomatoes under glass—one of America's largest tomato hothouses. Production is some 100,000 pounds annually. Each second Saturday in August, Vega stages its Oldham County Round-up—a parade and free barbecue on the courthouse lawn. At Vega, intersect US 385/Tour 60. Nearby also see Tascosa, Hereford.

Glenrio, 177 m., is a wayspot astride the New Mexico line.

☆

Tour 46

US 287
Wichita Falls,
Vernon, Childress,
Clarendon, Amarillo,
Dumas, Stratford, Oklahoma line,
328 m.

T his tour continues one of the longest US Highways in Texas, US 287 already having diagonalled up from the state's southeast corner at Port Arthur to reach Wichita Falls in the Red River Valley. Here you continue north of west, following the Red to its three forks, then veering up through the heart of the Panhandle to leave those Texas High Plains almost at their northwest corner.

Historically, you follow an old trail—the Red River route sought by Spain as a connecting link between her Texas missions and Santa Fe, later the route of the Texan expedition to that New Mexico capital.

In Indian eyes, this is the line of retreat for Plains warriors—Comanche, Kiowa, and Cheyenne—toward their last stand in Texas.

You travel across rolling prairies, flat grassy plains and past rough, eroded washes called "breaks"—land of the big ranch and its lonely first dugout shelters. Then, climbing the Cap Rock bluffs, you traverse the High Plains' greensward, once country so seemingly waterless and desolate that early U.S. exploration called it "The Great American Desert"—today, the great American "Breadbasket."

This is a land where friendliness is a way of life, perhaps because the country was once so lonely that any visitor received the best his host could offer: "Stranger, you take the wolf skin and the chaw of sowbelly," a host greets his guest in one old story, "I'll rough it."

Wichita Falls, 0 mi.—see Tour 1. Continue west from Tour 16.

Electra, 28 m. (alt. 1,229; pop. 3,113), is a prosperous-looking, pretty town in planted shade. It is on land of the old Waggoner Ranch, a 600,000-acre spread where oil was first detected in 1905 when ranch hands dug for water. Between Electra and Burkburnett northeast, the site of a prehistoric meteor strike was noted as early as 1772, when Indians were found worshipping the great metal mass, perhaps one source of the Thunderbird legend.

Oklaunion, 42 m., pop. 138, is a farming community. Merge with US 70/ Tour 47 to Vernon.

Vernon, 51 m. (alt. 1,205; pop. 12,001) expands spaciously from its big square, a solid, lived-in-looking town

which grew from a cattle camp on the Western and Dodge Trail, just short of the hazardous Red River Crossing. It was first called Eagle Flats for the number of birds nesting in the area. The Red River Valley Museum includes a big game exhibit, Indian artifacts, and history of the huge Waggoner Ranch headquartered here. Jack Teagarden, a jazz trombonist of fame and Vernon native, is also honored.

Each October, Vernon hosts the Greenbelt Fair, a six-county event, and follows that—the first weekend in November—with the International Barbed Wire and Antique Show, which attracts visitors from throughout the U.S. and many foreign countries. You need not be a collector to enjoy the exhibits.

North of the city 17 m. via US 283 is historic **Doan's Crossing,** where Texas' last trail drivers swam the Red River with their herds. Beside an old adobe in the riverbank elm and willow, a marker tells the crossing's story.

Beginning in 1874, more than six million cattle and 30,000 riders made this last stop before penetrating 300 m. of Indian country on the way to Dodge City's railheads. The adobe was Ohioan Corwin F. Doan's, who maintained two long barn stores with flour, grain, bacon, Stetsons, Colts and ammunition by freight wagon lots. Credit was universal, on a trail boss' word, and Doan knew every brand—from Richard King's and Shanghai Pierce's to the OX, the Pitchfork and the Matadors.

As barbed wire advanced on this last and biggest crossing, a remarkable proposal emerged at Doan's. In 1883, Texas cattlemen called on Congress for a fenced-off right-of-way, "The Great National Trail," beginning across from Doan's Crossing and extending north to Canada. Proposed was a 3 m.-wide highway complete with fencing, water tanks, bridges at all rivers, handling facilities at all rail crossings. Congress rejected the program, and the on-marching fence lines gradually ended the great drives.

The Doan's marker closes, "In honor of the trail drivers who freed Texas from the yoke of debt and despair (after Civil War)." Their longhorns quit only with the western ranges and city markets full, and nowhere left to trail.

The first weekend each May, a Doan's picnic recalls old trail drive days.

Chillicothe, 68 m. (alt. 1,406; pop. 816), shaded by elm trees and overshadowed by grain elevators, lies in rich bottomland between the Red and Pease Rivers; its red brick downtown indicates the prosperity of an earlier day.

Via FM 91 south 9 m., **Medicine Mounds,** pop. 50, is a tiny, old village beside four accurately-named Indian mounds—natural hillocks where Comanche and earlier Indians "made medicine" in worship. As you circle south or east, they stand apart in a

Medicine Mounds, between Chillicothe and Quanah.

spaced-out line—cedared hills, indeed, yet they seem something more: pyramid, mosque, canopied temple, square basilica, all in a row, suggesting an unusual parallel to the man-built pyramids of the Aztecs in Mexico. Numerous artifacts have been collected from this area.

At 78 m. Lake Pauline, immediately south, provides water recreation.

Quanah, 82 m. (alt. 1,568; pop. 3,413), with its neat brick homes set in planted elm shade, more resembles a midwestern than Texan town. It was settled in 1885 and named for Quanah Parker, a latter-day Comanche fighting chief whose white mother, Cynthia Ann Parker (see Groesbeck, Athens), kidnaped and married into the Comanche people, was recaptured just south of here. Time and again, this half-white chief flung his warriors against the white intruders until finally, realizing further resistance was useless, he returned to the Oklahoma reservation, taking his moth-

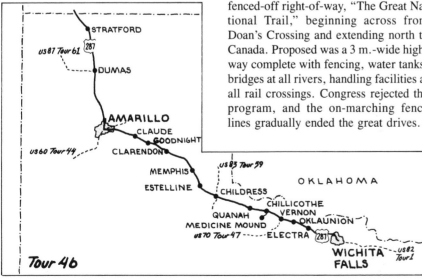

Tour 46

er's body, to live out his days. Informed that this settlement had been named for him, he blessed his namesake: "May the Great Spirit smile on you, town. May the rains fall in due season, may the earth yield bountifully. May peace and contentment dwell with you and your children forever." A county museum recollects regional history.

At Quanah, TX 6 leads south to **Copper Breaks State Park,** 12 m., with camping and all facilities. The area produced Confederate copper during the Civil War; after the war, Union General George McClellan formed a company which mined briefly near here. The site is more famous, however, for the Battle of the Pease River, where, in 1860, Cynthia Ann Parker was recaptured with her daughter, Prairie Flower. She had become completely happy, living as an Indian since her kidnaping; here her husband, Chief Peta Nocona, was reported killed in the battle. Neither Cynthia Ann, object of a long search by her family, nor her daughter could adjust to civilization, and both died shortly after her return.

Between Quanah and Vernon is the site of old Harrold community where a credo for the Texas Rangers was born. In the 1880s, Capt. Bill McDonald, already famed with the reputation of readiness "to charge hell with a bucket of water," learned that outlaws here planned to ambush him. Singlehanded, he confronted three of them on the town's street. In a blaze of gunfire, the ranger dropped one of the bad men but took bullets through his left and right side and his wrist. Able to use only one hand he refused to go down and was cocking his pistol with his teeth when the surviving outlaws fled. McDonald recovered, to coin the ranger watchword: "No man in the wrong can stand up against a fellow that's in the right . . . and keeps on a-comin'."

Despite its tiny population, this community decorates for Christmas like any big city. One of the citizenry hauls up a 10-foot mesquite tree, anchors it, and adorns it with home-made decorations.

Childress, 112 m. (alt. 1,877; pop. 5,055), "Gateway to the Panhandle," was once part of the big, early-day OX spread, a rough town in its latter 1880s youth—knowing the stamp of men like Frank James as guests. However, Childress has grown from its cluster about the old square to a small city of quiet, pleasant homes. Late in July, as it has done for almost a century, the town goes western with its Old Settlers Reunion and Rodeo—barbecue, fiddling, dancing. In mid March the city hosts a two-day Gospel Singing Convention. The pretty city park makes a fine picnic stop and nearby Lake Childress and Baylor provide fishing and water sports. In its old post office, Childress maintains an interesting Heritage Museum.

At Childress intersect US 83/Tour 59. In the area, also see Wellington and Paducah.

Estelline, 127 m. (alt. 1,759; pop. 194), edging the Red River, grew up around a salt spring just north of town and game trails—followed unerringly by cattle—that led to it. In the 1890s, most of West Texas drove for Estelline, the largest cattle shipping depot on the Fort Worth and Denver line; then the rails reached everywhere and the drives ended.

Turkey, pop. 507, 30 m. via TX 86, honors hometown singer Bob Wills with a reunion late each April and a Bob Wills Museum recalling the career of the Texas Playboys and the King of Western Swing.

Memphis, 141 m. (alt. 2,067; pop. 2,465) is the center of a diversified agricultural area. Its older buildings give the town an appearance of a much bigger city; in the early days city lots were priced so high that few builders settled for single-story structures. Those old days are recalled in the Hall County Heritage Hall here.

Each late September, Memphis observes Ernest Tubb Day, a country-western celebration honoring the singer who gave his last performance here before his death in 1984.

West of Memphis your road begins a perceptible climb toward the High Plains. The land grows rougher, with low mesas marching along the south horizon.

Clarendon, 169 m. (alt. 2,727; pop. 2,067), a mixture of old red brick and smart new structures, is the offspring of Old Clarendon, 6 m. north. That staunch settlement was founded in 1878 by Lewis H. Carhart, a Methodist circuit rider, at the very same time that Col. Charles Goodnight was pioneering his ranch in Palo Duro 20 m. west. The still-wild country had scarcely been cleared of the Comanche, yet Clarendon's settlers were determined to introduce cul-

ture with their town. The founders were a blend of Ivy League graduates and titled Englishmen insistent on ranching; they saw their town—with its charter prohibiting liquor and gambling—as "Athens of the Plains." Cowboys on neighboring ranges saw Clarendon as "Saint's Roost."

In good humor, the town preserves that heritage each July 4th with a Saint's Roost Celebration and Reunion, with all the western trappings. The Saint's Roost Museum, with displays of local history, is housed in the former Adair Hospital, founded by the wife of the owner of the JA Ranch and given to the town with the proviso that JA punchers get free care.

Via TX 70 north, Green Belt Reservoir, 6 m. provides all facilities. The lake is springfed; you can fish for trout and northern pike, along with catfish.

Fall hunters seek the canyon country southwest for the exotic auodad sheep.

Goodnight, 188 m. (alt. 3,145; pop. 25), is a scatter of frame structures around the old homesite of Col. Charles Goodnight, who pioneered plains ranching. Southward, FM 2889, largely unimproved, leads down into Palo Duro Canyon 20 m. and headquarters of still operating JA Ranch.

Claude, 200 m. (alt. 3,397; pop. 1,199), is the spread-out little seat of government for Armstrong County, here a lush green sea of agriculture, horizon to horizon. Claude's old county jail was so unused it was pressed into service for a time as the Methodist parsonage. FM 1151 leads west across the head of Palo Duro Canyon, providing access to the spectacular gorge (Tour 44); TX 207 leads south, plunging into Palo Duro abruptly—drive carefully. Farther south, TX 207 drops again, this time into the sheer-faced buttes of Tule Canyon. Nearby, also see Panhandle.

TX 207 skirts through Tule Canyon's striated buttes.

Amarillo, 228 m.—see Tour 44. Merge with US 87/Tour 61 and follow US 287 due north.

Dumas, 277 m. (alt. 3,668; pop. 12,871), is a clean, progressive, prospering little city; it is hard to drive the broad streets, past handsome homes and churches, and envision a struggling town that barely clung to life in the 1892 drought and grasshopper plague—a time when all but one family pulled out. Some of the very old-timers can remember the early 1900s when butter was so cheap it was better used to grease Dumas windmills. The town grew up with cattle and passed to the addition of oil, along with a smoky, ugly cloud from carbon black plants—all now briskly cleaned up. The Moore County Historical Museum recreates pioneering days with exhibits of an early plains kitchen, a general store, pharmacy, schoolroom and church. The Tumbleweed Gallery and Museum leans more toward area art and geology.

Each June, Dumas has fun with its heritage in a three-day celebration of Dogie Days. Veer north from US 87/Tour 61. Nearby, also see Lake Meredith and Alibates National Monument.

Stratford, 311 m. (alt. 3,695; pop. 1,781), on the distant horizon resembles a big city: its skyline is made up of lofty wheat elevators. In 1901 this county seat (Sherman Co.) had to take its records at gunpoint from the range settlement of Coldwater, now a ghost east on Coldwater Creek. The new town kept an armed posse on guard at the courthouse tent until quiet returned—times recalled in the old Sherman House, which serves as a historical museum.

At Stratford, your road bears northwest.

Okla. line, 328 m.

☆

Tour 47

US 70
Oklahoma line,
Oklaunion, Vernon,
Crowell, Matador,
Plainview, Muleshoe, Farwell, New
Mexico line, 253 m.

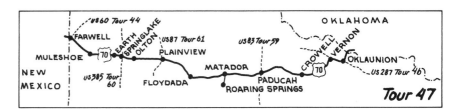

Tour 47

Entering Texas near the old Red River trail crossing, this tour turns west and crosses the state's northern region in two distinct halves. The first travels the gullied breaks country—rough, eroded and lonely land that still resists taming. The western half climbs atop the Cap Rock into the great green sea of the South Plains.

From Vernon west, you drive Big Ranch country—land little changed from the day of the Comanche. Behind U.S. troops, the rancher shot his way into this region, then drove out or killed off the buffalo, put up windmills and pasture fences, and forever changed the face of this wild landscape. Still, this part of Texas has changed less than others.

The western half of this region, like the Panhandle above it, was first believed unfit for human habitation. Today it is part of America's breadbasket. Settlement is recent enough that at many Old Settlers Reunions—and nearly every town has one—you can qualify with a residence of as little as 25 years.

Solitude there may be, but there is also a vigor to this land; and if the remoteness or infinite flatness begins to pall, contemplate the wide band of horizon, the giant bowl of the the the sky. Northwest Texans find a beauty here that they see nowhere else.

Okla. line, 0 m. Cross into Texas 14 m. south of Frederick.

Oklaunion, 7 m.—merge with US 287/Tour 46 to Vernon.

Vernon, 16 m.—see Tour 46. Follow US 70 west.

Crowell, 47 m. (alt. 1,463; pop. 1,230). A yellow brick courthouse, cupola atop, dominates a small business area. Interestingly, the little town maintains three area museums, all dealing with regional heritage. North of town, Copper Breaks State Park (Tour 46) is properly named—Union General George B. McClellan attempted to establish a copper mine there. Its ruins still known as the McClellan Mine, the project failed for lack of transportation and immediacy

of water. Nearby, also see Quanah and Medicine Mounds.

At 56 m. a mysterious marker stands 4 m. south of the highway—a 20-foot, manmade stone monument points an inexplicable finger at the sky. To this day, no one knows when or by whom it was fashioned, nor what it seeks to tell the traveler of this old Indian trail.

Paducah, 83 m. (alt. 1,886; pop. 1,788), nestles in low hills, county seat (Cottle Co.) of typical ranch country and a crossroads of two transcontinental routes: you travel the old Lee Highway from East to West Coast, and here you cross US 83 on its way from Canada to Mexico. Like others in this region, Paducah centers land once home to the buffalo and antelope. Buffalo-hunters, following old Indian trails (such as yours) were succeeded by hide-buyers, whose heavy wagons widened the trail. In the 1870s the big ranchers came—the Four Sixes and the Pitchfork south, the Spur southwest, the Matador to the west. Some of the brands have changed since then; the country, very little. Each April, for Cottle and neighboring King County, Paducah holds its Horse and Colt Show, together with an Old Settlers Reunion. Here you intersect US 83/Tour 59.

In the area also see Childress, Guthrie.

At 97 m., cross the South Pease River. North of here on Tee Pee Creek, near its junction with the Pease, is the ghost site of Tee Pee City (inaccessible to automobiles), a freighter depot in 1879 built squarely on the site of a just-deserted Comanche village, named for the then clearly visible tee pee circles. The old near-dead cottonwood marks the location of the hotel-saloon-gambling hall. Railroad extension southward killed the town and Matador took the county seat.

Matador, 115 m. (alt. 2,347; pop. 790), in its heaving sea of mesquite and broken land, is one of Texas' most typical cow towns—a dappling of roofs in pools of cottonwood shade and the feel of a line camp awaiting its riders.

The sidewalks, concrete now, still hold hitching rings from the old days.

This began as a make-believe town. In 1879, Henry H. (Paint) Campbell built a dugout headquarters for what was to become the giant Matador Ranch, at one time counting over a million acres. When Motley County was organized in 1891, there was no town for a seat of government; Matador's cowboys set about to solve this by "inventing" one. From the ranch commisary came a few cans of food—a grocery store; a few kegs of whiskey made a saloon, a roll of wire and some fence posts became a lumber yard, and Matador was born.

The old county jail has its hanging room, but Motley folks only aimed one man in that direction, and he failed to go all the way. That was a man named Digger Danby, whose worth for well-digging continually postponed his execution until, one day, Digger walked away and never returned.

The ranch is operated today as the Matador Cattle Company. Visits to its 1916-built headquarters may be arranged through the Community Associates organization.

Via TX 70 south, **Roaring Springs,** 8 m., pop. 264, on the South Pease River, an old Indian campground, has hosted Motley-Dickens county reunions for half a century.

At 123 m. the line of cliffs ahead is the edge of the Cap Rock. As you climb, look back on the broken land, then ahead to the magical transformation into lush green cropland.

Floydada, 146 m. (alt. 3,179; pop. 3,896), today is a neat, busy county seat which centers an enormously productive agricultural region. At harvest time, the many wheat elevators along your route are insufficient for production: freight cars are channeled in from across the nation to haul away this land's huge output.

The Floyd County Historical Museum recalls days when this city enjoyed no such prosperity: it was an 1890 land boomer whose first business establishment was a saloon—five kegs of whiskey on an open plain. Close beside was the town's waterworks, a public well. Early Floydadans can remember water distribution then—a rolling water keg. The settlement, originally Floyd City, won the county seat in a heated contest with nearby Della Plain (now a ghost).

The contested election went to Floydada only after a decision by the Texas Supreme Court. Nearby, also see Mt. Blanco, Estacado.

Plainview, 173 m. (alt. 3,366; pop. 21,700). This smaller city is 11 years senior to its big southern neighbor, Lubbock, having been founded as a dugout town in 1880, less than a decade after Comanche menace had been eliminated. All about are the almost traceless sites of early-century ghost towns which died because of wrong guesses as to the routes of the Santa Fe and the Fort Worth and Denver railroads. The town's name came from its magnificent view of surrounding plains in all directions. Today, Plainview yields a view of the very old and very new.

Here, in 1944–45, archaeologists identified the "Plainview Point," flintwork associated with an ancient culture of 8,000–10,000 years ago. Near the downtown area, fossil skeletons of some 100 giant bison were discovered, together with 22 artifacts, including flint points, knives and hide scrapers, indicating that a herd had been trapped and butchered. The point, of large and simple design, has been identified throughout the Southwest.

The "new" in Plainview is its atomic house, 4,000 square feet of its lower level entirely underground. Built to protect against the atom bomb, the private home today pays for itself in utilities economy, maintaining—as a cave does—an almost constant temperature through summer and winter. The William Hamman home is located on W. 20th Street. Plainview is also home of Wayland Baptist College, its Llano Estacado Museum with exhibits from archaeology to history, and its Flying Queens basketball team. The Runningwater Draw Arts and Crafts Festival is staged each mid-October.

At Plainview, intersect US 87/Tour 61. Nearby also see Tulia, Hale Center.

Olton, 197 m. (alt. 3,580; pop. 2,116), an agricultural center, serves as a good gauge of prevailing wind conditions. Old frame houses here lean to the north.

At **Springlake,** 208 m., pop. 132, intersect US 385/Tour 60.

Earth, 214 m. (alt. 3,550; pop. 1,228), offers two versions of how its name was derived. One is the natural richness of the region's soil; the other is that soil's penchant for blowing with the wind—the name settled upon during a dust storm.

Muleshoe, 232 m. (alt. 3,889; pop. 4,571), a rich cattle and farming center, took its name from the Muleshoe Ranch, one of the early spreads with its old headquarters 4 m. west. However, with typical West Texas humor, the community embraced the mule itself, a statue and plaque on the square saluting the bearer of man's burdens. "Without ancestral pride or hope for offspring, he made history."

Honoring the noble beast that helped build Texas is a life-size statue of a mule in Muleshoe. (Courtesy of Gil Lamb, KMUL radio)

When the idea of a life-sized statue was first announced, contributions for the mule memorial came in from across America, and one—a gift of 21 cents—from a mule driver from Samarkand, Uzbekistan, in the former Soviet Union.

The second Saturday in August each year is Mule Day in Muleshoe, with a mule rodeo, mule races, and other "mulish" events.

Via TX 214 south, 1 m., Blackwater Draw extends a mile-wide belt of sand hills across this area of the plains, west into New Mexico, a forbidding area in early times. Legend claims that long ago this valley was an Eden close beside a clear-running river; however, the people of the valley offended the Great Spirit with their arrogance, and a terrible sandstorm blotted them, their village and its river from the earth. Relenting, however, the Great Spirit allowed the river to continue flowing, hidden beneath the sand hills. Early day cowhands were told the legend by an ancient Indian and, on digging down, found the water he had told of. This hidden river today yields the free-flow-irrigation which has given Muleshoe its abundant crops. At Muleshoe, merge with US 84/Tour 53 northwest.

South 20 m. is the **Muleshoe National Wildlife Refuge,** oldest in Texas (1935). Upwards of 700,000 migratory birds arrive each late December, the beautiful lesser sandhill cranes in great numbers as early as mid-September.

Farwell, 253 m.—see Tour 44. Cross New Mexico line.

☆

Tour 48

US 82
Wichita Falls,
Seymour, Guthrie,
Crosbyton, Lubbock,
Brownfield, Plains, New Mexico line,
295 m.

More than any other, this route—a continuation west from Tour 1, Region I—displays the West Texas ranch as it was originally anchored in vast solitude. For some 50 m. on either side of Guthrie, you cross the land of the JY and Four Sixes, the Pitchfork and the Spur—ranches once so big that, in comparatively recent times, riders saddled out from headquarters for six months out on the range! From Crosbyton, atop the Cap Rock escarpment, to the New Mexico line, you encounter magnificent distances of an entirely different sort—the cultivated green sweep of Texas' South Plains.

Once, everything west of Wichita Falls was the domain of the first Plains horseman—principally the Comanche—and his buffalo. Then with blinding suddenness the Plains Indians were conquered by the United States Army, and the land accepted another rider, the leathery, horizon-eyeing rancher. With six-gun, windmill, and barbed wire the rancher established a domain that still holds sway, the rocky, rugged land unfit for the farmer's plow. Overwhelming in the beauty of its red soil and blue sky, this is the last stronghold of the big ranch in Texas.

Altogether, this tour will at least awe you—you cannot remain indifferent to its vastness. And within the lusty, glistening outreach of Lubbock, you may stop long enough to recall Guthrie's solitude, a few miles back. At the turn of this century the two differed from each

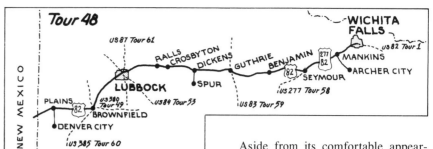

other little more than in the undulation of the terrain and in what man planned for each.

Wichita Falls, 0 m.—see Tour 1. Continue west on US 82 and merge with US 277/Tour 58 to Seymour. Southwest, you travel just under the old Waggoner Ranch which blocked out 30 m. square in early 1900. This is a region which paleontologists have explored, discovering fossil remains of giant reptiles and traces of immense insects, including a dragonfly with a two-foot wingspan.

At little **Mankins,** 19 m., pop. 20, TX 25 leads south to Lake Kickapoo, 7 m., providing water recreation. **Archer City,** 18 m. (alt. 1,041; pop. 1,748), centers an area where water conservation has received considerable attention. Five manmade lakes—Olney, Kickapoo, Diversion, Wichita, and Arrowhead (a state park with camping and all facilities)—are all in the immediate area. Drought caused the death in 1902 of nearby Geraldine, where only a few old water wells mark the site of a much-promoted Indian-settled turn-of-the-century development. The Archer County Historical Museum recollects pioneer days.

Seymour, 50 m. (alt. 1,291; pop. 3,185), at the intersection of four US highways, is a well-groomed little city of pretty, landscaped homes and—from the earliest times when it occupied the crossroads of the upper California Road and the Dodge-Western Trail—a good place to stop, at least to eat. Today, a new industrial park signifies healthy commercial growth.

The town was founded in 1876 when a group of Oregon families settled on the crossroads. The natural conflict between farmer and rancher erupted, the farmer gradually taking the land—as testified to by the prosperous stock farms in the area. However, most of the early Oregoners drifted away, their crops trampled.

Aside from its comfortable appearance, Seymour claims two notable distinctions—Texas' highest recorded temperature—120 degrees in August 1936—and a May 1 "Fish Day" when the town's entire population—fisherman or not—shuts down and repairs to big Lake Kemp (all facilities) just north.

Seymour's big city park is used by Texans from all across the state for family reunions. (Contact city hall.) The Baylor County Museum, housed in one of the town's earliest residences, reflects the earliest days of this area.

Each mid-July, Seymour stages its Old Settlers Reunion, together with a rodeo which—according to claim here—contests with both Pecos and Canadian for origin of the sport. Seymour's first took place in 1896. Here you veer west from US 277/Tour 58 and US 183. Westward, farmland gradually begins to thin out.

Seymour, which set the record high temperature for Texas, sits at the convergence of four US highways.

At **Benjamin,** 82 m. (alt. 1,456; pop. 225), you are on the edge of an emptiness that is the domain of the old, big ranches. The Knox County Museum recalls old times, when this little town was established in 1884, with lumber necessarily hauled from Wichita Falls—little more than a cover of cedar and mesquite tufts these low hills. One store, Uncle Bob Barton's General Mercantile, needed no lumber; the store was much traveled. It had stood in Arkansas awhile, then at Jacksboro, each time torn down for reassembly, at last here. Nearby, also see Rhineland.

At 87 m., a high ridge known locally as the Narrows crests along a hogback separating the Brazos and Wichita watersheds, south and north of you. Across this rough, wild country you are following an east-west trail worn by the Indian long before the white man's coming. Southward, Buzzard Peak and the Croton Breaks hide the site of a legendary lost lead mine, a valuable property in bullet-moulding days.

Guthrie, 115 m. (alt. 1,754; pop. 140). This tiny and remote seat of King County is a good place to put "population explosion" in focus—it is the capital of Big Ranch Country and the true cowboy town of Texas—for years without a newspaper or barber shop, the range its yielder of livelihood, the cattle and the cowboy its only tenants. With its land, Guthrie has declined to change, growing from a population of 101 near this century's turn to 140 today. Zane Gray used this locale for his epic, *Thundering Herd.*

At Guthrie, intersect US 83/Tour 59. To the west you may detect your road beginning a slight climb. Over the course of this tour, like a flat table elevated west, it will ascend almost a half mile. In the area also see Paducah, Aspermont.

At 130 m., the little settlement—almost as large as Guthrie behind you—is Pitchfork Ranch headquarters. The ranch has accepted some modern niceties since its founding in 1881—the big two-story building is one of a very few bunkhouses providing private quarters for its riders. Interestingly, you will note a different mount often tethered outside—today's rancher uses a pickup where roads let him.

Dickens, 146 m. (alt. 2,464; pop. 322), stands booted and unawed by the stern Cap Rock cliffs just west. In the campaign that finished the Comanche at Palo Duro to the north (Tour 44), Col. Ranald Mackenzie's troopers passed the peak immediately west—it bears his name—rode up the bluffs and joined a series of running clashes northward that, after 35 years of conflict, would drive the Comanche from Texas. The Dickens County Museum recalls pioneer days.

Via TX 70 south is **Spur,** 11 m. (alt. 2,291; pop. 1,300), shaded along a tributary of the Brazos' Salt Fork. At 6 m. you pass Soldiers Mound, site of Mackenzie's base fort in the climactic Comanche campaign—literally the end of the Mackenzie Trail, up from Central Texas Hill Country (see Forts McKavett, Concho), and for years the only road into the plains. After Indian withdrawal, this rough country saw the coming first of dugout line camps, then the big spreads themselves. Many notable western writers have chosen the Spur area—named for the immense Spur Ranch—as locale for their books. In the area also see Matador.

At 153 m., ascend the Cap Rock escarpment. The change from breaks to cropland is almost magical.

At 162 m. you drop suddenly into Blanco Canyon. The roadside park beside the White River, Silver Falls Park, is a big, scenic stop and provides hiking trails along the river.

Silver Falls Park near Crosbyton. Cool water and a sandy bottom make the White River an ideal place to wade.

Crosbyton, 170 m. (alt. 3,108; pop. 2,026), a brisk and prospering little county seat—its courthouse on the side of the square—won its existence from two now-ghost towns—Estacado northward, and Emma, below Ralls to the west. The beginning of Crosbyton in 1908 was marked by the literal hauling of buildings—over the level plain—from its defeated rival, Emma. The Crosby County Pioneer Museum displays many Indian artifacts and relics from pioneer days. The museum itself is a replica of the old Hank Smith rock house (see Mt. Blanco below), first homestead on the entire plains.

Via FM 651/193 north, **Mt. Blanco,** 12 m., in scenic Blanco Canyon, was site of the first building on the plains, and homestead of Henry Clay Smith (Uncle Hank), a rugged man who had done everything from Indian fighting to running a hotel at Frontier Fort Griffin (Tour 50). The old rock house was situated at the head of Mackenzie's trail from the south and was, for a time, the only gateway to the plains. Here, Paris Cox's Quakers (see Estacado, below) learned shallow-well irrigated farming; here was inn, fort and church for the plains-bound settler. Ruins of the old house still stand.

From Mt. Blanco via FM 193 west, near tiny Farmer, 18 m., is the site of **Estacado,** the plains' first settlement founded as Marietta in 1879 by North Carolinian Quaker, Paris Cox. The now-traceless site was the actual beginning of the Great American Desert's becoming this nation's breadbasket. Quaker farmers found shallow water, but the severity of weather and remoteness of location drove them out and left this first city a ghost.

South of Crosbyton 22 m., via FM 651/2794, White River Lake offers all recreation facilities, including cabins. Southwest of the lake some 6 m., near little Kalgary (and inaccessible to autos), Stampede Mesa flanks Blanco Canyon. The mesa, a hunched-over hill, is haunted: legend claims an early cattle herd as the ghost. The herd was run over a bluff, and now its ghosts ride the night ridges, carrying anyone on the mesa to death.

Ralls, 179 m. (alt. 3,108; pop. 2,172), centering a busy agricultural area, is just north of the site of ghost town Emma, which won the county seat from Estacado in 1891 and boomed for a time. When Crosbyton took the seat 20 years later, Emma's boom collapsed, her buildings literally hauled over to the new town. The Ralls Historical Museum displays relics from pioneer days.

Lubbock, 206 m. (alt. 3,241; pop. 186,206 city). It is hard to believe that this booming city—for many years voted Texas' cleanest—grew from the ghost of a Quaker settlement to the east, and an on-site collection of buffalo hunters, mustangers, traildrivers and ranchers. As recently as 1920 its population was only 4,051.

The cleanness of Lubbock's lines—from its broad, handsome business area to its landscaped boulevards—seems all the more remarkable in light of central city problems throughout the U.S., and particularly so when you recognize that the city has kept house while experiencing one of America's most rapid growth rates. The city's Fine Arts Center is an outstanding one, and its Llano Estacado Winery is one of Texas' largest. Its tasting room offers samples of local vintages, including Chardonnay, Chenin Blanc, and Reisling. Also in the area are Pheasant Ridge and Teysha Cellars wineries.

Lubbock openly seeks recognition as America's Chrysanthemum City. Spectacular displays feature many of Lubbock's parks and particularly the city's Garden and Arts Center, as well as the spacious Texas Tech University campus. For a week each October, the city revels in Chrysanthemum Colorama.

Here is the home of several outstanding institutions. Texas Tech, with an enrollment climbing past 23,000, occupies a campus notable for beauty of line and openness, and the Texas Tech Museum complex is housed in a $7-million installation. The completed museum and planetarium are outstanding, and the 76-acre complex also includes the Ranching Heritage Center. There, some two dozen structures have been grouped to display the development of Texas ranching from the original dugout, through the log cabin and stone fortress stage, finally to the elegant ranch home. At the museum, get directions (and map) to the nearby Lubbock Lake Landmark State Historical Park, an important archeological site that has yielded artifacts reported to be 12,000 years old. An interpretive center shows site artifacts.

Within the city is 500-acre Mackenzie State Park, one of Texas' most visited. The park provides all recreation and amusement facilities, including its most popular Prairie Dog Town. These inquisitively comic little creatures once burrowed throughout the West in countless millions but now exist in preserves like Mackenzie. Also within the park is the Yellow House Canyon site—once, according to tradition, a prehistoric Indian town. Early Spanish explorers named it "Casas Amarillas."

Lubbock Christian University and Reese Air Force Base are also here. The Buddy Holly Statue and Walk of Fame honors West Texas and Lubbock natives who succeeded in the entertainment industry. Each Sept. is Panhandle-South Plains Fair. Intersect US 84/Tour 53; US 87/tour 61. Follow US 82 as it bends southwest.

Prairie dogs convene over a snack in Prairie Dog Town, Lubbock.

Brownfield, 246 m. (alt. 3,312; pop. 9,560). Like so many of the plains' little new cities, Brownfield presents a neat, orderly appearance. Life and death of plains settlements is no better illustrated than by tiny, ghostlike Gomez, 6 m. west. In 1904 Brownfield won the Terry County seat from Gomez by just five votes.

Harvest Festival is celebrated each October, and the Terry County Historical Museum displays exhibits reflecting pioneering times. Intersect US 385/Tour 60. Merge with US 380/Tour 49 to Plains.

Plains, 278 m. (alt. 3,690; pop. 1,422), was a cowboy's town until 1935, when the Wassom Field blew in to the south, blending industry into the old range. The town occupies the head of Sulphur Draw, itself heading the Colorado River: from here, Comanche moved southeast down the river valley.

Via FM 214 south 10 m. is Inks Basin, with traces of ancient Indian-dug shallow water wells. Beyond, at 15 m., **Denver City** (alt. 3,550; pop. 5,145), shows different wells. This was empty rangeland until 1935, when the Wassom Field came in. Denver City was established in 1939 and within one year counted 5,000 population. It is center for the oilfield. At Plains veer southwest from US 380/Tour 49.

At 295 m., cross the New Mexico line.

Tour 49

US 380
Jacksboro,
Graham, Throckmorton,
Aspermont,
Post, Brownfield,
New Mexico line, 312 m.

One of the lesser-traveled Texas routes, westward from Tour 2/Region I, US 380 nonetheless traverses an interesting region—one that Spain in the 1700s sought to penetrate, seeking a Santa Fe road, and one that later was combed by U.S. troopers, northbound in the 1870s, for a Comanche showdown on the High Plains.

You begin in the very region where, after the Civil War, America determined to finish it with the raiding Plains Indians. The man who would finally bottle the Comanche, Col. Ranald Mackenzie, was commanding at Fort Richardson in Jacksboro when his Indian campaign was ordered. From there across to Graham and Throckmorton, you travel an area of bloody Indian attacks which invoked the hardline policy.

Throughout, the terrain is unspectacular—sparsely-timbered and rolling prairies that climb to more nearly flat ones—except for the sense of remoteness encountered west of Graham. The land rolls on and on, little changed since the coming of the white man. Then, at Post, you climb the Cap Rock escarpment and cross the great agricultural region of the South Plains. You encounter no big urban areas en route: your Texans are principally Anglo-Saxon ranchers or farmers, and their customs are those of rural folk.

Jacksboro, 0 m.—see Tour 2. US 380 pushes west over undulating terrain—thinly timbered with postoak and blackjack—enough cover to allow the bloody Indian raids of the 1860s. Massacres at Elm and Salt Creeks determined General

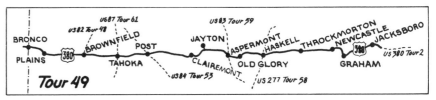

William T. Sherman, then investigating savage atrocities along the Texas frontier, to clear the state of hostiles. Fort Richardson's commander, Col. Ranald Mackenzie, was at hand; and he would be given the task, and—more than any other man—end the Comanche threat.

The first leg of your trip aproximates the old military road from Fort Richardson to Fort Belknap, then down to Fort Griffin, the upper end of Texas' western frontier.

At 18 m., FM 2075 leads northwest. North 7 m. near **Loving**, pop. 240, is the site of the Warren Wagon Train Massacre, May 18, 1871. An army supply train en route to Fort Richardson was ambushed here, seven teamsters mutilated and one man lashed to a wagon wheel and roasted. The raiding Comanche and Kiowa had unknowingly allowed the small troop escort of General Sherman to pass the day before. Survivors reached Fort Richardson and a convinced, if shaken, General Sherman ordered Mackenzie to clear West Texas. The Indian chiefs, Satank, Satanta and Big Tree, were apprehended in Oklahoma, and America's first Indian trial followed at Jacksboro (see Tour 2).

Graham, 28 m. (alt. 1,045; pop. 8,986), beside two small lakes in the broad, upper Brazos valley, is a wooded, handsome, small city. Graham survived a bloody frontier to prosper with a 1920 oil boom and, more recently, its role as gateway to big, scenic Possum Kingdom Lake. The shaded square has seen history—the 1879 Ryus Store building originally housed a district court which exercised jurisdiction over all of Texas north and west to New Mexico. Near on the square is Cattleman's Oak, where the Cattle Raisers Association was formed in 1877 to police ranching and specifically to halt rustling. Several fine old homes dating to the 1870s–80s, including that of the judge who presided over Graham's immense district, are close by. The modern courthouse has preserved the archway of its 1884 predecessor.

There are two pretty parks, and Lake Eddleman and Graham, nearby, provide water recreation.

Via TX 16/FM 1287 south, 20 m., **Possum Kingdom State Park,** with camping and all facilities, overlooks the big, wooded lake. Bass fishing is excellent and markers show the best areas to work. Many camps surround the deep Brazos reservoir.

Newcastle, 41 m. (alt. 1,126; pop. 505), shows signs of faded prosperity. It bloomed briefly from 1910–17 as a coal miner and was named for an English mining city. Oil production closed the mines where both iron and coal exist today.

The main building and water well at Ft. Belknap, near Graham.

Fort Belknap, just south on a great triple bend of the Brazos, was one of the anchors on an 1851 Red River to Rio Grande line, and was established specifically to guard over a premature Indian reservation here, and one westward near Throckmorton. The buildings remain in an excellent state of restoration, including the "Lee Well." With his famed 2nd Cavalry, Robert E. Lee commanded here for a time; in all, Fort Belknap saw the service of 17 men who would become generals during the Civil War—12 of them Confederate. Now a county historical park, Belknap is most notable for having launched in 1859 the "legal" exodus of Indians from Texas. Court-ordered, some 2,000 were uprooted from home and field and marched to Oklahoma reservations. The move failed of its purpose, Indian raids increasing in ferocity, particularly during the Civil War. The old commissary serves as an interesting museum; there are both Indian and old Army artifacts.

Profitt, 51 m., is a wayside farm community where, in 1864, the bloody Elm Creek Raid occurred. Indians hit the creekside settlement, killing 12 and abducting six women and children.

Throckmorton, 67 m. (alt. 1,441; pop. 1,036), is a shoulder-to-shoulder little town nestling in a valley and occupying the site of a campground on the old California-Western road. In early days it was notable for possessing the last house before reaching the New Mexico line, almost 300 m. distant. The town developed from Camp Cooper, 14 m. southwest, an establishment founded by Albert Sidney Johnston—later famed Confederate general—in 1856. Cooper's purpose was to guard an abortive attempt to place the Comanche on a four-league reservation, an effort which lasted five years but spun off this settlement as a ranching center, a role it continues today. Near-by Throckmorton Reservoir provides water recreation. In the area, also see Seymour, Fort Griffin.

Haskell, 100 m. (alt. 1,553; pop. 3,362), occupies the site of many crossroads—an ancient Indian campground and both Randolph Marcy's Forty-Niner and the later Butterfield-Overland stage route west. The first building here was a combination saloon and church—"The Road to Ruin."

Many springs in the area drew large herds of wild horses and pursuing mustangers, who captured them with corrals, by exhaustion and by "creasing"—a dangerous technique involving a shot across the neck, fine enough to stun the animal and yet not to kill.

Haskell's role as a mustanger shows in nearby place names—Wild Horse Mesa and Knob, Mustang Spring, Crossing and Hollow. It was also the area of sharp Indian fighting at such remote names as Paint Creek, California Creek, Double Mountain, and Lipan Point—all the sites of battles as buffalo hunters-turned ranchers took the land. At Haskell, the Fields Museum of Fine Living displays fine glass, china, furniture, and Oriental Rugs. Rice Springs Park, in the city, and Lake Stamford, southeast, have all facilities. At Haskell intersect US 277/Tour 58. Nearby, also see Stamford, Anson.

Old Glory, 121 m. (alt. 1,665; pop. 125), was settled by German farmers in 1903. In 1917 the village changed its name to show its loyalty. Just south is the site of **Rath City,** a now traceless dugout town which was 1870s headquarters for buffalo hunters and a hideout for outlaws.

Raynor, 124 m., a ghost today, was Stonewall County seat from 1888–1898, losing to Aspermont. The immense ranch home here—considered as a model for the film *Giant*—was that town's courthouse, then post office, church and school.

Aspermont, 131 m. (alt. 1,773; pop. 1,214). This little county seat (Stonewall Co.) and retail center mounts the divide between the Salt Fork of the Brazos to the north and Double Mountain Fork to the south, with massive Double Mountain itself looming southwest. This area was first crossed by white men in 1788, when Jose Mares—after countless Spanish attempts—finally opened a trail from San Antonio to Santa Fe. Thereafter, Double Mountain was a waymarker for every westward expedition and a rendezvous for buffalo hunters.

The old Spanish trail has given rise to many legends, chief among which connects Aspermont with the "Spider Rock." Allegedly, a Spanish treasure way station near here was wiped out by Indians, the treasure hidden—somehow with a map turning up. Northeast, near the Salt Fork, one treasure hunter in 1920 converted all his worldly goods into a 30-year search. Hermit-like, the man lived in a dugout he had dug into the side of the canyon. He is buried in one of the trenches he was convinced was just a shovel's length from bonanza.

Southwest, near Double Mountain, is the site of **Orient** (inaccessible to autos), a 1900 "silver strike" which boomed a promoter's town to several thousand population. The strike had been salted; the promoter disappeared, and so did the town.

At Aspermont, intersect US 83/Tour 59.

Jayton, 154 m. (alt. 2,015; pop. 608). North of this tiny county seat (Kent Co.) is a "salt lake," where stockmen for years have broken surface deposits with plows. That it has been used since dim past is evidenced by Indian artifacts dating back to the Folsom Man 10,000 years ago. Early buffalo hunters camped here to cure their meat. Nearby, also see Spur, Dickens.

Clairemont, 167 m. (alt. 2,727; pop. 35). Close below here is Treasure Butte, site of legendary buried Spanish treasure, also site of an 1872 battle with the Comanche during the Mackenzie campaigns.

Post, 210 m. (alt. 2,590; pop. 3,768). Walled north and west by the red-gray Cap Rock cliffs, this pin-neat little city was planned as a model by cereal king and philanthropist C. W. Post. In 1907,

supplies were hauled by wagon from rail head at Big Spring; shortly thereafter Post fought a battle for water, convinced that it would bring all the plains area to green life. For three years of drought, the inventor-industrialist staged perhaps the biggest rainmaking experiments this country has seen. He called them "rain battles" and fought them from the cliff over the town, tying dynamite sticks to kites and bombarding any likely overcast. Many of his rain-station ruins are visible on the Cap Rock bluffs: he ultimately built 12 stations, each firing 250 charges—one per minute—in the greatest peacetime barrage ever to shake an American city. The battles' rain production is debatable; however, the city held on and can justly boast on its city-limits sign, "Welcome to Post—gateway to the Plains."

Among several historic buildings are the 1912 Post home, the 1908 Algerita Hotel (now an art gallery for area works), and the 1912 Post Sanitarium (now the Garza County Historical Museum, reflecting this town's early days). Postex, an integrated textile mill conceived by the town's founder, is now used for warehousing cotton and other products.

Post rests atop the big Garza oilfield, which once boasted the world's only sextuple oil well—a single shaft drawing from six different pay zones. An excellent guide to the several historic sites in this area is available at the C of C.

Northeast some 30 m. White River Lake, with camping and all facilities, is probably the prettiest lake on the Plains. Southwest, via a private ranch road, Buffalo Point is a huge ledge over which early buffalo hunters, impatient with dropping their kills one by one, simply drove a herd over the edge, killing hundreds.

At Post, intersect US 84/Tour 53. Westward, you climb the Cap Rock escarpment and emerge on the rich green fields of the South Plains. In the area, also see Stampede Mesa, Gail and Lubbock.

Tahoka, 236 m. (alt. 3,090; pop. 2,868), took its name from the Indian word for sweet, deep water at Lake Tahoka, 5 m. northeast. Today's rich agricultural area was heavily camped by the Comanche, then by buffalo hunters and, in the 1870s, by Indian-pursuing troop-

ers. Northwest 5 m., at Double Lakes, one of the last Comanche raids resulted in the waterless ordeal known as Nolan's Expedition or the Lost Negro Expedition. Company A of 10th Cavalry, chasing Indians from a base on the lakes, were led in circles until they became lost. Waterless for 86 hours until they stumbled back on Double Lakes, Nolan's men lost every horse (most killed and their blood drunk) and four men. The Comanche escaped.

Tahoka stages Old Settlers Reunion late each June. The Harvest Festival, each fall, ends with a street dance. The city has given its name to the Tahoka Daisy, a pretty lavender wildflower discovered near Lake Tahoka, and one that often blankets the plains with its vibrant color. In town, the Pioneer Museum recalls old days.

At Tahoka intersect US 87/Tour 61.

Brownfield, 264 m.—see Tour 48.

Gomez, 270 m., a near-ghost, illustrates the fragility of early Plains settlement. In 1904, then-thriving Gomez lost the Terry County seat to Brownfield by 5 votes.

Plains, 296 m.—see Tour 48. Veer northward with US 380.

Bronco, 312 m., pop. 30, was the first town in this area, settled at the turn of the century. Its founder, namer and postmaster, H. (Gravey) Field delivered the mail free for six months, riding 90 m. to Portales, New Mexico periodically. The sunken bed of a wagon served as a store-post office. Gravey left the door open, and cowboys picked up what they needed, left a list of what they'd taken and every now and then settled up.

At Bronco, cross the New Mexico line.

☆

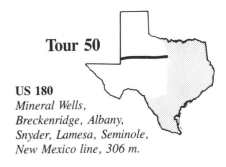

Tour 50

US 180
Mineral Wells,
Breckenridge, Albany,
Snyder, Lamesa, Seminole,
New Mexico line, 306 m.

Continuing Tour 3, Region I, this westward route is more varied than those to its north, ranging from hilly terrain in the east through rolling ranch country in its mid-reaches, finally to travel the long, sweeping vistas of West Texas.

You begin at Mineral Wells, just within the upper end of Texas hill country—the rugged and scenic Palo Pinto Mountains, which extend west almost to Breckenridge. There you cross the top of the old Ranger oilfield, which from 1917–24 saw one of Texas' greatest booms. Beyond, at Albany, you retreat in time, crossing the state's main north-south fort line, with Griffin just above and Phantom Hill below. Beyond Snyder, another scene of vast oil play (during the 1930s), you pass below the foot of the Cap Rock escarpment—a lonely land that has known only ranching. Far west near Lamesa you climb onto the South Plains and continue across that rich, green cropland until reaching the New Mexico line.

Mineral Wells, 0 m.—see Tour 3. Follow US 180 westward.

Palo Pinto, 12 m. (alt. 1,043; pop. 350), occupying a little valley, clusters modestly about a tan brick courthouse that could pass for a college administration building. A picturesque village of old-time white stone structures, Palo Pinto is old—settled in 1858 and named "painted post" for its valley's deposits of petrified wood. You can almost envision the Fort Worth-Fort Griffin stage pulling up on today's square, awaiting a team change; and the old stone county jail, now a museum, takes you back to an earlier time. West 3 m., Lovers Retreat is a very scenic maze of immense red boulders big as houses and honeycombed with paths and small caves—a fine picnicking park, but one which did not derive its name from romance—an early settler, Lovers by name, hid here from Indians. South 8 m. Lake Palo Pinto provides water recreation and several lakeside facilities. Nearby, see Thurber.

At **Caddo,** 36 m., pop. 40, park road 33 leads north 18 m. to big, scenic Possum Kingdom Lake and state park, with camping, all facilities, and good fishing.

Breckenridge, 50 m. (alt. 1,220; pop. 5,665), is one of those 1920 oil boomers that left itself looking larger than it is today. Established in 1876, this was long a frontier village, its outlying settlements centered on log forts. In 1917, oil play seeped gradually north from Eastland County below and by 1920 a boom was in full swing, the population leaping from 1,000 to 30,000, oil prospectors sleeping in shifts wherever room to lie down could be found. In the immediate area are ghost town sites from that boom—Jim Kurn, Necessity, Parks and LeeRay, all disappearing as the play ended. For a time prior to oil's discovery, Breckenridge knew a brief flurry in coal mining similar to that of Thurber to the southeast; and today it has satisfactorily substituted small industries for its once big oil income. Swenson Memorial Museum and Sandefer Oil Annex contains many interesting relics from early days, before and after oil. The Breckenridge Aviation Museum, at Stephens County airport, houses a dozen or more vintage warplanes and a large collection of historic photographs. On each Memorial Day weekend, thousands attend the city's Air Show, where more than a hundred of these flying veterans recreate the aerial combat of WW II. In August, Stephens County stages its junior rodeo here, and each early December sees Breckenridge's Christmas Parade. The city boasts an excellent Fine Arts Center at its new Library. West 4 m., Hubbard Creek Lake is one of West Texas' big, new water recreation areas.

In the area also see Graham, Ranger, Eastland and Cisco.

Albany, 74 m. (alt. 1,429; pop. 1,962). Nestled in choppy little hills, this heritage-minded old town was settled in 1875, taking the county seat from rawhide-famed Fort Griffin, immediately north. Close around its 1883 Victorian courthouse some 15 historic buildings have been cited. The town observes its ripsnorting early days in an annual latter-June "Fandangle," casting some 300 in an extravaganza of cowboys, Indians, and covered wagons—all to music

in Albany's "Prairie Theatre." Begun in 1938, the Fandangle—which regularly plays to an audience five times Albany's population—preambled the many musical historical dramas now shown across the country. The old M.K.T. depot houses Fandangle headquarters, as well as the C of C. Interestingly, Albany can draw first hand on its history—the *Albany News* having maintained its original files since its establishment in 1883.

In town, the 1878 jail has been restored to house some exceptional art exhibits. The Ledbetter Picket House, also restored, reflects earliest range days and, interestingly, Albany has erected a monument to the Georgia volunteers who fought for Texas independence. Dr. John Shackelford, for whom the county is named, was one of their number.

Via US 283 north 15 m. is **Fort Griffin State Park,** in partial restoration above the Clear Fork of the Brazos. Established in 1867 as a base for Col. Ranald Mackenzie's drive on the High Plains, Fort Griffin became Texas headquarters for cattle drovers, buffalo hunters, and fast guns like Billy the Kid, Bat Masterson and Pat Garrett. At

Ruins at Fort Griffin State Park near Albany.

one time buffalo hides were stacked a block square here, high as a two-story building! On the "Flat" below the mesa, where the old post stands, was another self-acknowledged "wickedest town on earth," known simply as The Flat and perhaps most notable for 34 on-the-street killings and the presence for a time of a mysterious and beautiful lady gambler, Lottie Deno. She was the best gambler in the West and, some said, a disillusioned Southern Belle; she disappeared as mysteriously as she came. The state park boasts a museum with instructive displays and, across from the fort, good camp-grounds along the Brazos. A herd of the famed Texas Longhorn is maintained.

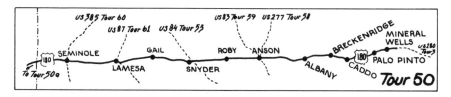

West of Albany, the hills lower to rolling, then level, prairies.

Anson, 112 m. (alt. 1,750; pop. 2,644), spreading around its yellow sandstone courthouse, occupies a cotton-producing area once devoted only to ranching. In 1881, with a total of four buildings and 14 people, the settlement still managed to name itself county seat and as it grew, entertained great ambition. Its old opera house, from the early 1900s, was "the finest showplace between Fort Worth and El Paso," and the city projects plans for its restoration. The old Bowyer store, a one-room boxed and stripped building, was one of Anson's original four.

Late August, the town stages its Jones County Fair; its most famed event, however, is the Cowboys Christmas Ball. Originated at the turn of the century, it drew cowhands from ranches throughout the region, decked in their best Ogden Mills trousers, their boots polished and Colts laid aside. The ball has become a tradition now staged in a rock building, Pioneer Hall, built specifically for the event.

At Anson, intersect US 277/Tour 58; US 83/Tour 59. Nearby, also see Stamford, Abilene.

Roby, 141 m. (alt. 1,990; pop. 616). Just west of TX 70 is a large display of true Western art, welded by a local blacksmith. The Hatahoe Drive-in just past is first in a chain started by a local boy who hated to hoe cotton and vowed when grown never to do so again.

Snyder, 174 m. (alt. 2,316; pop. 12,195). In the middle of one of America's richest oil-producing counties (Scurry Co., named for a Texas Confederate general), this handsome community was once little more than a rough and ready oil town that had grown from a dugout sprawl of 1877. That was when an ox-teamed supply train set up a buffalo hunters' camp here, sometimes dubiously known as Robbers Roost.

In 1967, Snyder determined to beautify itself and within two years of enormous refurbishing, earned All-American status, an accomplishment achieved without a penny of federal funds.

Snyder did not forget its early days, however, remembering that the most famed buffalo hunter of all, J. Wright Mooar (he killed 20,000 in one decade),

lived here and 10 m. northwest of town brought down a rare albino. A white buffalo statue stands on the square today. Snyder brought in oil in 1923, and 40 years later observed its billionth barrel produced, and has noted that achievement with a gold barrel, saluting the last Texas oil boom.

The Diamond M Foundation Museum reflects the city's maturing culture, with more than 300 paintings, 80 sculptures and 150 objects of jade, ivory and china. Western Texas College is a two-year accredited community institution stressing continuing education for everyone. The campus features an excellent planetarium. The C of C provides maps for a walking tour of downtown. At Towle Memorial Park, your youngsters can view the citizens of an intriguing Prairie Dog Town.

Near Snyder is the 1908 Mooar Mansion, an immensely handsome ranch-house built by the Vermonter who turned from Chicago streetcar conducting to buffalo-hunting and then ranching.

Lake J. B. Thomas, with camping facilities and water recreation, lies southwest. At Snyder, intersect US 84/Tour 53. In the area also see Colorado City.

Gail, 206 m. (alt. 2,530; pop. 189), lying close beside crouching Muchakooago Peak as it always has, is one of the smallest county seats in Texas. Like its county, named for Gail Borden, Texan Revolutionary and inventor of condensed milk, Gail has steadfastly resisted anything but ranching, boasting a town without a doctor, theater, newspaper or barbershop and a population unchanged since 1900. Its old handhewn rock jail was built escape-proof—apparently so foreboding that at last report it had held only one prisoner—an out-of-town bootlegger.

Adjacent to the courthouse is the excellent Borden County Historical Museum. Once a year, Gail holds an annual Quarter Horse Show and Junior Rodeo, but in this region of riders, you can find a good rodeo almost any night by driving to the arena—both young and old bring their horses and meet there.

The peak—actually a shoulder of the Cap Rock that has resisted erosion and pronunciation (it is called "Mushaway" locally)—was a landmark sighted by Capt. Randolph Marcy when blazing a Forty-Niner road, and by Robert E. Lee,

on an 1856 scouting expedition. It was a rendezvous for Comancheros trading stolen horses with the Indians and a base camp for expeditions hunting those Indians.

In the area also see Post, Big Spring.
Lamesa, 238 m. (alt. 2,975; pop. 10,809), is a bustling county seat (Dawson Co.) located on Sulphur Springs Draw, Colorado River headwaters and, from earliest time, head of a trail leading southeast into Central Texas. Once this was great grazing land for buffalo, replaced by ranchers' herds and, more recently, by excellent cotton production. When the county was organized, cowboys on the Barto Ranch, to secure a seat of government, wrote an actual wagonload of mail, hoping to impress postal officials. Pleased with their output, they suggested their city's name be Chicago. This tableland instead received the name "La Mesa" and a site some 2 m. distant from Chicago. In time the cowboys agreed and Lamesa absorbed Chicago.

The Lamesa Rodeo and Western Art Show is held each early August, and the Dawson County Fair is staged each mid-September; the county museum reflects early days on the range. Dawson County has the distinction of furnishing more men per capita for WW II than any other in Texas. At Lamesa, intersect US 87/Tour 61.

Seminole, 281 m. (alt. 3,312; pop. 6,342). This brisk county seat reflects a prosperous balance between rich oil production and agriculture—it is nothing to see a field veiled in sprinkler irrigation while between the crop rows oil pumps are working. Gaines County is Texas' fourth largest oil producer and shows 650,000 acres in crop cultivation as well. In September, Seminole stages Agriculture and Oil Appreciation Day. Here you intersect US 385/Tour 60.

At 289 m., FM 1757 leads northwest to Cedar Lake, 20 m., largest salt lake on the plains and the site, according to tradition, where Comanche Chief Quanah Parker was born to his white mother, Cynthia Ann Parker (see Groesbeck).

At 306 m. cross the New Mexico line. Hobbs, N. Mex. is 5 m. west, and US 180 continues through Carlsbad to emerge again in Texas, en route to El Paso (see Tour 50A).

Tour 50A

US 180
*New Mexico line,
Guadalupe Mountains
National Park, Salt Flat, El
Paso, 129 m.*

El Paso-bound, Tour 50A continues US 180 after that highway cuts 110 m. across the southeast corner of New Mexico, passing through Hobbs and Carlsbad (Carlsbad Caverns National Park) en route. The New Mexico leg begins in plains country and ends against the east wall of the Guadalupe Mountains, where this tour follows.

Throughout, your route displays scenic grandeur, starting with the skirting of Texas' highest peaks, descending for a mountain-girt desert run, and finishing in America's high, handsome international gateway to Old Mexico.

One of this state's most splendid views awaits your descent from Guadalupe Pass, at the outset of your trip—a long, twisting drop that unfolds the magnificence of view that you find only in America's West. From the foot of the Guadalupes, the 100 m. run to El Paso is a level, drumming drive across high terrain that you may dismiss as barren or—flanked by distant ranges that back away like stacked cardboard cutouts—find enchanting. After a rain, the desert springs to life in a profusion of crimson and yellow cactus blossoms. Awaiting you, El Paso backs against the silvery Mexican sierra, straddling its historic Pass of the North.

N. Mex. line, 0 m. South of Carlsbad Caverns 20 m., you cross into Texas. Directly ahead looms the east wall of the Guadalupe range, the sheer face of El Capitan, 8,078 feet, landmarking your gateway. Behind it, rounded, pine-clad Guadalupe Peak, Texas' highest, at 8,751 feet, seems from this perspective the lesser elevation.

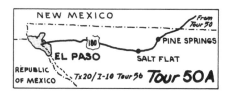

Pine Springs, 19 m., saw a 1980s battle between the National Park Service and owners who did not want to leave. In the late 1850s this was the site of one of Texas' most hazardous stage stations—the Apache watched from those heights above. One of their last strongholds in those mountains made this as dangerous for ambush as any point on the western road. Troops were often stationed here to escort the Butterfield stages through.

North via a park road is 77,000-acre **Guadalupe Mountains National Park,** with 80 miles of hiking and backpacking trails. Tent and RV camping is available at Pine Springs. The Guadalupes' walls conceal spectacular scenery, atop and within. The green tufts far above you are Ponderosa Pine and Douglas Fir—giant trees in forests that spill to chasm-slashed labyrinths, like beautiful McKittrick Canyon—a kind of close-quarter Yosemite—immediately north of El Capitan. High, fragile trails skirt

The rugged gorge of McKittrick Canyon, Guadalupe Mountains National Park. Accessible by foot only.

other canyons that are well named—Blue, Devil's Den. Bird and wildlife are profuse: often, elk and bobcat may be seen. If you have time and the legs for it, a day's hike is an experience.

These Guadalupes, unusual among mountains in that they were once a submerged ocean reef, were the last bastion of Apache Chieftain Victorio and, until recent National Park acquisition, were as wild as when a pursuing army cavalry troop lost itself within them. In a maze too rough for their mounts, the troopers left their horses and groped their way out afoot, and by compass.

At 23 m., the view from a roadside park is well worth your stop. Below, the land falls away like a roll of silk, south and west. Above you loom El Capitan (understandably once designated Signal Peak) and Guadalupe Peak. Somewhere

Giant El Capitan stands solemn guard along the southern tier of Guadalupe Mountains National Park, off US 180 near Pine Springs.

close behind El Capitan reputedly lies the legendary Ben (or Bill) Sublett treasure. In the 1880s, Willian C. Sublett, an old-time prospector, worked Texas and Pacific rail construction south at Van Horn, periodically disappearing into these mountains that were so dangerous to most white men. His friends, the Apache, showed him a cache of gold (doubtless hijacked from some Forty-Niner who hit it in California). Old Ben, as he was called, was prodigal with the solid nuggets he brought out—he startled an Odessa saloon crowd by spilling a handfull on the bar—and when he needed money, he made his lonely way toward the mountains. Men tried to follow; he eluded them or faced them down with drawn gun. Before his death in 1892, he showed his 14-year-old son the canyon-bottom cave and its treasure; but the boy—despite a near lifetime search—could never find it as a man.

Salt Flat, 42 m., pop. 35, edges a number of glistening white salt lakes, where not covered by inwashed silt, glaring beneath the sun or garishly white by night. Here is the cause of Texas' 1860s–70s Salt War, a dispute over the right to mine the deposits free. The trouble ended in violence in San Elizario (Tour 56), with the killing of a district judge and others by a mob, and for a time, the stationing of frontier troops at Fort Bliss in El Paso. Westward, you begin what was a difficult, parched journey in early stage or wagon train days: the desert is nearly waterless; its growth, mesquite and greasewood, cactus, tumbleweed and yucca or Spanish Dagger.

Hueco Tanks State Park, 103 mi. is a strange volcanic jumble that served as a prehistoric Indian campground—there are many pictographs—as well as a final Butterfield stage station (water collected in the cistern rock sinks within the formation) before reaching El Paso. The unusually scenic park provides camping and all facilities, with hiking and interpretive trails leading past some of the 14 areas of Indian pictographs.

El Paso, 129 m. (alt. 3,762; pop. 515,342 city). The Sun City boasts Texas' most spectacular metropolitan setting, meandering about the foot of the Franklin Mountains, fingering up their canyons, and perched along their slopes. Here is historically-famed Pass of the North—since 1598, gateway to Old Mexico. Across the Rio Grande is big Ciudad Juarez, Mexico's largest border city.

Proximity to the Mexican border can lead many tourists to overlook this city's natural beauty—few can equal its setting. There are more than 100 parks. The Transmountain Road (Loop 375) cuts across the midsection of the Franklin Mountains, topping out at near a mile high, while Murchison Park on Scenic Drive perches some 4,000 feet above the city at the mountains' southern tip, both affording sweeping vistas. The nighttime view from Murchison Park of El Paso and Juarez is especially impressive. West is Sierra Cristo Rey, with cross and Christ statue.

The aerial tram to Ranger Peak in the Franklin Mountains above El Paso.

There is an excellent tourist information stop westward on I-10 (Tour 56), and El Paso's C of C is one of the best—visit it. Downtown walking tours take you past such landmarks as the Notice Tree, a kind of pioneer bulletin board, and the site of Acme Saloon, where gunfighter John Wesley Hardin met death, shot in the back.

Mini-Tour Guide

Border Jumper trolley: Easy way to visit Juarez, lower valley missions. Depart from Civic Center, downtown.

Chamizal National Memorial: Border grant to Mexico. Paisano and San Marcial.

Centennial Museum: On U.T. El Paso campus.

El Mercadito: Collection of shops in recent adobe building; most items for sale made on site. 10189 Socorro Rd.

El Paso Museum of Art: Bi-cultural. 1211 Montana.

El Paso Museum of History: I-10 at Loop 375.

Missions: (See details, Tour 56.)

Placita Santa Fe: Southwestern arts, crafts. 5034 Doniphan.

El Paso Saddleblanket Co.: Largest collection of Indian, Mexican arts in the area. 601 Oregon.

Fort Bliss: Active duty post, home of Patriot missile crews of Gulf War fame. Base maintains four military museums (Air Defense and Artillery, Fort Bliss, Museum of the NCO, 3rd Armored Cavalry). Enter off US 54 N (Patriot Freeway).

Juarez: Many shops, fine restaurants, 1659 mission, historical museum, traditional market. Also Pueblito Mexicano, huge airconditioned mall fashioned after a Mexican village. Cross from downtown or ride Border Jumper trolley.

Magoffin Home: 1875 state historic structure. 1120 Magoffin.

Scenic Drives: Scenic Drive, Transmountain Road (Loop 375).

Sierra del Cristo Rey: Massive cross, statue, westward. Guided tours only.

Tigua Indian Reservation: (Ysleta del Sur Pueblo). 119 Old Pueblo Rd.

Wilderness Park Museum: Indian tribe artifacts. 2000 Transmountain Rd.

Zoo: Evergreen and Paisano.

The city's museums are varied. Wilderness Park explores pre-history, while Chamizal Museum is international. Handsome University of Texas at El Paso (15,000 enrollment) houses a Centennial Museum; and the city, a fine arts center. Fort Bliss, largest air defense center of the free world, displays a replica of the old frontier fort and a cavalry museum. Entertainment is equally abundant. All metropolitan facilities are here, bolstered by Ciudad Juarez (use a guide), and its attractions—bullfights (world's fourth largest ring) to greyhound races and restaurants to night spots. Sunland Park northwest features

horse races from October through May.

December (from November into January) is the month of Sun Carnival, climaxing with the major Sun Bowl football game. Early February sees a stock show and rodeo; July and August, festivals at the Chamizal and the Tigua reservation and production of *Viva!* at McKelligon Canyon. In October is the Border Folk Festival at the Chamizal.

East of the city (Tour 56) are the three white missions of Ysleta, Socorro and San Elizario, first Texas colonization and the beginnings of this city.

At El Paso intersect I-10/Tour 56.

☆

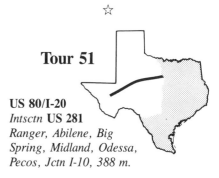

Tour 51

US 80/I-20
Intsctn **US 281**
Ranger, Abilene, Big Spring, Midland, Odessa, Pecos, Jctn I-10, 388 m.

This tour crosses a largely inhospitable land, but does it handsomely—a fine illustration of man's ability to build with a flourish in regions that seem at first glance defiant of habitation. Your westward interstate route traverses a procession of some of Texas' best-looking mid-sized cities.

Continuing Tour 3A, Region I, you begin at the intersection with Tour 17 south of Mineral Wells. From there you traverse a region of low hills, proven rich in minerals—the great coal boom at Thurber, and Ranger's even bigger oilfield.

At Abilene, immaculate on the rolling plains of West Texas, you enter a region of scant timber, broad horizons, crystalline air; and throughout your journey you continue in it. Midland's towers and the big new growth of Odessa occur in an area where once lone sentries stood guard over buffalo hides stacked against a treeless, empty horizon.

You pass a belt of desert sandhills at Monahans, and the Old-West-beginning barrier of the Pecos at that city; and then, at the junction of I-10 merging from the south, the minarets and spires of the Davis range mark the end of this tour. Enjoy it for what it is—brisk, invigorating country.

US 281/Tour 17, 0 m. You begin south of Mineral Wells, where Region I and IV meet.

Santo, 6 m. (alt. 970; pop. 312), in early days fought Indians to survive. Here was a makeshift 1865 fort bearing the sardonic name, "White's Town and Burnet Street; Stubblefield's Fort and Nothing to Eat." Northwest, Lake Palo Pinto provides water sports.

Thurber, 26 m. (alt. 1,150; pop. 8). Cupped in its crouching hills, this ghost miner is announced by the distant loom of a towering brick smokestack. Once a promising city of 10,000, a few weathered brick buildings and scarred hillsides remain. Beneath you is a reserve of bituminous coal estimated at 100 million tons; at its peak in 1919, Thurber mined 3,000 tons daily. Ruins are strung out on New York Hill, Silk Stocking Row and down in the flats where miners of every nationality saw labor trouble lead to America's first all-union town in 1917. In "The Snake," Thurber boasted the biggest horseshoe bar of any saloon between Fort Worth and El Paso, and her secondary industry—brickmaking—paved Austin's Congress Avenue and buttressed Galveston's seawall.

She became a ghost in strange fashion. A midwestern engineer, W. W. Johnson, saw coal here in the 1880s, hit it big with his first shaft and sold out to Texas and Pacific Coal company. As his town grew, however, Johnson's family saw tragedy, losing first a daughter, then, years later, a son. The grief-stricken man, unable to see his children buried, built a "small house," where he could watch them. Finally his wife, then he, died. The "house" was sealed—as his will required—and became the Johnson tomb looking out on the Thurber hills. Ironically, Thurber's discoverer died the very year that Texas and Pacific—seeing coal's end with the Texas oil boom—moved its headquarters from here to Fort Worth, its mines closed. By 1933, the town was abandoned, but every July 4th, old-timers return for reunion. The old company store (restaurant now) displays pictures of Thurber's boom days.

Ranger, 36 m. (alt. 1,429; pop. 2,803), in a hilly valley, is the great oil boomer of all times. Founded as a ranger outpost in 1881, Ranger in 1917 was a one-street, dusty, board-fronted town with Saturday band concerts and traveling medicine shows for entertainment. Then, in October, McClesky #1 (see site plaque) blew in and oil shot up, running down its hills and defying all efforts to dike it off. As wells multiplied, citizens literally tried to sweep the black flood from their doorways.

The town, population leaped from 1,000 to 40,000 in mere months and this city was a welter of roustabouts and carpenters, financiers and promoters, drillers and dressers, mule skinners and uniformed chauffeurs, gamblers and women. A hotel hall cot cost $10; a lobby chair, $5.

Famous people invested happily—men like Heavyweight champion Jess Willard, Circus boss John Ringling, oilman Harry Sinclair, and a new outfit called Humble Oil. Ex-President Taft walked the streets unnoticed.

Instant riches! A broke wildcatter kidnaped himself, made his well on his friends' kidnap ransom. One lease changed hands three times in a day, going from $1,500 to $15,000. Then, all at once after three years, the Ranger field went dry.

Today, Ranger looks like a city many times its modest population, and many solid buildings stand empty or have been demolished. Today, the city maintains Ranger Junior College. The old depot now houses the C of C, as well as the Roaring Ranger Museum, with recollections of the town's glory days. Immediately south, Lake Leon provides water sports.

Eastland, 46 m. (alt. 1,421; pop. 3,690), like its eastern neighbor, experienced the 1920s boom but today shows little effects of it. At its handsome courthouse the city preserves a legend—the tiny casket of Rip, the Horned Frog. In 1897 a youngster placed a horned frog in the metal container before the courthouse cornerstone was laid. In 1928–31 years later—a new courthouse was built. The container opened, Old Rip was found alive. Exhibited throughout the United States, he lived for 11 months.

Nearby is Merriman church and cemetery. A pioneer settlement, Merriman had dwindled to only its churchgrounds when the oil boom hit. Literally surrounded by wells, and a fortune for the asking by leasing the ground on which it stood, the Merriman congregation refused the money, kept their little church and cemetery "Not for Sale." Downtown, Eastland's post office displays an unusual historical mural, composed of some 12,000 stamps.

At 51 m., between Eastland and Cisco, the Kendrick Amphitheater stages giant religious dramas—an annual Easter pageant and, through summer, a portrayal of the life of Christ. The grounds can accommodate 100,000 and on them a museum displays dioramas tracing the growth of the Christian faith. Nearby, also see Breckenridge.

Cisco, 56 m. (alt. 1,608; pop. 3,813), absorbing part of Ranger's oil boom, once boasted the longest brick highway in the world—the 21 m. Ranger road. Many old homes have been preserved, and the Mobley Hotel, where Conrad Hilton began his hotel career, has been restored as C of C office, community center, and museum. North of town is the ghost of Cisco's predecessor, pioneering Red Gap, killed when railroads bypassed here.

Baird, 81 m. (alt. 1,708; pop. 1,658), Callahan County seat, began as a ranching center, cattle driving up the military road to Forts Phantom Hill and Belknap, northward; today, farming bolsters the economy. Immediately south are the ruins of Belle Plain, one of West Texas' early towns of great promise, boasting a school and college. By 1880, decline set in as Baird replaced Belle Plain, whose ruins stand in a field today. Lake Clyde, southward, provides water sports. Nearby, also see Albany.

Abilene, 102 m. (alt. 1,738; pop. 106,654 city). This vibrant city grew from an 1880 welter of tents and shacks along a Texas and Pacific rail siding. Located on the Western and Dodge cattle trail, it borrowed its name from the Kansas traildrive destination. Today it remains a primary livestock area, adding diversified agriculture, petroleum, and other industries to an economy which has produced a spacious, handsome city. Cultural influence is provided by three church schools—Abilene Christian University, Hardin-Simmons University, and McMurry College. Dyess Air Force Base is located here. The base offers interesting tours (advance arrangements) and displays about 25 World War II, Korean War, and Vietnam War planes along the main street entering the base. Planes of a wing of the Confederate Air Force are displayed weekends at the city airport.

A Fine Arts Museum and the excellent Abilene Zoo add to the city's spectrum of attractions. South at Buffalo Gap are an intriguing pioneer town and big, wooded Abilene State Recreation Area, with camping and all facilities. Just north is skeletal Fort Phantom Hill (Tour 58) and water sports on its lake.

Late each May, the Western Heritage Classic turns Abilene western with a ranch rodeo, campfire cookoff, sheep dog trials, cowboy horse races, bit and spur show, and western art show and sale. The West Texas Fair each mid-September is a big family affair. Each April and November arts and crafts shows come to town.

Old Abilene Town, a re-created village of the Old West in modern-day Abilene.

Cowboying is very much alive in this city, which makes boots, hats, and saddles, as well as boasting an authentic muzzle-loading gun shop.

At Abilene, intersect US 277/Tour 58; US 83/Tour 59; merge with US 84/Tour 53 west to Roscoe. In the area also see Anson, Stamford.

Sweetwater, 144 m. (alt. 2,164; pop. 11,967) spreads across low, rolling hills north of your road. In 1877 this was a dugout camp of buffalo hunters, its first frame structure being a saloon. The town nearly died along with surrounding ranches in the 1885 blizzard, followed by two years of fierce drought. Ironically, considering its name, the city's struggle for many years was for sweet water, citizens at the turn of the century building their own system.

In 1958 Sweetwater inaugurated its Rattlesnake Roundup, the world's largest, each second weekend in March. Substantial prizes are awarded for biggest and smallest snakes. A rattlesnake eating contest climaxes festivities; the show is heavily attended.

The massively handsome 1906 Ragland home serves as Sweetwater's Pioneer Museum.

Colorado City, 173 m. (alt. 2,067; pop. 4,749). On the Comanche Trail southeast toward Central Texas and once site of a substantial Indian village, this is the oldest town between Weatherford and El Paso. Lone Wolf Mountain, northeast, has long been a traveler's landmark. Southward, the famed Spade Ranch began when Isaac L. Ellwood, one of the inventors of barbed wire, bought an immense tract of land.

With railroad's arrival in 1881, the city boomed overnight, jumping to a rowdy 5,000 population. Today, the count remains the same; but the city has mellowed. South is Champion Creek Reservoir, water sports; southwest, Lake Colorado City State Park, with camping and all facilities.

The Colorado City Historical Museum downtown features artifacts from buffalo tracks to a horse-drawn hearse. Fort Wood, on I-20, recreates an Old West town.

Big Spring, 211 m. (alt. 2,397; pop. 23,093), with its big spring still bubbling south of town, has been a West Texas crossroads from prehistoric time: the Comanche Mexico-bound war trail came through, as did the Forty-Niner's California road. Early cattle ranching found some British investment. When rails came through in the 1880s, Big Spring was a tough gun town, its residences either tents or dugouts. Today it lies in a valley—you descend on the city from almost any direction—marked by a prosperous-looking business area. Signal Mountain, 10 m. southeast, is a prominent landmark.

The city's Heritage Museum boasts the world's largest collection of longhorn steer horns, and the lovely old Potton House is completely restored to reflect turn-of-the-century living. The Big Spring (in Comanche Trail Park) is surrounded by nature trails, golf course, and campgrounds, and Big Spring State Park (day use only) offers picnicking, jogging trails, prairie dog town, and scenic views. Moss Creek Lake, all facilities, is nearby.

Big Spring has square dances the first weekend each May. Latter June is Cowboy Reunion and Rodeo time; and late July sees the National Texas Style Domino Tourney. Late September, Howard County turns to the Fair Grounds.

At Big Spring intersect US 87/Tour 61. In the area also see Gail, Sterling City.

Stanton, 232 m. (alt. 2,664; pop. 2,576), near Mustang Spring, provided the best camp west of Big Spring on the New Mexico wagon road. It was originally settled by German farmers, railroad-induced from East Texas, and named Mariensfield—Field of Mary. There was the usual farmer-rancher trouble, and in 1890 the name was changed to Stanton. A museum here displays skeletal remains of the giant, prehistoric mastodon found nearby, and a gun collection is housed in the old jail on the square. Near Stanton is the 1890 Victorian Mulhollon Mansion, with which ghost stories are associated; the old house was used in the film, *Midnight Cowboy.*

Midland, 250 m. (alt. 2,779; pop. 89,443). A good-looking, shaded oasis in its bare, dun-colored plain, this is the "Tall City" of West Texas, with far more high-rise buildings than its size should promise: they house petroleum company offices, some 650 oil-related concerns listing Midland addresses.

Astride such early routes as the north-looping Chihuahua Trail and the Butterfield Overland, this was first buffalo-hunting country, then a ranch town, its famed Scharbauer Hotel (now gone), rancher's headquarters for years. On the nearby Scharbauer Ranch, archaeologists in 1954 discovered the "Midland Man," the skull of a female estimated some 12,000 years old. The Midland Museum displays a reproduction of that primitive being. The Museum of the Southwest offers a broad range of displays, from Indian artifacts and early day relics to objects of art and photographic exhibits. Most outstanding is the Permian Basin Petroleum Museum, Library and Hall of Fame, opened in 1975 just north of your highway: it traces the development of our Oil Age. Take time for it. The city also boasts a planetarium with intriguing presentations of each month's new sky.

At the Midland-Odessa Air Terminal, the Pliska Museum displays a restoration of the frail aircraft that Blacksmith Jan Pliska built and flew just a few years after the Wright Brothers' exploit. The Haley Library and History Center features collections on early Western history.

Odessa, 270 m. (alt. 2,890; pop. 89,699), the oil-well service capital of the Permian Basin oilfields, was seen by 1881 founding Methodists as a fertile farming region, by Slavic railroad workers as a duplicate of the steppes of Russia (thus its name). Today, Odessans have shrugged off their barren plains—a giant jackrabbit is the city's downtown statue—they've taken the underground wealth given them and have created an imaginatively handsome city that for four decades during oil boom times doubled in population every 10 years—a record.

Attractions are widely varied. At the other end of the spectrum from Odessa's tongue-in-cheek jackrabbit is the city's Globe Theater, a faithful model of the Avon playhouse, where Shakespeare is presented. The city's stress on the unique shows up everywhere—one of its most swank nightclubs is in an old depot, Victorian throughout. Another elegant one is housed within an oil storage tank. The Presidential Museum concentrates on that office, with each administration reflected in excellent displays. Also here is the University of Texas of the Permian Basin and Odessa College, which displays a planetarium. On the campus of U.T.P.B. is the ultramodern Art Institute, with outstanding galleries. Odessa also boasts a Prairie Pete (prairie dog) Park and an 18-acre (at the Air Terminal) Water Wonderland with slides and toboggan rides. Among Odessa's most special events are the Fiesta del Art, drawing from several states each March, and the Permian Basin Fair and Exposition each September. A Permian Basin Oil Show is staged in October, and a Music Festival

in July. At Odessa, intersect US 385/ Tour 60.

West of Odessa, 9 m., is the great meteor crater, second in size only to the Arizona giant, and the origin, some believe, of the Indian Thunderbird legend in its flaming plunge to earth. The meteor is still embedded more than 100 feet below the surface and its crater has largely been filled with blown-in dirt.

Monahans, 306 m. (alt. 2,613; pop. 8,101). In 1890, James Monahans had dug the only water well between Big Spring and Pecos, and this town began as a water stop on the Texas and Pacific Railroad. A 1930s oil boom jumped the population from that of a lonely village to a thriving little city. Some 35,000 wells operate within the area; downtown is the unusual arrangement of six pump jacks, side by side, each slanting its shaft far down and away from the city center. East of the city is Shell Oil's "Million Barrel Tank," built in 1928 before pipelines obviated such big storage. Abandoned because of leakage, it is now the site of a museum and amphitheater.

Over 4,000 acres of huge wind-sculptured sand dunes cover Monahans Sandhills State Park.

Just east on I-20 is **Monahans Sand Hills State Park,** centering a great mass of shifting, cream-colored dunes. A museum contains relics from early days when westbound wagons struggled across this wasteland where today you can frolic in 30-foot dunes. Interesting is the miniature oak forest—thousands of trees not three feet high but rooted 90 feet deep. The sandhills extend over some 40,000 acres.

Pyote, 321 m. (alt. 2,612; pop. 348), is a ghost site. Now housing the West Texas Children's Home, this was once Pyote (Rattlesnake) Air Base for bomber training. After WW II, more than 4,000 bombers and fighter planes were gathered here, horizon-to-horizon, to be melted down to scrap. "Enola Gay," the atom bomber, and "Swoose," General MacArthur's plane, among them, were sent on to the Smithsonian Institution, escaping the torch that consumed many another gallant warrior.

North via TX 115, **Kermit,** 25 m. (alt. 2,890; pop. 6,875), combines a rough-and-ready oiltown appearance on its outskirts with a new-looking and neat residential and downtown area. Before oil was discovered in 1926, early county records dealt with such things as fees for grubbing bear grass from the courthouse lawn and for wolf and wildcat bounties. The Medallion House Museum is maintained.

Pecos, 347 m. (alt. 2,580; pop. 12,069), originally ranching country, came into being with 1881 rails and was a tough guntown, known to the likes of Billy the Kid and Clay Allison, the "Shootist." "Pecosing" came to mean killing a man—usually ambush—then weighting him into the river. Pecos claims (along with Canadian and Seymour) the world's first rodeo, when local range hands matched skills on an open prairie in 1883. That event is observed in Pecos' famed rodeo each July.

An unusual installation—"West of the Pecos Park"—has been created on a downtown block. The Old Orient Hotel, which recalls life in the 1880s, is now the West of the Pecos Museum, where you will find the original old Number 11 Saloon, built in 1896, along with Clay Allison's grave and a replica of Judge Roy Bean's Jersey Lilly Saloon (see Langtry).

"Old Pecos" style storefronts in downtown Pecos.

In late June, a Night In Old Pecos turns the town back to its gunsmoke days and begins rodeo festivities. Today, this area is noted for its fine cantaloupes. For the youngsters, an excellent park and zoo also provides a child-sized replica of the Alamo, as well as a Prairie Dog Town.

Via US 285/TX 302 north, **Mentone,** 23 m. (alt. 2,683; pop. 50), tiny and sunbaked, is seat of Texas' last-organized and most sparsely-settled county—Loving Co. North of Mentone is Red Bluff Lake, with fishing, limited facilities. Beyond, your road drives northwest for Carlsbad Caverns or can angle across to Guadalupe Mountains National Park.

West of Pecos, your route crosses great, thinly-settled distances, and you approach mountain country, looming handsomely southward.

At 388 m., merge with I-10/Tour 56. The mountains southward are the Davis, among Texas' most beautiful. Those dead ahead are the rugged Apache Range.

☆

Tour 52

US 67
Stephenville,
Brownwood, Ballinger,
San Angelo, Big Lake,
McCamey, Fort Stockton, Alpine,
Marfa, Shafter, Presidio, 470 m.

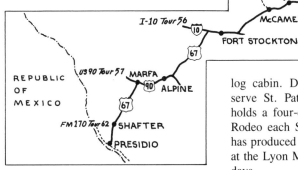

Continuing westward from Tour 2A, Region I, US 67 provides a long journey and an interestingly varied view of Texas. Crossing from the north central part of the state, it describes a sweeping diagonal south of west, finally

to veer due south to the tip of the rugged Big Bend country.

From Stephenville to Brownwood you travel a pleasantly wooded and undulating landscape dotted with well-maintained ranches and stockfarms. Edging across the top of Texas Hill Country there, you reach San Angelo and, beyond, open on westward plains—more sparsely populated, arid, and a region where substantial oil exploration intersperses with ranching. At Fort Stockton, as though drawn by southward mountains, you hug the east flanks of the Davis Range, circling around through Alpine to Marfa. From that high, handsome tableland you descend rapidly into the Big Bend for Presidio's lonely border on Old Mexico. This latter country is intriguing—its scenery is grand, and it is peopled with Indian spirits and ghost lights, and close-mouthed old ones who understand the ways of such things and know the locations of lost and haunted mines.

Stephenville, 0 m.—see Tour 2A, Region I. Follow US 67 southwest.

Dublin, 12 m. (alt. 1,461; pop. 3,190). With its downtown of square-cut limestone and its First Monday Trades Days, Dublin is the center of ranch country and not—despite its Gaelic street names—an Irish settlement. The Town's name came from the shouted warning of Indian attack—"Double in!," meaning to fort up in the town's stoutest log cabin. Dublin, however, does observe St. Patrick's Day and each fall holds a four-day fair. The Lightning-C Rodeo each St. Patrick's Day weekend has produced many fine riders. Exhibits at the Lyon Museum hark back to early days.

Via TX 6, **De Leon,** 12 m. (alt. 1,268; pop. 2,190), centers a rich, growing area, and ships out peanuts, pecans, fruits and melons. Each August since 1934 the little town has staged its Peach and Melon Festival.

Below Proctor, at 21 m., **Proctor Lake** provides good fishing, camping and all facilities.

Comanche, 33 m. (alt. 1,358; pop. 4,087). The Comanche courthouse square is a focus of interest in this area that knew both Indian depredation and outlaw trouble. On the southwest corner a large oak stands—once part of a big oak grove. In 1854 young Martin Fleming camped that grove, taking refuge from Indians behind this remaining tree. When the county determined to clear the grove and pave the square, workmen found gray-haired Uncle Mart—as he was by then known—barring their way with a rifle at full cock. The oak was spared and has become this town's living Christmas tree each season.

Gunplay of a different sort occurred one block north where a drug store now faces the courthouse. That store's service entrance once was entry to an early Comanche saloon. In 1874, John Wesley Hardin—only in his 20s yet already with a score of notches on his Colt and known as Texas' deadliest gunfighter—came to town to race horses. A Brown County deputy came to arrest or kill him. The two entered the saloon together, the deputy attempting to draw, Hardin whirling to shoot the lawman down. From then

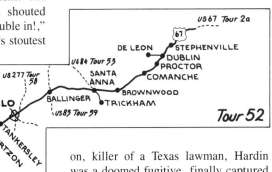

on, killer of a Texas lawman, Hardin was a doomed fugitive, finally captured in Florida, returned to the Comanche courthouse, convicted of murder and sent to Huntsville prison. He remained there 15 years, emerging as a man old and slow enough to be shot in the back in El Paso (Tour 50A) shortly afterwards.

Comanche lists other historical sites—its Episcopal and Presbyterian churches, some old homes dating to the later 1800s, and the old log courthouse built in 1856. The county museum displays a broad range of early pioneer relics. Each third weekend in June, Comanche stages a fine amateur rodeo.

Just northwest, Round Mountain served as the first field laboratory for the noted geologist, Dr. Robert T. Hill. After his death, his ashes were strewn there.

Brownwood, 59 m. (alt. 1,342; pop. 18,387). This city of shaded, dignified homes occupies an area hard hit by early Indian attacks, founded as it was in the heart of Comancheria. Originally open range, Brownwood also saw trouble in the 1882–83 "Bobwire War," when small ranchers sought to hold the open range against the fencing of large spreads. Damage was considerable before rangers and a law making fence-cutting a felony ended the war.

Brownwood is the home of Howard Payne University (merged now with Daniel Baker College), and its MacArthur Academy of Freedom. The academy, much visited, boasts five great halls and three rooms which inspiringly trace western man's search for freedom and his dependence on God. The three-story Wall of Light is the largest mural in Texas.

The city also houses the Brown County Historical Museum, as well as Camp Bowie Memorial Park, honoring men of the 36th (T-Patch) Infantry Division and exhibiting their WW II equipment. The 1876 Coggin Academy-McClelland Library is the oldest educational building still in use in Texas.

Among the city's historic buildings, St. John's Episcopal Church dates from 1892, and the 1902 jail is a grim, castle-like structure. There are many pretty parks.

Via TX 279 north, 23 m., **Lake Brownwood State Park** offers excellent fishing, all facilities, including good campsites, screened shelters and cabins.

The Texas geographical center, near Mercury, pop. 166, is 24 m. south via US 283.

At Brownwood, merge with US 84/Tour 53 to Santa Anna.

Santa Anna, 81 m. (alt. 1,743; pop. 1,249). The loom of its close-by mountain is visible for miles. Named for a Comanche chief, it was a landmark on 1835 Texas maps and a lookout for Texas Rangers. The mountain is of exceptionally high-grade silica; Santa Anna makes good glassware. Just below is the **Texas Ranger Memorial Park,** for years a reunion site. The old rock house, a museum now, was built in 1873. A .45 bul-

The cowboy and his horse, a team which figured prominently in settling the West, are memorialized in bronze at Ballinger.

let hole just above its mantel is an enigmatic recollection of the past. Southeast of Santa Anna is Coleman County's oldest settlement, Trickham (Tour 53).

Follow US 67 west. Nearby, also see Coleman.

At Valera, 96 m., FM 503 leads north to **Hords Creek Reservoir,** good fishing, lighted campgrounds, all facilities.

Ballinger, 121 m. (alt. 1,637; pop. 4,207). Its rough-cut rock buildings lend this Runnels County seat a solid if weathered look. With timber scarce, pioneers cut their stone and laid it like big bricks. Ballinger notes its origin as ranch country with a Pompeo Coppini statue of a cowboy and his horse. On the square, the bronze figures were erected by a father in memory of his range-riding son, killed in cattle-rounding. Nearby is hard-to-find Lake O.H. Ivie; ask for directions.

Churches and old homes here—the Miller and Gieschke houses particularly—are handsome. The Nancy Parker cabin dates from 1878. Each mid-June, Ballinger stages its Old Fiddlers Contest, and in late September, a Pinto Bean Cookoff. Nearby Rowena and tiny Olfin hold German church festivals with tasty cooking, and just west 6 m., Ballinger's City Park and Lake provide camping and all water sports. At Ballinger, intersect US 83/Tour 59. Also see Paint Rock, nearby.

San Angelo, 155 m. (alt. 1,847; pop. 84,474). Around its park-like courthouse square, this brisk and beautiful little city, greened by the Concho River's mid-town passage and crisscrossed by broad boulevards, is one of Texas' hand-

somest. In 1864, the first settler set down at the crossroads of western trails, but the beginning was inauspicious—for a time this site was overshadowed by the town of Ben Ficklin, three miles upriver, and was known only as "Over The River." In 1882, a flood devastated Ben Ficklin, and its survivors moved here.

The city grew up around Fort Concho, and it was nothing to see a herd of Longhorns driven down Chadbourne Street, one of today's main thoroughfares. The surrounding country proved excellent pasture, and San Angelo gradually became the world's largest wool market. Today it is home of 287-acre Angelo State University, a Texas A&M Research and Extension Center, and a big convention center impressively landscaped on the Concho's riverbanks.

Early each March the city hosts a five-day stock show and rodeo; its big, week-long Fiesta del Concho comes in mid-June, featuring a river parade. Old Fort Concho, 23 original and restored buildings, sits near downtown. Once home to black "Buffalo Soldiers," the fort today houses a Museum of Telephony, a Museum of Frontier Medicine, and a Museum of Fine Arts. A volunteer reenactment group often presents demonstrations in 1870s uniforms.

San Angelo has made its Concho River a showplace, with a 6 m. river walk for jogging or scenic walking. The river itself yields the famed Concho freshwater pearls, mussel-produced and ranging in color from pink to deep purple. A local jeweler specializes in mounting them, and the town's youngsters hunt them diligently.

In 1867, stone-walled Fort Concho was set as the mid-anchor on Texas' north-south frontier line. Ranald Mackenzie commanded here, as did William Shafter and Benjamin Grierson, both instrumental in ending the Indian threat in West Texas.

The headquarters building at frontier Ft. Concho, San Angelo.

Along Concho Street downtown is a historic district with a variety of antique shops and other stores along a boardwalk. Above one is a local landmark, Miss Hattie's Museum, a saloon and "parlor house" where ladies of the evening welcomed off-duty soldiers from Fort Concho. Texas Rangers closed the establishment in 1946. Miss Hattie's, restored with original furnishings, now welcomes visitors.

Nearby are five lakes providing camping and all facilities—O.C. Fisher, Nasworthy, Twin Buttes, E.V. Spence, and O.H. Ivie. Bass fishing is excellent. At San Angelo intersect US 277/Tour 58; US 87/Tour 61. In the area also see Robert Lee and Sterling City.

At wayside **Tankersley**, 169 m., **Twin Buttes Reservoir** lies just south. The two dominant hillocks recall an Indian legend where two sisters, sworn never to part, were given in marriage to different tribes. They prayed to the Great Spirit to keep them together and were transformed to these two buttes, seen clearly kneeling in prayer.

Mertzon, 181 m. (alt. 2,250; pop. 778). An oasis shaded by oaks, this county seat (Irion Co.) serves surrounding ranches. A small park makes a good picnic stop. Southeast is Indian Peak and site (on private land) of the Dove Creek Battle, January 8, 1865. A band of 1,200 Kickapoo Indians, circling to reach Mexico sanctuary, were attacked by Confederate home guards here. In a savage, day-long fight in deep snow, the Texans withdrew—a draw between two causes already lost—the Confederacy's and the Indian's.

The Irion County Museum is located here, and just northeast 1 m., the old Sherwood courthouse still stands in that tiny village.

Big Lake, 225 m. (alt. 2,678; pop. 3,672). A typical West Texas prairie town suddenly become oil center, this area is interesting for its invisible contribution to the state. Originally part of land granted to the University of Texas, ostensibly for grazing leases, it provided that institution with wealth to rank it among the nation's richest. A replica of Santa Rita No. 1, the basin's discovery well, stands in the city park.

Northwest 12 m., the near-ghost of Stiles still holds the two-story stone courthouse that governed Reagan County until bypassing railroads moved the seat to Big Lake at the turn of the century.

Best, 234 m., pop. 25, is a near-ghost that never lived up to its plans as a model oil camp. Instead it became a rough and ready center known in boom days as the "Best town with the worst reputation."

Texon, 238 m., pop. 35. Here in May 1923 Santa Rita No. 1 blew in and Texas education became wealthy. The town Texon was planned and built by an oil company—a model city for a 1930 population of more than 1,000. A school, church, hospital and all recreational facilities, including a golf course, were provided. Today the model town is gone.

Rankin, 253 m. (alt. 2,595; pop. 1,011), is a ranching trade center notable for the historic Yates Hotel, built by a tycoon. The restored lobby now houses a museum. The Mule Train Club, 4 m. west, also displays relics of the 1920s oil boom. Nearby are Iraan and Sheffield.

McCamey, 272 m. (alt. 2,441; pop. 2,493), occupies a land of long mesas and sun-baked buttes. This town boomed into existence in 1920 when Baker No. 1 hit big. Named for a well-driller, the site was marked only by a lone boxcar on the prairie, but within 24 hours streets were staked out and lots sold, provided building began in one hour. In a few months McCamey was a city of 10,000 in tents and shacks. Jail was a chain stretched between two deep-sunk posts and was occasionally pulled up and marched en masse to the nearest saloon. Today a quieter town recalls its heyday with Mendoza Museum and Adrian House. In town, 5th Street's false front row showcases the old boomtown itself. King Mountain, immediately north, provides a scenic drive, with fine, high views. At night, particularly, the city lights and myriad gas flares are beautiful from above.

At McCamey, merge with US 385/Tour 60 to Fort Stockton. Nearby, also see Horsehead Crossing.

Here FM 305 leads south to the Pecos River crossing, 12 m. Near here is the site of the old Pontoon Crossing of the Fort Concho-Fort Stockton military road. In one of the countless shallow caves in the low hills and canyons about, a treasure in silver bars has been the object of search since the 1900s.

At 297 m., the roadside park displays the clear three-taloned footprints of a flesh-eating dinosaur, kin to the terrible Tyrannosaurus Rex. It is difficult to visualize this barren, arid land as long ago swamp bottom; however, the footprints in solid rock remain as mute testimony to a grim time in the dim past.

At 304 m., merge westward with I-10/Tour 56.

Fort Stockton, 318 m. (alt. 2,954; pop. 8,524), is another sun-drenched town grown up around its westward road-guarding fort. Here is the site of historic Comanche Springs, a major water camp for Indian horsemen riding the Comanche Trail south through Big Bend to raid across Rio Grande in September-October, month of the Mexican Moon. The fort was established in 1859 to guard the springs and the old San Antonio-El Paso military road. It was abandoned in 1861 (Civil War) and reoccupied briefly from 1867 to 1886. The town centered some of the earliest Anglo irrigated farming, in 1877. Today the town is a treasure trove of historic buildings, beginning with the Annie Riggs Museum, once a pride-of-the-west hotel. Officers' quarters face the parade ground at the fort, and between the guard house and hospital was a 100-yard tunnel. The Episcopal and Mission churches, the 1880s jailhouse and Koehlers Store, the Grey Mule Saloon are landmarks, as is Youngs Store, with a gnarled and dead hanging tree. In the later 1800s, Fort Stockton had a sheriff so iron-handed—six gun notches—that the town feared him. In a macabre 1894 drawing of lots, one of six leading citizens was chosen to kill him, and the lawman died in a shotgun blast. His tombstone bears the verdict, "assassinated."

Annie Riggs Museum—the Old Riggs Hotel, a popular stop on the Butterfield Overland stagecoach route.

Special downtown signs will guide your historic tour, and an 11-foot-tall (20 feet long) statue of Roadrunner Paisano Pete makes a popular photo stop.

Each July, saluting its famed water hole (Comanche Springs), Fort Stockton stages an elaborate Water Carnival at its Olympic-sized swimming pool—a show worth seeing.

At 328 m. veer south from I-10 and continue on US 67.

At 376 m. merge with US 90/Tour 57 westward.

Alpine, 385 m. (alt. 4,481; pop. 5,637), spreads around the foothills of the Davis Range and is backdropped by high peaks north and west—perhaps the most typical mountain town in Texas, and the Brewster County seat, an area larger than Connecticut. Backing against the hills, Sul Ross State University is handsomely situated and offers an excellent geology department. For average tourists, this is good rock-hound country. (South on TX 118 16 m. is the Woodward Agate Ranch, where for a modest fee, you can collect those beautiful stones. On campus is the Museum of the Big Bend: see it before exploring that wilderness. Northwest, the Chihuahuan Desert Research Institute studies the barren southward terrain, America's second largest desert. The Apache Trading Post offers Indian handicrafts.

Founded as Osborne in 1882 with Southern Pacific rail arrival, this was later Murphyville, and finally Alpine. East of town, now dry, Kokernot

TX 118 channeling south from Alpine through beautiful, but desolate, rugged country near Big Bend National Park.

Springs was once a main watering hole—Charco de Alsate, for the last Chisos Apache chief—on the Indian war trail southward. Approximating that trail, TX 118 leads 78 m. to the west entrance of **Big Bend National Park.** Check automotive needs before leaving. For Big Bend, see Marathon, Tour 62. In the area also see Fort Davis and McDonald Observatory.

Marfa, 411 m., (alt. 4,688; pop. 2,424), is a clean, sunny ranch town situated on high plateau country. An invigorating climate, with fine scenery in all directions, attracts tourists here. The Davis range, Big Bend, and Mexico are close sidetrips. At the old Marfa air base, 9 m. east, is America's soaring capital: massive updrafts and sweeping terrain are ideal for gliders and sailplanes. Three American and one world championship meets have been held here. Also from the air base, the southward Chinati ghost lights (see Shafter) are often seen.

In town, the old courthouse reflects antique magnificence, the Paisano Hotel recalls old days when the big hotel was the town's activity center. Marfa boasts the highest golf course in Texas, its nine holes nearly a mile high.

At Marfa, veer south from US 90/Tour 57.

Fort D. A. Russell, 412 m., was formerly Camp Marfa. In 1911 cavalry patrolled here, watchful for border trouble stemming from Pancho Villa's revolutionists. The fort now houses handsome sculpture at the Art Museum of the Pecos.

San Esteban, 421 m. At this wayside ranch, your route here overlaps the ancient Chihuahua Trail, first traversed by Cabeza de Vaca in 1536, descending, as you do, on the site of Presidio. Wagon ruts are still faintly traced in the rock.

Shafter, 451 m., (alt. 4,000; pop. 31), is one of Texas' ghostliest ghosts, a tumbled rock ruin in the arroyos of Cibolo Canyon, under the looming Chinati Mountains. Once a rich silver miner, Shafter is largely abandoned today; silver recovery became too expensive. Use caution around open shafts.

Settlement here began with one of the first Anglo ranchers in the Big Bend, Milton Favor. In the 1850s he operated from three quadrangular adobe forts; ruins of all are in the immediate area. His

drives were the subjects of TV's *Rawhide* series.

Behind Shafter to the west the Chinatis rear. This is the land of inexplicable ghost lights, known for three generations, seen by thousands, and hunted by hundreds unsuccessfully for years. Old-timers credit them to ghosts of Apache chiefs or to other-world beings, but insist they are friendly. Best seen nights from the old Marfa Air Base, toward Alpine, the lights glow brightly until approached, then disappear.

Cactus blooms over faded, ghostly Shafter.

Presidio, 470 m., (alt. 2,594; pop. 3,072). You descend sharply on this city, the broad valley spilling down some 1,500 feet over the last 20 m. The town is old and squats like an ancient man within its riverbank cottonwoods. A single main street heads for the river, and many adobes are scattered about.

Cabeza de Vaca found a fairly civilized friendly pueblo here and, from its inhabitants, the route to safety in Mexico. Here later were placed Spanish missions and a guarding fort, Presidio del Norte, its site on the east edge of the little town. Across river is quaint Ojinaga, Mexico. On the gray sierra above Ojinaga, legend insists that early priests imprisoned the Devil in a cave by building huge fires at its entrance. Each spring natives reenact the fire-rite pilgrimage.

At Presidio, intersect FM 170. Westward it leads to **Ruidosa,** 29 m., pop. 43, and to remote **Candelaria,** 39 m., pop. 55. Beyond Candelaria (and now on private land), Capote Falls is a thin veil of water falling against colored cliffs— Texas' highest.

Eastward, FM 170 is the spectacularly scenic Camino del Rio leading to Big Bend National Park (see Tour 62). Nearby, see Fort Leaton State Historical Park.

☆

Tour 53

US 84
Evant,
Goldthwaite, Brownwood,
Coleman, Abilene,
Sweetwater, Lubbock, Littlefield,
Muleshoe, New Mexico line, 400 m.

As Tour 52 diagonals from Central Texas southwestward to end in the Texas Big Bend, this route slants in an opposite direction—northwest—to finish in the Panhandle.

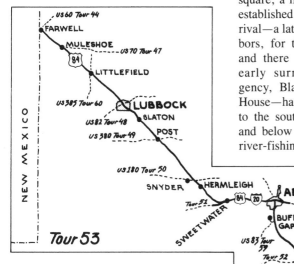

Continuing Tour 7 (which has crossed Region I from the Louisiana line) US 84 enters Region IV in rolling ranch and stockfarm country, emerges on the plains at Abilene and pursues them, topping the Cap Rock at Post, thence through Lubbock and the lush South Plains, to finish on the New Mexico line at little Farwell, just east of Clovis.

The early miles of your trip cross a land timbered in postoak and blackjack. Beyond Abilene, except for the few watersheds crossed, terrain is open. En route, you travel a region of modest towns, encountering only two cities. These, however, are Abilene and Lub-

bock, two of this state's most attractive and prospering.

Evant, 0 m.—see Tour 7. Follow US 84 westward.

At 9 m., **Center City,** pop. 15, a scatter of buildings and an immense oak 50 feet south of your highway mark a site of ambition denied. In the 1870s this was believed to be the geographical center of Texas, and the big tree took the name "Center Oak." Here, Mills County planned its seat of government—a 50-acre town was platted, a square laid out, and many buildings including a hotel, erected. While awaiting construction, the oak did double duty as shelter for court. Then rails by-passed the town, and Goldthwaite emerged. In the 1930s, the highway threatened the old tree, but county folk protested its destruction. The highway moved north just enough to leave Center Oak with what was intended to be a thriving city.

Goldthwaite, 25 m., (alt. 1,580; pop. 1,658), is quiet around its spacious square, a little town of weathered stone established in 1885 with railroad's arrival—a later founding than many neighbors, for this was Comanche country, and there was Indian fighting. Many early surrounding settlements—Regency, Blanket Spring and Clements House—have faded away. San Saba Peak to the south is a prominent landmark, and below it the Colorado offers good river-fishing (secure permission). Late

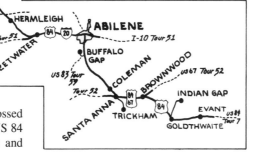

each May the town stages Old Settlers Reunion and "County Fare."

In the area also see Comanche, Hamilton, Lampasas.

Via TX 16/FM 218, **Indian Gap,** 21 m. north, pop. 36, is a wayside spot and site of an 1850 Indian fight. Above the old stone building occupying the gap, a 22-foot shaft high up the hill marks a pioneer grave. The shaft is set on a flat-rock Indian ceremonial site, for this was a Comanche stronghold

threatening the entire region. As late as 1867, a minister and teacher were killed nearby.

Brownwood, 60 m.—see Tour 52.
Santa Anna, 82 m.—see Tour 52.

Via FM 1176 south, **Trickham,** 15 m., pop. 12, is a sturdy ghost, oldest town in Coleman County. Traildriver John Chisum began it when he herded his thousands of cattle in the valley of the Mukewater Creek there and needed a long cabin to store his supplies. His employee storekeeper was a practical joker and gave the settlement its title "Trick'em" from jokes played on Chisum cowboys. The town grew and old-timers claim that the teacher one year was John Wilkes Booth under an assumed name (see Bandera, Glen Rose). Indians raided the village constantly and in the streets of Trickham today, five Indian victims' graves lie. Growth of nearby towns and railroad by-pass faded the town.

Coleman, 90 m., (alt. 1,710; pop. 5,410). This leisurely town is notable for wide streets so designed that the early freighter teams could turn about without difficulty. A good county museum reflects early days, itself a replica of C.O. headquarters at nearby ghost Camp Colorado, a frontier outpost. Pioneer blacksmith shop, picnic grounds, and playground are part of the complex. World War II and Korean War planes are refurbished, displayed, and flown at the Warbird Museum at the airport. Lakes Coleman and Hords Creek offer fishing.

Via TX 206 north, **Camp Colorado,** 10 m., was cavalry outpost commanded by names later distinguished in the Confederacy—Earl Van Dorn, Edmund Kirby Smith, John Bell Hood and Fitzhugh Lee. From 1857 to 1861 this was center of county settlement, a telegraph line connecting to San Antonio, and a Yale graduate teaching school under an elm tree. Fading after the war, it became part of a ranch in the 1870s.

At 126 m., merge with US 83/Tour 59 to Abilene.

Via FM 613 west is **Buffalo Gap,** 13 m. pop. 499. Under the mesas of Callahan Divide and beautifully nestled in big cottonwoods, this town that might have been Abilene takes you back a century. In the 1870s, this was a buffalo hunter's town and a decade later heatedly resisted Abilene's taking the

Looking west down FM 613 toward Buffalo Gap in the Callahan Divide.

county seat. Wisely, the village has maintained its pioneer flavor: the reunion grounds, old courthouse-jail (housing a museum), the wagon yard and some new buildings designed in keeping with the old, make a pretty little village that edges, to the north, fine homes outspilling from Abilene. Considerable restoration here has added several new enterprises—a restaurant and handicraft shops. To the south is big-shaded Abilene State Recreation Area (camping and all facilities) a surprising woodland on the otherwise open plain. Legend insists that somewhere in the gap, Forty-Niner gold was ambushed and buried.

Abilene, 142 m.—see Tour 51.
Sweetwater, 184 m.—see Tour 51. Just southeast, Lake Sweetwater provides water sports, campsites. At 192 m., veer north at Roscoe.
Hermleigh, 211 m., (alt. 2,442; pop. 725). Just southeast is Sandstone Canyon, marked with Indian pictographs, names of early hunters and ranchers, even ranch brands. The canyon floor was once deep in round, marble-sized stones called buckshot rocks.
Snyder, 222 m.—see Tour 50.
Post, 267 m.—see Tour 49. Here your highway climbs the Cap Rock escarpment. Atop, just west, a roadside park provides a scenic overlook and an interesting cactus garden. A total of 28 varieties are exhibited. As you resume the highway, the rich green croplands of the South Plains magically reappear.
Slaton, 293 m. (alt. 3,085; pop. 6,078), a division terminal of the Santa Fe line since 1910, marks its heritage with a museum and old Engine 1809 lodged on the city hall square. The town grows as a neighbor to mushrooming Lubbock.
Lubbock, 309 m.—see Tour 48.

Littlefield, 347 m., (alt. 3,556; pop. 6,489), is a good-looking little city with a particularly modern business area—an open shopping mall with piped music and attractive landscaping. Littlefield is one of the plains' "instant" cities, having been laid out on an empty prairie as recently as 1912. Recalling its earlier past, the city displays the "world's tallest windmill," originally located on the Yellowhouse Ranch, a division of the legendary, mammoth XIT. Comanche and Comanchero campgrounds were at Bull and Illusion Lakes—both gypsum water—just west of town. With an immense textile mill (tours available), Littlefield considers itself the denim capital of the west.

At its community center, the little city stages a country-western, bluegrass, gospel music show on the first Saturday evening of each month. A free campground with necessary facilities is provided on US 385.

At Littlefield, intersect US 385/Tour 60.
Muleshoe, 379 m.—see Tour 47.
Farwell, 400 m.—see Tour 44. Cross the New Mexico line 9 m. east of Clovis.

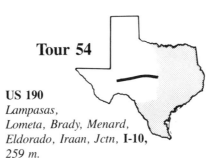

Tour 54

US 190
Lampasas,
Lometa, Brady, Menard,
Eldorado, Iraan, Jctn, **I-10,**
259 m.

This tour, westward from Tour 18, Region II, may be divided into two distinct regions. Beginning at Lampasas, on the border of Regions I and II, the first half extends to the clear-running San Saba headwaters beyond Menard— the pleasantly-wooded upper reaches of the Texas Hill Country. It is scenic—

green hills and long valleys, a land for hunters, fishermen and campers. Within the watersheds of the Colorado and San Saba it is also notable for its pecans— you pass many stands of the great trees, and in the fall you can see tree-shaker tractors working the planted orchards.

Beyond Menard, from Eldorado to Iraan, the terrain rolls out in arid prairies that roughen beyond the Devil's headwaters to a country of low buttes and mesas. Here, however, scenic shortcomings are offset by rich oil production, and at the end of your trip you are near West Texas' handsome mountains.

Before the white man, the entire region was the domain of the deadly Lipan Apache until the mid-1700s, when he was replaced by the even fiercer horseman, the Comanche. Taking part in that Indian struggle, Spain began the decline which would finally drive her from Texas. At Menard, ruins of the fortress that brought on Spanish retreat exist today—as do persistent tales of buried treasure somewhere near it.

Lampasas, 0 m.—see Tour 18. Northeast of you lies Region I; Southeast, Region II. Follow US 190 westward.

Via FM 580 west 22 m., **Bend,** pop. 115, rests remotely scenic in a land of high-tilted valleys and distant, notched mountains. At the bluffside head of Lake Travis, the village is a fisherman's haven; under mossy, springspilling banks, the Colorado is a beautiful stream, with Gorman Falls just downriver. The little village is gateway to one of Texas' newest state parks, Colorado Bend. Beyond, 5 m. on FM 501, is tiny **Chappel,** pop. 25, four-generation home of a camp meeting arbor since 1858, when worshippers came armed and posted guards against the Comanches during services.

Lometa, 17 m. (alt. 1,484; pop. 625), is an agricultural shipping center. Due to an 1885 founders' pledge, it has never known an open saloon. Also see nearby Goldthwaite.

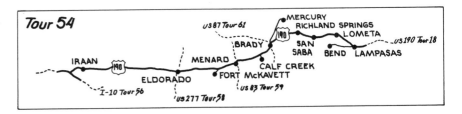

Via FM 581 southwest, **Senterfitt,** 3 m., on the Fort Worth-Fort Mason stage line, boomed from 1881–85. Railroad by-pass moved most citizens to Lometa. Some traces remain.

At 32 m., the hill just north was a Comanche signal station until the 1870s.

San Saba, 37 m. (alt. 1,210; pop. 2,626), reposes prettily in a pecan woodland where the San Saba River joins the Colorado. A frontier settlement in 1854, this little town laid its claim early as "Pecan Capital of the World," making the nut a cash crop within three years. It was an early cattledriver, later introducing sheep and angora goats. It suffered some of the violence of neighboring Mason County's "Hoodoo War," essentially a Reconstruction feud after the Civil War, survived a disastrous 1938 flood, and today thrives quietly with the influx of hunters and fishermen adding to its agribusiness base. A number of interesting buildings of the 1880s are displayed on a walking tour (C of C maps), from the Log Cabin Museum and the old jail to the Mill Pond House. The Wedding Oak, where many turn-of-the-century marriages were performed, stands on the northwest edge of town. The surrounding area is good rock-hunting country. See the C of C.

Via FM 1480 9 m., at the junction of the San Saba and Colorado Rivers, is the San Saba Mother Pecan, source of more important varieties than any pecan tree in the world. From it have come the Liberty Bond, Jersey, No. 60, San Saba Improved, Texas Prolific, and the internationally-famed Western Schley.

Richland Springs, 52 m. (alt. 1,375; pop. 344), a sheep and goat raiser, is the site of John Duncan's 1858 fort. Through 1865, settlers wintered here for protection from the Comanche.

Brady, 80 m. (alt. 1,670; pop. 5,946), a jaunty little western city, rambles over its hilly terrain, spreading out from a white stone, castle-like courthouse. Near Texas' center, Brady grew up on the military road from Fort Mason to Fort Griffin, then drove cattle up the Dodge Trail. The city has converted its twin-towered old red brick jail into a museum recollecting pioneer days.

Headquarters for deer hunters in the hills about and for fishermen bound for Lake Brady, just west, the town is home of the Texas Muzzle Loaders Rifle Association, with shoots in February, June and October—the contestants firing in authentic costume. The Santa Fe Center, a restored depot, houses an art gallery as well as a working studio. Each Labor Day weekend Brady stages "The World Championship Barbecue Goat Cookoff" and associated arts and crafts fair and street dances. Some 10,000 attend.

At Brady intersect US 87/Tour 61.

Via US 377 north, near tiny **Mercury,** 23 m. pop. 166, is the Heart of Texas Oak, marking the state's geographic center. The big live oak stands on coordinates that divide Texas into four equal areas. Beyond Mercury is the ghost of **Milburn,** once a prospering 1890s town with a 577-foot bridge spanning the Colorado River. A flood took the bridge, and by-pass withered the town.

Calf Creek, 93 m., pop. 23, is one of the disputed sites where famed Jim Bowie and his brother Rezin are reputed to have stood off some 200 Indians in 1831. With 10 companions, Bowie was in search of an Indian treasure cache known today as the "Lost Jim Bowie Mine." Somewhere in the area of the Spanish mission at Menard, that site is still lost, as is that of this eight-day stand against savage and relentless attack. Many historians claim the site here, others hold it nearer Menard.

Menard, 115 m. (alt. 1,960; pop. 1,606). In its heavily wooded, parklike San Saba valley, the town was settled in 1858 on already historic land. In 1757, attempting to extend a road from San Antonio to Santa Fe, Spain established a Lipan Apache mission 3 m. east of town (no trace), and a guarding Presidio San Saba on the northwest edge of today's city. Under immediate and almost continual Comanche attack, the mission was burned and most of its neophytes and priests slaughtered. The fort stood off increasing Comanche pressure for 11 years but was finally abandoned, along with Spain's attempt to extend its Texas foothold. The rock ruins are formidable and the old depot museum nearby contains many artifacts. In the river fronting the presidio, faintest traces of the old dam may be seen; until some 40 years ago, the Spanish irrigation ditches were still used by area farmers. Enhancing the claim that the "Lost Jim Bowie Mine" lies close by is the enigmatic "Bowie" signature carved on the right-hand bottom stone of the presidio's west entrance. On the south edge of town is the "Country Store," offering local handicraft and interesting browsing.

At Menard, intersect US 83/Tour 59. In the area also see Paint Rock, Junction.

At 127 m., cross **Dry Creek.** A local road north leads to one site (of many, including that at Calf Creek) where Bowie supposedly located a great silver treasure and, returning for it in 1831, fought a savage battle with Indians. Much searching has occurred here, and traces of several fruitless shafts can be found.

At 132 m., via FM 864, is **Fort McKavett,** 6 m. south, pop. 103 (day use state park). This post occupies the

Ruins at the site of Old Ft. McKavett are the object of a major restoration project.

beautiful headwater valley of the San Saba. The fort was established in 1852 and, after the Civil War, was reoccupied from 1868–83, serving as base for Col. Ranald Mackenzie's drive on the High Plains. At its peak it was considered Army's handsomest Texas post, even more than celebrated Fort Sam Houston in San Antonio. The ruins have been restored or stabilized.

Eldorado, 166 m. (alt. 2,410; pop. 2,019), is a lonely town in remote ranch country. In 1876, William Black, a New Yorker, paid 10 cents an acre for 30,000 acres nearabouts and was considered foolish: he could have ranged the land at no cost. However, Black stocked the land with Angora goats and soon had so many he built a cannery and in one year slaughtered and canned 7,000 goats, labeling the cans "Roast Mutton." Some say the meat fed American troops in the Spanish-American War. Schleicher County Museum, intersection with US 277/Tour 58 are here.

From here westward you traverse a sparsely populated and gradually roughening country. Here and there solitary buttes and mesas rise as you progress toward the Pecos River. About midway across this 79 m. stretch, oilfields begin to appear, the pumps nodding and bowing at their work. In the area also see San Angelo, Sonora.

Iraan, 245 m. (alt. 2,590; pop. 1,322), is a sun-drenched little oil town in a land of long mesas shouldering up the rough Pecos River valley. The town was born in 1926 when the Yates No. 1 blew in—a 70,000-barrel producer that, in the West Texas wind, sprayed crude over tents some 4 m. distant. A later well was accounted America's greatest, with a 170,000-barrel-a-day production. The field today remains one of North America's biggest producers.

Alley Oop Fantasyland is located here, coming about because V. T. Hamlin was inspired to write his comic strip "Alley Oop" while working as a reporter in Iraan during the boom. The park is west of town, containing a replica of Dinny, an 80,000-pound dinosaur, and other children's playground facilities. The park also includes an excellent archaeological museum displaying artifacts of prehistoric man.

If the Pecos valley here seems drab, drive a local road to the top of one of the mesas: from there, the view is breathtaking. Nearby, also see Sheffield, Fort Lancaster.

Beyond Iraan you climb from the Pecos lowlands and at 259 m. merge with I-10/Tour 56, westbound.

☆

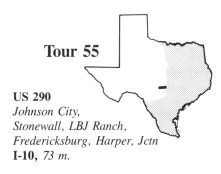

Tour 55

US 290
*Johnson City,
Stonewall, LBJ Ranch,
Fredericksburg, Harper, Jctn*
I-10, *73 m.*

This brief extension of US 290/Tour 19, across to westbound I-10/Tour 56, crosses some of Texas' most gracious land, the heart of the state's Hill Country. More specifically, it explores

what has come to be known in recent years as LBJ Country—the region around little Stonewall and the late president's ranch on the Pedernales.

You begin at Johnson City, the president's schoolboy hometown, named for his pioneering family, pass through picturesque little Hye, then the LBJ Ranch at Stonewall. Beyond is old German Fredericksburg, probably the most charming little city in the Southwest. West of there 41 m. you merge with broad westbound I-10.

President Lyndon B. Johnson's ranch home near Hye.

However, to appreciate more fully this Hill Country beauty, a short side tour extends north from Fredericksburg to Llano in the rugged granite hills of the Central Mineral Region—the land where Texas' scenic Highland Lakes begin.

Johnson City, 0 m.—see Tour 32. The Pedernales valley here, particularly as approached from the south or east, offers a sweeping vista, its rimming hills hazy along distant horizons. Also see nearby Blanco.

Hye, 11 m. (alt. 1,475; pop. 105) is a wayside village perched on a rim overlooking the broad valley situating the LBJ Ranch. The old general store-post office, colorfully painted, is for photography buffs. At the foot of the hill the famous Stonewall peach orchards begin; in season many roadside stands offer the fruit. Ranch Road 1 veers slightly north of your highway to parallel the Pedernales and lead directly past the LBJ

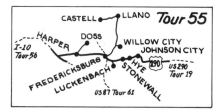

Ranch, the big two-story Texas White House easily viewed just across river.

Your highway passes Lyndon B. Johnson State Park (day use), with an interpretive center, a "living history farm" with many authentic structures and an accurate recreation of turn-of-the-century farmlife—the chores exactly duplicated, from soap-making and meat-smoking to gardening and canning. Native animals roam a preserve here. From park headquarters the National Park Service operates tours of the LBJ ranch, stopping at the farmhouse replica where President Johnson was born, and the family cemetery where he is buried. The tour is unique in that the full lifespan of one American president can be gauged in this single area.

Stonewall, 16 m., pop. 245. The big, colorful shed of the Gillespie County fruit growers provides souvenirs of this peach country, as well as a successful processing and marketing outlet for its members. Two pretty churches, Trinity Lutheran and St. Francis Xavier Catholic, stand near the Pedernales River.

Stonewall Peach Jamboree, Stonewall.

At 26 m., FM 1376 leads south 4 m. to **Luckenbach,** pop. 25, originally settled in the 1850s and recently a near-ghost revived as a haunt for young people staging such events as armadillo races and various "almost-world's-fairs," all under the slogan, "In Luckenbach, everybody is somebody." The town was home of scientist Jacob Brodbeck who—a quarter-century before the Wright Brothers—invented an airplane powered with coiled springs. In 1865 San Antonio he briefly flew the craft to tree-top heights, but the plane crashed and his experiment was abandoned. The "town," made famous by Texas humorist Hondo Crouch, consists of a weathered general store, a rural dance hall, and a blacksmith shed.

FM 1376 winding casually through the country between Luckenbach and Boerne.

Close by is the ghost of **Cain City,** a prosperous town in 1912, when Fredericksburg finally achieved railroad connections with San Antonio.

At 28 m., cross the Pedernales River. In the field just north is the traceless site of Zodiac, an 1850 Mormon settlement (see Mormon Mills). For almost five years the town prospered here, with two mills, a smithy, church and irrigated farming, but a flood destroyed it, and the settlers moved on, finally to Bandera.

Fredericksburg, 32 m. (alt. 1,742; pop. 6,934), is a historic and quaint Old-World city, one of Texas' most fascinating. Steepled and snug in a ring of hills, and scrupulously clean with extraordinarily wide streets, the town was founded in 1846 by a German baron who chose to become plain John O. Meusebach. The colony found itself purchaser of land deep within Comancheria, where most Texans had to shoot their way in. Meusebach led Fredericksburg's men,

Children costumed for the Easter Fires Pageant at Fredericksburg.

unarmed to show good faith, deep into Indian country, signed and kept a friendship treaty with the Comanche (see Camp San Saba).

From that ordeal of waiting and watching Indian watchfires on the surrounding hills has come this town's Easter observance of hillfires and the tales which long-ago mothers told their frightened young: the lofty fires were made by Easter bunnies to mix the paint for their eggs.

Many in-town homes are tourist delights, particularly the "Sunday House," a dwelling in-city where farm families could spend weekends shopping and churchgoing. The entire city should be toured leisurely. Begin at the octagonal Vereins Kirche, 1847, Fredericksburg's first building—church, school, meetinghouse, fort. Here, an excellent C of C will chart your tour, 45 carefully-routed stops that cover the enchanting old homes, large and small, and such landmarks as the 1850 Pioneer Museum, historic old St. Barnabas and St. Mary's Churches, the 1882 courthouse (now a library), and the **Admiral Nimitz State Historic Site,** a museum restoration in the old Nimitz Hotel, whose original dated back to 1852 and was built, prophetically, in the shape of a ship—the center honors Fleet Admiral Chester W. Nimitz of WW II fame, a native son. Also on Main Street within the town's National Historical District is the Keidel Drugstore and the White Elephant Saloon. Individual homes—too many to mention—are opened in tours during Easter and Christmas, the latter a candlelight pilgrimage.

There are countless local events— Sangerfests (for singing), Schuetzenfests (for target shooting); in June, a Walk Fest; July, a Night in Old Fredericksburg; and in August, the state's oldest county fair (since 1888). You will want to browse through some of the more than 20 antique, art and gift shops and you will find restaurants generally excellent. West of the city is the pretty Lady Bird Johnson Park, with camping and all facilities. Quarter horse racing (parimutuel betting) takes place at the adjacent fairground. North via FM 965 is Enchanted Rock State Park, one of Texas' prettiest.

East of the city is the site of Fort Martin Scott (1848–52) which for a time protected against Indians. Trouble came in a different form, however: during the

Civil War, Fredericksburg's area was torn, loyalties divided. Many of these new Americans tried to march south to Mexico and Union service; one group of them was cut down near Uvalde on the Nueces River (see Comfort). Here you intersect US 87/Tour 61.

Via TX 16 north, your road leads into granite hills: secure C of C listings for rock hunting sites. At 16 m., just east, **Willow City,** pop. 75, is a near-ghost in rugged country, and one of Texas' most extravagant displays of bluebonnets, an area abounding in wildlife. Rock hunting is good near (not within) the serpentine quarry close by. From here northward you are in Rockhound Country.

At 23 m., FM 965 leads west to **Enchanted Rock** (State Park), a round red mass of solid granite, second in size only to Georgia's Granite Mountain. An Indian legend forbade these heights, where the ghost of an ancient chief nightly walks penance. It was this belief that allowed famed Texas Ranger Jack Hays to singlehandedly hold that summit against 100 Comanche warriors circling the 3 m. base below—they feared to set foot on the forbidden rock. The dome is 500 feet high and an easy trail tops it. Below is the park with camping facilities.

At tiny Oxford, 28 m., pop. 33, a local road leads west. Near Bear Mountain is perhaps the likeliest site of the **Lost Jim Bowie Mine** (see Menard). Inaccessible without special permission (inquire at Llano), ruins of a Spanish mine exist. Under collapsed beams bearing Spanish writing, the shaft is very dangerous.

Llano, 39 m. (alt. 1,029; pop. 2,962). Beside its small, clear lake (Llano—camping facilities), and under the eastern loom of Packsaddle Mountain and the Riley range, this town centers one of Texas' most scenic areas. Established in 1855, Llano, in an area where Spain reportedly mined gold and silver, knew its own boom in the 1880s, reaching an 1890 population of 7,000. Aside from granite and some marbles, mining has proven an illusory pursuit and the town today is a tourist and hunter headquarters, and a ranching center. The western gateway to Highland Lake country, Llano claims the capital of Texas deer-hunting—over 400,000 acres under hunting lease.

Centering this mineral region, Llano is a mecca for rockhounds who search the area for specimens of quartz, amethyst, serpentine, opal, tourmaline, garnet, and even gold, found in traces. Llanite, a pink granite with blue quartz crystals, is found nowhere else. The Llano County Museum displays stones as well as historical items. Inquire at the C of C for places where rock hunting is allowed.

Awakening to its historic and scenic setting, Llano's C of C provides an excellent guide for a downtown walking tour. Several pretty campsites (all facilities) lie along the river, and the 1891 Badu House provides delightful bed-and-breakfast accommodations. Llano boasts a good county museum and interesting exhibits at its Fine Arts Guild Gallery.

Southeast is humpbacked Packsaddle Mountain, site of an 1873 Indian fight that cleared the country of Comanche. Much prospecting took place here, one of several sites where Bowie's legendary lost mine was "discovered" by a prospector who could not find his way back. West, on the Llano River, 18 m., is secluded **Castell.** Here and at the ghost sites of Bettina and Leiningen, close by, were German colony experiments in 1850 communistic living. The settlements were planned by German nobility, providing a careful selection of all skills or a share-and share-alike operation. Descendants of original families remain on the land where the settlements failed—some colonists worked and some did not. Those who did, stayed.

Eastward from Llano 15 m. is the clear blue expanse of Lake Buchanan, first in the chain of Highland Lakes descending through Lakes Inks, LBJ (Granite Shoals), Marble Falls, Travis, Austin, and Town Lake at Austin, all facilities provided at each lake. Bluebonnet Trails, early each April, ascend the lake route to Llano.

Nearby, also see Mason.

West of Fredericksburg, your route traverses hilly country, paralleling the upper Pedernales to its headwaters.

Harper, 56 m. (alt. 2,100; pop. 383), flanked by low hills, strings along the highway. A sleepy little town, Harper swells to several times its usual size during periodic auctions of exotic animals. Anything from aoudad to zebras can be bought here. Most area ranches are leased for deer hunting. excellent hereabouts.

Via FM 783 north, **Doss,** 14 m., pop. 75, within a long valley, is close by old Lange's Mill, built by the Doss brothers in 1849. Threadgill Creek was dammed and, with the gristmill and

sawmill, a distillery was operated for a time until flood carried away much of the works. The old mill, mill run and dam are still in existence (private property).

At 73 m., merge with I-10/Tour 56.

☆

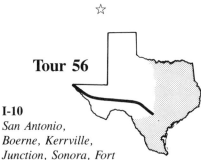

Tour 56

I-10
San Antonio,
Boerne, Kerrville,
Junction, Sonora, Fort
Stockton, Van Horn, Sierra Blanca, El
Paso, New Mexico line, 587 m.

F or the lover of wide-open spaces, this southernmost American Interstate—from Jacksonville, Fla. to Los Angeles, Calif.—nowhere displays more grandeur than along its reach through Region IV of Texas. The landscape is varied—from hills to high plateaus to long mountain-girt valleys—yet from beginning to end, one sense grips you: that of vast distances and boundless horizons.

Leaving San Antonio (from Tour 20, Region II), you climb directly into Texas' Hill Country, opening a succession of long, hill-rimmed valleys and clear-running streams. West of Kerrville, the road rides the high rims, and the regularly-spaced scenic overlooks should be enjoyed.

At Junction you veer due west to parallel the limpid North Llano to its headsprings, then cross a high plateau from Sonora, beyond Ozona, to the deep-cut Pecos gorge, near Sheffield. Following the old military road there, you traverse a broad stretch of rolling range shouldered by choppy hills and mesas; and west of Fort Stockton, you edge along the north foot of the scenic Davis Range. The last 200 miles wind through handsome mountains to enter El Paso by way of the upper Rio Grande Valley.

For the first half of your journey—to Fort Stockton—you travel within the domain of the Comanche horseman. Once within the mountains you are in the realm of his mortal enemy, the Apache. Along your route are some of the old

forts which blazed this nowadays safe passage for you.

San Antonio, 0 m.—see Tour 33.

At 30 m., Cascade Caverns lies just east. Within the unusually-lighted cave is a waterfall. Campgrounds are available.

Boerne, 34 m. (alt. 1,405; pop. 4,274), nestles in the hills beside scenic Cibolo Creek, an old town with several interesting buildings, including one-time headquarters of Robert E. Lee, the home of George W. Kendall, an old bakery, stagecoach stables, and an interesting Catholic church. Boerne grew from 1847 Tusculum, a communal settlement established by five families from Communist Bettina (see Castell), the venture failing within five years and the new town replacing it. Kendall, co-founder of the New Orleans *Times Picayune* and America's first "war correspondent"—covering the Texan Santa Fe Expedition and the Mexican War—retired to ranch here, introducing angora goats and promoting the little town. The county, named for him, stages its fair early each September. In June, Boerne hosts a Berges (Hill) Festival.

The 1859 Kendall Inn is a Texas historic landmark, and from Boerne's highest hilltop, the ornate (1911) Kronkosky Mansion and its tower (now a Benedictine school, visitors welcome) look down. In town, the Historical House Museum reflects early times.

Via TX 46, 13 m. east, Guadalupe River State Park offers camping and all facilities in a pretty setting.

Via TX 46 west 24 m., **Bandera** (alt. 1,258; pop. 877), jaunty as a Stetson crease, is Texas' dude ranch capital. Founded in 1850 as a shingle camp, it was expanded by Mormons (see Mormon Mills), then by Poles. A legend persists that John Wilkes Booth for a time operated a successful school here under the name of William J. Ryan, disappearing when his identity was threatened in the early 1880s (see Glen Rose). North of the courthouse is Frontier Times Museum, an excellent display of Old West relics, and nearby, Bandera Downs offers parimutuel betting on quarter horse races. Near the square is 1876 St. Stanislaus Church, serving America's second oldest Polish parish (see Panna Maria). Outlying and along the scenic Medina River are several handsome guest ranches. Hunting, fishing, and scenic horseback riding are amply available. South of Bandera, the

FM 470, between Bandera and Tarpley, is a rewarding drive, shooting along the southeastern rim of the Edwards Plateau.

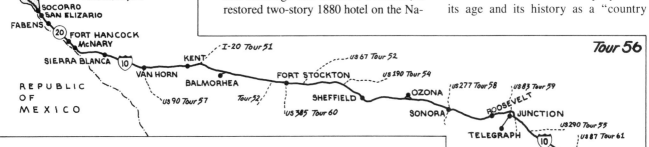

the experiment actually succeeded. However, Civil War intervened and the camels here were killed or loosed, some wandering as far as Arizona. From here, TX 173 leads on to Kerrville (see below).

Comfort, 51 m. (alt. 1,437; pop. 1,477), is a pretty little German town on the Guadalupe, its colonization directed from New Braunfels. Many of Comfort's 100-plus pre-1900 buildings have been restored, affording one of the most interesting walking tours in Texas (Visitors Information Center). The 800 block of High Street is one of the state's outstanding 19th century business districts still standing. The Comfort Common, a restored two-story 1880 hotel on the National Register, offers guest rooms furnished with period antiques, as do a number of area bed and breakfasts.

The town boasts a monument, rare in the South: "True to the Union." This memorializes 65 German colonists from the Hill Country who, in 1862, tried to march to Mexico and Union service (see Fredericksburg). Many were cut down near Uvalde by Confederate irregulars. Beneath the monument is their common grave.

At Comfort, intersect US 87/Tour 61.

Via FM 473 east, **Sisterdale,** 13 m., pop. 63, is a tiny hamlet on the Guadalupe's timbered banks. German intellectuals founded the village in 1847: living here were noblemen, an author, scientist, geographer, and congressman-to-be. The German king's brother visited here in the 1850s, finding the colony at peace with the Comanche, reading Goethe aloud, discussing science, philosophy, and the rights of man, while the bemused Indian peered through their windows.

Kerrville, 67 m. (alt. 1,645; pop. 17,384). Once tucked quietly in the deep and beautiful upper Guadalupe valley, this resort city remains one of Texas' handsomest, boasting a delightful climate and growing rapidly. Many sum-

mer camps surround its area; there are three small lakes along the Guadalupe, **Kerrville State Park,** with camping and all facilities, fronting Flat Rock Lake just southeast of the city. Here is located Presbyterian Schreiner College, a four-year institution named for Capt. Charles A. Schreiner, the area's most noted pioneer, and established by his family. Late each May, Kerrville hosts the big Texas State Arts and Crafts Fair. Nearby Quiet Valley Ranch hosts a concurrent Folk Festival, followed by a June County Fair, a July Gospel Jubilee and a September Bluegrass Festival.

Downtown, the handsome appearance of the Charles Schreiner Company belies its age and its history as a "country store." It was established in 1869 and, one of Texas' most successful such ventures, by 1919 had pushed its annual sales over the $600,000 mark.

Kerrville boasts a handsome Cowboy Artists of America Museum showcasing works by many noted artists such as Joe Beeler, James Boren, Robert Duncan, and Melvin Warren. Downtown, the Hill Country Museum, housed in Captain Schreiner's home, reflects the area's early days.

The city is also home of Mooney Aircraft and James Avery, Craftsman—manufacturer of unique religious jewelry; and at close-by Ingram is the riverbank-situated Hill Country Arts Foundation and summer Point Theater. Above Ingram, scenic Hunt centers the youth camp area, and all along the Guadalupe's two branches are scenic drives, crossing and recrossing that clear stream. On the upper branch, 25 m. west of Kerrville, is MO Ranch, once an oil man's 6,500-acre estate, now the property of the Presbyterian Synod of Texas, its 35 buildings serving as a Christian

river forms hill-girt Medina Lake. Upstream and west is the pretty little town of Medina. The river itself was viewed by Spain in the 1700s as western boundary of Texas, Mexico later shifting that boundary to the more westerly Nueces.

Southwest, where the hills lower to brush country, is Ney Cave, 13 m. (private), one of the largest bat caves in America. The Confederacy mined its guano for gunpowder and during WW II a top-secret experiment—Project X-Ray—was designed to drop clusters of dormant bats (5,000 per canister) carrying self-igniting thermite bombs on Japan. But escaped bats burned down their base, ending the experiment.

North via TX 173 is Bandera Pass, 11 m., a narrow, quarter-mile cut through steep hills. Here in the 1700s, Spain defeated the Apache; in the 1840s, some 40 Texas Rangers beat off a Comanche ambush in hand-to-hand fighting.

At 14 m., **Camp Verde,** pop. 41, now primarily a private ranch, was the mid-1800s scene of an extraordinary experiment conceived by Jefferson Davis. During the Mexican War, noting the army mule's difficulty with rough, arid terrain, he conceived a U.S. Camel Corps; Camp Verde was its caravansarai. The balky animals were brought from Africa and Asia Minor. Preceding Britain's camel corps by several years,

Education center and retreat. Also see Fredericksburg, nearby.

At 99 m. intersect US 290/Tour 55.

Junction, 121 m. (alt. 1,742; pop. 2,654), is a ranchtown-resort deep in the scenic Llano valley alongside that clear stream; your road descends steeply into it. The town lies directly on the old Spanish route aimed from San Antonio to Sante Fe and to Spain's ill-fated fort and mission at Menard, to the north.

Originally called Kimbleville for an Alamo hero, the settlement took roots in 1876 after the Texas Ranger Frontier Battalion swept the area not only of Indians but of outlaws who found the rough country ideal for hideout. Literally combing every draw, rangers rounded up all men found, cut them out like cattle at round up, chained the hardcases to trees, then convened court to run them out of the county. The old Kimble Court Oaks stand today near the airport.

US 290 descends into Junction in the pretty Llano River valley.

Overlooking the town from the south is a steep bluff—a "Lover's Leap" from Indian legend, and a scenic overlook. The small lake below provides all recreational facilities, good campsites. In town, the Old Rock Store and a log cabin hark to early days and the Kimble County Historical Museum displays relics from the past. Junction stages a beautiful outdoor Easter Pageant each year and in August, the annual Hill Country Race Meet. The town also makes an unusual boast—its location is most withdrawn from any Texas metropolitan hubbub. Here, you intersect US 83/Tour 59.

In the area also see Menard, Mason.

South 16 m. via US 377 at **Telegraph,** pop. 11 (which does not possess one, but furnished timber for poles) in the pastoral South Llano valley is the scenic site of Seven Hundred Springs, a veil of water spilling down rocky cliffsides. Floods have reduced the flow. The region is wooded with pecans.

Roosevelt, 140 m., pop. 98, is the site (private land) of old frontier Fort Terrett, its ruins still traceable. A little east, FM 1674 approximates the old military road north to Fort McKavett. The road south to Fort Clark cuts around the mesas directly below you. Some of Terrett's stone buildings serve a ranch today.

Sonora, 178 m. (alt. 2,120; pop. 2,751), is a ranchers' town of big, handsome homes on wide, shaded streets. Settled in 1889, a survey error later disclosed the little town to be on land owned by a New York company; citizens were obliged to repurchase their own homesites. Here, from 1910–21, was the terminus of an intriguing "railroad"—a financial success without track or ties or trains. Called Tillman's Lane for its creator, the "line" resulted from railroad efforts to reach sparsely settled Hill Country ranches for cattle shipments. Convinced that rails would lose money, the road instead bought right of way and opened a 250-foot-wide, 100-mile-long "lane," all fenced with holding pens, wells, windmills and—until rails finally reached the area—operated in the black, as many as 50,000 cattle at one time marching from here to railroad at Brady. Today, Sonora concentrates more on sheep and goats, especially the long-haired angoras, descended from stock brought from Turkey in 1849—a gift from the Sultan in appreciation for an American professor teaching his people how to grow cotton. Today a 100-mile circle around Sonora produces 95 percent of the nation's mohair, the name for the hair of the Angora goat. The Old Sonora Trading Company offers items made from Texas wool and mohair. At Sonora intersect US 277/Tour 58.

At 187 m. FM 1989 leads south to the **Caverns of Sonora,** 8 m., which have been called "the world's most beautiful" by the founder of America's speleological society. Not large, but exquisite, a mile of well-lighted passageway leaves the viewer with no sense of confinement underground but rather with that of traveling through a delicately

silver-frosted fairyland. Picnic and camping facilities are available.

Westward your road traverses a sweeping plateau, apparently empty. A quarter million stock are ranging that emptiness.

Ozona, 215 m. (alt. 2,348; pop. 3,181), like its distant neighbor, is a rancher's town—big homes in planted pecan shade, the only city in a county larger than Delaware. The park on the square honors Alamo's hero, Davy Crockett; a walking tour from there leads past the county museum, the vine-covered old jail with a hanging tower (never used), the 1893 hotel, and Davy's statue. A leading wool producer, Ozona stages a July Junior Rodeo and weekly roping contests.

Slightly west of south, the old westbound military road crossed this lonely land searching for water and finding it at Howard Wells (inaccessible). In 1861 the Confederate invasion of the Far West drove 4,000 cavalrymen and a 10-mile-long wagon train over this road, the only near water for this vast cavalcade being this one well and its bucket.

Westward, your road crosses a rough, arid high plateau dotted with hills and mesas. Between Ozona and the Pecos canyon, occasional storage tanks and working pump jacks show oil activity: actually you pass through some 20 producing fields. At 248 m. a scenic overlook yields a panoramic view of the Pecos canyon, broadening to a deep valley here. South of your highway, you can still make out the ruts dug by wheellocked wagons careening down these precipitous walls; descending far more gradually than the old-time trains, your road still clings to the cliffside.

At 251 m., Fort Lancaster has been restored as a state historical park (day use). The interpretive center presents an authentic picture of this old post which held the southmost passable ford of the Pecos from 1855–61. The river, just west, is much reduced from early days; upriver dams and irrigation reduce today's flow.

Sheffield, 256 m., pop. 300, looks the part of a western town, occupying an area where the Blackjack Ketchum gang operated along the Pecos (see Dalhart). For years, an old treasure map here showed a cache at the military road pontoon crossing, up FM 349 near Iraan.

Searchers have hunted the area since 1900. Nearby, also see Horsehead Crossing.

At 279 m., merge with US 190/Tour 54.

At 314 m., merge with US 67/Tour 52; US 385/Tour 60.

Fort Stockton, 328 m.—see Tour 52. Tour 60 veers south. At 338 m., Tour 52 veers south. At 340 m., the Firestone 7.7 m. test track lies just north.

Balmorhea, 380 m. (alt. 3,205; pop. 765), centers a farming area irrigated by artesian springs.

Via TX 17 South 4 m. **Balmorhea State Park** (camping and all facilities), is an oasis around San Solomon Springs, a mighty outpouring (20,000 gallons per minute) of crystalline water. Long an irrigated valley with old Mexican towns on earlier Indian campsites, the lake has been converted into one of the country's largest swimming pools. TX 17 leads south into the beautiful Davis Mountains, looming immediately ahead (see Tour 57). Just within the shoulder of the range is Phantom Lake (private property), a hidden body of water and an old Indian campground.

At 400 m., merge with I-20/Tour 51. Immediately south, the prominent mountain thrusting out from the Davis range is Gomez Peak, rising to 6,323 feet.

Beyond **Kent,** 410 m., pop. 60, mountains rise to either side of you: the rugged crests northward are the Apache; your road begins a perceptible climb. At 440 m. a roadside park offers an exceptional view. Southward the Wylie Mountains where rock is crushed for purposes ranging from highway construction to cosmetics. To the northwest, close at hand, are the Baylor Mountains. East of them, far distant in a north-reaching line, are the Delawares. Between the two, faint on the horizon, are the Guadalupes, Texas' highest; and you are sighting them across a 60 m. distance.

Van Horn, 447 m. (alt. 4,010; pop. 2,930). Under its range at the end of a long valley, the town grew from a stage stop when rails came through in 1881. Van Horn still caters to travelers: there are many motels. Here TX 54 leads due north to Guadalupe Mountains National Park. In this area for years swirled the last savage fighting against the Apache; at nearby Bass Canyon, a company of

black soldiers was wiped out, and estimates place casualties at the hands of Victorio's warriors at some 4,000 before he was cut down, across in Mexico. The Sierra Diablos, west of north, are notable for Indian pictographs and prehistoric cave dwellings. The Culberson County Museum, with a good arrowhead collection, is located in town.

Each June, Van Horn celebrates Frontier Days. Here you merge with US 90/Tour 57. Immediately west, change to Mountain time.

Sierra Blanca, 480 m. (alt. 4,512; pop. 573). Perched near the top of its pass through the "White Mountains," the town takes its name from the silvery mountain just northwest. This pass represented a difficult climb for the old military road. Here also was the end of the giant railroad struggle between Southern Pacific and Texas Pacific, each seeking the first southern transcontinental line and building from opposite directions. At Sierra Blanca, January 1, 1882, the lines met and the continental link was complete. Interestingly, the Hudspeth County Courthouse here is the only such structure in Texas built of adobe. The Abstract Building houses an unusual collection of relics of frontier lawmen.

South via unimproved local roads through the Quitman Range is Indian Hot Springs, 33 m., once a flourishing little resort hotel, now a near-ghost. In this range are several abandoned lead, silver and zinc mines.

Beyond Sierra Blanca, a sweeping descent lowers you into the upper Rio Grande Valley; you turn into it just a few miles across from Old Mexico. At the head of the valley is the site of old Fort Quitman, traceless today. A replica of the fort serves as a museum. At

I-10 sweeps toward the Rio Grande in the vast, lonely expanses between the Quitman and Sierra Blanca Mountains west of Van Horn.

McNary, 508 m., pop. 250, TX 20 veers slightly west to hug the Rio Grande—slower going but a better view of the old towns of the valley.

Fort Hancock, 514 m. (alt. 3,517; pop. 400), was an 1882 outpost of El Paso's Fort Bliss. Near the river some foundation traces remain.

At **Fabens,** 538 m. (alt. 3,612; pop. 5,599), FM 258 veers alongside the Rio Grande, passing in succession the famed white missions of El Paso.

San Elizario, 9 m. (pop. 4,385) farthest east, nestles sleepily and almost unchanged around its 1777 plaza. The white church is of a period later than the two ahead of you, resembling more the California missions than those at Socorro and Ysleta. Not a mission but a presidio chapel, the structure, along with the others in the area, sat on an island in the Rio Grande until a mid-1800s flood changed the river's course and left them on the Texas side. Here took place America's first Thanksgiving, when Juan de Onate led a 1598 celebration after crossing the desert en route to New Mexico. Here also was the scene of the bloody Salt War (see Salt Flat.) Today a dinner theater, gallery, and other shops front the square. A block away is the old jail from which Billy the Kid reputedly sprang a friend.

Socorro, 14 m. (pop. 22,995) with its snow-white La Purisma Church, was founded a year later than Ysleta, just ahead, in 1682. The mission church contains the original hand-hewn roof beams. Legend claims the statue of St. Michael was bound for New Mexico but bogged down here and miraculously refused to budge, thus becoming patron saint of the parishioners.

Ysleta, 17 m., now part of El Paso, is Texas' oldest community, founded in 1681 when Spain fell back from New Mexico's bloody Pueblo revolt. In the silver-domed Mission Ysleta (Nuestra Senora del Carmen), through flood and fire, services have continued from the date of founding, just as the adjacent land has been cultivated from the beginning. Across the plaza is the Tigua Indian Reservation where authentic crafts, food and a museum await the visitor.

El Paso, 568 m.—see Tour 50A.

Above **Anthony** (pop. 3,328) cross the New Mexico line. A Texas Travel Information Center, just short of the line, provides incoming visitors with complete tourism information.

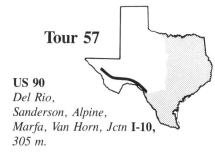

Tour 57

US 90
*Del Rio,
Sanderson, Alpine,
Marfa, Van Horn, Jctn I-10,
305 m.*

Until the more northerly routing of I-10, US 90 was the principal artery westbound from San Antonio to El Paso. For this tour, westward from Tour 34, you begin at Del Rio on the Rio Grande and hug that river route for virtually all of your journey, leaving it only to cut across the top of its great, south-looping Big Bend.

Nearly all of your trip traverses desert mountain country and reflects the wild beauty peculiar to such arid regions—sweeping sun-colored valleys, vast vistas rimmed by mountain ranges folding against the distance like cardboard cutouts. Your high crossing of the Pecos gorge alone is worth the journey to reach it.

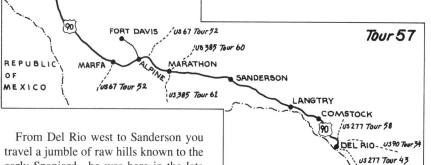

From Del Rio west to Sanderson you travel a jumble of raw hills known to the early Spaniard—he was here in the late 1500s—as *malpais*, or badlands. Beyond Sanderson, mountains loom as you approach Alpine, nestled against the foot of the Davis Range, where a side trip explores those delicately-spiring peaks and their historic ground. South of Marathon and Alpine, the immense Big Bend Country and its awesome Chisos Range—a national park—is reserved for a separate tour (62).

Beyond Alpine, a lofty plateau extends to Marfa, where you veer northwest up a succession of mountain-rimmed valleys to merge with I-10, El Paso-bound.

Del Rio, 0 m. (alt. 948; pop. 30,705), sun-drenched, friendly and informal, is discovering itself as an international vacationland today—its Mexico gateway now bolstered with the sporting appeal of big Amistad Lake and National Recreation Area.

Originally San Felipe del Rio, the border city centers an area crossed early by Spain—Cabeza de Vaca in 1535 and Gaspar Castano de Sosa, blazing America's first wagon road (your route west to the Pecos), in 1590. In 1849 the westward military road turned north here, up the Devil's River to avoid the Pecos gorge, due west.

The town grew from San Felipe Springs, an immense outpouring of 90 million gallons daily, forming an oasis welcome to early travelers; today Del Rio caters to tourists. South of the springs—on the city's east edge—is a new river walk park and amphitheater for special events. The C of C maps some 72 historic structures from century-turn and earlier, including the Whitehead Museum in its 1870 building, and the intriguing old Val Verde Winery. The museum, in an old mercantile building, displays exhibits ranging from archaeology to border Texana—Judge Roy Bean is buried on the grounds—while the winery has been operated by the same family since 1883: you'll want to visit its cellars. Del Rio is also home of Laughlin Air Force Base, credited in 1962 with proving the presence of Soviet missile build-up in Cuba. Across the river, Ciudad Acuna offers interesting shops, good restaurants and bright nightlife.

Amistad (Friendship) Dam, just west, a joint U.S.-Mexico project, impounds a bluewater lake reaching 74 m. up the Rio Grande, 25 m. up Devil's River, and 14 m. up the distant Pecos. The National Park Service administers U.S. facilities which include marinas and limited-facility campsites. Numer-

US 90 crosses the Devil's River arm of 67,000-acre Amistad Reservoir near Del Rio.

ous Indian pictographs can be found in cliff caves along the lakeshore, accessible only by boat. Amistad's fishing is justly famed.

At Del Rio, intersect US 277/Tour 58, Region IV; Tour 43, Region III; and US 90's eastward continuation, Tour 34, Region III. In the area also see Brackettville, Eagle Pass.

Beyond the Devil's River arm of the lake, 12 m., your route traverses rough, arid ranchland.

Comstock, 32 m. (alt. 1,550; pop. 375) is a sunbaked, shouldered-together ranchtown in an area of prehistoric cave shelters (private property). Here TX 163 leads north up the Devil's River, approximating the old military road. About 20 m. upstream is the site of Camp Hudson, an 1857–68 outpost guard. Somewhere nearby, the Devil's River took its name when Ranger Jack Hays—told the river's name was San Pedro—peered into its canyon and remarked, "St. Peter's River, Hell! It looks more like the Devil's." Nearby, numerous cave dwellings have been explored, dating back thousands of years, and in this wild region has grown the legend of the Wolf Girl, an early 1800s newborn babe whose mother died in childbirth. The girl was reared by wolves, goes the story.

Seminole Canyon, 40 m., is a picturesque rocky site, now a state park. Numerous cave dwellings exist, and guided hiking tours (up to 3 m.) take you to 4,000-year-old rock art. The Visitors Center displays the lifestyle of these early people. Camping and all facilities are available.

Pecos Gorge, 45 m. The scenic overlook (east side) offers a spectacular view. Southward, the Pecos canyon joins that of Rio Grande and beyond loom the mountains of Mexico. All along the bluffs are cave dwellings; one directly beneath this park was excavated by the Smithsonian Institute, tracing the 8,000-year-old culture of the ancient cliff-dwelling "Basketmaker." The high bridge is 273 feet above the riverbed. Across, a marker cites the location of the silver spike noting the Southern Pacific Railroad's Pecos River crossing and linkage of east and west portions of its Sunset Route.

Langtry, 60 m. (alt. 1,315; pop. 45), rocky and barren, houses the restored Jersey Lilly Saloon and home of Judge Roy Bean, self-proclaimed Law West of the Pecos. He named his saloon for Lily Langtry, famed actress, whose first name Bean's sign-painter misspelled. The judge held two-fisted court here, once fining a dead man $40 for carrying a pistol, then confiscating the gun. He also outwitted Texas law here by staging a heavyweight boxing match—then banned in Texas—on the Mexican sand-pit directly across the Rio Grande behind his town.

Whether the town itself was actress Lily's namesake, no one knows for sure. Bean said he named it for her, but many credit the town's name to a civil engineer named Langtry who worked for the Galveston, Harrisburg and San Antonio Railroad when it came through town.

In a handsome Texas Travel Information Center, Judge Roy Bean's colorful ca-

Judge Roy Bean's Jersey Lilly saloon and courtroom, Langtry.

reer is interpreted through dioramas with sound and music. The old saloon, meticulously restored, literally breathes its frontier times. Adjacent is an exceptional cactus garden, whose self-guiding tour identifies the many unusual desert plants of this region—from the spindly ocotillo to the barrel cactus. All in all, this is a must-stop if you would experience the feel of old and remote West Texas.

Sanderson, 120 m. (alt. 2,980; pop. 1,128). For relative newness, the town centers old country, for Cabeza de Vaca toiled westward here in the early 1500s. The land remained empty until the railroad made this a water stop in 1882. It became a rough guntown with cattle smuggled up from the Rio Grande, with outlaws and gunfighters like Bat Masterson frequent visitors. Charlie Wilson's Old Cottage Bar was widely known, and Roy Bean for a time maintained a saloon here. The town was headquarters over a period of years for expeditions in search of a lost mine across in the Fronteriza Range in Mexico. A Negro, far removed from his camp, stumbled on the mine and, according to legend, celebrated his discovery so completely that he fell asleep with his feet in the campfire and died without telling companions of the mine's location. The searches probed Maravillas Canyon south of here.

Marathon, 174 m. (alt. 4,043; pop. 800), a scatter of dwellings edging the Glass Mountains, is notable primarily as gateway to Big Bend National Park, via US 385, 80 m. south. (However, the historic old Gage Hotel, restored now, offers ranchstyle lodging. Campgrounds are available nearby, and the C of C can arrange guided tours of the Big Bend as well as Rio Grande float trips.) See Tour 62. US 385 north is Tour 60. At 196 m. merge with US 67/Tour 52 as far as Marfa.

Alpine, 205 m.—see Tour 52. TX 118 leads south to Big Bend's west entrance, 78 m. (Tour 62).

Via TX 118 north, **Fort Davis,** 26 m. (alt. 5,050; pop. 900), grew up around its fort, a major anchor on the California road. In 1854 the fort was established under fire in a running fight to clear Limpia Canyon of Apache. The Eighth Infantry dug in and the fort remained in almost continual Apache warfare until 1880 when its mountains finally were cleared. Now a National

Historic Site, much has been restored, much stabilized in the dignity of ruin. There is an excellent park museum and an elaborate sound re-creation of a military retreat parade. Echoing over an empty parade ground, its effects are moving. With the fort's abandonment in 1891, the little hamlet remained.

There are two museums: the Overland Trail building takes you back to 1883, outside and within; the Neill Museum in historic Trueheart House exhibits antique toys, dolls. The Limpia Hotel (1912), now restored, provides lodging and meals in an interesting old country inn. Lodges are available at the state park, just west.

Looping west, a beautiful 74-m. Scenic Loop (TX 118/166) passes big **Davis Mountain State Park,** with camping and all facilities, its road-climbing mountain overlook immediately east, and dominant Mt. Livermore (8,362 feet), Texas' second highest peak, to the west. The loop passes below McDonald Observatory, one of America's most powerful, twin tiny white thimbles atop Mt. Locke, a scenic road ascending to it, and visitors' tours daily. Four nights a week at the visitor center, staffers host "star parties" featuring viewing through small telescopes and astronomical explanations. Nearby is Harvard University's Radio Astronomy Observatory.

TX 118 offers scenic vistas as it courses through the Davis Mountains northwest of Alpine.

Returning to Fort Davis, the scenic drive passes Skillman Grove, site of Bloys Cowboy Camp Meetings since 1889. Each August, West Texans gather by thousands for a week of interdenominational, open-sky worship. On the edge of town is Mt. Dolores, atop which a lovely Mexican girl kept tragic vigil with her lover—killed by Indians. Each night for 30 years, until her death, she climbed to light a beacon fire on the peak. Westward, toward Valentine, is the rocky slope of El Muerto, where the legend of buried treasure and its death curse persists. Here, one man dug all his life, certain he was close to great riches.

To the north, via TX 17, is Wild Rose Canyon, 18 m., a spectacular entry to the mountains where the old road may be seen climbing rockily below you. Here Butterfield Overland stages could expect Apache ambush, and near here famed Texas Ranger Bigfoot Wallace is said to have dropped a deer from the peak above, picking it up without stopping the stage he guarded. Toward Toyahvale and Balmorhea (Tour 56) beyond, but back in the lowering hills, is the ghost resort of Madera Springs, a 1920–30 spa now on private land.

From Alpine, your road cuts through the lower Davis Mountains past the site of the old Marfa Air Base, 222 m. From here on occasional nights the "Marfa Ghost Lights," known by many names, may be seen against the looming Chinati Mountains, southward (see Shafter).

Marfa, 231 m.—see Tour 52. Proceeding northwestward you pass **Valentine,** 261 m. (pop. 217) flanked westward by the Sierra Vieja (Old Mountains) range, a wild, empty county once the hideout of outlaws and renegades. At tiny Lobo, 288 m., pop. 40, is the site of old Van Horn Wells, a remote stage stop and a dangerous one on the western road.

Van Horn, 305 m. Merge with I-10/Tour 56, westbound for El Paso.

☆

Tour 58

US 277
Oklahoma line,
Wichita Falls, Seymour,
Haskell, Abilene, Bronte,
San Angelo, Sonora, Del Rio, 403 m.

From north to south, US 277 crosses the midsection of Texas, a great unchanged ranch country: you begin on the rolling prairies north of Wichita Falls and end on similar plains at Del Rio at the Mexican border. Except for artesian wells and manmade lakes, it is a dry country that, when won from the Comanche, had to be won again from drought. In later years oil has enriched some of the route; however, the Texan

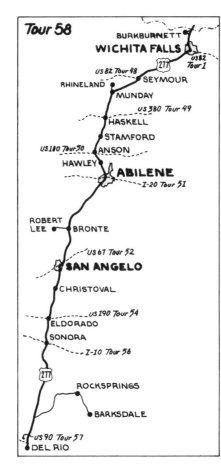

that you meet along this road is essentially the same rancher that his grandfather was—his mount instead is a pickup.

Interestingly, you approximate the main line of frontier forts that stood guard when Texas changed from a republic to a state. You veer west of Fort Belknap, below Wichita Falls, then pass Phantom Hill and Chadbourne near Abilene, and Concho at San Angelo—ghosts at parade rest today, yet in their time bulwarks against the hard-riding and desperate Indian.

On the whole, this is a tour more for feel than for seeing—there is a sameness in the rolling, thin-timbered terrain, yet at the same time you can sense a vigor in land fought for and won, and in large and small cities that look new because they are still pioneering today.

Okla. line, 0 m. You cross into Texas 42 m. south of Lawton.

Burkburnett, 2 m. (alt. 1,040; pop. 10,145), is a clean and handsome little city on the Red River, bordering Oklahoma—one that must rank with Ranger (Tour 51) as one of the riproaringest oil

boomers Texas has known. In 1918 it gushed from a few hundred population to a sprawling roughhouse of 30,000 in less than a year, its land jumping to as much as $40,000 an acre. The former cowboy town on Samuel Burk Burnett's Four-Sixes Ranch became the brawling locale for Rex Beach's novel, "Flowing Gold"; and from this field, where gusher followed gusher, Wichita Falls built its future. Many ghost town sites (see Tour 1) lie forgotten in the brush.

There is a legend, discounted today but worth repeating, that Burk Burnett's vast 6666 holdings came about because of a poker hand that read just that way.

Wichita Falls, 14 m.—see Tour 1. Here you merge with Tour 48 to Seymour.

Seymour, 64 m.—see Tour 48. Veer southwest.

Munday, 87 m. (alt. 1,460; pop. 1,600), is a ranch and stockfarm center that seems almost by design to have stayed precisely the same for half-a-century. Texas A&M University maintains a vegetable research station here. At Miller's Creek Reservoir, 12 m. southeast, fishing is good.

Via FM 267 north, **Rhineland,** 6 m., pop. 196, is notable for its delicately tall-steepled church. From clay in a nearby pit, German parishioners made some 100,000 bricks to hand-build their place of worship—a good place to contemplate faith.

Haskell, 108 m.—see Tour 49.
Stamford, 123 m. (alt. 1,603; pop. 3,817), is a town of red brick and white stone with a comfortable sturdiness built by its Swedish settlers. The rangetown grew up around the famed Swenson SMS ranch and Swedish immigrants brought to Texas by Swen Magnus Swenson, in 1838 first of his breed in the state. The town, early each July, is the three-day home of Cowboy Reunion, one of the nation's leading rodeo and western celebrations. The reunion is no trick-riding floorshow, but a determined and successful effort to preserve the history and culture of the real Texas cowboy. At the first reunion in 1897—actually held in Haskell, just north—some 15,000 range riders came to select the West's finest cutting horse, and to talk of a West that they saw slipping into the past. Despite pickups for mounts today, the reunion's

philosophy remains unchanged. The land about bears the Swenson backward SMS—today one of Texas' leading brands. Suitably, there is an excellent Cowboy Museum here, as well as a monument to the Indian fighters who rode the Mackenzie Trail. In the area also see Albany, Aspermont.

Anson, 140 m.—see Tour 50.

At little **Hawley,** 150 m., pop. 606, FM 1082 leads east to **Fort Phantom Hill,** well-named, for it stands one of the state's ghostliest guards—lonely, rock-walled commissary, guardhouse and magazine and a skeletal array of solitary chimneys. The site was ill-chosen in 1851—water was gyp—and by 1854 abandonment was ordered. Mysteriously, the fort burned, and to this day Phantom Hill has remained an enigma—thronged with ghost legends, one of them dealing with a scalp hunter. Apparently the phantom was the hill itself: its mirage-like quality making it higher than it is. Ironically, the water lack that caused its abandonment is abundant in Lake Phantom Hill today. The lake is a popular water recreation area.

Abilene, 163 m.—see Tour 51. At 177 m., FM 1235 leads east to Buffalo Gap and Abilene State Recreation Area (camping and all facilities, an excellent park—see Tours 51 and 53).

At 211 m. Oak Creek Reservoir provides water sports, camping facilities. Immediately south (on private ranch) are the ruins of **Fort Chadbourne,** established in 1852 to guard the Butterfield Overland stage route. Taken over with Texas secession, it was Confederate-occupied for a time and never regarrisoned

The ruins of Ft. Chadbourne, just west of US 277 north of Bronte, near Oak Creek Reservoir.

after the Civil War, Fort Concho at San Angelo replacing its function. The old buildings still stand duty as structures for the ranch and are visible from this highway and TX 70.

At Chadbourne, bored troopers spent much time racing their mounts—traces of the old track remain. In the mid-1850s, Comanche Chief Mulaquetop, drifting by with a party of braves, suggested that his tribe owned a horse that might match with Chadbourne's blooded champion—it appeared a miserable, shaggy mustang. Bets were laid and thunderstruck troopers saw the Indian mount change to a lightning bolt, its rider saddled backwards and thumbing his nose at cavalrymen who had lost their bets.

Bronte, 220 m. (alt. 1,893; pop. 962), occupies a land of notched mesas and takes its name from the English novelist, Charlotte Bronte. Via TX 158 west is **Robert Lee** (alt. 1,780, pop. 1,276), also famously named. Its close-by Spence Reservoir provides good fishing, campsites. Also see Ballinger and Paint Rock, nearby.

San Angelo, 254 m.—see Tour 52. Numerous nearby lakes provide all facilities.

Christoval, 274 m. (alt. 2,000; pop. 216), is a beautifully-shaded little hamlet on the South Concho River, which happens to run north here. Toenail Trail is the relic of an old military road crossing this region.

Eldorado, 297 m.—see Tour 54.
Sonora, 318 m.—see Tour 56.

At 344 m. TX 55 leads southeast to **Rocksprings,** 33 m. (alt. 2,450; pop. 1,339). This is a sheep-and-goat little town, its reason for being—mohair. In 1927 it was almost destroyed by a tornado which killed 67 people.

The Angora Goat Breeders Association maintains a Rocksprings museum and the only place of registry for that industry in all of America.

Just east of town on a working ranch (accessible with permission) is the awesome **Devil's Sinkhole,** a sudden abyss yawning in otherwise level land, apparently a collapsed subterranean cavern. The result is an almost circular opening some 50 feet wide, over a vast upside-down, funnel-shaped pit, the sides sloping sharply outward. Below is a "mountain," the total depth, 400 feet. At the bottom is a lake which some believe heads the Nueces River, emerging miles below. It is best to peep over only; descent is most hazardous; trying to return to the surface, even more so.

South 25 m. via TX 55 is **Barksdale,** pop. 71, within the scenic Nueces canyon. The settlement dates from 1880, holding on despite savage Indian attacks. Nearby are numerous Indian caves in the canyon wall.

Del Rio, 403 m.—see Tour 57.

☆

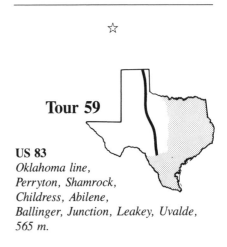

Tour 59

US 83
Oklahoma line,
Perryton, Shamrock,
Childress, Abilene,
Ballinger, Junction, Leakey, Uvalde,
565 m.

U S 83, called "Backbone of the Continent," is one of the longest north-south highways in America, running from Canada to the very tip of Texas at Brownsville. Across Texas its length is almost 900 m., the longest reach lying within Region IV. Here it begins above Perryton at the top of the Panhandle and ranges southward to leave this region at Uvalde (where it continues south as Tour 42).

Skirting east of the Cap Rock escarpment and the flat plains beyond those bluffs, your route traverses rolling, sparsely-timbered prairies which descend imperceptibly as you drive south. The Panhandle region, once vast ranches, now boasts great fields of wheat and grains, stockfarming and some oil production. Below Childress, where the pan's handle extends north, you encounter the traditional solitude of West Texas ranch country. South of Abilene, particularly as you near Brady, you climb into the scenic Hill Country, and from Junction south along the Frio, you can enjoy some of Texas' handsomest vistas—rugged hills, wooded, clear-running streams. At Uvalde, you emerge from the hills and leave Region IV.

Throughout, you cross a land long dominated by the Comanche. Southward, you approximate his 1700s invasion routes as he swept down from Yellowstone country to confound Spain's colonization plans. Along the way you also reverse his fighting retreat before Texas pressure, beginning your tour, in fact, among the scenes of his bitter last stand on the High Plains.

Okla. line, 0 m. You cross into Texas over a narrow strip of Oklahoma, only 35 m. south of Liberal, Kan.

Perryton, 7 m. (alt. 2,942; pop. 7,607), with its towering grain elevators, calls itself "Wheatheart of the Nation." With its broad streets and neat residential areas, it is hard to envision a 1919 settlement where men lived in boxcars building a town along a new railroad. That year, Perryton took the county seat from now-ghost Ochiltree, then a thriving little settlement 8 m. south where TX 70 veers west.

Towering grain elevators around Perryton, the "Wheatheart of the Nation."

This northernmost of Texas county seats boasts the Museum of the Plains, a good one; and each September stages its Golden Spread Antique Machinery Show, displaying such equipment as a 1916 Waterloo Boy Tractor, the forerunner to famed John Deere products.

South 18 m. and via a local road is **Wolf Creek Park.** Near here in 1909 a buried Indian pueblo was excavated; some traces remain. Recent archaeological digs have revealed a 700-year-old Indian house in this enigmatic "buried city." Southward your road passes big wheat fields and widely spread oil and gas development.

Southwest of Perryton is the site of famed Adobe Walls battleground. Follow TX 15 to **Spearman,** 26 m. (inquire there), then south via FM 760 and local roads (marked). Close by the Ca-

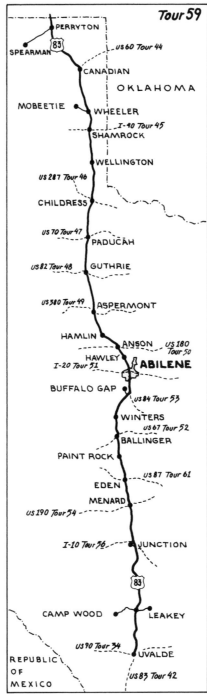

Tour 59

nadian in 1874, 28 buffalo hunters, including famed marksmen Billy Dixon and Bat Masterson, fought off a three-day attack by a force of Comanche, Kiowa and Cheyenne, determined to wipe out the hunting camps—this one at the ruins of an 1843 trading post. During the fight, Dixon, with an open-sight Sharps Big Fifty, made one of history's most incredible shots, dropping a Cheyenne chief from his horse at a range slightly under one mile!

The same site, ironically, served as an earlier battleground when Col. Kit Carson led some 400 troopers from Fort Union, N. Mex. against Indians entrenched here. Despite Carson's cannon, he could manage no more than an all-day draw, retreating to New Mexico. Carson's fight preceded Dixon's by 10 years. There are two markers here—one, interestingly, salutes the Indian who fought for land he believed his.

Canadian, 53 m.—see Tour 44.

At 60 m. TX 33 leads east 8 m. toward tiny **Gem.** South of here near the Washita River, the army wagon train of Capt. Wyllys Lyman stood off a combined Comanche and Kiowa assault for five days in September, 1874. Cut off from water, 100 yards distant, Lyman's men subsisted on canned tomatoes and a pool of rainwater and beat off five-to-one odds. This was one of several clashes occurring as US troops drove from all directions to complete the clearing of these high plains of their last Indian warriors.

At 68 m. FM 277 leads east 5 m. to the site of the Buffalo Wallow Fight. Here, almost simultaneously with Lyman's stand to the north, Scout Billy Dixon (see Adobe Walls) and five couriers, all wounded, held a 10-foot-wide buffalo wallow for three days against Comanche and Kiowa from the same band that had hit Lyman. All of them—one buried where he died in the wallow—received the Congressional Medal of Honor, rare for civilians.

Wheeler, 87 m. (alt. 2,600; pop. 1,393), in the red-jumbled, hilly breaks above the North Fork of the Red is an agribusiness center with many large cattle feedlots. Begun as an 1880 dugout community, the town grew from Old Mobeetie, westward.

Via TX 152 west 11 m., **Old Mobeetie** was a buffalo hunters camp called Hidetown until taking the Indian name for sweet water. In 1875 it was as tough a guntown as westerly Tascosa (Tour 60). That year saw Texas' last frontier post, Fort Elliott, established here. The town itself, the Panhandle's capital, was a one-street, cottonwood picket and raw frame shebang frequented by gunfighters. There is a legend that Bat Masterson, surveying the area, killed a renegade for molesting a young Mobeetie girl. The girl is believed buried in the ghost town cemetery on the hill. Several original buildings remain, and "New" Mobeetie, pop. 154, hangs on nearby. The Old Mobeetie Museum reflects these old days.

Shamrock, 103 m.—see Tour 45.

Wellington, 128 m. (alt. 2,078; pop. 2,456) is today a farming community which took its lofty name for a reason, being an offspring of the old Rocking Chair Ranch, called by Texas cowboys the "Nobility Ranch." Owners of the Rocking Chair included the First Baron of Tweedmouth and the Earl of Aberdeen. Unable to cope with the land, the English lost control of the Rocking Chair, itself ultimately divided into townsites. During the early 1900s, Wellington's outreaching phone system was strung along ranch barbed wire. The Collingsworth County Historical Museum reflects the area's early days.

Childress, 158 m.—see Tour 46.

Paducah, 188 m.—see Tour 47.

Guthrie, 216 m.—see Tour 48.

At 235 m. cross the Salt Fork of the Brazos. Near here is the legendary site of the Spider Rock Treasure, allegedly old Spanish gold en route from New Mexico. Particularly by one man who lived like a hermit, digging for 30 years before he died, the area has been combed without known success (see Aspermont).

Aspermont, 250 m.—see Tour 49.

Hamlin, 269 m. (alt. 1,705; pop. 2,791), is a neat little city shaded with mesquite and locust trees, a former railroad division point within an area of Swedish settlement. The little city displays three beautifully-landscaped parks.

Via TX 92 west 5 m. is the site of near-ghost **Swedona,** a rural community of Swedes, many of whom came through the influence of S. M. Swenson, noted pioneer. Closely-knit families farmed here and well into the 1900s maintained Swedish customs—Saturday night family socials with fiddle and harmonica accompaniment.

Anson, 287 m.—see Tour 50.

Abilene, 311 m.—see Tour 51. See Abilene State Park, Buffalo Gap.

At 327 m. veer west from US 84/Tour 53.

Winters, 352 m. (alt. 1,860; pop. 2,905), is a relatively old town (1880)

with a clean, new look. It prospers in a rich agricultural region and feels the effect of nearby oil production. Birthplace of baseball's great, Rogers Hornsby, this little city also boasts the state's first charter granted to its Future Farmers of America chapter (1930).

Nearby, the fishing at fairly new Elm Creek Reservoir (5 m. east on TX 53) is one of West Texas' best-kept secrets. Try it! Just west is the site of Fort Chadbourne (Tour 58).

At 364 m., the ghost site of old Runnels City lies just west (FM 2887). Once a prospering county seat, forerunning Ballinger, it was railroad by-passed. The city knocked down most of its stone buildings, hauled them in wagons to the new town and built Ballinger. A few tumbled stones mark the old site.

Ballinger, 368 m.—see Tour 52.

Paint Rock, 384 m. (alt. 1,639; pop. 227) is a drowsy town beside the shallow Concho River Canyon, taking its name from one of the remarkable displays of Indian pictographs in America—some 1,500 of the hieroglyphics inscribed along a mile of canyon wall. The pictograph served as a kind of almanac-newspaper for primitive Americans—with signs of drought, good harvest, war, celebrations, tragedy. One record is that of the Comanche massacre of the Spanish mission at Menard, just south, in 1757 (see Tour 54). It shows a mission afire and a priest beheaded.

Northeast of Paint Rock, where the Concho joins the Colorado (FM 1929 and local roads) is the 1683 site of one of Spain's earliest missions, a temporary one "ordered" by the miracle of the "Lady in Blue." Mother Maria de Agreda, who never left her convent in Spain, is credited with the miracle of bilocation: she was able to describe in detail areas of the Southwest—particularly Texas—and ask of the Franciscan order that missions be established among the savages. That she "visited" the New World was proven many times to Spain's satisfaction—Texas Indians, "to whom she came from the sky" could describe her in detail. This mission was one of the first she sought. Nearby, also see San Angelo.

Eden, 405 m. (alt. 2,048; pop. 1,567), oak shaded in its hills, is a ranch center crossroads. Eden was the home of WW II's famed General Earl Rudder, who led his men up the savagely-con-

tested cliffs at Omaha Beach, and later headed Texas A&M University. Intersect US 87/Tour 61.

Menard, 427 m.—see Tour 54.

Junction, 458 m.—see Tour 56.

Leakey, 524 m. (alt. 1,609; pop. 399), is a little resort town in some of the handsomest Texas Hill Country, centering the Tri-canyon vacationland of the Frio, Nueces and Sabinal. An old town, Leakey has existed since 1857, fighting Comanche for its foothold. Its remote and hard-bitten early days are reflected in the death of an eastern visitor whose family requested embalming. Lacking facilities, the citizens placed the man in a smokehouse.

Immediately north, Horsecollar Bluff offers a beautiful view of the Frio River.

South 10 m. is **Garner State Park** on the Frio, with camping and all facilities, in a forest of giant cypress trees. Nearby are the resort towns of Concan, pop. 71, and Rio Frio with guest ranches and summer camps.

Via FM 337 west, one of Texas' most scenic drives climbs to and descends from the pass to **Camp Wood,** 21 m., pop. 595, in the equally scenic Nueces Canyon. Long before this little town was an 1857 outpost garrison, it housed Spanish Mission San Lorenzo in 1762. A Lipan Apache installation, it failed and was abandoned under Comanche attack, as was its companion Mission Candelaria, 10 m. south at tiny Montell. Camp Wood boasts a jewel-like lake on the Nueces with limited camping facilities but all water sports. South of Montell, a commercial campground

Floating the shallow rapids of the clear, cool Frio River at Garner State Park.

at Chalk Bluff occupies a beautiful site on the Nueces, also the site of an early-day Indian massacre.

Via FM 337 east from Leakey, scenery is equally handsome. Tiny **Vanderpool**, pop. 20, 17 m., is gateway to beautifully-secluded Sabinal Canyon with its mossy bluffs, contorted rock and its "lost maple trees," now a scenic state park with camping and all facilities. Below, 8 m., is little Waresville. Settled far beyond the then frontier in 1852, it saw bloody Indian fighting. The Ware cabin is preserved today.

South of Leakey on your highway, Garner State Park is 534 m.

Rolling Hill Country landscape along FM 337, between Leakey and Vanderpool.

Uvalde, 565 m.—see Tour 34. Enter Region III, where your road becomes Tour 42.

☆

Tour 60

US 385
Oklahoma line, Dalhart, Hereford, Levelland, Seminole, Odessa, McCamey, Fort Stockton, Marathon, 505 m.

Southbound from the Dakotas, US 385 hugs the western edge of the Texas plains for some 300 m. of America's breadbasket—the great green sea, so rich today, once considered uninhabitable by man. Below Seminole, unlike more easterly routes, this road does not drop from the Llano Estacado at a bluff line, but rather descends gradually into

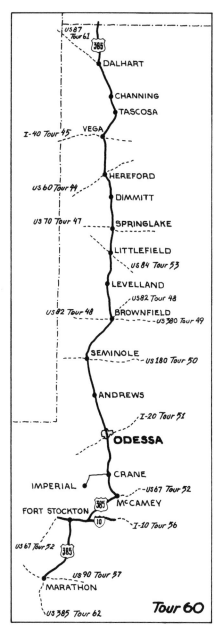

Tour 60

more arid land, where it continues across a terrain that also has enriched Texans: from Andrews to well south of Odessa, you cross the great Permian Basin, one of this state's greatest oil-producing areas.

Still southbound, you cross the Pecos beyond McCamey's long mesas, veering through Fort Stockton to skirt the eastern foot of the Davis range and, at Marathon, lodged against the Glass Mountains, you drive straight south for the mighty Chisos peaks and Big Bend National Park. Because of its spectacular scenery, this last leg is treated as a separate tour (62).

In a general sense and even before entering Texas, your highway follows the old Comanche war trails. Drifting south in the 1700s, he fanned out across much of West and Central Texas. However, one of his most valued raiding targets remained northern Mexico. Each fall—he called it the Month of the Mexican Moon—the Comanche rode a trail south to the Rio Grande, a trail US 385 follows closely from Fort Stockton (Comanche Springs) south to Big Bend.

Okla. line, 0 m. You cross into Texas some 10 m. south of Boise City and within a very few miles of the states of New Mexico, Colorado and Kansas.

Dalhart, 31 m. (alt. 3,985; pop. 6,246), highest and northwesternmost of our plains, is also the city most closely associated with the gigantic XIT Ranch, three million acres deeded for the construction of the Texas Capitol in 1881–82. Originally sprawling 30 m. wide from near Lubbock to the Okla. line, it embraced all or part of 10 counties, once boasting 3,000 m. of fenceline and its initials XIT loosely—and, in fact, mistakenly—translated to "Ten in Texas." First headquarters were at Buffalo Springs, 32 m. north, but Dalhart is XIT town. For three days early each August since 1936, the XIT Reunion and Rodeo has returned the old-timers here. In town, an "Empty Saddles" monument salutes XIT's departed. The August celebration includes one of the world's largest amateur rodeos and free barbecues. Dalhart maintains an XIT Museum, and closeby is Rita Blanca Lake and Park, with camping and all facilities.

Early days were not easy going—notorious Black Jack Ketchum (see Sheffield) operated in the area and—to the accompaniment of a string band—was hanged just across the border in Clayton, N. Mex.

At its peak, XIT was divided into seven divisions, each with its own headquarters; however, by the 1900s it began to sell off sections and by 1912 sold its last cattle, its acreage much reduced. At Dalhart, merge with US 87/Tour 61 to Hartley.

Channing, 61 m. (alt. 3,817; pop. 277), rests on a plain just north of the rugged Canadian River valley. It originated as a northern headquarters for the XIT; and the county seat was dragged here from northward Hartley on wheels, XIT cowboys manning drag ropes. The old headquarters building still exists, as does an 1898 church, oldest north of the Canadian.

Via FM 767 west 36 m. **Romero,** a near-forgotten wayspot, was founded about 1800 by New Mexicans from the Taos area. Partners with the Comanche, they were Ciboleros (buffalo hunters with lance) and Comancheros (Indian-traders). As Indians retreated, the settlers became shepherds, giving way in turn to the onrush of the great ranches.

Tascosa, 73 m. (alt. 3,176; pop. 410), in the Canadian valley breaks, was perhaps Texas' most violent guntown and second to Mobeetie, eastward, in date of founding. As an early Mexican shepherd camp, it took its name from the boggy Canadian crossing which attracted cattle and freighter trails, then big ranches. With this, Tascosa became cowboy capital and sometime residence of men like Billy the Kid, Temple Houston (Sam's son), Bat Masterson, Frank James and Pat Garrett. Here also was the battleground of the 1880 Cowboy Strike, essentially a struggle between big and little ranchers (and rustlers), which produced Tascosa's Boot Hill, the only one in Texas, with 28 known graves—five of them coming in one one-minute-long gunfight. The railroad killed the town, but Amarillo business and philanthropic interests revived it in establishing a Boy's Ranch on the townsite. Boot Hill and some old buildings are preserved (notably the old courthouse, now the Julian Bivins Museum). Old streets are marked. A visit here is a must.

West of Tascosa via local roads are the ruins of the 1875 Torrey Ranch with 30-inch rubblestone walls. Billy the Kid ran this new Englander rancher out.

Vega, 97 m. (alt. 4,030; pop. 840), deep in ranchland, offers a surprise—five acres of tomatoes in a giant greenhouse, one of the biggest. Annual yield is 100,000 pounds per acre. See Tour 45.

Hereford, 127 m.—see Tour 44.

Dimmitt, 148 m. (alt. 3,854; pop. 4,408), on a trail Coronado followed in 1542 is today a land to color green, growing everything. Its $45 million Amstar Plant makes high fructose syrup (sweeteners) from corn. Tours are inter-esting. Big feedlots, including one for sheep, are numerous in the area.

Springlake, 170 m. Intersect US 70/Tour 47.

Littlefield, 191 m.—see Tour 53.

Levelland, 215 m. (alt. 3,523; pop. 13,986), centers an area long-known and long-deserted by history. Tradition holds that Yellow House Canyon, just north and crossing east-to-west (see Lubbock), was named by Coronado's scouts—*casas amarillas*, for prehistoric dwellings, traceless today. After Comanche withdrawal, the area marked the lower end of the XIT Ranch, with other large spreads nearby. In 1921 population swelled with the arrival of rails. The first commissioners court here was convened on Texas Independence Day, March 2, 1921, in an automobile in the middle of a bald prairie.

Table-flat high plains spread to infinity around Levelland and Littlefield.

Consider that as you scan the maze of towers, silos, scaffoldings that testify to the earth's wealth above and below. The South Plains College (two years) is here; the South Plains Museum displays regional history with some excellent exhibits.

Brownfield, 245 m.—see Tour 48.

Seminole, 285 m.—see Tour 50.

Andrews, 313 m. (alt. 3,190; pop. 10,678), a new-looking town with broad streets, was born in 1910 when the county was organized. It came into its own when oil was discovered in the Deep Rock Pool, Permian Basin, in 1930. Today, Andrews boasts one of the wealthiest school districts in the nation. There is a nearby prairie dog town, and a new amphitheater, which the "can-do" resolve of this bustling little city converted from a raw caliche pit in just five weeks.

Odessa, 348 m.—see Tour 51.

Crane, 380 m. (alt. 2,555; pop. 3,533), on a rolling prairie in the midst of one of Texas' biggest oil-producing areas, is the only town in a county that until 1918 could claim not one single road.

Via TX 329 west/FM 1053 south, 19 m. below **Imperial,** pop. 720 (seek local road directions), is **Horsehead Crossing,** which had been a major ford of the Pecos since prehistoric times. Named for skeletons of horses and cattle found there by early travelers, Horsehead was one site where the Pecos banks were gradual enough to permit passage. Below here, the gorge and then deep-running river were virtually impassable. The buffalo and its Indian hunter came first, then Spain, and finally the Westbound trains and stages on Emigrant, California and Chihuahua Trails.

From Crane south at 390 m., **Castle Gap** lies east, a rampart-like gateway through the Castle Mountains. The gap opened on Horsehead Crossing and was a primary point of ambush, both by Indians and by bandits preying on gold-laden, returning Forty-Niner wagons. Belief in legendary buried gold is strong here; some tell of treasure buried by Maximilian. Clearly visible from the crossing, or your nearer highway, the Gap is on private land.

Castle Gap, corridor to the Castle Mountains, lies east of US 385 between Crane and McCamey.

McCamey, 401 m.—see Tour 52. The C of C here can furnish information on Horsehead Crossing and Castle Gap.

At 433 m., merge with I-10/Tour 56 to Fort Stockton.

Fort Stockton, 447 m.—see Tour 52. Follow US 385 south.

Marathon, 505 m.—see Tour 57. Here US 385 continues south for Big Bend as Tour 62. Check automotive needs.

Tour 61

US 87
New Mexico line,
Dalhart, Dumas,
Amarillo, Lubbock, Lamesa,
Big Spring, San Angelo, Eden, Mason,
Fredericksburg, Comfort, San Antonio,
659 m.

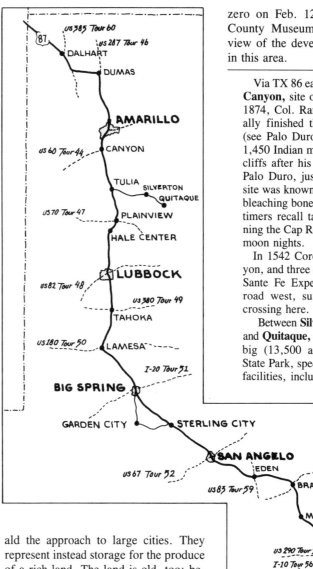

Descending along the eastern ramparts of the Rocky Mountains, from Montana through Colorado and New Mexico, US 87 enters Texas' Region IV at the northwest corner of the Panhandle and angles generally southeast through San Antonio to end on the Gulf Coast at Port Lavaca. Through Region IV, from Texline to San Antonio, your route is this tourguide's longest, a total of 659 miles.

In reverse, it is a primary route for those South Texans bound for mountain vacations in the upper New Mexico or Colorado Rockies.

Roughly, the first half of your journey traverses the green heartland of the upper Texas plains, rich in agriculture and oil, dropping down from the Cap Rock escarpment between Lamesa and Big Spring. From there you travel rolling ranch and stockfarming country beyond San Angelo, entering the Texas Hill Country at Eden and leaving it immediately north of San Antonio, where Region IV ends, and US 87 becomes Region III's Tour 33.

Although spanning great distances and much broad and open countryside, your route also visits a number of principal Texas cities—Amarillo and Lubbock on the plains, San Angelo on the edge of the Hill Country, and San Antonio at tour end.

N. Mex. line, 0 m. You cross into Texas 10 m. east of Clayton and about 100 m. east of the mountain gateway of Raton Pass, bordering New Mexico and Colorado.

Texline, 1 m. (alt. 4,694; pop. 425), occupies the northwest corner of the vast old XIT Ranch. It is older than Dalhart, preceding it as Dallam County seat until 1893. From here southeastward you enter a land of towering grain elevators, along the horizons ahead seeming to her-

ald the approach to large cities. They represent instead storage for the produce of a rich land. The land is old, too: between here and Dalhart, traces of the Folsom Man date back more than 12,000 years.

Dalhart, 37 m.—see Tour 60. Follow US 87 east, merging with US 385 to Hartley, 15 m.

Dumas, 76 m.—see Tour 46. Merge south with US 287 to Amarillo, 49 m.

Amarillo, 125 m.—see Tour 44. Merge south with US 60 to Canyon, 16 m.

Canyon, 141 m.—see Tour 44. Spectacular Palo Duro Canyon lies just east.

Tulia, 179 m. (alt. 3,501; pop. 4,699), is a busy and thriving farm center with neat homes surrounding a spread-out business area where big farm machinery seems arrayed before many buildings. Tulia boasts the dubious distinction of recording one of the coldest days on Texas record—23 degrees below

zero on Feb. 12, 1899. The Swisher County Museum here affords a good view of the development of agriculture in this area.

Via TX 86 east 12 m. is colorful **Tule Canyon,** site of much history. Here in 1874, Col. Ranald Mackenzie effectually finished the long Comanche war (see Palo Duro) by slaughtering some 1,450 Indian mustangs herded up these cliffs after his victory at the Battle of Palo Duro, just north. For years, this site was known as "Bone Ford" for the bleaching bones of the ponies, and old-timers recall tales of ghost herds running the Cap Rock rims on dark-of-the-moon nights.

In 1542 Coronado visited Tule Canyon, and three centuries later the Texan Sante Fe Expedition, blazing its own road west, suffered a major ordeal, crossing here.

Between **Silverton,** 29 m., pop. 779, and **Quitaque,** 46 m., pop. 513, is new, big (13,500 acre) Caprock Canyons State Park, spectacular scenery, and all facilities, including good hiking trails.

Little Silverton offers the Briscoe County Museum, and the entire area, some spectacular scenic drives. Beyond **Quitaque** is equally small **Turkey,** pop. 507, which boasts a granite monument and museum to native country-western pioneer Bob Wills. Each late April, some 10,000 c-w devotees descend on the little town for a festival honoring the singer.

Plainview, 201 m.—see Tour 47.
Hale Center, 212 m. (alt. 3,423; pop. 2,067), is a pin-neat agricultural center that grew from two ghosts—New

Epworth and Hale City, both close by and for a time fierce rivals for survival through drought and only the hope of a railroad. Tiring of dual upkeep, the rivals joined midway at Hale Center which itself nearly succumbed to drought, fading in 1898 to two businesses and one residence. In 1909 the Santa Fe came through and Hale Center avoided joining its dead founders. There is a farm and ranch museum here. In the area also see Floydada, Estacado.

Lubbock, 248 m.—see Tour 48.

Tahoka, 277 m.—see Tour 49.

O'Donnell, 292 m. (alt. 3,110; pop. 1,102), squarely on the Lynn-Dawson county line, is the hometown of the late TV star Dan Blocker (Hoss Cartright of *Bonanza*), with his statue in a local park to prove it. The O'Donnell Museum is interesting, including an early day telephone system and much other memorabilia.

Lamesa, 308 m.—see Tour 50. Here, agriculture has shifted from emphasis on grains to the growing of fine cotton. Along the road are many wire-sided trailers, wispy with past cargo.

Big Spring, 353 m.—see Tour 51. Southeast along your route, 363 m., Signal Mountain is an old Indian lookout where you enter the valley of the North Concho River.

FM 33 leads south to **Garden City,** 26 m. (alt. 2,630; pop. 293). This quiet county seat (Glasscock Co.) saw one of West Texas' earliest oil booms promise riches, then fade away. Land prices soared from $1 an acre to $1,000 in 1917, and towns like Drumwright (north, close by Lees) sprang up and flourished briefly. Close by the ghost of Drumwright is another, Konohassett, a 1907 philanthropic settlement established by a doctor. Competition with Big Spring was too much and Konohassett's new buildings—school, gin, two-story residences and the townsite itself were plowed under. Of all the booms, Garden City alone remains.

Sterling City, 396 m. (alt. 2,294; pop. 1,096). Under a hilly rampart, this quiet ranching center lies on the route of 1654 Spanish explorers who were hunting pearls on the Concho River. Toward San Angelo is James Hollow, just off Sterling Creek, where Jesse and Frank James are believed to have hidden out in the 1870s.

At 404 m., **Tower Hill** looks down from the west. An enigmatic, block-like ruin is discernible atop the hill, and its legend has persisted, unsolved, for a century. Early 1864 settlers found a rock fort ruin, complete with firing ports and, within the bullet-pocked walls, muzzle-loading rifle barrels. Nearby was a small cave with a skeleton in a beaded mantle and wearing jewelry. There was also a silver goblet engraved "For best Carlisle Colt, 1830." Who fought and died here, and for what, has never been completely determined.

San Angelo, 439 m.—see Tour 52. Veer eastward with US 87.

Eden, 483 m.—see Tour 59. Beyond Eden, the land becomes hilly and broken.

Brady, 515 m.—see Tour 54. Brady Lake, camping and all facilities, lies just west. At Brady you turn southward directly into the upper Texas Hill Country.

Camp San Saba, 526 m., pop. 36, was the 1862 site of a frontier Ranger outpost protecting Texas' western frontier from Indian depredation during the Civil War. Just east is the old flatrock crossing of the military road from Fort Mason to Griffin. East of that, near tiny Voca, is the ruin of an old gristmill. Near Camp San Saba—and well before its time, Fredericksburg's John O. Meusebach struck his historic treaty with the Comanche which allowed that settlement to live in peace (see Fredericksburg).

Mason, 543 m. (alt. 1,550; pop. 2,041). This hill-perched little town grew from Fort Mason, on Post Hill on the south side of town, many local buildings later erected with stone taken from the fort.

Fort Mason, a big establishment with 23 buildings, was a principal anchor on the initial western frontier before U.S. troopers pushed westward. Built in 1851, it knew such famed names as Albert Sidney Johnston and Robert E. Lee. John Bell Hood, operating from here, led one of the post's most daring sweeps against the Comanche. It was at Fort Mason, in 1860, that Lee agonized over impending Civil War, his duty to country and to his native Virginia. Here he received the telegram ordering him to Washington, where he would be offered supreme command of U.S. armies but would decline it and cast his lot with the South. The nearby Mason County Museum displays memorabilia from the old fort.

The town counts many historic old buildings dating before turn of the century, among them the Reynolds-Seaquist Home (tours). *Old Yeller* author Fred Gipson was reared here, and an exhibit outlining his career is at the new library. Artist Gene Zesch's collection of hand-carved caricature art is at the Commercial Bank. May to October you can visit a bat cave with 5 million bats exiting nightly.

Mason is headquarters for rock hunters. Here may be found the famous blue and clear topaz as well as other semi-precious stones. Seek rockhound sites at the C of C: one is the Seaquist Ranch—a small fee allows rock-hunting, camping.

Specimens of the fine topaz that attracts rock-hunters to the Mason area.

Loyal Valley, 562 m., pop. 150, cupped in the hills, is an old German settlement overflowing from Fredericksburg. In and around here in 1875–76 occurred the bloody Mason County or "Hoodoo" War—a clash between Germans, predominantly Unionists, and ranchers, returning Confederates—a feud that finally enveloped much of this country with mob-hangings, ambushes, even scalpings, until Texas Rangers restored order.

Cherry Spring, 567 m., pop. 75, is another 1850 German settlement in this area marked by sturdy rock homes. Fredericksburg's founder, John O. Meusebach, is buried here.

Fredericksburg, 585 m.—see Tour 55. Your road to Comfort crosses a scenic divide between the Pedernales and Guadalupe valleys.

Comfort, 608 m.—see Tour 56. An excellent museum of German pioneer days is located here. At Comfort, merge southward with I-10.

San Antonio, 659 m.—see Tour 33. Enter Regions II and III. US 87 continues as Tour 33; I-10, with which you have merged, turns east as Tour 20.

☆

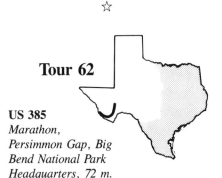

Tour 62

US 385
Marathon,
Persimmon Gap, Big
Bend National Park
Headquarters, 72 m.
FM 170
(Camino del Rio), Study Butte, Lajitas,
Fort Leaton, Presidio, 68 m.

This tour has been separated from others—it continues south from Tour 60—simply because in its lonely grandeur it knows few equals in America. From Marathon south you penetrate the Chihuahuan Desert, America's second largest, your road closely following ancient trails—that of the early Spaniard who sought and failed to subdue the land, and—not long afterward—that of the Comanche horseman hammering south for his raids on upper Mexico during the autumnal "Month of the Mexican Moon."

At Persimmon Gap, northeast entrance to Big Bend National Park, pause for a moment as the Comanche must have done two centuries earlier. Ahead crouch the Chisos, that foreboding mass of Ghost Mountains. Southeastward rear the spectacularly-colored precipices of the Sierra del Carmen, across in Mexico. Through what appears to you an impenetrable southward wall, the Comanche knew the trail. Today you can find your way by following the well-marked paved park roads.

Bounding the 1,100-square-mile park, established in 1944, 107 m. of Rio Grande canyon-cutting river lie behind the ranges confronting you. Three canyons—Santa Elena, Mariscal, and Boquillas—west to east—are prodigal chasms, and the lofty basin within the

Chisos is red-rock-rimmed magnificence. Various locations provide all facilities: for lodges or cabins, arrange advance reservations.

You will leave the park by way of Camino del Rio, judged one of America's 10 most scenic highways—68 m. northwest to old Presidio.

Marathon, 0 m.—see Tour 57. Continue south from Tour 60.

At 2 m., Camp Pena Colorado, an 1879 outpost of Fort Davis, lies 3 m. west (private ranch). The old post was established to hold the Apache (Mescalero and Chisos) in check. For some distance southward through a succession of long valleys, mountainously flanked in all directions, your road parallels Maravillas Creek—your Indian predecessor knew not to let his road stray far from water.

Southwest, like a giant black pyramid cut off at the top, is Santiago Peak, dominating your horizon for many miles and seeming much higher than its 6,521-foot altitude. Its flat top was an Apache lookout and ceremonial ground. In the early 1900s West Texas promoters conceived the incredible land-scheme "town" of Progress City which, in fact, lay along the steep face of that peak. More than that, they managed to sell many town lots to easterners who wanted a bit of scenic western land. The new citizens took one look at their "town," another for the already-disappeared promoters, and left.

Your road parallels this south-running Santiago range, low mountains to either side of you crouching like giant spine-backed prehistoric creatures.

At 40 m. Persimmon Gap pierces the range at the entrance to **Big Bend National Park.** Through this gap came the Comanche war trail and from here you catch your first good view of the fortress-like Chisos, massing ahead. From here you aim directly at them, crossing desert vegetation of sotol, lechuguilla, cenizo, blackbrush and almost every species of cactus. Early morning and late evening are the best times of approach—the coloring is splendid. Dominating the Chisos is Casa Grande, the castle-like battlement fronting the range; the average altitude of these mountains is some 7,000-plus feet, but above your low desert, their relative height seems enormous. Dagger Flats and Dog Canyon (for a dog found guarding the wagon of a never-found owner) lie eastward, near the Sierra del Carmen. Closer, to the west, are the reddish Rosillos peaks.

At 69 m., the Boquillas park road leads southeast. For now, however, veer right to Park Headquarters at Panther Junction. Here all information, maps, and literature are available, and there is a big broadscale map which spreads the entire park before your eyes.

Boquillas, 28 m., rests a century ago just across river. This is a primitive village, and a visit yields only the sense of deep interior Mexico. On the park side, Rio Grande Village offers a year-round campground, at this 3,500-foot elevation, pleasant in any season. The village has all facilities, including gas, phone, groceries, campsites and nature

Looking across the Rio Grande at the Mexican village of Boquillas and the Sierra del Carmen range, Big Bend National Park.

trails. Facing you from the east is Boquillas Canyon's mouth, longest of the three and easiest to manage by a raft-float (canoes are for the skilled; permission is a must). It is a two-day run, spectacularly walled, with primitive campsites along the way and a takeout at the Adams Ranch immediately below the canyon or at the bridge beyond.

At Panther Junction headquarters, inquire as to access roads—some are closed—to such locales as Glen Springs Draw, southeast, a painted desert of its own and scene of a Mexican bandit raid in 1916. South of Glen Springs, across the river is the ruin of Mexico's Presidio San Vicente, dating from the 1750s. Just west is lonely Mariscal Canyon, most

difficult to reach, shortest of the three for a river run, at the very bottom of the Bend. When mounted for trailride, you can see the slash of the canyon clearly from the high rims of the Chisos.

From headquarters again, a steep climb northwest 10 m. puts you into the Chisos Basin, heart of the park—a simply magnificent giant amphitheater walled by Casa Grande, Lost Mine Peak, Pulliam, Emory and others. Westward, the Window provides a spectacular view of far-below desert. You can trail-hike up Lost Mine Peak (there's a treasure up there that only the Apache knows) or you can take one of several saddle trips provided by the Chisos Remuda—they've mounted riders from age 6 to 80 without mishap. Lodges are available, as are campgrounds with all facilities. You are high here: the nights are brisk and—if you're lucky enough to catch one—the thunderstorms are awesome.

West of Panther Junction 12 m. is a park road intersection. The south road leads 22 m. to Castolon under its strangely-colored peak, an old cavalry outpost. Close by is Cottonwood Camp, with limited but adequate facilities. Under the immense wall of Mexican cliffs along the River, Santa Elena Canyon and its primitive camp are 8 m. west. The gorge—you face its outlet—is breathtaking, its sheer sides rising 1,500 to 1,800 feet, its rock-cut length 15 m. The float-through (put in near Lajitas, see below) is hazardous: attempt it only with skilled boatmen. Within is a rock collapse that can suck you under.

From the intersection northward, your park road skirts Burro Mesa to Maverick, 9 m., the western entrance, and FM 170, the beginning of Camino del Rio.

Study Butte, 1 m. (alt. 2,500; pop. 120) is a ghost town that mined cinnabar for quicksilver until shafts flooded. Awaking to tourism, there are some small shops. You can arrange Rio Grande canyon float trips (1–9 days) here.

Terlingua, 5 m. (alt. 2,720; pop. 25), is a formidable ghost, scores of tumbled rock and melting adobe climbing a raw yellow hill up to an iron-steepled church and a gaunt white house—once the owner's mansion—at the summit. Here once was America's quicksilver capital, dating from the 1890s, pop. 2,000. Its miners worked the scores of miles of later-

What's left of Study Butte, once a mining town, near the western entrance to Big Bend National Park.

als, naked in black heat, lived and died there for the meager pay of $1 a day while the mine's owner lived in opulent fashion aboard his New England yacht.

An annual chili cookoff—at last count there were three rival organizations claiming to be the original—has brought fame to Terlingua but has failed to daunt its handful of hardy locals, who tend to go into hiding when thousands of "chiliheads" descend.

The ghost town is owned by the Ivey family, which has undertaken much restoration. The Terlingua Trading Company, housed in the old mining company store, offers souvenir and gift items and has an art gallery. Down the way is the Star Light Theatre, a steakhouse and dinner theater. For local flavor, the Desert Deli and Diner is hard to beat, a place where you can watch the Chisos bask in the setting sun and the locals howl at the full moon.

Lajitas, 13 m. (alt. 2,200; pop. 48) boasts a modern motel and resort complex around a newly-built "old west" town put up on the foundations of an old cavalry post. Here is headquarters for float trips down the Rio Grande as well as back-country four-wheel-drive trips to abandoned mines, horseback trips, and even mountain bike trips through the desert.

Under the hill is the historic Lajitas Trading Post, an area institution that serves people on both sides of the Rio Grande as it has for a century. The trading post carries everything from caviar to washboards and is home to a beer-drinking goat, heir to the deceased and far-famed Clay Henry.

On the east edge of town is the Barton Warnock Center, a fine area museum and headquarters for the Big Bend Ranch State Natural Area, Texas' largest state park, which begins just west of Lajitas and spreads over a vast area of magnificent scenery and splendid isolation. Your route passes through the park; no fee is required

FM 170 travels the wild country west of Lajitas.

unless you visit park sites. Inquire at the Warnock Center.

At 17 m. cross Contrabando Creek, the wild area's source of livelihood speaking for itself. At 20 m. "Penguin Rocks," erosion-formed, make this rugged riverbluff road a miniature Bryce Canyon. Just across is the remote Mexi-can village of Flores.

At 28 m. a 15 percent grade tops the "Big Hill." The view is spectacular. Block your wheels when you park.

At 38 m., Close Canyon can be reached (Eagle Crack) by a short lateral.

At 38 m., Closed Canyon can be reached via a hiking trail (park permit required). It is a towering slit piercing a razor-thin cliff. Wear boots if you explore the river.

At 42 m., Tapado Canyon, a red gorge, cuts north. Below on the river are great balanced rocks; good picnicking.

At 45 m. descend from the mountains onto river plain. At 47 m., pass Redford, a small farm-ranch center that is home to a member of the Texas Women's Hall of Fame. The local woman started a library in her husband's store; now donated books number in the tens of thousands, and the library, free and open to all, serves residents on both sides of the Rio Grande.

Fort Leaton, 64 m., a State Historical Site, is a restoration of Ben Leaton's 1848 adobe home and fort, one of the largest adobe structures known, its walls enclos-ing one acre. One of the area's first ranchers, Leaton continually lost livestock to the Apaches. Finally he invited their chiefs to dinner, seated them at a long table, then unveiled a cannon which cleared the table with one blast. Thereaf-ter, goes the story, Leaton's troubles di-minished.

An excellent interpretive center tells the story of Fort Leaton, its role as a stopping point on the Chihuahua Trail, and the occupation of this area at the junction of the Rio Grande and Rio Conchos since prehistoric times.

Presidio, 68 m.—see Tour 52. West-ward, FM 170 continues to tiny Ruidosa, 29 m. and via an unimproved road be-yond to remote Candelaria, 39 m., and Capote Falls. See Tour 52.

At Candelaria a tiny trading post serves both sides of the river. Half a mile south of the trading post lies perhaps the shortest international bridge in the world, a 50-foot span built by local people that links Can-delaria with the village of San Antonio del Bravo on the other side of a channelized, 12-foot wide Rio Grande.

Appendix—
Texas Lakes

Locations

This is an alphabetical list of cities/towns and the lakes that are nearest them. For the facilities and activities available at these lakes, see the following section.

Abilene: Abilene, Ft. Phantom Hill
Amarillo: Meredith
Archer City: Kickapoo
Arlington: Arlington, Grapevine
Athens: Athens, Cedar Creek
Atlanta: Wright Patman
Austin: Austin, Town, Travis, Walter B. Long

Ballinger: O. H. Ivie
Balmorhea: Balmorhea
Bandera: Medina
Bastrop: Bastrop
Belton: Belton, Stillhouse Hollow
Big Spring: J. B. Thomas
Bonham: Bonham
Borger: Meredith
Bowie: Amon G. Carter
Brady: Brady
Brenham: Somerville
Breckenridge: Hubbard Creek
Bridgeport: Bridgeport
Brownwood: Brownwood
Burnet: Buchanan, Inks

Caldwell: Somerville
Canadian: Marvin
Carthage: Martin Creek, Murvaul
Childress: Childress, Greenbelt
Cisco: Cisco
Clarendon: Greenbelt
Cleburne: Pat Cleburne
Coleman: Coleman, Hords Creek
Colorado City: Champion Creek, Colorado City
Comanche: Proctor
Conroe: Conroe
Corsicana: Navarro Mills
Crockett: Houston County

Dallas: Lewisville, Mountain Creek, Ray Hubbard, White Rock
Daingerfield: Ellison Creek, Lake O'the Pines
Del Rio: Amistad
Denison: Texoma
Denton: Grapevine
Dublin: Proctor

Eagle Lake: Eagle
Eastland: Leon
Edna: Texana

Fairfield: Fairfield
Fort Stockton: Imperial
Fort Worth: Benbrook, Eagle Mountain, Grapevine, Lewisville, Worth

Gainesville: Moss, Texoma
Georgetown: Georgetown
Gilmer: Lake O'the Pines
Glen Rose: Squaw Creek
Goliad: Coleto Creek
Graham: Eddleman, Possum Kingdom
Granbury: Granbury
Granger: Granger
Greenville: Tawakoni
Groesbeck: Limestone

Haskell: Stamford
Hemphill: Toledo Bend
Henderson: Martin Creek, Striker
Hillsboro: Aquilla, Whitney
Houston: Clear, Houston, Livingston
Humble: Houston

Jacksonville: Jacksonville, Palestine, Striker
Jasper: B. A. Steinhagen (Martin Dies St. Pk.)

Karnack: Caddo
Killeen: Belton, Stillhouse Hollow

La Grange: Fayette
Laredo: Casa Blanca
Livingston: Livingston
Llano: Buchanan, Inks
Lubbock: Buffalo Springs
Lufkin: Sam Rayburn

Marble Falls: Marble Falls
Mathis: Corpus Christi
Mexia: Mexia
Mineola: Hawkins, Holbrook
Mineral Wells: Mineral Wells, Palo Pinto, Possum Kingdom
Monahans: Imperial
Mt. Pleasant: Bob Sandlin, Monticello, Welsh
Mt. Vernon: Cypress Springs

Nacogdoches: Nacogdoches
New Braunfels: Canyon
Nocona: Nocona

Orange: Sabine

Palestine: Palestine
Palo Pinto: Palo Pinto
Pampa: McClellan
Paris: Crook, Pat Mayes
Pecos: Red Bluff
Perryton: Fryer
Pittsburg: Cypress Springs, Welsh
Plano: Lavon
Pt. Arthur: Sabine
Post: White River

Quanah: Pauline
Quitman: Fork, Quitman, Winnsboro

Ranger: Leon
Robert Lee: E. V. Spence
Rockwall: Lavon, Ray Hubbard
Round Rock: Travis

San Angelo: Nasworthy, O. C. Fisher, Twin Buttes
San Antonio: Braunig, Calaveras, Medina
San Augustine: Sam Rayburn, Toledo Bend
San Marcos: Canyon
Seymour: Millers Creek
Silverton: Mackenzie
Spur: White River
Stamford: Stamford
Sulphur Springs: Sulphur Springs, Tawakoni
Sweetwater: Oak Creek, Sweetwater, Trammell

Taylor: Granger
Texarkana: Wright Patman
Three Rivers: Choke Canyon
Tilden: Choke Canyon
Tyler: Tyler

Victoria: Coleto Creek
Waco: Brazos, Waco
Waxahachie: Bardwell
Weatherford: Weatherford
Whitney: Whitney

Wichita Falls: Arrowhead, Diversion,
   Kemp, Kickapoo, Wichita
Winnsboro: Winnsboro

Zapata: Falcon

Facilities and Activities

Legend:	F-Fishing;		S-Swimming;	B-Boating;	*-Facilities
Lake	**Sport**	**Camping**		**Near**	**State Park**
Abilene	F/S/B	*		Abilene	*
Amistad	F/B	*		Del Rio	
Amon G. Carter	F/S/B	*		Bowie	
Aquilla	F	-		Hillsboro	
Arlington	S/B	-		Arlington	
Arrowhead	F/S/B	*		Wichita Falls	*
Athens	F/S	*		Athens	
Austin	S/B	-		Austin	
B. A. Steinhagen	F/S/B	*		Jasper-Woodville	*
Balmorhea	F/B	-		Balmorhea	
Bardwell	F/S/B	*		Waxahachie	
Bastrop	F/S/B	-		Bastrop	
Belton	F/B	*		Belton	
Benbrook	F/S/B	*		Ft. Worth	
Bob Sandlin	F/B	*		Mt. Pleasant	
Bonham		*		Bonham	
Brady	F/B	*		Brady	
Braunig	F/B	-		San Antonio	
Brazos	F/B	*		Waco	
Bridgeport	F/S/B	*		Bridgeport	
Brownwood	F/S/B	*		Brownwood	*
Buchanan	F/S/B	*		Burnet-Llano	
Buffalo Springs	F/B	-		Lubbock	
Caddo	F/B	*		Karnack	*
Calaveras	F/B	-		San Antonio	
Canyon	F/S/B	*		New Braunfels/San Marcos	
Casa Blanca	F/S/B	-		Laredo	
Cedar Creek	F/S/B	*		Athens	
Champion Creek	F/S/B	*		Colorado City	
Childress-Baylor	F/B	*		Childress	
Choke Canyon	F/S/B	*		Tilden/Three Rivers	*
Cisco	F/S/B	-		Cisco	
Clear	F/B	-		Houston/NASA	
Coleman	F/S/B	*		Coleman	
Coleto Creek	F/B	*		Goliad-Victoria	
Colorado City	F/S/B	*		Colorado City	*
Conroe	F/B	*		Conroe	
Corpus Christi	F/S/B	*		Mathis	*
Crook	F/S/B	*		Paris	
Cypress Springs	F/S/B	*		Pittsburg-Mt Vernon	
Diversion	F/S/B	-		Wichita Falls	
E. V. Spence	F/B	*		Robert Lee	
Eagle	-	-		Eagle Lake	

Lake	Sport	Camping	Near	State Park
Eagle Mtn	F/S/B	*	Ft. Worth	
Eddleman-Graham	F/B	*	Graham	
Ellison Creek	F/S/B	-	Daingerfield	
Fairfield	F/B	*	Fairfield	*
Falcon	F/B	*	Zapata	*
Fayette	F	-	La Grange	
Fork	F/B	-	Quitman	
Ft. Phantom Hill	S/B	*	Abilene	
Fryer	F/S/B	*	Perryton	
Georgetown	F/B	*	Georgetown	
Granbury	F/S/B	*	Granbury	
Granger	F/S/B	*	Granger-Taylor	
Grapevine	F/S/B	*	Ft. Worth-Grapevine	
Greenbelt	F/S/B	*	Clarendon	
Hawkins	F/B	*	Mineola	
Holbrook	F/S/B	*	Mineola	
Hords Creek	F/S/B	*	Coleman	
Houston County	F/B	*	Crockett	
Houston	F/S/B	-	Houston-Humble	
Hubbard Creek	F/S/B	*	Breckenridge	
Imperial	F/S/B	-	Monahans-Ft. Stockton	
Inks	F/S/B	*	Burnet-Llano	*
J. B. Thomas	F/S/B	*	Big Spring	
Jacksonville	F/S/B	*	Jacksonville	
Kemp	F/B	*	Wichita Falls	
Kickapoo	F/S/B	*	Archer City	
Lake O'The Pines	F/S/B	*	Gilmer-Daingerfield	
Lavon	F/S/B	*	Rockwall-Plano	
Leon	F/B	*	Eastland-Ranger	
Lewisville	F/S/B	*	Dallas-Ft. Worth	
Limestone	F/B	-	Groesbeck	
Livingston	F/S/B	*	Livingston	*
Lyndon B. Johnson	F/S/B	-	Marble Falls	
McClellan	F/S/B	*	Pampa	
Mackenzie	F/S/B	*	Silverton	
Marble Falls	F/S/B	-	Marble Falls	
Martin Creek	F/B	-	Tatum	
Marvin	F/B	*	Canadian	
Medina	F/S/B	*	San Antonio-Bandera	
Meredith	F/B	*	Amarillo-Borger	
Mexia	F/S/B	*	Mexia	
Miller's Creek	F	-	Seymour	
Mineral Wells	F/S	*	Mineral Wells	*
Monticello	F/B	*	Mt. Pleasant	
Moss	F	-	Gainesville	
Mountain Creek	F/B	-	Dallas	
Murvaul	F/S/B	*	Carthage	
Nacogdoches	F/S/B	-	Nacogdoches	
Nasworthy	F/S/B	*	San Angelo	
Navarro Mills	F/B	*	Corsicana	
Nocona	F/S/B	*	Nocona	
O. C. Fisher	F/S/B	*	San Angelo	
O. H. Ivie	F/S/B	*	Ballinger	
Oak Creek	F/S/B	-	Sweetwater	
Palestine	F/S/B	*	Jacksonville	
Palo Pinto	F/S/B	-	Palo Pinto-Mineral Wells	
Pat Cleburne	F/S/B	*	Cleburne	

Lake	Sport	Camping	Near	State Park
Pat Mayes	F/B	*	Paris	
Pauline	F/S/B	*	Quanah	
Possum Kingdom	F/S/B	*	Graham-Mineral Wells	*
Proctor	F/S/B	*	Comanche-Dublin	
Quitman	F/S/B	*	Quitman	
Ray Hubbard	F/B	-	Dallas, Rockwall	
Red Bluff	F/B	-	Pecos	
Sabine	F/B	-	Pt. Arthur-Orange	
Sam Rayburn	F/S/B	*	Lufkin-San Augustine	
Somerville	F/B	*	Brenham-Caldwell	*
Squaw Creek	F/B	-	Glen Rose	
Stamford	F/S/B	*	Stamford-Haskell	
Stillhouse Hollow	F/B	*	Belton-Killeen	
Striker	F/B	*	Henderson-Jacksonville	
Sulphur Springs	F/S/B	*	Sulphur Springs	
Sweetwater	F/S	-	Sweetwater	
Tawakoni	F/S/B	*	Greenville	
Texana	F/B	*	Edna	*
Texoma	F/B	*	Denison	*
Toledo Bend	F/B	*	San Augustine-Hemphill	
Town	F	-	Austin	
Trammell	F	-	Sweetwater	
Travis	F/S/B	*	Austin-Round Rock	
Twin Buttes	F/S/B	*	San Angelo	
Tyler	F/B	*	Tyler	
Waco	F/S/B	*	Waco	
Walter B. Long	F/B	-	Austin	
Weatherford	F/B	-	Weatherford	
Welsh	F/B	*	Mt. Pleasant-Pittsburg	
White River	F/B	*	Post-Spur	
White Rock	F/B	-	Dallas	
Whitney	F/S/B	*	Hillsboro-Whitney	
Wichita	S	-	Wichita Falls	
Winnsboro	F/S/B	*	Winnsboro-Quitman	
Worth	S/B	-	Ft. Worth	
Wright Patman	F/S/B	*	Texarkana-Atlanta	*

Index

--- **Let Gulf Publishing Company show you the best of Texas:** ---

The Alamo and Other Texas Missions to Remember

Amazing Texas Monuments and Museums

Backroads of Texas/2nd Edition

Beachcomber's Guide to Gulf Coast Marine Life
    2nd Edition

The Best of Texas Festivals

Bicycling in Texas

Birder's Guide to Texas, 2nd Edition

Camper's Guide to Texas Parks, Lakes, and Forests
    3rd Edition

Diving and Snorkeling Guide to Texas

From Texas Kitchens

Frontier Forts of Texas

Great Hometown Restaurants of Texas

A Guide to Fishing in Texas

A Guide to Historic Texas Inns and Hotels
    2nd Edition

A Guide to Hunting in Texas

A Guide to Texas Lakes

Hiking and Backpacking Trails of Texas/3rd Edition

Historic Homes of Texas

A Guide to Texas Rivers and Streams

A Line on Texas

Ray Miller's *Eyes of Texas*® *Travel Guides:*
    Dallas/East Texas, 2nd Edition
    Houston/Gulf Coast, 2nd Edition
    Panhandle/Plains
    San Antonio/Border, 2nd Edition

Ray Miller's *Galveston*

Ray Miller's *Houston*

Ray Miller's *Texas Forts*

Ray Miller's *Texas Parks*

Rock Hunting in Texas

Texas—Family Style/2nd Edition

Traveling Texas Borders

Unsung Heroes of Texas

Why Stop? A Guide to Texas Historical Roadside Markers
    3rd Edition